Market Failure or Success

Market Failure or Success

Success

The New Debate

Edited by

Tyler Cowen and Eric Crampton

A BOOK FROM THE INDEPENDENT INSTITUTE

Edward Elgar

Cheltenham, UK • Northampton, MA, USA

Published by
Edward Elgar Publishing Limited
Glensanda House
Montpellier Parade
Cheltenham
Glos GL50 1UA
UK

Edward Elgar Publishing, Inc.
136 West Street
Suite 202
Northampton
Massachusetts 01060
USA

A catalogue record for this book
is available from the British Library

Library of Congress Cataloging in Publication Data

Market failure or success: the new debate/edited by Tyler Cowen and Eric Crampton.
   p. cm.
  'In association with the Independent Institute.'
  Includes bibliographical references and index.
  1. Capitalism. 2. Economic policy. 3. Central planning. 4. Business cycles.
5. Welfare economics. 6. Information theory in economics. 7. Economics – History
– 20th century. I. Cowen, Tyler. II. Crampton, Eric.

HB501.M33124 2003
330.12′2 – dc21   2002067152

ISBN 1 84376 025 8 (cased)
    1 84376 085 1 (paperback)

Typeset by Cambrian Typesetters, Frimley, Surrey
Printed and bound in Great Britain by MPG Books Ltd, Bodmin, Cornwall

The **INDEPENDENT INSTITUTE**

THE INDEPENDENT INSTITUTE is a non-profit, non-partisan, scholarly research and educational organization that sponsors comprehensive studies of the political economy of critical social and economic issues.

The politicization of decision-making in society has too often confined public debate to the narrow reconsideration of existing policies. Given the prevailing influence of partisan interests, little social innovation has occurred. In order to understand both the nature of and possible solutions to major public issues, The Independent Institute's program adheres to the highest standards of independent inquiry and is pursued regardless of prevailing political or social biases and conventions. The resulting studies are widely distributed as books and other publications, and are publicly debated through numerous conference and media programs.

Through this uncommon independence, depth, and clarity, The Independent Institute pushes at the frontiers of our knowledge, redefines the debate over public issues, and fosters new and effective directions for government reform.

THE INDEPENDENT INSTITUTE
100 Swan Way, Oakland, California 94621-1428, U.S.A.
Telephone: 510-632-1366 • Facsimile: 510-568-6040
E-mail: info@independent.org • Website: http://www.independent.org

INDEPENDENT STUDIES IN POLITICAL ECONOMY

For further information and a catalog of publications, please contact:
THE INDEPENDENT INSTITUTE
100 Swan Way, Oakland, California 94621-1428, U.S.A.
510-632-1366 • Fax 510-568-6040 • info@independent.org • www.independent.org

Contents

ix

Figures

Tables

Acknowledgements

The Editors and publisher wish to thank the following who have kindly given permission for the use of copyright material.

American Economic Association for 'Toward a general theory of wage and price rigidities and economic fluctuations', J. Stiglitz, *American Economic Review* 89: 2 (1999): 75–80; 'An empirical examination of information barriers to trade in insurance', John Cawley and Tomas Philipson, *American Economic Review* 89: 4 (1999): 827–46; 'A direct test of the "lemons" model: the market for used pickup trucks,' Eric W. Bond, *American Economic Review* 72: 4 (1982): 836–40; 'Cooperation in public-goods experiments: kindness or confusion?', James Andreoni, *American Economic Review* 85: 4 (1995): 891–904.

Basil Blackwell Publishers for permission to draw upon 'The demand for and supply of assurance', Daniel B. Klein, *Economic Affairs* (2001): 4–11.

Cambridge University Press for 'Public Choice Experiments', Elizabeth Hoffman, in *Perspectives on Public Choice*, 1997, edited by Dennis Mueller, 415–26. Cambridge, MA.

Edward Elgar Publishers for 'Path dependence, its critics and the quest for "historical economics" ', Paul David, in *Evolution and Path Dependence in Economic Ideas: Past and Present*, P. Garrouste and S. Ioannides (eds), 2001.

Elsevier Science for 'Group size and the voluntary provision of public goods', R. Mark Isaac, James M. Walker and Arlington W. Williams, *Journal of Public Economics* 54 (1994): 1–36; 'Non-prisoner's dilemma', Gordon Tullock, *Journal of Economic Behavior and Organization* 39: 4 (1999): 455–8.

Independent Institute for 'Beta, Macintosh, and other fabulous tales', in Stan J. Liebowitz and Stephen E. Margolis, *Winners, Losers and Microsoft: Competition and Antitrust in High Technology* (2001), 119–34. Oakland, CA.

MIT Press for 'The market for "lemons": quality uncertainty and the market mechanism', George A. Akerlof, *Quarterly Journal of Economics* 84 (1970): 488–500; excerpts from Chapter 2 and Chapter 3 of *Whither Socialism?* (1994), Joseph E. Stiglitz, Cambridge, MA.

Ohio State University Press for 'Do informational frictions justify federal credit programs?', Stephen D. Williamson, *Journal of Money, Credit, and Banking* 26 (1994): 523–44.

Oxford University Press for 'Efficiency wage models of unemployment – one view', H. Lorne Carmichael, *Economic Inquiry* 28 (1990): 269–95.

University of Chicago Press for 'Some evidence on the empirical significance of credit rationing', Allen N. Berger and Gregory F. Udell, *Journal of Political Economy* 100: 5 (1992): 1047–77; 'Information and efficiency: another viewpoint', Harold Demsetz, *Journal of Law and Economics* 12: 1 (1969): 1–22.

Introduction

1. Introduction

Tyler Cowen and Eric Crampton

Market failure remains one of the most influential arguments for government intervention. Throughout the twentieth century, most of the market failure arguments were based on theories of public goods and externalities. These theories suggest that market participants will fail to produce certain mutually beneficial goods and services. To provide a simple example, individuals may not voluntarily contribute towards a protective missile system because they hope to free-ride on the contributions of others.

Although aspects of these theories can be traced back to the beginnings of economics, the modern formulations were laid down by Paul Samuelson, James Meade, Francis Bator and others in the 1950s. Since that time, and despite some significant differences (for which see Cowen, 1988), a consensus developed that governments should provide at least a few basic public goods, such as national defense, but that markets do the best job of providing most goods and services.

This consensus fell apart in the 1970s and 1980s, as economists constructed new market failure arguments. These new challenges were based on the idea of information and informational imperfections. And in these arguments, more than just a few markets are bound to fail. Rather, if these arguments are correct, we can expect market failure whenever information is imperfect or distributed asymmetrically.

The new wave of market failure ideas included Stiglitz's 'efficiency wage' hypothesis, George Akerlof's 'market for lemons' model, Oliver Williamson's notion of opportunistic behavior,[1] and network and lock-in effects, stressed by Paul David and others. The first two economists on this list were rewarded with the Nobel Prize in 2001, precisely for their work on market failure and the economics of information.

The new market failure economists have pointed to information problems in virtually every sector of the economy. In the Western world, governments account for about 40 to 60 percent of gross domestic product, depending on the country. Regulation makes the scope of government intervention even greater, as over the last 20 years most government growth in the United States has come in this form. Virtually all of these expenditures and regulations have been defended with market failure arguments. Critics allege that significant market failures are widespread in the labor market, the health sector, in agriculture, in education, in basic scientific research, in electricity and in many other sectors. It is hard to think of any area where market failure arguments would not apply. Indeed the work of Joseph Stiglitz suggests that market failure will occur whenever the price system is used.

The 'information economy' of course has made the economics of information all the more important. The growth of services relative to manufacturing, the Internet, e-commerce, computer and software networks, and the move away from 'mass production' have dramatically changed the American economy. New ideas are more important than ever before and there has been a corresponding interest in how ideas are produced and traded. The advent of new technologies built on standards such as the personal computer, HDTV, wireless telephones and the Internet, had also brought new attention to the fear that markets might lock-in to the wrong standard or technology. When Paul David first used the example of the QWERTY keyboard (see further below) to illustrate this possibility, lock-in seemed like an interesting but esoteric idea of most relevance to economic historians. Lock-in took on new importance in the 1990s when a host of new standards were developed that may be with us for decades to come. The epic antitrust battle between Microsoft and the US Department of Justice, sometimes labeled 'the antitrust trial for the new century,' also brought home the relevance of David's ideas.

As late as the 1970s, it was a common criticism that neoclassical economics neglected both information and informational asymmetries. In the socialist calculation debate of the 1930s, Friedrich A. Hayek, Ludwig von Mises and others in the 'Austrian' tradition stressed imperfect information, and dispersed knowledge as fundamental arguments for the market and a liberal order (Boettke, 2000). Most of the economics profession, however, did not take up the challenge of analyzing decentralized knowledge and information. As late as 1976, Rothschild and Stiglitz were able to argue that 'economic theorists traditionally banish discussions of information to footnotes.' This state of affairs, of course, changed rapidly. But the new contributions to economics did not typically follow a Hayekian tack. Instead they emphasized market failure rather than market success.

In essence the new market failure arguments turned Hayek's insights on their head. Information problems were now a cause of market failure, rather than a reason for praising markets.

Hayek and the new market failure theorists focus on different aspects of information. For Hayek, the central problem is to mobilize widely dispersed information to maintain an extended order of sophisticated capitalist production. For the new market failure theorists, however, the key aspect of information is not dispersal but 'asymmetry' – some people have information that others do not. Information dispersal and asymmetry are two sides of the same coin, one must accompany the other. The difference between Hayek and the market failure theorists is that in Hayek's view markets eliminate asymmetry by revealing relevant aspects of information in market prices. The Canadian plumber's knowledge of substitutes for copper piping influences the French electrician's choice of home wiring through its effect on the market price of copper. For the market failure theorists, however, asymmetry cannot be overcome by exchange precisely because the unequal distribution of information interferes with mutually beneficial exchange.

A second difference exists between Hayek and the new theorists. Hayek prefers the word 'knowledge' to 'information.' The term information suggests a well-defined 'bit' or datum while the word 'knowledge' allows greater scope for practical wisdom, tacit knowledge, and the notion of understanding.

These two visions of markets, and knowledge, stand in tension. Both theories begin with the raw fact that information and knowledge are not centralized, but they reach for different conclusions. Understanding how markets overcome and are overcome by problems of information is perhaps the central problem in economics today. Yet in the economics profession, the new market failure theorists have taken over the debate. Their perspective has received more attention, and more pages in the journals, than has the Hayekian vision of market success. The purpose of this volume is to remedy this imbalance and to examine the new market failure arguments critically, often from a Hayekian perspective.

We do not seek to dismiss market failure arguments, or to argue that markets always do the best job, amongst competing institutional alternatives. We do, however, believe that the strength of the new market failure arguments has been overstated, and that the new market failure arguments are applied without sufficient discrimination. We are seeking to improve the intellectual debate by collecting and reprinting some of the key articles in the more recent debates on market failure. We believe that these articles, on examination, should produce greater skepticism of market failure claims.

In 1988, George Mason University Press, in conjunction with the Cato Institute, published *The Theory of Market Failure: A Critical Examination*, edited by Tyler Cowen, one of the editors of this collection. (The book was later republished by Transactions Books as *Public Goods and Market Failures*.) This volume reprinted some of the original articles on public goods and market failures and collected the major rebuttals. The selection of pieces suggested that many observers had overrated the strength of public goods and externalities arguments, on both theoretical and empirical grounds. Due to publication delays, the book, while published in 1988, contained nothing on the new market failure arguments. Hence the need for the present volume. We seek to examine where market failure arguments have headed and how much validity the new market failure arguments hold. More generally, we seek to evaluate the relative efficacies and drawbacks of voluntary exchange, operating under a system of private property and rule of law.

THE NEW MARKET FAILURE ARGUMENTS

The new theoretical arguments for market failure rose to prominence in the 1980s, although their roots can be traced back much earlier, arguably to Adam Smith. They tend to focus on problems of agency, information and coordination.

Economist Joseph Stiglitz has held a special importance in the new market failure theories. Stiglitz's productivity, brilliance and expositional talent have made him the leading figure in the new market failure arguments. His stint in government, especially as Chief Economist at the World Bank, and as Chairman of the Council of Economic Advisors under President Bill Clinton, has extended his influence further. His receipt of the 2001 Nobel Prize in Economics for the economics of information will bring renewed attention to his views.

Stiglitz developed a new way of thinking about market prices. The older view, as found in Hayek, stresses how prices create and communicate information about resource scarcity and help markets economize on information. A price, for Hayek, clears the market and tells distant buyers and sellers about the relative scarcities of differing goods and services. Stiglitz, in contrast, emphasizes how prices are used to solve problems of agency and quality verification. In these models, quality is a function of price. That is, the higher (or lower) the price, the higher the quality of goods and services that buyers can expect to receive. When prices are used to signal or guarantee quality, however, they cannot also clear the market and will not properly measure the relative scarcities of goods and services.

The Stiglitzian worldview is understood best by example. Stiglitz presents credit rationing and efficiency wages – both based in imperfect information – as two clear examples of how markets may misfire.

His credit rationing model starts with the claim that the probability of borrower default is related to the rate of interest charged on the loan. Stiglitz argues, for instance, that at high rates of interest the borrowing pool will be composed of an especially high percentage of deadbeats. Note how asymmetric information enters the argument. Stiglitz assumes that borrowers have a better idea of their likelihood of default than do lenders. High rates of interest therefore scare off the good borrowers, who expect to repay the loan. In contrast, high rates of interest do not scare off the deadbeats, who know their chance of having to repay the money is slight in any case. This principle then imposes a constraint on how high rate of interest a lender will charge. Many lenders will keep loan rates artificially low, to maintain a higher quality pool of borrowers and to increase their chance of being paid back.

In this setting the rate of interest will not necessarily clear the market for borrowing and lending. Banks keep interest rates down, but at those low rates demand exceeds supply. Lending must then be rationed. Banks will use non-price criteria, such as their estimation of borrower quality, or perhaps simple favoritism, to determine who can borrow how much money.

Stiglitz emphasizes that interest rates are a special kind of price. Most ordinary business firms are happy to sell as much as possible at going prices. No bank, however, wishes to loan as much as possible at posted rates of interest. In fact banks invest a good deal of time and energy into limiting the amount that their customers can borrow.

Whether credit rationing is in fact a market failure remains an open question, as we will see further below. One possibility is that credit rationing is an optimal response to the problem of loan deadbeats and involves no special social costs, other than reflecting a general imperfection of the world. At the very least, however, credit rationing, to the extent it is practiced, shows that prices do not always clear the market. Furthermore the social rate of return on investment will exceed the private rate of interest, which might be used to argue for government investment programs.[2]

Credit rationing models usually rely on a mechanism known as 'adverse selection.' George Akerlof's 'The market for "lemons" ', reproduced in this volume, was the first explicit exposition of this mechanism. Akerlof's piece was published in 1970, but it did not attain its full influence until the 1980s and later.

Adverse selection occurs when a voluntary market mechanism tends to attract the 'wrong' buyers and sellers, typically for reasons of asymmetric information. Akerlof cites the used car market as a possible example of this principle. The model assumes that sellers know the quality of the used car they are selling, but buyers do not know the quality of what they are getting. Buyers, then, will only be willing to pay a price conditioned on the probability of receiving a lemon – a price that will necessarily be lower than the value of a good used car. This makes potential sellers of good used cars more reluctant to offer them for sale, lowering average quality in the marketplace even further. In equilibrium, only the lemons are sold, making it impossible to get a good used car simply by paying a higher price. The potential for adverse selection crops up in insurance markets as well. When a firm offers insurance, for instance, it might expect that only the worst risks will be interested in purchasing the contract. The contract therefore must be structured to pay for these high-risk individuals, which will further discourage low-risk individuals from buying insurance. Adverse selection models imply that low-risk individuals have a hard time finding fairly priced insurance in the marketplace.

'Efficiency wage' theory concerns labor markets rather than credit markets. Building on suggestions from Adam Smith, Stiglitz notes that higher wages cause individuals to work harder. Asymmetric information is rife in labor markets, as the boss does not always know how hard the employees are working. If we imagine a hypothetical situation where an individual is paid the same wage as he or she could get in the next-best job, that individual would tend to shirk rather than to work hard. The worst that could happen is that the individual would be fired, but this would occasion no great loss. The fired individual would move into the next job with no loss in pay.

Employers therefore must pay workers a certain premium if they expect to get good effort. When every employer pays a premium, however, some unemployment will result, due to the higher overall level of wages. In some efficiency wage models the unemployment is itself the disciplining device that induces extra effort (Shapiro and Stiglitz, 1984). At the going wage rate, more workers would like to have jobs than can find them. The market price fails to clear the market and to coordinate all buyers and sellers, again contra Hayek.

Note that adverse selection may lie behind efficiency wage arguments as well. Higher wages will attract a higher quality of job applicants in the first place. Offering the market-clearing wage rate may attract only those individuals who do not have jobs, have been fired or cannot command a high premium for their skills, all of which may serve as examples of labor market 'lemons.'

Both credit rationing and efficiency wage theories have had influence on economic policy. Economists at the Department of Labor cited the efficiency wage argument when pushing for an increase in the minimum wage under the Clinton administration. The claim was that in an efficiency wage model a higher real wage would not put as many people out of work as otherwise might be expected. Credit rationing models have been used to justify a number of interventions into credit markets, including usury laws (maximum ceilings on interest rates), fairness in lending regulations, and government investment subsidies. Credit rationing also has been used to argue for a more activist monetary policy, to encourage banks to lend more to customers. Most generally, Stiglitz (1988) has tried to use both efficiency wage and credit rationing theory to restructure the foundations of macroeconomics and the theory of business cycles.

CRITICS OF CREDIT RATIONING AND ADVERSE SELECTION

The volume at hand offers several criticisms, both theoretical and empirical in nature, of the new market failure ideas. These critics have argued that the models are not very general but rather rest on very specific assumptions. Other scholars have questioned the empirical relevance of the anti-market mechanisms. It is one thing to argue that credit rationing and efficiency wages are theoretical possibilities, but it is quite another to argue that they are significant phenomena in the real world. Since Stiglitz has never presented empirical work on his basic mechanisms, many economists have been skeptical about the relevance of the research.

The current volume collects two differing critics of credit rationing. Stephen Williamson, in his 'Do information frictions justify federal credit programs?' argues that credit rationing is not a market failure that government intervention can improve on in significant fashion.

Williamson addresses credit rationing by building a formal model and then seeing whether government policy, in the form of federal credit lending, will actually improve on the equilibrium. He adds the explicit assumption that government cannot verify the quality of a lender any better than the private sector can. With this assumption, government lending will simply displace private lending, rather than alleviating credit rationing. Some borrowers will be drained from the private markets, and brought into the public sector markets, but the remaining private borrowers will still be rationed. The total amount of lending will not go up. Under some assumptions, 'the [government] program lowers the interest rate faced by lenders, raises the interest rate faced by borrowers, and increases the probability that a borrower is rationed' (Williamson, 1994: 525).

Williamson does show that a sufficiently complex tax and subsidy scheme can improve welfare and alleviate credit rationing to some extent. Nonetheless the informational requirements of such schemes would be daunting, and in any case such schemes do not match current policy. A government that had enough information to implement such a scheme also would be capable of direct central planning, which we know is not the case. In comparative institutional terms, credit rationing may not be a market failure at all.

Credit rationing has come under fire on empirical grounds as well. Berger and Udell (1992) conduct a systematic examination of whether markets do in fact ration credit, looking at over one million commercial bank loans from 1977 to 1988. The authors do find some evidence that commercial loan rates are 'sticky,' as credit rationing theories would indicate. Nonetheless the data do not support most other implications of credit rationing models.

Berger and Udell note the distinction between loans issued 'under commitment' and loans issued without commitments. The former set of borrowers cannot be rationed, since, with the loan, they also receive an option to borrow more. Only lenders who borrow without commitment can be rationed in subsequent time periods. Credit rationing theories typically would predict that when credit markets are tight, a greater percentage of extant loans would result from previous commitments (borrowers without such commitments presumably would be excluded from the market to some extent, thus raising the percentage of extant loans *with* commitment). Yet the data show no such relationship, inducing Berger and Udell (1992, p. 1047) to conclude: 'Overall, the data suggest that equilibrium rationing is not a significant macroeconomic phenomena.'

The phenomenon of adverse selection has received empirical attention as well. Eric Bond studies the used car market in 'A direct test of the "lemons" model: the market for used pickup trucks', and concludes that trucks purchased on the used car market required no more maintenance than other trucks of similar age and mileage. If the used trucks market suffered from Akerlof's lemons problem, truck owners would keep high-quality older trucks while selling lemons on the used truck market. Yet data collected by the US Department of Transportation reveal no significant differences in maintenance costs between trucks kept by their original owners and trucks sold on the used car market. In the market used as exemplar by Akerlof, Bond finds no empirical support for the lemons hypothesis.

Keep in mind that the lemons argument, in its most extreme form, predicts that it is impossible to buy a good used car. This prediction is countermanded by the millions of used cars that are bought and sold in the United States each year, frequently to the satisfaction of both buyer and seller.

It has been equally difficult to prove that adverse selection is a serious problem in insurance markets. Cawley and Philipson test the implications of the asymmetric information model in the term life insurance market and find no evidence of market failure. Where asymmetric information predicts increasing unit prices for insurance purchases, quantity-constrained low-risk individuals, and prohibitions on the purchasing of multiple small contracts to prevent arbitrage, Cawley and Philipson find robust evidence for decreasing unit prices, for low-risk individuals holding larger policies than high-risk customers, and for frequent multiple contracting.

The authors suggest that it is cost efficient for insurers to overcome informational asymmetries. Insurers deal with applicant information all the time, both in their role as insurers and as underwriters. It may not be true that the insurance purchasers have superior information; in fact the company may have better estimates of an individual's health risks than does the individual himself or herself. In Hayekian terms, the knowledge may be so decentralized that individuals themselves do not have easy access to it. The insurance company, however, has a greater ability to process actuarial statistics and hire specialists for advice. Once the underlying informational asymmetry goes away, the adverse selection argument does not get off the ground.

Other researchers find little evidence of adverse selection or asymmetric information in insurance markets, though for reasons of space we have not included their contributions. Chiappori and Salanie (2000) test for asymmetric information in the French market for automobile insurance and echo the conclusions of Cawley and Philipson. Where asymmetric information models predict that, among observationally identical individuals, those with more coverage should have more accidents, Chiappori and Salanie find no correlation between unobserved riskiness and accident frequency. Similarly, Browne and Doerpinghaus (1993) find no evidence that risky individuals purchase more medical insurance. They do find that legal obstacles prevent insurers from using all relevant observable information about risk characteristics in setting premiums; that they also find low risk individuals implicitly subsidizing higher risk individuals in a pooling equilibrium then seems unsurprising.

Hemenway (1990) takes the argument against adverse selection in insurance markets one step further. If individuals are consistent in risk preferences across physical and financial dimensions, then propitious selection ensues: people with higher levels of risk avoidance 'are more likely both to buy insurance and to exercise care. Those with low levels, or who are actually risk seeking, will tend to do neither.' While his empirical evidence is less rigorous than that of the other authors citied,[3] it is suggestive. Where adverse selection would lead motorcyclists to purchase more insurance than other drivers, Hemenway argues that motorcyclists admitted to hospital after accidents are more likely than car drivers similarly admitted to have no insurance at all, and that unhelmeted motorcyclists are the least likely to carry any insurance. Automobile associations, which provide insurance in the form of assistance to member drivers in distress, should be comprised of young risky drivers with unreliable cars but in fact mostly count richer, older drivers as members. While propitious selection does nothing to eliminate the moral hazard problem of insurance markets, it does render far less likely insurance market failures associated with adverse selection.

In retrospect, it may not be surprising that adverse selection fails to hold in many markets. Taking the used car market as an example, let us accept that sellers know more about the value of their car than buyers. We may still ask how much more do they know and how costly is it for buyers to learn? Visual inspection and a test drive will already tell a buyer about many major problems. Services like *Consumer Reports* give buyers ready access to information about the average quality of cars of that year and model.[4] CARFAX, a recent creation of the Internet, allows consumers to find out information about specific cars – information such as odometer readings, major accident and fire histories, types of previous owners – for example rental companies, and more (gathered from state title reports, insurance companies, auto rental companies, fire and police stations and so on). A buyer can also pay for a mechanic to examine a car at a price that is usually low relative to the value of the car.

Certified used cars, available with a warranty from car dealers, are today a common phenomenon and attract millions of buyers each year.

Not all of these services were available when Akerlof wrote his paper but this only reminds us that markets constantly innovate. In any case, the lesson to be drawn from the above examples is not simply that services exist to alleviate the lemons problem in the used car market. Rather, the lesson is that informational asymmetries (and simple lack of information) create a demand for product assurance that entrepreneurs can profit from by meeting. This is the subject of Daniel Klein's chapter.

Before turning to Klein, however, it is worth asking one more question about the Akerlof lemons model. Why don't sellers *tell* buyers about the true history of their cars? To an economist, the answer is obvious – sellers don't have an incentive to tell buyers bad news. Yet, in experiments by James Andreoni and others, which we discuss at greater length in the next section, individuals often behave in ways that run against their narrowly defined self-interest. People care about their reputation and their self-image, and for many sellers, honesty is the best policy.

In what is probably the most explicitly Hayekian piece in this volume, Daniel Klein looks for the institutions that have arisen spontaneously in the market system to mitigate problems of information, quality and certification. In his examination of quality certification, Klein provides some general presumptions against the strength of asymmetric information in markets.

Buyers and sellers are willing to pay to overcome the problems that information asymmetries cause. Buyers seek assurance that purchased products will meet expectations, and sellers know that confidence in product quality generates sales. Several mechanisms have emerged to meet the demand for assurance. At the most basic level, extended dealings and firm reputation, coupled with a low enough discount rate, can engender cooperative transactions and trust. Firms go to considerable expense to foster such extended dealings. The emergence of brand names also makes repeated dealings more frequent and communicates information to consumers about product quality.

Trusted middlemen emerge between buyers and sellers who would otherwise find it too costly to investigate the trustworthiness of each other. Car dealers transform the set of isolated dealings that could otherwise lead to a lemons market into a nexus for repeated transactions. In some cases, the only product provided by the middleman is assurance – the bridging of the information asymmetry that allows trade to take place. *Consumer Reports*, Underwriters Laboratories, CARFAX and a multitude of credit bureaus reduce information asymmetries between buyers and sellers of products and credit. Market failure theory predicts massive deadweight losses accruing from the trades that fail to take place because of informational asymmetries. In reality, alert entrepreneurs see deadweight losses as potential profits to be earned by removing the impediment to trade.

CRITICS OF EFFICIENCY WAGES

Like credit rationing, the efficiency wage doctrine has proven the subject of much controversy. H. Lorne Carmichael, in his 'Efficiency wage models of unemployment: one view,' tries to show that the theoretical case for the efficiency wage phenomenon is weaker than is commonly believed. Efficiency wage arguments require numerous and detailed assumptions, either explicit or implicit, about why markets cannot handle the basic monitoring problem. In Carmichael's view, efficiency wage models explain some facts about labor markets, but do not account for either wage rigidity or persistent involuntary unemployment. They are the exceptional case, rather than the standard account of how labor markets work.

Efficiency wage models make worker productivity a function of wage rates. Firms increase profits by paying a wage higher than the market-clearing rate in order to induce optimal work effort. In the aggregate, these actions create involuntary unemployment by keeping wage rates above those expected in competitive equilibrium. An unemployed worker may offer his or her services for less than the going wage rate, but that prospective worker's marginal product would drop more than proportionately with the decrease in the wage rate, dissuading firms from accepting the offer.

Carmichael examines the various efficiency wage models and finds them less than sound. Some models simply assume that workers wish to return the 'gift' of above-market wages with extra effort. Restrictions on worker utility functions, however, do not make for satisfying economic models. Furthermore, if efficiency wages do in fact increase worker utility, above and beyond the transfer of additional income (perhaps because of pride), they are all the more likely to be second-best efficient, rather than a market failure.

The mechanisms underlying more complex models also are suspect. Allowing entrance fees and bond posting typically overturns the conclusions of efficiency wage models. Shirking models posit that firms pay efficiency wages to increase the costs to workers of being fired and thereby reduce shirking. Unemployed workers in such markets should be willing to pay entrance fees in order to get valuable jobs, just as prospective tenants in New York are willing to pay apartment move-in fees for rent-controlled flats. In turnover models firms pay efficiency wages to avoid costly worker quits after the firm has invested in worker training. Again, unemployed workers should be willing to pay an upfront fee to the company to compensate the firm for hiring costs. This would again eliminate involuntary employment within the context of the model. Note that in this context 'entrance fees' can take many forms, including a salary structure that penalizes new workers and rewards seniority.

Note that Gary Becker and George Stigler presented the efficiency wage mechanism (1976) before Stiglitz published his work in the area. In their treatment, however, efficiency wages are not necessarily a cause of market failure. Instead efficiency wages (they do not use the term) help motivate market participants to achieve commonly agreed-upon ends. Becker and Stigler also note how bonding can serve many of the functions of efficiency wages, and avoid related market failure problems. The treatment of Becker and Stigler received less attention, in part because they pointed out a solution to the problem at the same time as they pointed out the problem itself.

Adverse selection models provide a more plausible mechanism for the creation of efficiency wage markets. In these models, firms pay higher wages to attract a more desirable pool of job applicants, as individuals with higher opportunity costs will apply for higher-paying positions. This model, however, like the other models of efficiency wages, does not generate either downward wage rigidity or an unemployment rate that fluctuates across the business cycle in the expected manner.

While efficiency wage models predict above-market wage rates leading to unemployment, they do not predict wage rigidity. First, the model determines the real wage, whereas we usually observe rigidity in nominal terms. More importantly, in such models, the optimal efficiency wage premium will fluctuate pro-cyclically, increasing wage volatility rather than inducing wage rigidity. In gift models, the size of the optimal 'gift' will vary with prevailing wage rates and unemployment levels. When unemployment rises, a smaller wage premium would result in optimal mitigation of both shirking and quitting. A downturn in the business cycle will increase the pool of applicants for open positions, reducing the wage premium necessary to generate the desired number of applicants. In all of these cases, the efficiency wage will fluctuate with the business cycle and efficiency wage models therefore fail as explanations of either nominal or real wage rigidity. Efficiency wage models then lose much of the power that they had claimed in explaining labor markets.

Unfortunately the efficiency wage arguments have not proven easily amenable to more direct empirical tests, and thus we provide no empirical article in this volume on efficiency wages. Krueger and Summers (1988) have argued that strong evidence of the efficiency wage phenomenon exists, but their work is not very convincing. They set up a wage equation and treat the unexplained residual as evidence for the efficiency wage phenomenon. More plausibly, this suggests that an econometric model cannot capture every determinant of the wage rate. Even if we accept this evidence, however, it does not show efficiency wages to be a market failure; it would simply show that the wage structure is one tool that employers use to control shirking. We have seen already that this may be a first- or second-best market response to a serious institutional problem.

Moreover, market failure in the labor market would not necessarily imply more government intervention. For example, the basic Shapiro–Stiglitz efficiency wage model (1984) predicts that increases in unemployment benefits will increase unemployment not only by directly reducing the downside risk of shirking but also by increasing the efficiency wage premium that must be paid in order to prevent shirking (p. 439). This might suggest that unemployment benefits should be reduced. While it has been argued that efficiency wages mitigate the employment effects of minimum wage increases, alternative models show that minimum wage increases lead to higher unemployment when the efficiency wage phenomenon is present, because of the required increase in efficiency wage premiums. In any case, efficiency wage models do not provide unequivocal support for government intervention into labor markets.

Some of the more general empirical patterns of business cycles tend to militate against the relevance of the efficiency wage phenomenon. For instance, productivity tends to rise with the business cycle, whereas the efficiency wage model suggests that people will work hardest in depressions, when they are most afraid of losing their jobs. To the extent efficiency wages exist, they are more likely a useful market institution than a fundamental cause of unemployment or economic downturns.

LOCK-IN

The lean mathematical models that have characterized the bulk of economic theory since the Second World War necessarily abstracted away from historical context. Paul David brought the notion that 'history matters' back to economics in the mid-1980s as a theory of market failure. David combined theories of network effects, path dependence and lock-in to argue for the strong likelihood of market failure in technological markets requiring coordination to a common standard.

The basic argument behind lock-in is simple: collective action problems may cause individuals to end up stuck in a technology that is less than optimal. When compatibility plays a role in determining value, switching from an established standard to a superior standard may become very difficult. The market may fail to abandon the inefficient standard because it has no mechanism to coordinate the move to a new standard. When compatibility effects are strong, the private gains of an individual switch would be lower than the social gains of the switch. Each individual fails to take into account that a successful collective switch would yield significant benefits for others as well. This makes individuals more reluctant to switch than they should be, and the market may become 'locked in' to an inefficient standard. In the absence of a centrally coordinated move, individuals and firms would stay with the old standard.

The QWERTY keyboard is often cited as the classic example of lock-in. According to legend, the QWERTY keys were first laid on the top row of the keyboard *to slow typists down*, not to help them type faster. Early typewriters sometimes jammed when multiple type bars hit the ribbon in too short a period of time. The QWERTY keyboard, it has been argued, slowed typists down enough to prevent the keys from jamming. This same QWERTY keyboard, efficient in its day, persists as the dominant technology and now slows down current typists, who obviously do not have to worry about jamming type bars. The critics claim that numerous alternative keyboards, such as Dvorak, in fact allow today's typists to work at a much faster rate.

This story sounds intriguing but in fact it appears to be false. Indeed, the QWERTY keyboard did not slow down early typists at all. Rather, it prevented type bar jamming by separating type bars corresponding to common letter combinations, forcing those type bars to approach the ribbon from different angles and reducing their chances of jamming together. Consequently, Dvorak typists enjoy few or no advantages against their QWERTY-trained counterparts. In *Winners, Losers & Microsoft*, Stanley Liebowitz and Stephen Margolis examine QWERTY and other cases held as examples of market lock-in and find little evidence for the phenomenon.

Liebowitz and Margolis's 'Fable of the keys'[5] questions whether David succeeded in living up to Cicero's dictum, cited by David in his initial exposition of the QWERTY story, that historians must tell true stories. Where David cites US Navy experiments demonstrating the superiority of the Dvorak keyboard, Liebowitz and Margolis point out the biases in those studies, which had been conducted by Lt. Cmdr. Dvorak himself. They also note a more rigorous examination of the two typewriter layouts performed in 1956 for the US government's General Services Administration which concluded that Dvorak keyboards were no better than the standard QWERTY design and that retraining on Dvorak would never amortize its costs. David concludes his 1985 work by expressing his belief that 'there are many more QWERTY worlds lying out there' (1985: 336), but we still cannot confirm even the QWERTY keyboard as a market failure.

Liebowitz and Margolis systematically examine other cases held as examples of lock-in to an efficient standard. In each case they fail to find evidence of serious market failure. VHS-based videocassette recorders succeeded over Betamax recorders in the consumer market because the VHS standard offered consumers a superior bundle of characteristics, especially longer recording time, rather than because of any initial market dominance. In the professional market, where the ease of editing film is important, Betamax is the standard. The command line interface of Microsoft's DOS system taxed computer system resources less than Apple's graphical user interface in the era when processing speed, memory and hard disk capacity were hard and binding constraints. DOS allowed users to run more powerful programs more quickly, leading consumers to prefer DOS to Apple. Apple's failure to incorporate backward compatibility into system upgrades meant that existing Apple users faced higher costs than Microsoft users in keeping their systems current, ensuring Microsoft's continued popularity when hardware improvements made graphical user interfaces the norm across both platforms.

The popularity of Microsoft's operating system has not, however, translated into the automatic dominance of other Microsoft software packages. Instead, Liebowitz and Margolis point out that Microsoft's market share in a wide range of software product categories seems closely tied to user and reviewer evaluations of the relative quality of Microsoft's products. When Microsoft offers a poor product, as it did with Excel prior to 1992 and Internet Explorer prior to 1996, it has a much lower market share than its competitors. When the Microsoft product improves, so does its market share.

Even the software market provides evidence against the phenomenon of lock-in. WordPerfect dominated the market for word processors from the 1980s through the early 1990s, with a market share rising to almost 50 percent in 1990. WordPerfect users, as many readers will recall, invested significant resources in learning the WordPerfect system's complex array of command keys and functions. WordPerfect would have seemed a likely candidate for market lock-in, but by 1994 Microsoft Word for Windows had grown to command a larger market share than the DOS and Windows versions of WordPerfect combined. WordPerfect dominated the word processing market only as long as its product beat out its competitors in user evaluations and magazine reviews. When Microsoft produced a better product, Word supplanted WordPerfect as the preferred word processing program. The same story plays out in each of the software markets Liebowitz and Margolis examine: the better product wins, regardless of initial market share.

Given the paucity of identifiable market failures through lock-in, Liebowitz and Margolis adopt a cautious theoretical approach. They present a taxonomy of path dependence based on appropriate policy responses. For instance simple path dependence – when a company's current production decisions depend in part on capital investment undertaken in previous periods – is of no policy consequence. A more significant form of path dependence results when *ex ante* rational investment decisions are found *ex post* to have been inferior to other previously available options. Liebowitz and Margolis argue, however, that markets may remedy this problem relatively well. Though the *ex ante* decision may be regrettable, it is not inefficient. If the benefits of switching are, *ex post*, high enough, markets can coordinate to new standards. Finally, agents may choose an *ex ante* sub-optimal option. While unlikely, in theory such a situation could emerge from a coordination failure where agents expect the sub-optimal option to become the standard.

David criticizes Liebowitz and Margolis for grounding their argument too firmly in the world of policy analysis. We argue to the contrary. The theory of market failure must be viewed within a comparative institutional framework; as Harold Demsetz warns us, assertions of failure outside of such a framework slide easily into the 'nirvana' fallacy. A failure of market mechanisms to deliver as high a level of welfare as other feasible institutions would be a more powerful and relevant critique than simply noting divergences from competitive equilibrium. By focusing on the policies that would be required to remedy the market failures identified by David, Liebowitz and Margolis thrust us back into the world of comparative institutional analysis. Where David argues that lock-in induced failures should pervade technological markets and justify government intervention to slow down the adoption of any technical standard, Liebowitz and Margolis demonstrate the rarity of potentially remediable cases of lock-in, both in theory and, *a fortiori,* in practice.

The mitigation of lock-in induced inefficiencies can take two forms – comprehensive reforms and selective interventions. David proposes comprehensive measures to improve 'the informational state in which choices can be made by private parties and governmental agencies' and to delay market commitment to any particular technological standard. Yet the case for such comprehensive measures seems weak. Information improves the workings of markets, but governments are rarely superior predictors of quality. Comprehensive efforts to delay the adoption of any particular standard will necessarily reduce consumer welfare by the discounted value of the network benefits that would have accrued during the delay period. Furthermore, consumers would only enjoy offsetting benefits from the delay when delay prevents them from choosing the inferior standard. But usually we do not know which standard is better until we start experimenting. The fundamental questions about standards often relate to their practical efficacy, rather than their abstract theoretical properties. The market is a discovery process, as Hayek has stressed, and much of this discovery results from learning by doing. Though David argues that static welfare analysis lies at the root of opposition to the concept of path dependence and to the policy consequences he sees as flowing from it, a Hayekian dynamic market process approach to economic analysis makes his case all the more tenuous. It therefore remains to be seen whether David's delay proposals would survive a cost–benefit analysis.

A second form of potential mitigation would take the form of selective government intervention when market failure from lock-in had been identified. In some obvious cases of coordination failure, for example, the government could facilitate standard switching by itself adopting the more efficient standard. Government action would thus coordinate consumer expectations on the best technological standard.

While this sounds good in theory, everyone has their favorite candidate for an inferior standard (for example, there are still partisans of the Beta format) and what one person regards as an obviously inferior system is, to an aficionado, the best. The case that is supposedly most obvious, QWERTY, turns out to be illusory or at least hard to pin down. More generally, government does not do a good job of 'picking winners,' whether it be backing companies, industrial sectors or standards. Liebowitz and Margolis note Zinsmeister's (1993) chronicle of the failures of Japan's Ministry of International Trade and Industry (MITI) in picking winners: '[v]ery simply, MITI, which may well have had the best shot of any government agency at steering an economy toward the best bets, was no substitute for the interplay of multitudes of profit-seeking rivals competing with each other to find the best mousetrap' (1999, p. 131). MITI, for instance, originally recommended that Japanese firms abandon both automobiles and consumer electronics.

The failures of politics are often no accident, but rather result from the power of special interest groups. The owner of a winning standard is likely to reap large profits, thus creating an incentive for lobbying, bribery, rent-seeking and other distortions of the political process. For these reasons government intervention could easily make things worse rather than better.

Note also that private market participants can settle on their own standards, and change standards, without government intervention. Railroad gauges became mutually compatible in the interests of commerce. The railroads even succeeded in introducing standard time zones across the United States, a particularly interesting example because government did not make the zones official until after three decades of evolution, the market had decisively locked-in – the precise opposite of the process that David recommends.[6] The MP3 format has become commonplace in digitally distributed music, without government assistance. Yet if the major music companies come up with something better, they will have every opportunity to market it to their consumers. These same companies are also using consortia (SDMI, Secure Digital Music Initiative) to introduce new standards for encrypted music that cannot be distributed over Napster-like services. The companies may not beat the hackers, but there is no doubt that they have worked together to introduce new standards. Similarly, we see Hollywood moving towards digital filming of movies, and away from the previous medium of celluloid film.

Lock-in theories have influenced real world economic policy, most notably in the realm of antitrust. Antitrust lawyers argue that network effects give incumbent firms too large an advantage over their competitors or potential competitors. Liebowitz and Margolis point out that, to the contrary, multiple standards are common in many markets. While competition within a proprietary standard is negligible, competition among standards can be fierce and need not lead to 'winner-take-all' dominance. Apple remains a strong player in the computer market, especially among those involved in graphic design, despite its smaller market share than Microsoft. VHS dominates consumer videocassette markets while Betamax is the choice of those involved in film production and editing, though DVD technology may yet supersede both formats. Suppliers that rest on their laurels usually receive a come-uppance at the hands of a very dynamic marketplace. Microsoft must constantly improve its product or lose market share to another fierce competitor.

How, then, can the debate over QWERTY-nomics be resolved? Evidence for the phenomenon seems weak, but the existence of the phenomenon cannot be ruled out on aprioristic grounds. QWERTY was a plausible story when first told and continues to hold influence despite the criticisms of Liebowitz and Margolis. David argues that, because his theory predicts pervasive inefficient market lock-in, the burden of proof must lie on Liebowitz and Margolis to show that lock-in does not exist. Liebowitz and Margolis, in turn, contend that David's theory is not strong enough for him to assert that market failure in this context is the null hypothesis; consequently, he must provide sufficient proof of its empirical significance.[7]

Harold Demsetz, in his 1969 classic 'Information and efficiency: another viewpoint,' offers clues as to how we might resolve such disputes. Demsetz reminds us of the dangers of moving from the identification of an imperfection to the belief that government can usefully improve matters. Attempting to remedy all observed imperfections is dangerous and costly, in terms of both efficiency and liberty. The burden of proof should therefore lie on those who assert market failure, and they have failed to make a convincing case in the areas cited above.

Demsetz argues that economic analysis cannot consist of simply pointing out that the real world fails to conform to a theoretical ideal, which he calls the 'nirvana' approach to economics. Reducing economic analysis to nirvana theorizing leaves great scope for political mischief. In the absence of a comparative institutional framework, simple identification of inefficiency amounts to a cry that 'Something must be done!' – a call that politicians and regulators are only too ready to respond to, with an armory of 'somethings' always at the ready. Comparative institutional analysis moves beyond the identification of discrepancies between the ideal and the real, examining instead the relative merits of feasible alternative institutional arrangements for dealing with identified economic problems.

Though Demsetz's critique of nirvana theorizing was directed at earlier market failure theories advanced by Kenneth Arrow, it applies just as strongly against the information-based market failure theories currently popular. Demsetz lays out three fallacies that are commonly found in public policy discourse. The 'grass is always greener' fallacy arises when it is simply assumed that government can improve on free enterprise. Far more pages in economic journals have been devoted to technical expositions of why markets might fail than have been used to explain why we might expect better results from government interventions. Echoes of the fallacy can be heard in David's calls for government delays of technological standard adoption. If public choice theory teaches us anything, it is that we have reasons to believe that the grass may be less lush when watered by a government bureaucracy.

Similarly, inefficiency claims flowing from Stiglitz's efficiency wage theory arguably rest upon two additional fallacies identified by Demsetz: the 'free lunch' fallacy and the 'people could be different' fallacy. If we assume for the moment that efficiency wages are a common phenomenon and that they are a result of firms mitigating shirking (both contentious claims) we must remember that we cannot eliminate the desire to shirk and that we cannot do away with efficiency wages without incurring the resulting reduction in work effort. The alternative to existing market structures is not some theoretical ideal achieved by sleight of hand and good intentions, it is some other institution whose feasibility and efficiency require careful examination. Demsetz's points are simple, and his targets obvious, but these remain some of the most important, and underappreciated, contributions of the economic way of thinking.

In lieu of these fallacies, Demsetz proposes that economists conduct comparative institutional analysis. That is, we should consider which real world alternatives actually do a better job at solving problems. While the economics profession has moved a long way towards Demsetz's perspective, there is still a long way to go.

EXPERIMENTAL INVESTIGATIONS OF PUBLIC GOODS THEORY

The market failure literature has evolved methodologically as well as theoretically. In the last 20 years we have seen a spate of articles testing market failure and game-theoretic propositions using the method of experimental economics. While the experimental method has offered varied results, the thrust of the literature has been to revise some of our previous beliefs. In particular, economists now see voluntary cooperation as more likely than before.

The experimental revolution has been one of the most important developments in recent economics. In this approach the economist adopts some of the methods of the natural scientist. He or she creates a controlled experiment using actual subjects and real dollar prizes. The economist designs 'rules of the game' and communicates those rules to the participants. Individuals then play the game, knowing they can keep their winnings. Variations in the experiment then allow us to better see how markets work, how individuals make decisions and how institutions matter.

Elizabeth Hoffman, in her 'Public Choice Experiments,' surveys the contributions of the experimental method to issues of public goods and politics. The first and most basic result was to establish that free-riding behavior is not universal. When individuals are given the opportunity to free-ride in experiments, many of them cooperate or contribute to the production of a public good. Individuals are also more likely to contribute when they see others contributing as well. This suggests that ongoing reciprocity is possible, even when a prisoner's dilemma might otherwise appear to hold. Individuals follow 'rules of thumb' that allow both small and large groups to sometimes reach cooperative solutions. Casual empiricism had already led us to suspect this result, but it is welcome to see it confirmed repeatedly in a laboratory setting.

Hoffman also surveys the literature on bargaining experiments. When individuals are put in isolated, stylized settings and allowed to strike bargains, they tend to strike good bargains. More specifically, they tend to strike the bargain that maximizes joint profits. This is consonant with a belief in the power of markets to encourage value-maximizing outcomes.

Some of the research surveyed by Hoffman reveals the limitations of many experimental studies. The constructed experiment does not exactly match any set of real world institutions. The experimental subjects sometimes know they are being 'watched.' The 'prizes' are often smaller than real world rewards. Yet the experimentalists have, over time, responded to many of their critics effectively. Experiments have been set up where individuals sit at a computer terminal and play anonymously. Many results are robust to the size of the prizes, or even become stronger as the prizes become more valuable. Experiments have moved closer and closer to reflecting some institutional structure. The robustness of many experimental results – including the finding of cooperative behavior – is a central reason why the experimental method has become increasingly popular and influential (see Kurzaban, McCabe, Smith and Wilson, 2001, as well as Smith, 1992 and 2000).

The other experimental pieces in this section look at how cooperative behavior varies under various assumptions and experimental designs. Gordon Tullock, in his 'Non-prisoner's dilemma,' allows the experimental participants to communicate, and he allows them to 'fire' their partners if they find the person insufficiently cooperative. Under these assumptions individuals cooperate with a much higher degree of frequency than most other experiments have found. Tullock's experiment is a very simple one, but also a powerful one. His design comes closer to real world institutions than do many other experiments about cooperation, and he finds that those changes bring more cooperation. Tullock (p. 456) notes that: 'most of our normal dealings do not meet the rather stringent conditions of the prisoner's dilemma.'

Isaac, Walker and Williams, in their 'Group size and the voluntary provision of public goods,' vary yet another aspect of experimental design. They look at how the extent of cooperation changes as the number of players in a game changes.

Under the standard market failure story, small groups might manage to cooperate successfully, but large groups almost certainly will not. When the group is small, the contribution of any single person still affects the overall outcome. Furthermore it would appear that small groups use norms, sanctions and informal codes of behavior more easily than can large groups, due to the lesser degree of anonymity in small groups. This also would militate in favor of more cooperation in small groups than in large ones.

While these kinds of stories have long commanded assent from many economists, they do not necessarily fit the data. The authors of this chapter, for instance, found that groups of four and ten persons provide public goods less effectively than do groups of 40 and 100. This is directly contrary to what standard theory would have led us to expect.

It remains an interesting question why the experiments indicate that large groups cooperative more successfully than do small ones. The authors suggest several reasons why people cooperate at all, but they make little attempt to explain their result of more cooperation with greater numbers of people. It appears clear that people reject the 'backwards induction' reasoning of the Nash equilibrium concept in game theory. (Backwards induction suggests that people see they will not cooperate in the last period of some game, and thus do not cooperate at all, once they see the breakdown in cooperation coming.) Yet why should they reject backwards induction even more when the number of players is large?

The answer to this question is likely to await further experimental work. The authors hint at one possibility but without exploring it. They suggest that individuals may cooperate to signal their trustworthiness to others. The value of this signal may be larger, the greater the number of people playing the game. There is yet another hypothesis, not considered by the authors. Cooperation may bring feelings of belonging and group solidarity, almost like that of a fan club or mass movement. Again, the value of these benefits may be greater, the larger the number of individuals playing the game.

James Andreoni, in the final experimental piece in our book, looks at why individuals tend to cooperate more than standard theory had predicted they would. Andreoni distinguishes two hypotheses (though more hypotheses may be relevant): an 'error' hypothesis, and a 'warm glow' hypothesis. The error hypothesis states that people cooperate because they do not really understand the nature of the game. The implication is that learning the nature of the game, and extended play, will bring less cooperation over time. The 'warm glow' hypothesis is that people simply enjoy cooperating, helping others, or being kind.

Andreoni's experiment reveals that at least half of all observed cooperative behavior comes from the 'warm glow' hypothesis. That is, individuals persist in this behavior, even once they understand that they might do financially better by free-riding. Again, this suggests that cooperation is relatively robust, more robust than traditional models would indicate. Cooperation is not just a matter of making a mistake.

CONCLUDING REMARKS

Our world is a highly imperfect one, and these imperfections include the workings of markets. Nonetheless, while being vigilant about what we will learn in the future, we conclude that the 'new theories' of market failure over-state their case and exaggerate the relative imperfections of the market economy. In some cases, the theoretical foundations of the market failure arguments are weak. In other cases, the evidence does not support what the abstract models suggest. Rarely is analysis done in a comparative institutional framework.

The term 'market failure' is prejudicial – we cannot know whether markets fail before we actually examine them, yet most of market failure theory is just theory. Alexander Tabarrok (2002) suggests that 'market challenge theory' might be a better term. Market challenge theory alerts us to areas where markets might fail and encourages us to seek out evidence. In testing these theories, we may find market failure or we may find that markets are more robust than we had previously believed. Indeed, the lasting contribution of the new market failure theorists may be in encouraging empirical research that broadens and deepens our understanding of markets.

We believe that the market failure or success debate will become more fruitful as it turns more to Hayekian themes and empirical and experimental methods. Above, we noted that extant models were long on 'information' – which can be encapsulated into unambiguous, articulable bits – and short on the broader category of 'knowledge,' as we find in Hayek. Yet most of the critical economic problems involve at least as much knowledge as information. Employers, for instance, have knowledge of how to overcome shirking problems, even when they do not have explicit information about how hard their employees are working. Many market failures are avoided to the extent we mobilize dispersed knowledge successfully.

It is no accident that the new market failure theorists have focused on information to the exclusion of knowledge. Information is easier to model, whereas knowledge is not, and the economics profession has been oriented towards models. Explicitly modeling knowledge may remain impossible for the immediate future, which suggests a greater role for history, case studies, cognitive science and the methods of experimental economics.

We think in particular of the experimental revolution in economics as a way of understanding and addressing Hayek's insights on markets and knowledge; Vernon Smith, arguably the father of modern experimental economics, frequently makes this connection explicit. Experimental economics forces the practitioner to deal with the kinds of knowledge and behavior patterns that individuals possess in the real world, rather than what the theorist writes into an abstract model. The experiment then tells us how the original 'endowments' might translate into real world outcomes. Since we are using real world agents, these endowments can include Hayekian knowledge and not just narrower categories of information.

Experimental results also tend to suggest Hayekian conclusions. When institutions and 'rules of the game' are set up correctly, decentralized knowledge has enormous power. Prices and incentives are extremely potent. The collective result of a market process contains a wisdom that the theorist could not have replicated with pencil and paper alone.

NOTES

1. Williamson's theory of post-contract opportunism (1976) was directed against Demsetz's 1968 argument that franchise bidding could be used to solve the problem of natural monopoly regulation. In Demsetz's view, a competitive bidding arrangement for the awarding of monopoly privileges in natural monopoly industries would lead to efficient results. Williamson argued that the inevitable incompleteness of contracts would cause the winning companies to shirk on every available margin, leading to undesirable results. Though we have not included this debate in our current volume, readers are encouraged to consult the two seminal papers noted, as well as Zupan's (1989) examination of franchise bidding in the American cable industry. Where Williamson predicts competitive underbidding of franchise contracts in anticipation of chiseling opportunities, Zupan finds no evidence for the phenomenon.

2. Theories of credit rationing have been around for much longer than the work of Stiglitz, and some individuals have suggested that Stiglitz does not give his precursors (for instance, Barro, 1976; and Jaffee, 1976) sufficient credit. Stiglitz, however, gives the clearest theoretical account of the mechanism behind credit rationing, and sets it in the broader context of a non-Hayekian theory of prices.

3. Hemenway's evidence consists of various sets of descriptive statistics; a thorough econometric test of propitious selection remains to be conducted but seems a fruitful line of enquiry for an econometrician with an appropriate data set.

4. Recall that a 'lemon' is a specifically bad car, not a low-quality brand or model (low-quality brands, at low prices, are not a market problem). A 'lemon' in this sense may be more of a statistical fallacy, a failure to recognize that in any random experiment some cars will turn out to have more problems than others, similar to the 'hot hand' in basketball, than a fact. Even

if sellers know that their car has a long history of repairs this may say very little, after factoring in information about model and brand, about the future expectation of repair which is what buyers want to know and what drives the lemons model.
5. Liebowitz and Margolis (1990), reproduced as Chapter 2 of *Winners, Losers & Microsoft.*
6. The contra-David process in which governments officially sanction a standard that the market has chosen has not been well studied but is not uncommon. In law, for example, governments and private bodies such as the American Law Institute periodically restate and codify law that is developed in a decentralized manner.
7. See Peter Lewin (2001) for an extended discussion of these issues.

REFERENCES

Akerlof, George. 1970. 'The market for "lemons": quality uncertainty and the market mechanism.' *Quarterly Journal of Economics* 84:3 (August): 488–500.

Akerlof, George. 1982. 'Labor contracts as partial gift exchange.' *Quarterly Journal of Economics* 97:4 (November): 543–69.

Andreoni, James. 1995. 'Cooperation in public-goods experiments: kindness or confusion.' *The American Economic Review* 85:4 (September): 891–904.

Barro, Robert J. 1976. 'The loan market, collateral, and rates of interest.' *Journal of Money, Credit, and Banking* 8:4 (November): 439–56.

Becker, Gary S. and George J. Stigler. 1974. 'Law enforcement, malfeasance, and compensation of enforcers.' *Journal of Legal Studies* 3:1 (January): 1–18.

Berger, Allen and Gregory F. Udell. 1992. 'Some evidence on the empirical significance of credit rationing,' *Journal of Political Economy* 100:5 (October): 1047–77.

Boettke, Peter, ed. 2000. *Socialism and the Market: The Socialist Calculation Debate Revisited.* London: Routledge.

Bond, Eric W. 1984. 'A direct test of the 'lemons' model: the market for used pickup trucks.' *American Economic Review* 72:4 (September): 801–4.

Browne, Mark J. and Helen I. Doerpinghaus. 1993. 'Information Asymmetries and Adverse Selection in the Market for Individual Medical Expense Insurance.' *Journal of Risk and Insurance* 60:2 (June): 300–312.

Carmichael, H. Lorne. 1990. 'Efficiency wage models of unemployment: one view.' *Economic Inquiry* 28:2 (April): 269–95.

Cawley, John and Tomas Philipson. 1999. 'An empirical examination of information barriers to trade in insurance.' *American Economic Review* 89:4 (September) 827–46.

Chiappori, Pierre-Andre and Bernard Salanie. 2000. 'Testing for asymmetric information in insurance markets.' *Journal of Political Economy* 108:1 (February): 56–78.

Cowen, Tyler. 1988. *The Theory of Market Failure: A Critical Examination.* Fairfax, Virginia: George Mason University Press and the Cato Institute.

David, Paul A. 1985. 'Clio and the economics of QWERTY.' *American Economic Review* 75:2 (May): 332–7.

David, Paul A. 1997. 'Path dependence and the quest for historical economics: one more chorus of the ballad of QWERTY.' *University of Oxford Discussion Paper in Economic and Social History*: 20.

Demsetz, Harold. 1968. 'Why regulate utilites?' *Journal of Law and Economics* 11 (April): 55–66.

Greenwald, Bruce and Joseph Stiglitz. 1988. 'Examining alternative macroeconomic theories.' *Brookings Papers on Economic Activity.* 1988:1. 207–60.

Hayek, F.A. 1945. 'The use of knowledge in society', *American Economic Review.* 35:4 (September): pp. 519–30.

Hemenway, David. 1990. 'Propitious selection.' *Quarterly Journal of Economics* 105:4 (November): 1063–69.

Hoffman, Elizabeth. 1997. 'Public choice experiments', 415–26 in Dennis C. Mueller, ed. *Perspectives on Public Choice: A Handbook.* Cambridge: Cambridge University Press.

Isaac, R. Mark and James M. Walker, Arlington W. Williams. 1994. 'Group size and the voluntary provision of public goods.' *Journal of Public Economics.* 54:1 (May): 1–36.

Jaffee, Dwight M. 1976. 'Imperfect information, uncertainty, and credit rationing.' *Quarterly Journal of Economics* 94:4 (November): 651–66.

Katz, Lawrence F. 1986. 'Efficiency wage theories: a partial evaluation.' *NBER Working Paper* 1906.

Klein, Daniel. 2001. 'The demand for and supply of assurance.' This volume.

Krueger, Alan, and Lawrence Summers. 1988. 'Efficiency wages and the inter-industry wage structure,' *Econometrica* 56:2 (March): 259–93.

Kurzban, Robert O. and Kevin McCabe, Vernon L. Smith, Bart J. Wilson. 2001. 'Incremental commitment and reciprocity in a real time public goods game.' *Personality and Social Psychology Bulletin* 27(12): 1662–73.

Lewin, Peter. 2001. 'The market process and the economics of QWERTY: two views.' *Review of Austrian Economics* 14:1 (March): 65–96.

Liebowitz, Stan J. and Stephen E. Margolis. 1990. 'The fable of the keys.' *Journal of Law and Economics* 33:1 (April): 1–26.

Liebowitz, Stan J. and Stephen E. Margolis. 1999. *Winners, Losers & Microsoft: Competition and Antitrust in High Technology.* Oakland, CA: Independent Institute.

Rothschild, Michael and Joesph Stiglitz. 1978. 'Equilibrium in competitive insurance markets: an essay on the economics of imperfect information.' *Quarterly Journal of Economics* 90:4 (November): 629–49.

Samuelson, Paul A. 1954. 'The pure theory of public expenditure.' *Review of Economics and Statistics* 36 (November): 387–9.

Shapiro, Carl and Joesph E. Stiglitz. 1984. 'Equilibrium unemployment as a worker discipline device.' *American Economic Review* 74:3 (June): 433–44.

Smith, Adam. 1998 (1776). *An Inquiry into the Nature and Causes of the Wealth of Nations.* Oxford and New York: Oxford University Press.

Smith, Vernon. 1991. *Papers in Experimental Economics.* New York: Cambridge University Press.

Smith, Vernon. 2000. *Bargaining and Market Behavior: Essays in Experimental Economics.* New York: Cambridge University Press.

Spence, M. 1973. 'Job market signalling.' *Quarterly Journal of Economics* 87:3 (August): 355–74.

Stiglitz, Joseph E. 1981. 'Credit rationing in markets with imperfect information.' *American Economic Review* 77:1 (March): 228–31.

Stiglitz, Joseph E. 1984. 'Theories of wage rigidity.' *NBER Working Paper* 1442.

Tabarrok, Alexander. 2002. 'Market challenges and government failure,' in *The Voluntary City*, edited by D. Beito, P. Gordon and A. Tabarrok. Ann Arbor, MI: University of Michigan Press.

Tullock, Gordon. 1999. 'Non-prisoner's dilemma.' *Journal of Economic Behavior and Organization* 39:4 (August): 455–58.

Williamson, Oliver E. 1976. 'Franchise bidding for natural monopolies – in general and with respect to CATV.' *Bell Journal of Economics* 7:1 (Spring): 73–104.

Williamson, Stephen D. 1994. 'Do informational frictions justify federal credit programs?' *Journal of Money, Credit, and Banking* 26:3 (August): 523–44.

Zinsmeister, Karl. 1993. 'MITI mouse: Japan's industrial policy doesn't work.' *Policy Review* 64 (Spring): 28–35.

Zupan, Mark. 1989. 'The efficiency of franchise bidding schemes in the case of cable television: some systematic evidence.' *Journal of Law and Economics* 32:2 (October): 401–56.

PART 1

New Market Failure Theories

2. Toward a general theory of wage and price rigidities and economic fluctuations

Joseph E. Stiglitz[1]

This chapter begins with the hypothesis that large economic fluctuations, the marked changes in the unemployment that characterize market economies, are a consequence of problems of adjustment to disturbances, especially adjustments of wages and prices. Two strands of work have addressed these problems of adjustment. One focuses on rigidities: downward rigidities in wages are at the center of traditional Keynesian models. The other focuses on the consequences of rapid changes, particularly in asset prices, in the context of markets with incomplete contracting (imperfect indexing) and imperfect capital markets. While the second tradition traces its origins at least back to Irving Fisher's debt-deflation theories, it has been revived in the new-Keynesian work of Bruce Greenwald and Stiglitz (1988, 1989, 1990b, 1993, 1995) and others. The fact that wages and prices did fall dramatically in the Great Depression (by more than a third in the United States) provided some of the impetus to the latter theory. The major economic downturn this year in East Asia, with unemployment in Indonesia soaring from 4.7 percent to 14.3 percent and output falling by at least 16 percent, was accompanied by huge changes in prices: over the first year of the crisis, the current best estimate is that Indonesian real wages fell by 40–60 percent (World Bank, 1998, p. 105). This result, I would argue, is better interpreted through the second strand of thought.

I. ASYMMETRIES IN ADJUSTMENT SPEEDS

This chapter carries the analysis one step further. It argues that, because different prices (including prices of labor and capital) are determined in different ways, shocks lead to marked changes in relative prices, and those disturbances in relative prices greatly exacerbate economic fluctuations. The determination of asset prices is often best described by the auction markets emphasized in traditional economics texts. These prices adjust quickly; and because the value of assets today depends on expectations of future values, current prices can be highly volatile, as those expectations change. On the other hand, prices of most products, wages, and bank interest rates are set by firms (and banks), albeit in the context of markets. Firms face downward-sloping demand curves for their products in the short run and upward-sloping supply curves for factors. These slopes can be explained in part by imperfections in competition due to product differentiation or to the small number of firms in the market and in part by information imperfections.

The importance of downward-sloping product demand (at least in the short run) has been brought home forcefully by the recent crisis in East Asia. Consider the example of Thailand, which, with less than 1 percent of world GDP, is a small player in the world economy. Under standard theory, it would face a horizontal demand curve for its products; certainly a 30 percent real devaluation should lead to huge increases in the demand for its products. Exports would quickly fill up any loss in domestic demand. Yet in fact, the value of Thai exports actually declined in the aftermath of the crisis (Greenwald, 1998).

For price- and wage-setting firms, the consequences of changes in prices and wages are uncertain, not only because prices and wages have to be set before demand and supply curves are fully known, but also because the reactions of other agents in the market are uncertain. The uncertainty arises for two reasons: first, because changes in a firm's circumstances (including the signals they receive) are only imperfectly known by other firms; and second, because firms receiving the same information or the same shocks will react differently, depending on their circumstances and characteristics (which are not common knowledge). Both because of agency problems and imperfections of capital markets, which lead to firms acting in a risk-averse manner (Greenwald and Stiglitz, 1990a), firms are sensitive to the risks associated with different decisions. The problem of price- and wage-setting thus should be approached within a standard dynamic portfolio model, one that takes into account the risks associated with each decision, the nonreversibilities, as well as the adjustment costs associated with both prices and quantities (see Figure 2.1). My earlier papers (with Greenwald) have argued that (a) the risks associated with wage and price adjustments may well be larger than those associated with output adjustments, at least for goods that could be stored; and (b) there were fixed costs associated with hiring and firing, and those costs were often asymmetric. These asymmetries helped explain the pattern of hours and employment over the cycle, with increases in hours (entailing high overtime payments) typically preceding increases in employment, and with labor-shedding typically lagging downturns (giving rise to the phenomenon described as labor-hoarding).

In the following sections, I look more closely at the price-setting process, providing further insights into why prices exhibit rigidities and why different prices may adjust at different rates. I then explore the consequences of asymmetric price responses.

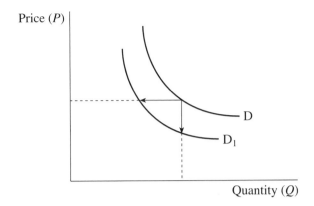

Price (*P*)

D

D$_1$

Quantity (*Q*)

Notes: If there is a shift in the demand curve, either price or quantities must change. The smaller the adjustment of prices, the larger is the adjustment of quantities. With uncertainty in the demand curve, different adjustments in prices impose different risks on the firm.

Figure 2.1   Price versus quantity adjustment

II.   SIGNALING AND RIGIDITIES

Earlier analyses explained why the level of wages or prices might affect the quality of the labor hired or of the good purchased. These effects have profound implications for the shape of the demand and supply curves, and they imply that wages and prices may not adjust to market-clearing levels. Here, however, the concern is with how economies respond to shocks. Efficiency-wage theories, for instance, argue that, while real wages may not adjust to a change in the supply of labor, they will typically change in response to other changes in economic circumstances, including information (e.g., about the productivity of workers). In a dynamic economy, changes in prices and wages may convey information, about both the characteristics of a firm and changes in those characteristics. For instance, if a firm responds quickly to the lowering of prices by a competitor, this action may convey information about the firm's willingness to meet or its ability to withstand competition. By the same token, given asymmetries of information about a firm's balance sheet, large changes in prices may convey information of particular importance to a firm's creditors (e.g., that the firm needs to liquefy assets quickly). (Firms facing the threat of bankruptcy are often forced to engage in quick inventory reductions; the fact that the signal is costly makes it a very effective signal.) It is the *change* in observable behavior that conveys information.

The information conveyed by changes in prices is all the greater when there are costs to changing prices, as in the menu-cost literature. In this case, the change conveys information that the shock to the environment (e.g., to the net worth of the firm) is greater than some critical threshold level.

Signaling theories thus suggest that, to the extent that it is changes in behavior that convey relevant information, there will be strong rigidities in variables that are publicly observable. While inventories and much of the internal workings of firms are not observable, by their very nature, prices have to be at least partially observable to outsiders (to those engaging in the trade). Similarly, layoffs may convey a strong signal, especially to other workers at the firm, that may induce those not laid off to commence searching for alternative employment. The recognition that various actions can convey information may provide an incentive for secrecy and for firms to take actions to otherwise obfuscate signals and their interpretations. Like other attempts to block information flows, this practice may interfere with overall economic efficiency (see Aaron S. Edlin and Stiglitz, 1995).

Much of the signal is related to deviations from norms. That is, if all firms are increasing prices by 3 percent, or if the firm has always increased its price in line with the rate of inflation, then deviations from either norm will convey information about the changed circumstances of the firm. Since norms can differ in different countries and can change dramatically, it may be difficult to relate price-setting processes just to fundamentals.

The state of the economy may affect the information conveyed by a particular action, causing more rigidities in some circumstances than others. Thus, if the state of the economy is such that bankruptcy is a real danger, a firm may have a strong incentive to avoid signaling that it faces a higher probability of bankruptcy; as a result, prices may be relatively rigid in this situation. On the other hand, if the state of the economy is such that most firms are markedly decreasing prices, then the signal conveyed by a price decrease by a firm may be weaker, and it could simply be interpreted as reflecting lower costs of production or an effective response to competitive pressures.

Firms may, of course, be uncertain about the full implications of signals conveyed by wage and price changes, including how competitor firms, customers, or suppliers (including creditors) will respond to those changes. This risk, combined with firm risk aversion, reinforces the reluctance to change prices.

III.   SEARCH AND RIGIDITIES

Search is costly, and the extent of search depends on perceptions of whether the offered price (wage, interest rate) deviates from that being offered by others. Elsewhere (Stiglitz, 1987), I have shown that this can give rise to a kinked demand curve in product markets. The reasoning is as follows: When a firm raises its price (by more than the 'norm'), the firm's customers immediately

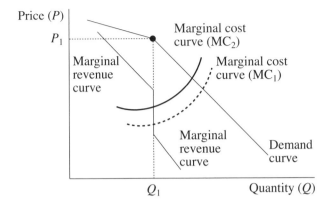

Notes: Conventional search models give rise to firms facing kinked demand curves. The gains to lowering prices may be markedly lower than the losses from raising prices.

Figure 2.2   Kinked demand curves

know it and are induced to search for alternative suppliers. But if it lowers its price, then unless it expends resources on advertising, its action induces no new customers to launch a search; and while it will glean more customers (as those currently searching are more likely to settle on this firm), the increased sales under plausible conditions will be markedly less than the loss in sales from price increases (see Figure 2.2). Similar arguments hold in other markets. The location of the kink and how it changes over time depend on expectations. If most individuals expect most firms to be adjusting prices with inflation, and if there are shared views about the rate of inflation, then the price at the kink will move up with inflation: only deviations from expectations (from the norm) give rise to search. Norms can change and change quickly.

The consequences of actions are not only uncertain, but they can also not be costlessly reversed: it will be costly to recruit back a customer who has found another supplier or a good worker who has found another employer. Together, risk and adjustment costs imply that there may be an option value in delaying wage decreases and price increases, which gives rise to further rigidities in price-setting in markets.

IV.   UNCERTAINTY AND THE WAGE- AND PRICE-SETTING PROCESS

In the price-setting sectors of the economy, differences in the implied risk aversion of firms (resulting in part from differences in net worth) lead to differences across firms in price and wage responses to similar shocks. This increases the possibility that different wages and prices will adjust differently in response to shocks to the economy. This effect is, of course, exacerbated by shocks that have large and differential effects on the net worth of different firms. On the other hand, greater uncertainty may lead to more risk-averse behavior on the part of firms, thus contributing to greater wage and price rigidities (i.e., smaller deviations from perceived norms of adjustments).

Ex ante, it is not possible to ascertain which effect will predominate. But large shocks, such as those facing East Asia, are more likely to result in a change in norms; and indeed, these markets have been characterized by rapidly falling wages and prices. This is especially the case in Indonesia, where it has been estimated that almost two-thirds of the firms are bankrupt; thus the marginal adverse signaling effect of lowering one's price may, at this juncture, be minimal.

V. INTERACTIONS BETWEEN ASYMMETRIES IN RESPONSES AND IMPERFECTIONS IN INFORMATION

The rapid response of asset prices and interest rates to shocks, combined with the imperfections in capital markets that limit the ability of firms to divest themselves of risks, and with the imperfect indexing of debt contracts, has profound implications for the economy's aggregate supply curve. The net worth of firms can change very quickly (Greenwald and Stiglitz, 1993). With risk-averse firms and imperfect risk markets, decreases in net worth lead to large leftward shifts in supply curves. Moreover, the concavity of the supply functions implies that even in a closed economy, where producers of a given product gain from a price rise what purchasers lose, large price changes have macroeconomic effects. Again, East Asia provides an illustration of the phenomenon, as well as a confirmation of the predictions of the theory. There, the increases in interest rates, which were both unexpected and very large, quickly eroded the net worth of the already highly indebted firms. They also reduced net worth through another channel: many firms held substantial wealth in the form of assets like land and stock in other firms, the value of which was adversely affected by the increased interest rates and the associated economic decline. More broadly, to know the impact of a shock on the net worth of any firm requires enormous information, not only about its asset position, but also about the adjustments in prices of the goods it sells and the factors it purchases. A full accounting of net worth requires not only knowing the value of those variables today, but also an estimate of how they will move through time. The larger the disturbance to the economy, the greater the uncertainty.

If all wages and prices were to fall proportionately, matters would be grave enough. But in the previous section, I argued not only that different prices are determined by different adjustment mechanisms, but also that for wage and price-setting firms, patterns of adjustment of their wages and prices will depend on factors idiosyncratic to each firm (such as the change in its net worth and its implicit degree of risk aversion). Therefore prices and wages do not all fall proportionately. And even if there were indexed debt contracts (so that interest rates adjusted to changes in inflation or deflation), different firms would still find their net worth affected differently, and relative prices could deviate significantly from those associated with traditional equilibrium theories, which ignored these effects. Because interest-rate increases have such a large impact on asset values and on the dynamics of adjustment, the large increases in interest rates lead to marked increases in uncertainty.

Increased uncertainty and lower net worth affect the macroeconomy through several channels: through the decreased willingness of risk-averse firms to hire labor, to hold inventories, to produce (except in response to orders), or to invest. At the same time, agency problems in the economy are likely to increase, one consequence of which is that credit flows get choked off. Aggregate demand and supply are both adversely affected.

Reduced credit flows reinforce all of these effects. Consider trade credit. Firms can be viewed as engaged in both 'production' and 'financial' activities. Their reduced net worth makes them less willing and able to absorb risk. And the greater uncertainty about their borrowers' position (together with the decline in average net worth of their borrowers) means that lending through trade credit will now be a more risky activity. Reduced lending on the part of banks (a result of tighter supervision, the closure of many banks, and the decreased net worth and increased risk exposure of banks that remain open) reinforces these effects (Greenwald and Stiglitz, 1990b).

As noted earlier, the overall patterns observed in East Asia closely match those predicted by these theories, with four additional observations. First, earlier models focused on closed economies. Because the East Asian economies were open economies, some of the price adjustments (such as the large increases in interest rates) represented redistributions to those outside the economy; there was thus an aggregate-net-worth effect, which reinforced the internal redistributive effect Greenwald and I had earlier emphasized. Second, our earlier models did not focus on the impact of devaluations. As noted, risk-averse firms would typically have cover for their foreign exchange liabilities, so that devaluations would help exporters. Under perfectly flexible wages and prices, nontraded-goods industries would be affected only in the intended way, that is, through a shift of resources from the nontraded to the traded sector. But with relative price rigidities, some nontraded-goods firms may find their input prices rising faster than the prices for the goods which they sell; these firms may thus experience large negative net-worth effects. Third, poor accounting practices (i.e., a lack of transparency) increased the uncertainty: not only were there on average large changes in net worth, but it was also difficult for suppliers of capital to ascertain the magnitude of those changes. Fourth, firms in East Asia were typically highly leveraged, making them even more sensitive to changes in interest rates. The high levels of debt (especially short-term) were far greater than could be explained by an interaction between rational risk-averse borrowers and rational risk-neutral or risk-averse lenders. These deviations from expected behavior can perhaps be interpreted as evidence of moral hazard; lenders, both domestic and foreign, apparently expected to be bailed out. (In cases when the high levels of short-term debt and low levels of transparency are important features of the private-sector landscape, policy should presumably take into account the fact that large increases in interest rates may have particularly large adverse effects.)

Note, however, that it was the large adjustments in some prices that played as important a role in propagating and amplifying the disturbance as did the relative rigidity in other prices. Would still greater flexibility of wages and prices enable the economy to maintain itself at close to full employment? Not obviously: an increased pace of wage and price adjustment, given the contractual rigidities already in place, would have led to even more bankruptcies, greater erosion of net worth, and a more adverse effect on aggregate supply. Nor would indexing have fully resolved these problems, given the large changes in relative prices (e.g., real interest rates and exchange rates).

VI.   CONCLUDING REMARKS

This chapter has attempted to provide insights into the three key macroeconomic questions. Why do wages in the labor market not adjust to clear the labor market? How can we explain the magnitude of the changes in the demand curve for labor, which seem to necessitate such large changes in real wages to equilibrate that market? And why do adjustments in person-hours take the form they do, with a disproportionate share of the adjustment in downturns occurring in the form of employment? In addressing these questions, I have unified the two alternative strands in new-Keynesian economics, one focusing on rigidities, the other on the adverse consequences of downward movements in prices. I have argued that asymmetries of adjustment and imperfections of information are key; the asymmetries are particularly pronounced between those markets (like assets) where auction processes prevail and those in which firms engage in price-setting. It is relative rigidities, not absolute ones, that matter. In the case of price-setting firms, a dynamic portfolio theory of adjustment that (i) incorporates both prices and quantities, (ii) takes into account nonlinearities, fixed costs, and irreversibilities, and (iii) incorporates signaling impacts of changes and option values can explain not only slow speeds of adjustment, but even rigidities. (Specifically, it explains rigidities of the sort where changes in the environment lead to no change in firm behavior: for example, because of kinks in the perceived demand curves facing firms.) I have argued that it is not just the price of goods and labor relative to money that matters in determining macroeconomic fluctuations; disturbances ('deviations from full equilibrium') of other relative prices may matter even more.

The theory has, at the same time, strong policy implications. It agrees in some respects with traditional Keynesian prescriptions and differs in others, but most importantly it calls attention to aspects of policy that are too often ignored and that have played out with a vengeance in East Asia. Falling wages and prices (increased price flexibility) in the presence of incomplete contracting may have negative impacts that far outweigh positive real-balance effects. Impacts on asset values and cash flows of different policies have first-order effects. Monetary policy has impacts not only through channels traditionally emphasized, including credit availability, but also through changes in asset values and cash constraints facing firms. Aggregate demand and aggregate supply are intimately intertwined, so that demand shifts that reduce the net worth of firms have significant impacts on aggregate supply in subsequent periods. The fact that these effects are persistent and hard to reverse in turn has strong implications for the design of the appropriate macroeconomic policies. While there is always some uncertainty about the future position of the economy and the consequences of alternative policies, risks are asymmetric. This is perhaps one of the central lessons to emerge from the crisis in East Asia.

NOTE

1. World Bank, Washington, DC 20433; on leave from Stanford University. The views expressed are solely those of the author and do not necessarily represent those of any organization with which he is or has been affiliated. This paper is based on joint research with Bruce Greenwald.

REFERENCES

Edlin, Aaron S. and Stiglitz, Joseph E. 'Discouraging rivals: managerial rent-seeking and economic inefficiencies.' *American Economic Review*, December 1995, 85(5), pp. 1301–12.
Greenwald, Bruce C. 'International Adjustment in the Face of Imperfect Capital Markets.' Unpublished manuscript presented at the 1998 Annual Bank Conference for Development Economics, World Bank, Washington, DC, 1998.

Greenwald, Bruce C. and Stiglitz, Joseph E. 'Examining Alternative Macroeconomic Theories.' *Brookings Papers on Economic Activity*, 1988, (1), pp. 207–60.

Greenwald, Bruce C. and Stiglitz, Joseph E. 'Toward a Theory of Rigidities.' *American Economic Review*, May 1989 (*Papers and Proceedings*), 79(2), pp. 364–69.

Greenwald, Bruce C. and Stiglitz, Joseph E. 'Asymmetric Information and the New Theory of the Firm: Financial Constraints and Risk Behavior.' *American Economic Review*, May 1990a (*Papers and Proceedings*), 80(2), pp. 160–65.

Greenwald, Bruce C. and Stiglitz, Joseph E. 'Macroeconomic Models with Equity and Credit Rationing,' in R.B. Hubbard, ed., *Asymmetric information, corporate finance, and investment*. Chicago: University of Chicago Press, 1990b, pp. 15–42.

Greenwald, Bruce C. and Stiglitz, Joseph E. 'Financial Market Imperfections and Business Cycles.' *Quarterly Journal of Economics*, February 1993, 108(1), pp. 77–114.

Greenwald, Bruce C. and Stiglitz, Joseph E. 'Labor Market Adjustments and the Persistence of Unemployment.' *American Economic Review*, May 1995 (*Papers and Proceedings*), 85(2), pp. 219–25.

Stiglitz, Joseph E. 'Competition and the Number of Firms in a Market: Are Duopolies More Competitive Than Atomistic Markets?' *Journal of Political Economy*, October 1987, 95(5), pp. 1041–61.

World Bank. *Global economic prospects and the developing countries 1998/99: Beyond financial crisis*. Washington, DC: World Bank, 1998.

3. Keynesian economics and critique of first fundamental theorem of welfare economics

Joseph E. Stiglitz

KEYNESIAN ECONOMICS

Of all the market failures the one whose impact in eroding public confidence in market processes was the greatest was the Great Depression, the worst example of the periodic slumps that had plagued market economies throughout the centuries of capitalism. The existence and persistence of unemployment can be viewed as providing a convincing refutation of the neoclassical model: for in that model, all markets, including the market for labor, clear.

Curiously the debate on market socialism did not focus on the relative macroeconomic merits of the alternative systems, and the historical evidence is of limited value. Though the socialist economies 'solved' the unemployment problem, their solution *may* have been to make it disguised rather than open. The socialist economies did not seem to exhibit fluctuations in growth rates, evidence of fluctuations in economic activity.

Still there are theoretical reasons to think that market socialism would alleviate the underlying problem. One of the central themes in recent macroeconomic work has traced economic slumps to 'coordination failures.' To put the matter baldly, there are no jobs because there is no demand for the output of firms, and there is no demand for the output of firms because people do not have jobs. *If* the economy was well described by the Arrow–Debreu model, *if* there were, for instance, a complete set of markets, then these coordination failures presumably would not occur. Advocates of market socialism argue that it can overcome the coordination failure problem, and thus avoid the huge loss of economic efficiency associated with the periodic downturns that have characterized market economies.

Another recent theme has seen economic downturns as a consequence of capital market imperfections, which inhibit the economy's ability to spread and diversify risks.[1] Thus, if firms perceive an increase in risk, they will reduce the level of their investment. Reductions in cash flow may force a reduction in investment, if firms face credit rationing and if there are impediments to their raising capital in other forms (e.g., through equity). Again, market socialism, with its direct control of investment, would seem to alleviate these problems; it would presumably set investment at the level required to sustain full employment.

During the 1970s and early 1980s there was another strand of work in macroeconomics which suggested that these macroeconomic concerns were not of much importance. Market economies quickly adjusted to disturbances. The tendency in American universities not to include economic history as part of the study of economics has reinforced a shortness of memory, leading many American academic economists to conclude that recessions were a problem of the past – if they were a problem then. But unfortunately, the major recession of the early 1980s, the recession of the early 1990s, and the persistence of high unemployment rates in Europe provided a rude awakening to those who believed that cyclical unemployment was a thing of the past. These experiences should have sent one message: Something was fundamentally wrong with the Arrow–Debreu model. If that model were correct, unemployment would not exist, and it would be hard to explain the volatility of the economy, given the role of prices in absorbing shocks and given the role of inventories, savings, and insurance markets in buffering both individual firms and households from the impact of shocks.

But while Keynes as well as the subsequent research in new Keynesian economics has provided an explanation for both unemployment and economic volatility – while it has attempted to identify precisely what is wrong with the Arrow–Debreu model that can account for these observations – there was another message of Keynes that was clearly heard: the macroeconomic ills of capitalism were curable. One didn't need to institute fundamental reforms in the economic system. One only needed selective government intervention. It is in this sense that Keynesian economics greatly weakened the case for market socialism.

. . .

CRITIQUE OF THE FIRST FUNDAMENTAL THEOREM OF WELFARE ECONOMICS

In this chapter I argue that the first fundamental theorem of welfare economics – asserting the efficiency of competitive economies – is fundamentally flawed. Quite contrary to that theorem, competitive economies are almost never efficient (in a precise sense to be defined below). I focus on the problems that arise from the assumptions of perfect information and a complete set of markets. Other problems, such as those associated with other assumptions of these theorems like the absence of endogenous technological change, are taken up in Stiglitz (1994).

The first fundamental theorem asserted that every competitive economy was Pareto efficient. This is the modern rendition of Adam Smith's invisible hand conjecture:

> Man has almost constant occasion for the help of his brethren, and it is in vain for him to expect it from their benevolence only. He will be more likely to prevail if he can interest their self-love in his favor, and show them that it is for their own advantage to do for him what he requires of them . . . It is not from the benevolence of the butcher, the brewer, or the baker that we expect our dinner, but from their regard for their own interest. We address ourselves, not to their humanity but to their self-love, and never talk to them of our own necessities but of their advantages.

Smith went on to describe how self-interest led to social good:

> He intends only his own gain, and he is in this as in many other cases, led by an invisible hand to promote an end which was no part of his intention. Nor is it always the worse for society that it was no part of it. By pursuing his own interest he frequently promotes that of the society more effectually than when he really intends to promote it.[2]

It is the first welfare theorem that provides the intellectual foundations of our belief in market economies. Like any theorem, its conclusions depend on the validity of the assumptions. A closer look at those assumptions, however, suggests that the theorem is of limited relevance to modern industrial economies.

The Greenwald–Stiglitz Theorems on the Efficiency of Competitive Markets[3]

It is often interesting to note which assumptions an author highlights, by labeling them 'assumption A.1 . . . A.10' and which assumptions are hidden, whether deliberately or not: the unspoken assumptions that go into every model, the assumptions that are made in passing, as if they were no more than a reminder of conventional usage, or the assumptions that are embedded in certain basic definitions. The notion that market equilibrium should be characterized by demand equaling supply is, for instance, presented as part of the definition of equilibrium in the standard competitive model. It is implied that it should be obvious that if demand were not equal to supply, there would be forces for change, so that the situation would not be an equilibrium.[4] More recent work in economies with imperfect information has shown that that conclusion is not correct; competitive[5] market equilibrium may be characterized by demand exceeding supply (as in the Stiglitz–Weiss 1981 models of credit rationing) or by supply exceeding demand (as in the Shapiro–Stiglitz 1984 model of unemployment with efficiency wages).[6] Similarly the standard competitive model begins with the implicit assumption of a linear price system (a fixed price per unit purchased), while we now know that competitive markets with imperfect information may be characterized by nonlinear price systems, where there may, for instance, be quantity discounts.[7] The standard assumption that competitive equilibrium drives profits to zero can also be shown not to be valid in models with imperfect information.[8]

The Importance of Informational Assumptions

The fact that so many of the standard results do not remain valid when the extreme assumptions of perfect information are dropped serves to emphasize the general – and until recently, insufficiently recognized – importance of informational assumptions in competitive equilibrium analysis. The concerns about unspoken assumptions are of equal importance to the question at hand – the evaluation of alternative ways of organizing the economy. The first fundamental theorem of welfare economics is based on the assumption that there is perfect information, or more accurately, that information is fixed – and in particular unaffected by any action taken by any individual, any price, or any variable affected by the collective action of individuals in the market – and that there is a complete set of risk markets. Whenever these conditions are not satisfied the market is not constrained Pareto efficient; that is, there are interventions by the government that could be unambiguously welfare improving. These interventions respect the same limitations on markets and costs of information (and marketing) that affect the private economy. Indeed government intervention can be shown to be desirable, even if the government is extremely limited in its instruments, for instance, if the government is limited to simple (linear) price and uniform lump-sum[9] interventions. Beyond that, the nature (and even the magnitudes) of the desirable interventions can be related to observable market parameters, such as how different groups in the population respond to changes in wages and prices.[10]

In a sense Debreu and Arrow's great achievement was to find that almost singular set of assumptions under which Adam Smith's invisible hand conjecture was correct.[11] There are, to be sure, a few other singular cases in which the market might be constrained Pareto efficient. For instance, the absence of risk markets would have no consequences if everyone were identical and faced identical shocks, so that even if there were risk markets, there would be no trading in them;[12] or if the quantities of all goods consumed by all individuals were observable, then economies of all goods consumed by all individuals were observable, then economies in which there were moral hazard would be constrained Pareto efficient.[13] (The welfare economics of economies with moral hazard is explored in greater detail by Prescott and Townsend, 1984. The differences in conclusions between Greenwald and Stiglitz and Prescott and Townsend is attributable to the fact that the latter focus on this special case which Arnott and Stiglitz 1985 as well as Greenwald and Stiglitz had shown to be efficient.)

Externality Effects in the Presence of Imperfect Information and Incomplete Markets

The essential insight of Greenwald and Stiglitz was that when markets are incomplete and information is imperfect, the actions of individuals have externality-like effects on others, which they fail to take into account. (The externalities are generally like 'atmospheric' externalities in that their level depends on the actions of all individuals together.) Some examples may help illustrate what is at issue:

1. *Incomplete risk markets.* Suppose that there are many states of nature, but only one risky asset, apple trees. The number of apple trees planted determines (stochastically) the number of apples produced next year, and this in turn determines the price and profitability, in each state of nature, of owning an apple tree. As individuals plant more apple trees, the probability distribution of the returns from planting apple trees changes, and since apple trees are, by definition, the only risky investment, it is as if one asset (the old probability distribution) is replaced by a new one. Each investor of course takes the probability distribution of returns as given, even though it changes as more trees are planted. The effect of each individual's action on that probability distribution can thus be viewed as an externality.[14]

2. *Variable labor quality (adverse selection).* Consider the problem of imperfect information about the quality of laborers. Firms may know the average quality of labor being offered in a union hiring hall. They may even know how that quality is affected by the wage paid.[15] Their demand for labor, at each wage, will depend on this quality variable. On the other hand, each worker, whether of high or low quality, does not take into account the effect of his or her decisions concerning the amount of labor to supply on the average quality of labor (and accordingly on the demand for labor). In effect, if low-quality laborers were to decide to supply more labor, at any given wage, it would lower the profits of the firm. Their actions would have an externality effect on firms. By the same token, it is easy for the government to affect the quality mix, for instance, by taxing or subsidizing commodities that have a differential effect on the labor supply of low and high-ability individuals.[16]

3. *Incentive (moral hazard) problems.* Individuals buy insurance because they are risk averse. But insurance means that they do not have to bear the full consequences of their actions: Their incentives to avoid the insured-against event are attenuated. Each individual takes the insurance premium as given. Of course, if all take less care, the insured event will occur more frequently, and premiums will rise. This example also shows how the government can effect a Pareto improvement. By taxing and subsidizing various commodities, the government can encourage individuals to take greater care. Suppose that the insured-against event is damage from fire, and one of the major causes of fires is smoking in bed. Smoking in bed is particularly dangerous if the individual also drinks too much. One might imagine, in principle, an insurance contract requiring that the individual not smoke in bed after drinking, but this would be hard to enforce. (The insurance company could install TV monitors in every bedroom, but some might view this as an intrusion on privacy.) But by taxing cigarettes and alcohol, the government can discourage smoking and drinking in general, and as a by-product, smoking in bed after drinking would be discouraged as well. For at least small taxes, the welfare gains from the reduced 'moral hazard' would more than offset the welfare losses from the distortions (deadweight loss) in consumption patterns induced by the taxes.[17] It should be clear that taxes and subsidies should be set so as to encourage care, for instance, by subsidizing goods that are complements to taking care, and taxing substitutes. The optimal tax rates are set so that at the margin, one balances the benefits of induced care with the marginal deadweight loss. Both of these can be related to empirically observable magnitudes (e.g., the compensated [own and cross] price elasticities of demand and the elasticities of 'care' with respect to various prices). Thus, while government and private insurers lack the information necessary to prevent moral hazard – they cannot directly control actions – the government has the instruments with which to alleviate the effects of moral hazard and the information required to use those instruments.[18]

Powers of the Government

This example also serves to illustrate the powers that the government may have that the private sector does not. There is a 'folk theorem'[19] (or what would be a folk theorem, were it true) that says that anything that the government can do, the private sector can do as well or better: Alleged advantages of the government only arise from 'unfair' comparisons, for instance, a government with costless information can improve on market allocations when markets face costly information. It was to avoid this criticism that I focused on the concept of *constrained* Pareto efficiency.

But the question still needs to be addressed: how does the government differ from other economic organizations? Why can it do things that others cannot? This is the question I addressed in my book *The Economic Role of the State*, where I argued that the government's power of compulsion (associated with its property of universal membership) gave it distinct advantages (and concern about abuses of those powers gave rise to constraints that resulted in distinct disadvantages). Thus the government can prohibit the manufacture of cigarettes – no private individual or group of individuals can do this. (Of course, to enforce this prohibition, the government must have the power to observe the production of cigarettes. If there were not economies of scale in production, then it might be difficult for the government to enforce this prohibition. But with significant economies of scale, if the government could not enforce the prohibition, it could at least increase the costs of cigarettes significantly.) By the same token, the government can impose a tax on the production of all cigarettes. It may be possible to observe, and hence to tax, the production of cigarettes even if it is not possible to observe individual consumption levels (it is impossible to monitor secondary trades). No private insurance firm or collection of insurance firms could 'force' all cigarette companies to pay a tax on their production. Suppose that they bribed them, by offering them a payment conditional on their increasing the price. Then a new company could come along, charge a slightly lower price, take away all of their customers, and make a profit. This is just an illustration of the fact that the government does have powers that the private sector does not have, powers that in certain instances (if well used) could result in a Pareto improvement. (For other examples, see Stiglitz, 1989b and 1991a.)

Some Cautionary Notes on the Interpretation of the Greenwald–Stiglitz Theorems

The Greenwald–Stiglitz and related theorems have three interpretations. First, as we have seen, in certain cases they provide well-identified forms of welfare-enhancing government intervention. Second, they suggest that it may not be possible to decentralize efficiently, in the manner suggested by the fundamental theorems of welfare economics. I will return to this theme later in the chapter. Third, and perhaps most important, they *remove* the widespread presumption that markets are necessarily the most efficient way of allocating resources. There is, to repeat, no general theorem on which one can base that conclusion. (There may of course be other bases for reaching that conclusion, a point to which I will come shortly.)

In this perspective the Greenwald–Stiglitz theorems should not primarily be taken as a basis of a prescription for government intervention. One of the reasons that they do not provide a basis for prescription is that doing so would require a more detailed and formal model of the government. When the central theorem of economics asserted that no government – no matter how benevolent, no matter how rational – could do any better than the market, we had little need for a theory of the government: It could only make matters worse. But the Greenwald–Stiglitz theorems assert that there is a *potential* role for government. Whether and how the government should intervene is a question to which I will return later. (Presumably, since governments are political institutions, the answer will depend in part on the form that those institutions do or can take. The theorems do tell us, if the government decides to intervene through, say, taxes and subsidies, the critical parameters on which the rates of those taxes and subsidies should depend.)

Other Reasons Why Market Economies with Imperfect Information May Not Be Pareto Efficient

While the Greenwald–Stiglitz theorems provide the most forceful refutation of the first fundamental theorem of welfare economics, several other results of the information paradigm provide equally fundamental criticisms. I want to draw attention to but three, two of which have to do with how information-theoretic considerations lead to the conclusion that other assumptions of the standard competitive model (which underlie the fundamental theorem of welfare economics) will not be satisfied. The list below is not meant to be exhaustive. I have tried to focus on what I see as the central economic assumptions.[20]

Incompleteness of Markets

The assumption that there is a complete set of markets, including a complete set of risk and futures markets is important in the standard competitive paradigm but unrealistic.

Transaction costs
The incompleteness of markets can itself be explained by transaction costs, an important component of which is information costs. There are costs associated with establishing a market. If there were markets for each of the millions of commodities, each of the billions of contingencies, each of the infinity of future dates, then so much of societies' resources would be absorbed in organizing these transactions that there would be little left over to be bought and sold on each of these markets!

Once we recognize the myriad events that affect us, we recognize the impossibility of having even a complete set of risk markets (insurance against all contingencies). Each firm is affected not only by the events that affect the industry but by idiosyncratic events – the illness of its president, a breakdown in one of its machines, the departure of a key salesperson. The firm itself can buy insurance for many of the risks it faces, such as that its trucks get into accidents or that its factories burn down, but most of the risks it faces cannot be insured against. The notion that there be markets for each of these risks is mind-boggling.

Inconsistency between assumptions of 'complete markets' and 'competitive markets'

Just as the high dimensionality of the 'states of nature' makes it obvious that a complete set of securities simply cannot exist, so too the high dimensionality of the product space makes it obvious that a complete set of markets for commodities cannot exist once we remember that products are defined by a complete specification of their characteristics: Products of different quality are treated as different commodities, and products delivered at different dates and locations are treated as different commodities. Arrow and Debreu's idea of treating commodities at different dates and in different states of nature as different commodities seemed like a nice mathematical trick, enabling the extension of the standard model to a new, much wider range of problems, but upon closer examination the underlying spirit of the model was vitiated: Either there simply could not exist a complete set of markets (there would have to be a *perfectly competitive* market for the delivery of a machine of a particular specification to a factory at a particular date at a particular time) or, if there did exist a complete set of markets, it is hard to conceive of each of those markets as being 'perfectly' competitive (i.e., that there be so many traders on both sides of the market that each trader believes it has a negligible effect on price). Of necessity, the markets would have to be thin and imperfectly competitive.[21] Consider, for instance, the market for labor. Each individual is different, in myriad ways. A complete set of markets would entail there being a different market for each type of labor – a market for Joe Stiglitz's labor, which is different from the market for Paul Samuelson's labor, which in turn is different from the market for plumbers, which in turn is different from the market for unskilled labor, and so on. If we are careful in defining markets for homogeneous commodities (Joe Stiglitz's labor delivered at a particular date, in a particular state, at a particular location), then there is only one trader on one side of the market (Joe Stiglitz). If we expand the markets to embrace all theoretical economists, then it is obviously more competitive. But we have had to drop the assumptions that commodities are homogeneous and that the set of markets is incomplete; there is not a separate market for each homogeneous commodity.

Asymmetric information and complete markets

Imperfect information obviously serves to ensure that the set of securities cannot be complete, since individuals can only trade in commonly observed states.[22] If I promise to deliver to you something in a particular set of states, it has to be observable to both of us that the state has occurred; to use the legal system to enforce such a contract, it has to be verifiable to an outside, third party. The inability to do so clearly limits the set of securities.

But beyond that, asymmetries of information greatly limit the opportunities to trade, a notion captured in the familiar maxim: I wouldn't want to buy something from someone who is willing to sell it to me. Of course the old principles concerning differences in preferences and comparative advantage providing motives for trade still remain valid, but there is another motive for trading, which can be put baldly as 'cheating.' While in traditional exchanges both parties are winners, I can get you to pay more for something than it is worth – to buy a used car that is a lemon – I win and you lose. Farmers have a strong incentive to sell their crops on futures markets, but most do not avail themselves much of this opportunity, and for good reason. Those markets are dominated by five large trading companies, who have every incentive to be more informed than the small farmer. The differential information means the farmer is at a disadvantage; the trading companies can make a profit off of the farmer's relative ignorance. Knowing this, a choice is made to bear the risk rather than pay the price.

Asymmetries of information give rise to market imperfections in many markets, other than the insurance market, futures markets, and the market for used cars. Consider, for instance, the market for 'used labor,' workers who already have a job. Their present employer normally has more information concerning their abilities than do prospective employers. A prospective employer knows that if it makes an offer to attract an employee from another firm, the other firm will match it, if the worker is worth it, and will not if the worker is not. Thus, again, the prospective employer is in a heads you win, tails I lose situation: it is only successful in hiring the new employee if it has offered higher wages than the current (well-informed) employer thinks the worker is worth. To be sure, there are instances when the prospective employee's productivity at the new firm will be higher than at the old job – the employee is better matched for the job – or where there are other (nonpecuniary) reasons why the individual may wish to move (to be near relatives, or get away from them). As a result there is *some* trade in the used labor market, but apart from younger workers who are trying to get well matched with a firm, these markets tend to be thin.

Similarly equity provides more effective risk distribution between entrepreneurs and suppliers of capital than does credit; providers of equity share the risk, while with credit (bank loans and bonds) the residual risk is borne by the entrepreneur or the firms' original shareholders.[23] Yet equity markets are notoriously imperfect; only a small fraction of new investment is provided by equity.[24] One of the reasons for this is asymmetries of information: the sellers of equity are better informed than potential buyers; they are most anxious to sell shares in their company when the market has overpriced their shares. Buyers know this. Thus the willingness of firms to issue shares sends a signal to the market, that the sellers think that the shares are overpriced. The market responds, and the price of shares falls.

There are, to be sure, other reasons – besides a firm's shares being over-priced – for a firm to issue shares. The owners of a firm may be risk averse, and as we have noted, equity provides a more effective method of sharing risk than do other methods of raising capital. (In some sectors, like insurance, regulations require that firms raise capital via equity.) Outsiders ('the market') cannot, however, tell whether the reason the firm is selling shares is that its shares are overpriced, that its bankers refuse to lend it money, or that the firm's owners recognize that equity is a more effective way of distributing risk. In fact, when firms issue shares, on average, the price falls (on average, the decline in value of existing shares equals about 30 percent of the amount raised;[25] in some cases the decline is far greater than the amount raised): the market assigns some probability to the chance that the firm is issuing shares because they are overpriced. From the perspective of the firm this makes issuing shares very costly. And it is this which (at least partly) explains the relatively little reliance on equity as a means of raising new capital.

Moral hazard

Asymmetries of information give rise to two problems, referred to as the (adverse) selection[26] and the incentive or moral hazard problems.[27] Both are seen most clearly in the context of insurance markets, but they arise in a variety of other contexts as well. The first problem results in firms being unable to obtain insurance on their profits: clearly the firm is more informed about its prospects than any insurance firm could be, and the insurance firm worries that if the firm is willing to pay the premium, it is getting too good of a deal. That is, there is a high probability that the insurance firm will have to pay off on the policy.

Moral hazard also leads to limited insurance. The more complete the insurance coverage, the less incentive individuals or firms have to take actions that ensure that the insured-against event does not occur. Because the actions that would be required to reduce the likelihood of the insured-against even occurring are often not observable (and/or it cannot be verified that the insured took the requisite actions), the payment of the insurance cannot be made contingent on the individual or firm taking those actions. Thus health insurance firms would like those they insure not to smoke or to be in places where they suffer the consequences of 'second-hand smoke,' that is, smoking by others. But insurance firms cannot observe these actions, and hence cannot require those they insure not to smoke.[28]

The provision of *complete* insurance would greatly attenuate incentives, so much so in many cases that for the insurance firm to break even would require charging such a high premium that the policy would be unattractive. Thus, in general, whenever there is moral hazard, there will be incomplete insurance.[29] Analogous incentive issues arise in many other markets. In most firms pay is not just paid on performance. Input (effort) is not easily monitorable. It may be possible to monitor output, but if pay is based solely on output, compensation would be highly variable, since there are many determinants of output, besides effort. In effect, by making pay depend only partially on performance, firms are providing some insurance to their workers, though incomplete insurance. If pay did not depend at all on performance, workers would have no incentive to provide any effort at all.[30] Thus both moral hazard and adverse selection provide reasons for markets to be *thin*; in some cases the market might actually be closed. When combined with other transactions costs, they reinforce the conclusion that we expect markets to be incomplete.

Inconsistency between assumptions of perfect information and complete markets

Somewhat more subtly, the number of markets that exist affects the information structure of traders; that is, prices in different markets convey information. If the futures price of wheat is very high, one can infer that informed individuals in the market either believe that demand in the future will be high or supply low. Uninformed traders can thus glean some information from informed traders by looking at prices; and just how much information they can glean depends on what markets exist. In some cases uninformed traders can glean all of the information from informed traders. (The discussion of academic economists sometimes seem to recall the religious debates of the Middle Ages on how many angels could dance on the head of a pin: there was a long discussion of whether one could infer from market prices the state of nature of the economy.[31] If, for instance, there were a single random variable affecting the return to a particular security, and if there were some informed individuals who knew the value of that random variable, then the price would fully reveal that random variable. If that were true for *every* risky security, prices would fully reveal the state of nature. But the 'event' space is so much larger than the price space – there are hundreds of variables that affect the profitability of a firm – that it seems absurd to hope that anyone by looking at prices could infer the state of nature.)

It should be clear of course that for traders to have incentives to gather information required that information not be perfectly disseminated in the market. If, simply by looking at market prices, those who do not spend money to acquire information can glean all the information that the informed traders who have spent money to acquire information have, then the informed traders will not have any informational advantage; they will not be able to obtain any return to their expenditures on information acquisition. Accordingly, *if there were a complete set of markets, information would be so well conveyed that investors would have no incentives to gather information.* (Of course with all participants having the same [zero] information, incentives to trade would be greatly reduced.) To put the matter differently, the assumptions of 'informed' markets[32] and 'a complete set of markets' may be mutually exclusive.[33]

Conceptual impossibility of a complete set of markets

The problems with the assumption of a complete set of markets run deeper. In Stiglitz (1994) I emphasize the importance of innovations, but it is hard to conceive of here being markets for contingencies (states) that have not yet been conceived of: surely an event such as the discovery of the principles underlying atomic energy and the subsequent development of commercial atomic power is an event of immense economic importance, in particular for owners of other energy resources. Yet how could markets in these risks – or in the risks associated with lasers or transistors – have existed before the under-lying concepts had been developed? This is a fundamental incoherence between the ideas of a complete set of markets and notions of innovation.[34]

I have detailed several of the fundamental reasons why markets are likely to be incomplete. For many purposes it does not matter why they are incomplete. It only matters that they are incomplete.

Absence of Competition

Another critique of the fundamental theorem of welfare economics is that it *assumes* that there is perfect competition, that every firm is a price taker. Most markets are in fact not perfectly competitive. One reason is that when information is imperfect and costly, markets will normally not be perfectly competitive. Imperfect information confers on firms a degree of market power. Though there is competition, it is not the perfect competition of textbook economics, with price-taking firms; it is *more* akin to monopolistic competition, of the kind discussed a half-century ago by Chamberlin.[35] (I will return to this point later; for now I simply want to emphasize that the welfare results are strongly dependent on firms being price takers, that is, on there being *perfect* competition.) Because of imperfect information, if a firm raises its price, not all the firm's customers will immediately be able to find a firm that charges a lower price for the same commodity: indeed customers may well infer that other firms have raised their prices as well. By the same token, if it lowers its price, it does not instantly garner for itself all the customers from the higher-priced stores. Search is costly, and so those in the market rarely know the prices being charged by all the firms selling every good in which they are interested.

The imperfections of competition arise not only, however, from imperfect information but also from fixed costs, many of which are information-related costs. There are fixed costs that arise directly in production – the overhead costs of running a firm – and fixed costs associated with acquiring information about how to produce. This means that there is unlikely to be a very large number of firms producing every quality of every good at every location at every date in every state of nature. As we noted before, with even small fixed costs, many of these 'markets' will have relatively few suppliers.

For these and other reasons, firms face downward-sloping demand curves. Markets may be highly competitive – but not perfectly competitive. Each of the deviations from perfect competition may be small, but when added up, they may amount to something – a myriad of small deviations leads to a picture of the economy that is markedly different from that of the standard paradigm. In particular, only under highly stringent conditions is the economy (constrained) Pareto efficient.[36]

The reason for this can be put simply. With downward-sloping demand curves, price – which measures consumers' marginal benefit or willingness to pay – exceeds the marginal cost. Lerner (1944) pointed out that if all firms faced the same elasticity of demand, were produced by labor alone, and the elasticity of supply of labor were zero, then even with monopolies the economy could be Pareto efficient. But this is a singular case. In general, the supply of labor is not inelastic, so monopoly in the goods market affects real wages and, in turn, the supply of labor; likewise the degree of monopoly (the elasticity of demand) differs across products.

Lerner (and other early writers) focused on the relative quantities of different goods that would be produced under imperfect competition. It is also the case that the set of goods that is produced may not be the most desirable set. A firm produces a product if the revenues it attains exceed the costs. In making its decision, the firm does not care to what extent its profits are garnered at the expense of other firms. If it produces a new commodity, it will shift the demand curve of other firms to the left as in Figure 3.1. It may shift some firm's demand curve to the left enough that it no longer is profitable for it to produce. There is a loss of consumer surplus (the shaded area ABC). The consumer surplus lost may exceed the consumer surplus gained from the production of the new commodity.

Markets Create Noise

Finally, we think of one of the great virtues of market economies is its ability to 'solve' information problems efficiently. Yet when information is costly, firms act to take advantage of that. In doing so, they may *create* noise[37] – they create, some times deliberately, information problems for consumers.

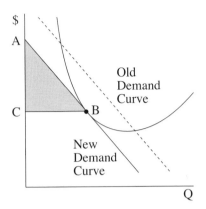

Notes: The new commodity shifts the demand curve to the left, making it no longer profitable to produce. The loss in consumer surplus (the shaded area ABC) may be greater than the consumer surplus associated with the new product.

Figure 3.1   Introducing a new commodity may not increase social welfare

Temporary price reductions ('sales'), though we normally do not view them from this perspective, create price dispersion. Costly search gives firms good reason to charge different prices, or to temporarily reduce prices. Low-priced firms can gather themselves a larger customer base, but the high-priced firms can still survive, serving only those who have high search costs and who have not had the good fortune to find a low-priced firm. The high-priced firms compensate for the smaller scale of their sales with a higher profit (price) per sale. Figure 3.2 shows a case where the only equilibrium must entail price dispersion. Suppose that all firms were to charge the same price. Each firm contemplates what would happen should it lower (or raise) its price. If it raises its price, it loses customers to other firms. If it lowers its price, it 'steals' customers away from other firms. It steals those who have easiest access to information (low-cost searchers). There may be relatively few of these (for a small decrease in price) at any firm, but there are many firms from which it can steal customers. The total percentage increase in its sales from a 1 percent decrease in its price may be either smaller or larger than the decrease in its sales from a 1 percent increase in its price, depending on the number of other firms from which it can steal customers, and the number it steals from each firm (which in turn depends on how many low-search-cost individuals there are). Figure 3.2 depicts the case where the percentage increase in sales from a decrease in price is quite large, relative to the percentage decrease in sales from an increase in price: the demand curve has a kink. But it is clear that if this were the case, there could not exist a zero-profit, single-price equilibrium.

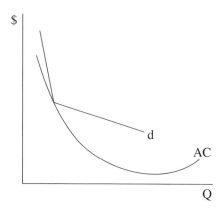

Notes: With costly search, the increase in sales from lowering prices may be greater than the loss in sales from increasing prices. If all firms charged the same price, there would be a kink in the demand curve at that price. There cannot then exist a single-price, zero-profit equilibrium: At the point of tangency between the demand curve and the average cost curve, it pays the firm either to increase or decrease the price charged.

Figure 3.2   The unique equilibrium may entail price dispersion

We have drawn the average cost curve through the posited single price – the point where there is the kink in the demand curve. It clearly pays the firm either to increase or decrease its price. Either way, it makes a profit.

Thus, while price dispersion gives rise to search and other activities directed at reducing the 'noise' of the market, and search limits the extent to which prices may differ in the market, the fact of the matter is that the existence of imperfect information – costly search – is what creates the price dispersion in the first place. The price dispersion itself arises, in part, not in response to exogenous changes in economic circumstances, or the differences in economic circumstances facing different firms, but endogenously, as part of the market equilibrium where each firm recognizes the consequences of the fact that search is costly. (That is, while Grossman and Stiglitz, 1976 and Lucas, 1972 emphasized the role of costly information in limiting the extent of arbitrage, reducing the differential impact of exogenous shocks, it is actually the case that markets create noise.)

The New and the Old Market Failures

These results, combined with the Greenwald–Stiglitz theorem, reduce the confidence we have in the presumption that markets are efficient. There are two important differences between the new market failures, based on imperfect and costly information and incomplete markets, and the older market failures associated, with, for instance, public goods and pollution externalities: the older market failures were, for the most part, easily identified and limited in scope, requiring well-defined government interventions. Because virtually all markets are incomplete and information is always imperfect – moral hazard and adverse selection problems are endemic to all market situations – the market failures are pervasive in the economy. The Greenwald–Stiglitz analysis of these market failures is designed not only to identify the existence of the market failure but also to show the kinds of government interventions that will be Pareto improvements. Their analysis goes beyond this to identify the behavioral parameters (e.g., supply and demand elasticities) that determine the optimal corrective tax rates. Yet a full corrective policy would entail taxes and subsidies on virtually all commodities, based on estimated demand and supply elasticities for all commodities (including all cross elasticities). The practical information required to implement the corrective taxation is well beyond that available at the present time, and the costs of administering such corrective taxation (which were ignored in the Greenwald–Stiglitz analysis) might well exceed the benefits when the markets' distortion is small. Thus it seems reasonable that the government should focus its attention on those instances where there are large and important market failures – say, in the major insurance markets (for health care, perhaps even automobile insurance), risks associated with job security, and imperfections of capital markets. I will return to these practical considerations later in this book. For now I simply want to emphasize the essential difference between the new and the old market failures: the pervasiveness of the problems posed by imperfect information and incomplete markets.

Information, Prices, and the Efficiency of Market Economies

To some readers the claim that market economies are inefficient in the presence of imperfect information may seem curious, and quite at odds with the Austrian tradition. One of the claims frequently made of the price system is its informational efficiency. As we tell students in the basic introductory courses, no firm has to know even how to make a pencil; no firm need know the scarcity of any of the inputs that go into pencils, or the preferences of consumers. All that each person needs to know is the price received for outputs and the price paid for inputs. The great insight of the first fundamental theorem of welfare economics, of Adam Smith's invisible hand, is that even with access to this extremely limited information, markets can produce Pareto-efficient outcomes.

To be sure, there is great informational efficiency: under the idealized conditions of the Arrow–Debreu model, prices do convey information efficiently from producers to consumers, and vice versa. Yet this is an extremely limited information problem. When a heavier informational burden is placed on market – when it must sort among workers of different ability or securities of different qualities, when it must provide incentives to workers in the presence of imperfect monitoring, when it must obtain and process new information about an ever changing environment – markets do not perform so well, even in terms of our limited welfare criterion of constrained Pareto efficiency.

Market Socialism and Market Failures

This chapter has explained the importance of imperfect information and incomplete markets as an explanation of why market economies fail to be (constrained) Pareto efficient, why they fail to attain the standards of economic efficiency predicted by the neoclassical paradigm. Socialism, and market socialism, was intended to achieve greater economic efficiency without the attendant social costs of capitalism. But market socialism, in assigning to the government the responsibility for running 'markets' (or 'as if' markets), when such markets did not function well in the private sector, did not resolve these problems: the theory of market socialism, for the most part, was not based on an analysis of these market failures, and of the reasons why government might be able to resolve them, but rather on the naïve comparison of the actual performance of market economies and the hypothesized performance of a market socialist economy with an idealized view of government. This idealization not only failed to take into account the political realities, but more important from the perspective of this chapter, failed to take into account essential economic realities.

The new information paradigm has revealed that 'market failures' are indeed pervasive in the economy. They appear in virtually every transaction among private parties in the economy, and while they may be small in each case, cumulatively they are important. Moreover the market failures are not like those concerning air pollution, for which a well-defined and effective government policy can often easily be designed. This pervasiveness of failures, while it reduces our confidence in the efficiency of market solutions, also reduces our confidence in the ability of the government to correct them. Most important from our perspective, neither the theory nor the practice of socialism paid any attention to these problems.[38]

NOTES

1. For an overview, see Greenwald and Stiglitz (1993) or Stiglitz (1992b).
2. A. Smith, *Wealth of Nations*, bk. 1, ch. 2.
3. Greenwald and Stiglitz (1986, 1988) develop a general methodology for analyzing the welfare consequences of imperfect information, limited markets, and other market imperfections. They apply their methodology to economies facing problems of adverse selection,

signaling, imperfect risk markets, moral hazard, costly transactions, efficiency wages, and search. Unpublished work shows how the analysis can be extended in a simple way to models with incentive compatibility (self-selection) constraints. (See Arnott, Greenwald, and Stiglitz, 1992).

4. It is perhaps remarkable that not only does Debreu (1959), in his classic statements of the competitive model, pay no attention to the implicit information assumptions, but does not even seem to recognize this as an important limitation of the theory. For instance, in concluding the basic statement of the theory, he lists what he considers to be (presumably) the two most important limitations of the theory: the failure to integrate money into the theory of value and the exclusion of indivisible commodities.

    The *economic* significance of the assumption of a complete set of future and risk markets is passed over with the statement, 'The assumption that markets exist for all the uncertain commodities . . . is a natural extension of the usual assumption that markets exist for all the certain commodities' (p. 102).

5. Using the term 'competitive' in the natural way, referring to a market in which there are a large number of participants on both sides. Of course some equilibrium theorists take it as a *definition* of competitive markets that there be perfect information. This assertion can be thought of as either a semantic quibble or an admission that, unless it could have been shown that markets with imperfect information behave very much like markets with perfect information, competitive equilibrium theory is of limited relevance as a description of actual economies.

6. In these cases prices (interest rates, wages) affect the quality of what is being traded (the risk of the borrower not repaying the load, the productivity of the labor). It does not pay firms to raise interest rates charged, even when there is an excess demand for credit (so that it could do so, and still make all the loans it wished to); doing so would result in a higher probability of default, and thus a lower expected return. It does not pay firms to lower wages, even when there is an excess supply of workers; doing so would result in a labor force of lower productivity. In chapter 4 of Stiglitz (1994) I discuss these issues at greater length.

7. Firms make prices depend on quantity in order to discriminate among different kinds of customers. Insurance firms thus use the quantity of insurance purchased as a basis in making inferences concerning the likelihood of having an accident. On average, those more prone to having accidents will want to have more extensive coverage (see Rothschild and Stiglitz, 1976; C.A. Wilson, 1977). In other cases firms may simply do this to increase their profits: With perfect information they would engage in perfect price discrimination. With imperfect information they can glean information about individuals from the quantity that they purchase. For instance, if those who buy large quantities have a lower consumer surplus per unit purchased than do those who buy small quantities, a nonlinear price system, with charges per unit purchased declining with quantity purchased, may yield a monopolist higher profits than would a conventional 'linear' price system. This issue too is discussed at greater length in chapter 4 of Stiglitz (1994). See also Stiglitz (1977) and the vast subsequent literature. The same argument also applies in cases where there is some, but imperfect, competition. See, for example, Salop (1977) or Salop and Stiglitz (1982).

8. In standard reputation models profits are necessary to induce firms to produce high-quality goods (otherwise there is no penalty for producing shoddy merchandise). In the context of adverse selection, the argument is more subtle. The equilibrium contracts, say, in the insurance market with two types of risks, can be described as follows: the high-risk individual gets complete insurance, at his or her actuarially fair odds. The contract for the low risk is that policy that maximizes the low-risk individual's expected utility, subject to the high-risk individuals preferring their own policies to this policy (the self-selection constraint) and the policy's profits being nonnegative. If the low-risk individual is more risk averse than the high-risk individual, the later constraint may not be binding. The equilibrium policy offered to the low-risk individual makes a profit, but were a firm to lower the premium or raise the benefit, all the high-risk individuals would demand the policy, and with that mix of applicants (remember, it is assumed that the insurance firm cannot distinguish between high-risk and low-risk individuals) the expected profits of the policy drop precipitously: the slight reduction in premium or increase in benefits results in the policy now making an absolute loss.

Precisely the same reasoning applies in the context of moral hazard. Suppose that individuals have the choice of two different activities, a 'safe' activity or a risky activity. Which activity the insured undertakes depends on the insurance policy. With more complete insurance, the insured undertakes the risky activity. The equilibrium insurance contract may be described as that contract that maximizes the expected utility of the insured, subject to the insured undertaking the safe activity and subject to profits being nonnegative. Again the solution to this maximization problem may entail the latter constraint not being binding. The equilibrium contract makes a profit but a slight increase in benefits, say, results in the insured's switching from the safe activity to the risky activity, with profits dropping precipitously from positive to negative. For a fuller discussion, including the formal argument, and a more complete statement of the assumptions, see Arnott and Stiglitz (1988a).

9.   The lump-sum transfers are identical for *all* individuals, regardless of differences in observable characteristics.

10. The general analysis is due to Greenwald and Stiglitz (1986, 1988). The first paper shows the constrained Pareto inefficiency of market economies in which markets are clear, and the second (1988) shows the result in efficiency wage, search, and other models in which markets do not clear. (For a more extensive discussion of market equilibrium when markets do not clear, see Stiglitz, 1987.) A third paper (Arnott, Greenwald, and Stiglitz, 1992) extends the analysis to models with self-selection and incentive compatibility constraints.

     The more general Greenwald–Stiglitz results were anticipated by a number of papers considering special cases. These papers provide insight into the nature of the market failure in each of these instances. For the analysis of inefficiency in the presence of moral hazard, see Arnott and Stiglitz (1985, 1986, 1989, 1991); for the analysis of inefficiency in stock market models, see Stiglitz (1972, 1982); for the analysis of inefficiency in more rudimentary economies, in which there is not even a stock market, see Newbery and Stiglitz (1982, 1984); for the analysis of inefficiency in models with implicit contracts, see Newbery and Stiglitz (1987); for the analysis of inefficiency in search models, see Mortenson (1989); for a discussion of the inefficiency within efficiency wage models, see Shapiro and Stiglitz (1984). A more thorough discussion of the general problems of welfare economics in the presence of asymmetric and imperfect information is contained in Stiglitz (1991b).

11. See below for further elaboration on the sense in which popular interpretations of the insights provided by the Arrow–Debreu models are and are not correct.

12. Thus the Greenwald–Stiglitz analysis explains why representative agent models are simply of no use in evaluating the efficiency of market economies. (Of course a result establishing conditions under which markets with representative agents should turn out to be inefficient would tell us something, but results showing that a particular representative agent model is efficient are of little, if any, value.)

13. Still a third example is the stock market economy with no bankruptcy and a single good studied by Diamond (1967). Stiglitz (1982) showed that with just two goods, the stock market economy was essentially never constrained Pareto efficient. Greenwald and Stiglitz showed how the Stiglitz (1982) result could be seen as a special case of their more general theorem. Other, rather different problems with the efficiency of economies with an incomplete set of risk markets (e.g., the possibility of multiplicity of equilibria, one of which might be Pareto dominated by another) were studied by Stiglitz (1972), Drèze (1974), and Hart (1975).

14. This example helps clarify the special nature of Diamond's results, showing the constrained Pareto efficiency of stock market economies with a single good. In his model the actions of each investor has no effect on the probability distribution of returns, since the relative prices of different goods are, *by assumption*, fixed.

15. This is the case in the standard adverse selection model. See Akerlof (1970).

16. It is a somewhat more subtle matter to show that the government can effect these changes in such a way as to make everyone better off – given that the government faces the same limitations on information that employers do. But if there are enough different commodities (over which the groups with different abilities differ in their preferences), then one can show that the government can indeed attain a Pareto improvement.

17. This discussion makes clear why earlier results, such as that of Shavell (1979) asserting the

constrained Pareto efficiency of market economies with moral hazard with a *single* good are not general: With a single good there is no scope for government policy to induce greater care through differential tax rates on different commodities.

18. For a deviation of the optimal rates of taxes/subsidies, see Arnott and Stiglitz (1986).

19. A folk theorem is a widely known theorem, the origins of which cannot easily be traced. It is part of the oral tradition in a particular field. The most famous folk theorem of recent vintage is that in repeated games, which states that for an infinitely repeated prisoner's dilemma, the strategy 'cooperate–cooperate' is a subgame perfect equilibrium of the supergame.

20. Several years ago, when I was assigned the task of setting the comprehensive Ph.D. exams in microeconomics, I was so foolish as to ask what were the central economic assumptions of the fundamental theorems of welfare economics that might be questioned. At least a third of the students, well trained in the mathematics of the theorem, responded with an extended discussion of the role of the nonsatiation assumption, totally omitting any discussion of the issues with which I have been concerned.

21. If there were no nonconvexities, as assumed by the standard theory, then presumably there could be many firms producing at each date, location, and state of nature. In a sense, the theory is consistent in making a series of unreasonable, but 'coherent,' assumptions. With small fixed costs associated with the production of each of these state-location-time dated commodities (or with each set of such commodities), not only will there not be many firms producing each, many such commodities will not even be produced.

22. This point was first made by Radner (1968).

23. This is not quite accurate. So long as there is some chance of default, creditors bears some residual risk.

24. See Stiglitz (1992).

25. See Asquith and Mullins (1986a and b).

26. This is sometimes referred to as the problems of 'hidden knowledge,' as opposed to the moral hazard problem, which is referred to as one of 'hidden action,' but I think the description is somewhat misleading. The moral hazard problem arises because of a particular type of hidden knowledge problem – hidden knowledge concerning the actions taken by the individual.

    Why we use the terms 'selection problem' or 'screening problem' can be seen most clearly in the context of the insurance or labor market. The insurance firm wishes to select (or screen) for the lowest risks; the employer wants to select (or screen) for the product market the buyer of used cars wishes to select for the most underpriced car, that is the car that represents the greatest value. All of these problems share in common that there is a characteristic of the commodity relevant to one side (e.g., the buyer that is not costlessly or directly observable to that individual).

    The term *adverse selection* is used to denote the fact that as certain terms of the contract change, there is an adverse effect on the quality mix of those offering themselves on the market; for instance, raising the premium adversely affects the mix of those who wish to buy insurance, raising the interest rate charged on a loan adversely affects those who apply for a loan, with an increase in the proportion of those who are bad risks – who have a high probability of default.

27. This is sometimes referred to as the hidden action problem because one side of the contract cannot observe the actions taken by the other side, and accordingly cannot make contracts contingent on those actions. Contracts can only be made contingent on the observable outcomes, or on observable actions (which may be related to the hidden actions).

28. Curiously some insurance firms do attempt to distinguish between smokers and non-smokers, trusting that those that it sells insurance to will report honestly whether they do or do not smoke.

29. A more rigorous development of this point is contained in Arnott and Stiglitz (1988a, 1990a and b), where it is shown that not only is insurance, in general, incomplete, but in some instances no insurance may be provided. (At a more technical level, in some cases no competitive equilibrium exists. The reason for the failure of equilibrium to exist is quite different from that noted in Rothschild and Stiglitz 1976.)

30. Moral hazard arguments also are used to explain the thinness of the equity market: the fixed obligations associated with debt provide an incentive for managers to work hard.

31. This discussion has a curious history. Grossman (1975) and Grossman and Stiglitz (1976), after setting out some simple models in which prices fully revealed all the relevant information, viewed these as 'limiting cases' helping us to fix our ideas on how to construct more relevant modes of how prices convey information; we quickly moved on to construct such models. A subsequent literature (see, e.g., Radner, 1979) seemed to get fixated on what we viewed as the wrong question: the conditions under which price could convey all the relevant information.

    It should have been obvious from our analysis that not only were the assumptions concerning the dimensionality of the commodity-marketed security space critical but so too were the assumptions concerning the utility function. For instance, we explored one model in which different farmers had information about their own crops. This affected their demand for futures, and *with a constant absolute risk aversion utility function*, the futures price conveyed all the relevant information, that is, provided a perfect predictor of the future supply. The reason was simple: demand for futures was linear in each farmer's crop size, and hence the equilibrium futures price could be shown to be a function only of total crop size. With virtually any other utility function, demand for futures will not be linear in crop size, so that a low price might represent either a higher aggregate supply, or a more or less disparate distribution in crop sizes. (See Jordan, 1983 or Gale and Stiglitz, 1985.)

32. That is, markets in which participants have information other than that which arrives at zero cost.

33. See Grossman and Stiglitz (1980a).

34. Of course, in principle, the Arrow–Debreu model involves states of nature that are exogenous, and it is not apparent whether we should take the discovery of atomic energy as 'exogenous.' To the extent that it depends on the allocation of resources to research, it is endogenous. But the outcome depends not only on the allocation of resources but on an underlying unknown 'state' – the world that the research is supposed to uncover. Thus there are formalisms that would embrace these risks – if they could have been articulated – within the state-of-nature formulation. Nonetheless, research will alter subjective probabilities concerning the various states of nature, and those endogenous changes in the probabilities are themselves precluded from the theory. Thus these formalisms fail to rescue the central results of the conventional paradigm.

35. With the dominance of Keynesian economics within macroeconomics and the perfect competition paradigm within microeconomics, the monopolistic competition model remained relatively unexplored until its formal revival by Spence (1976) and Dixit and Stiglitz (1977). The similarities (and differences) between these models and the imperfect competition generated by imperfect information is evident in the studies by Salop (1976), Salop and Stiglitz (1977, 1982, 1987), Stiglitz (1986a, 1989a), Wolinsky (1986), and Diamond (1971). These results were anticipated by Arrow (1988) and Scitovsky (1950). For other references, see Stiglitz (1989a).

36. See Dixit and Stiglitz (1977).

37. See Salop and Stiglitz (1977, 1982).

38. Except to the extent that market socialism emphasized the market's failure to allocate investment efficiently, partly as a result of the absence of the requisite futures and risk markets.

REFERENCES

Akerlof, G. 1970. 'The market for "lemons": quality uncertainty and the market mechanism.' *Quarterly Journal of Economics* 86: 488–500.

Arnott, R., B.C. Greenwald and J.E. Stiglitz. 1992. 'Information and economic efficiency.' Paper presented at AEA annual meeting in New Orleans.

Arnott, R. and J.E. Stiglitz. 1985. 'Labour turnover, wage structure and moral hazard: The inefficiency of competitive markets.' *Journal of Labour Economics* 3: 434–62.

Arnott, R. and J.E. Stiglitz. 1986. 'Moral hazard and optimal commodity taxation.' *Journal of Public Economics* 23: 1–24.

Arnott, R. and J.E. Stiglitz. 1988a. 'The basic analytics of moral hazard.' *Scandinavian Journal of Economics* 90: 383–413.

Arnott, R. and J.E. Stiglitz. 1989. 'The welfare economics of moral hazard.' in *Risk, Information and Insurance: Essays in the Memory of Karl H. Borch*, Henri Louberge (ed.). Kluwer Academic Publishers, Norwell, MA, pp. 91–122.

Arnott, R. and J.E. Stiglitz. 1990a. 'Price equilibrium, efficiency, and decentralizability in insurance markets.' Working Paper, Stanford University.

Arnott, R. and J.E. Stiglitz. 1990b. 'Equilibrium in competitive insurance markets with moral hazard.' Working Paper, Stanford University.

Arnott, R. and J.E. Stiglitz. 1991. 'Moral hazard and non-market institutions: dysfunctional crowding out or peer monitoring.' *American Economic Review* 81: 179–90.

Arrow, K.J. 1988. 'Toward a theory of price adjustment.' In *The Allocation of Economic Resources*, P.A. Baran, T. Scitovsky, and E.S. Shaw (eds) Stanford: Stanford University Press.

Asquith, P. and D.W. Mullins. 1986a. 'Equity issues and stock price dilution.' *Journal of Financial Economics* 13: 296–320.

Asquith, P. and D.W. Mullins. 1986b. 'Equity issues and offering dilution.' *Journal of Financial Economics* 15: 61–89.

Debreu, G. 1959. *The Theory of Value*. Wiley, New York.

Diamond, P. 1967. 'The role of the stock market in a general equilibrium model with technological uncertainty'. *American Economic Review* 57: 759–776.

Diamond, Peter A. 1971. 'A model of price adjustment.' *Journal of Economic Theory* 3: 156–68.

Dixit, A. and J.E. Stiglitz. 1977. 'Monopolistic competition and optimal product diversity.' *American Economic Review* 67: 297–308.

Drèze, J. 1974. 'Investment under private ownership: optimality, equilibrium and stability.' In *Allocation under Uncertainty: Equilibrium and Optimality*, J. Drèze (ed.). Macmillan, New York, pp. 261–97.

Gale, I. and J.E. Stiglitz, 1985. 'Futures markets are almost always informationally inefficient.' Princeton University Financial Research Center Memorandum No. 57. February.

Greenwald, B. and J.E. Stiglitz. 1986. 'Externalities in economies with imperfect information and incomplete markets.' *Quarterly Journal of Economics* 101: 229–64.

Greenwald, B. and J.E. Stiglitz. 1988. 'Pareto inefficiency of market economies: search and efficiency wage models.' *American Economic Association Papers and Proceedings* 78: 351–5.

Greenwald, B. and J.E. Stiglitz. 1993. 'Financial market imperfections and business cycles.' *Quarterly Journal of Economics* 108: 77–114.

Grossman, S.J. 1975. 'The existence of futures markets, noisy rational expectations and informational externalities.' Ph.D. dissertation. University of Chicago.

Grossman, S.J. and J.E. Stiglitz. 1976. 'Information and competitive price systems.' *American Economic Review* 66: 246–53.

Grossman, S.J. and J.E. Stiglitz. 1980a. 'On the impossibility of informationally efficient markets.' *American Economic Review* 70: 393–408.

Hart, O. 1975. 'On the optimality of equilibrium when the market structure is incomplete.' *Journal of Economic Theory* 11: 418–43.

Jordan, J.S. 1983. 'On the efficient markets hypothesis.' *Econometrica* 51: 1325–43.

Lerner, A.P. 1944. *The Economics of Control.* Macmillan, New York.

Lucas, R.E., Jr. 1972. 'Expectations and the neutrality of money.' *Journal of Economic Theory* 4: 103–24.

Mortensen, D. 1989. 'The persistence and indeterminacy of unemployment in search equilibrium.' Scandinavian Journal of Economics 91: 367–72.

Newbery, D. and J.E. Stiglitz. 1987. 'Wage rigidity, implicit contracts, unemployment and economic efficiency.' *Economic Journal* 97: 416–30.

Prescott, E.C. and R.M. Townsend. 1984. 'Pareto optima and competitive equilibria with adverse selection and moral hazard.' *Econometrica* 52: 21–45.

Radner, R. 1968. 'Competitive equilibrium under uncertainty.' *Econometrica* 36: 31–58.

Radner, R. 1979. 'Rational expectations equilibrium: generic existence and the information revealed by prices. *Econometrica* 47: 655–678.

Rothschild, M. and J.E. Stiglitz. 1976. 'Equilibrium in competitive insurance markets.' *Quarterly Journal of Economics* 90: 629–49.

Salop, S. 1976. 'Information and monopolistic competition.' *American Economic Review* 66: 240–45.

Salop, S. 1977. 'The noisy monopolist: imperfect information, price dispersion and price discrimination.' *Review of Economic Studies* 44: 393–406.

Salop, S. and J.E. Stiglitz. 1977. 'Bargains and ripoffs: a model of monopolistically competitive price dispersions.' *Review of Economic Studies* 44: 493–510.

Salop, S. and J.E. Stiglitz. 1982. 'The theory of sales: a simple model of equilibrium price dispersion with identical agents.' *American Economic Review* 72: 1121–30.

Salop, S. and J.E. Stiglitz. 1987. 'Information, welfare and product diversity.' In *Arrow and the Foundations of the Theory of Economic Policy.* G. Feiwel (ed.). Macmillan, London, pp. 328–40.

Scitovsky, T. 1950. 'Ignorance as a source of oligopoly power.' *American Economic Review* 40: 48–53.

Shavell, S. 1979. 'On moral hazard and insurance.' *Quarterly Journal of Economics* 93: 541–62.

Shapiro, C. and J.E. Stiglitz. 1984. 'Equilibrium unemployment as a worker discipline device.' *American Economic Review* 74: 433–44.

Spence, A.M. 1976. 'Production selection, fixed costs, and monopolistic competition.' *Review of Economic Studies* 43: 217–35.

Stiglitz, J.E. 1972. 'On the optimality of the stock market allocation of investment.' *Quarterly Journal of Economics* 86: 25–60. (Shortened version of a paper presented at the Far Eastern Meetings of the Econometric Society, June 1970. Tokyo.)

Stiglitz, J.E. 1977. 'Monopoly, nonlinear pricing and imperfect information: the insurance market.' *Review of Economic Studies* 44: 407–30.

Stiglitz, J.E. 1982. 'The inefficiency of the stock market equilibrium.' *Review of Economic Studies* 49: 241–61.

Stiglitz, J.E. 1986a. 'Towards a more general theory of monopolistic competition.' In *Prices, Competition and Equilibrium.* M. Peston and R. Quandt (eds). Allan, Oxford, pp. 22–69.

Stiglitz, J.E. 1986b. 'Theory of competition, incentives and risk.' In *New Developments in the Theory of Market Structure*, J.E. Stiglitz and F. Mathewson (eds). MIT Press, Cambridge, pp. 399–449.

Stiglitz, J.E. 1987. 'The causes and consequences of the dependence of quality on price.' *Journal of Economic Literature* 25: 1–48.

Stiglitz, J.E. 1989a. 'Imperfect information in the product market.' In *Handbook of Industrial Organization*, vol. 1. Elsevier Science Publishers, Amsterdam, pp. 769–847.

Stiglitz, J.E. 1989b. 'On the economic role of the state'. In *The Economic Role of the State*, A. Heertje (ed.). Basil Blackwell, Oxford, pp. 9–85.

Stiglitz, J.E. 1991a. 'The economic role of the state: efficiency and effectiveness.' *Efficiency and Effectiveness*, T.P. Hardiman and M. Mulreany (eds). Institute of Public Administration, Dublin, pp. 37–59.

Stiglitz, J.E. 1991b. 'Welfare economics with imperfect and asymmetric information.' New York: Oxford University Press.

Stiglitz, J.E. 1992. 'Capital markets and economic fluctuations in capitalist economies.' *European Economic Review* 36: 269–306.

Stiglitz, J.E. 1994. *Whither Socialism?* Cambridge, Mass.: MIT Press.

Wilson, C.A. 1977. 'A model of insurance market with incomplete information.' *Journal of Economic Theory* 16: 167–207.

Wolinsky, A. 1986. 'True monopolistic competition as a result of imperfect information.' *Quarterly Journal of Economics* 101: 493–512.

4. The market for 'lemons': quality uncertainty and the market mechanism

George A. Akerlof[1]

I. INTRODUCTION

This chapter relates quality and uncertainty. The existence of goods of many grades poses interesting and important problems for the theory of markets. On the one hand, the interaction of quality differences and uncertainty may explain important institutions of the labor market. On the other hand, this chapter presents a struggling attempt to give structure to the statement: 'Business in underdeveloped countries is difficult'; in particular, a structure is given for determining the economic costs of dishonesty. Additional applications of the theory include comments on the structure of money markets, on the notion of 'insurability,' on the liquidity of durables, and on brand-name goods.

There are many markets in which buyers use some market statistic to judge the quality of prospective purchases. In this case there is incentive for sellers to market poor-quality merchandise, since the returns for good quality accrue mainly to the entire group whose statistic is affected rather than to the individual seller. As a result there tends to be a reduction in the average quality of goods and also in the size of the market. It should also be perceived that in these markets social and private returns differ, and therefore, in some cases, governmental intervention may increase the welfare of all parties. Or private institutions may arise to take advantage of the potential increases in welfare which can accrue to all parties. By nature, however, these institutions are nonatomistic, and therefore concentrations of power – with ill consequences of their own – can develop.

The automobile market is used as a finger exercise to illustrate and develop these thoughts. It should be emphasized that this market is chosen for its concreteness and ease in understanding rather than for its importance or realism.

II. THE MODEL WITH AUTOMOBILES AS AN EXAMPLE

A. The Automobiles Market

The example of used cars captures the essence of the problem. From time to time one hears either mention of or surprise at the large price difference between new cars and those which have just left the showroom. The usual lunch table justification for this phenomenon is the pure joy of owning a 'new' car. We offer a different explanation. Suppose (for the sake of clarity rather than reality) that there are just four kinds of cars. There are new cars and used cars. There are good cars and bad cars (which in America are known as 'lemons'). A new car may be a good car or a lemon, and of course the same is true of used cars.

The individuals in this market buy a new automobile without knowing whether the car they buy will be good or a lemon. But they do know that the probability q it is a good car and with probability $(1 - q)$ it is a lemon; by assumption, q is the proportion of good cars produced and $(1 - q)$ is the proportion of lemons.

After owning a specific car, however, for a length of time, the car owner can form a good idea of the quality of this machine; i.e., the owner assigns a new probability to the event that his car is a lemon. This estimate is more accurate than the original estimate. An asymmetry in available information has developed: for the sellers now have more knowledge about the quality of a car than the buyers. But good cars and bad cars must still sell at the same price – since it is impossible for a buyer to tell the difference between a good car and a bad car. It is apparent that a used car cannot have the same valuation as a new car – if it did have the same valuation, it would clearly be advantageous to trade a lemon at the price of new car, and buy another new car, at a higher probability q of being good and a lower probability of being bad. Thus the owner of a good machine must be locked in. Not only is it true that he cannot receive the true value of his car, but he cannot even obtain the expected value of a new car.

Gresham's law has made a modified reappearance. For most cars traded will be the 'lemons,' and good cars may not be traded at all. The 'bad' cars tend to drive out the good (in much the same way that bad money drives out the good). But the analogy with Gresham's law is not quite complete: bad cars drive out the good because they sell at the same price as good cars; similarly, bad money drives out good because the exchange rate is even. But the bad cars sell at the same price as good cars since it is impossible for a buyer to tell the difference between a good and a bad car; only the seller knows. In Gresham's law, however, presumably both buyer and seller can tell the difference between good and bad money. So the analogy is instructive, but not complete.

B.   Asymmetrical Information

It has been seen that the good cars may be driven out of the market by the lemons. But in a more continuous case with different grades of goods, even worse pathologies can exist. For it is quite possible to have the bad driving out the not-so-bad driving out the medium driving out the not-so-good driving out the good in such a sequence of events that no market exists at all.

One can assume that the demand for used automobiles depends most strongly upon two variables – the price of the automobile p and the average quality of used cars traded, μ, or $Q^d = D\,(p, \mu)$. Both the supply of used cars and also the average quality μ will depend upon the price, or $\mu = \mu\,(p)$ and $S = S(p)$. And in equilibrium the supply must equal the demand for the given average quality, or $S(p) = D(p, \mu(p))$. As the price falls, normally the quality will also fall. And it is quite possible that no goods will be traded at any price level.

Such an example can be derived from utility theory. Assume that there are just two groups of traders: groups one and two. Give group one a utility function

$$U_1 = M + \sum_{i=1}^{n} x_i$$

where M is the consumption of goods other than automobiles, x_i is the quality of the ith automobile, and n is the number of automobiles.

Similarly, let

$$U_2 = M + \sum_{i=1}^{n} 3/2x_i$$

where M, x_i and n are defined as before.

Three comments should be made about these utility functions: (1) without linear utility (say with logarithmic utility) one gets needlessly mired in algebraic complication. (2) The use of linear utility allows a focus on the effect of asymmetry of information; with a concave utility function we would have to deal jointly with the usual risk-variance effects of uncertainty and the special effects we wish to discuss here. (3) U_1 and U_2 have the odd characteristic that the addition of a second car, or indeed a kth car, adds the same amount of utility as the first. Again realism is sacrificed to avoid a diversion from the proper focus.

To continue, it is assumed (1) that both type one traders and type two traders are von Neumann-Morgenstern maximizers of expected utility; (2) that group one has N cars with uniformly distributed quality x, $0 \le x \le 2$, and group two has no cars; (3) that the price of 'other goods' M is unity.

Denote the income (including that derived from the sale of automobiles) of all type one traders as Y_1 and the income of all type two traders as Y_2. The demand for used cars will be the sum of the demands by both groups. When one ignores indivisibilities, the demand for automobiles by type one traders will be

$$D_1 = Y_1/p \qquad \mu/p > 1$$

$$D_1 = 0 \qquad \mu/p < 1.$$

And the supply of cars offered by type one traders is

$$S_2 = pN/2 \qquad p \le 2 \tag{1}$$

with average quality

$$\mu = p/2. \tag{2}$$

(To derive (1) and (2), the uniform distribution of automobile quality is used.)
Similarly the demand of type two traders is

$$D_2 = Y_2/p \qquad 3\mu/2 > p$$

$$D_2 = 0 \qquad 3\mu/2 < p$$

and

$$S_2 = 0$$

Thus total demand $D(p, \mu)$ is

$$D(p, \mu) = (Y_2 + Y_1)/p \qquad \text{if } p < \mu$$

$$D(p, \mu) = Y_2/p \qquad \text{if } \mu < p < 3\mu/2$$

$$D(p, \mu) = 0 \qquad \text{if } p > 3\mu/2.$$

However, with price p, average quality is $p/2$ and therefore at no price will any trade take place at all: in spite of the fact that *at any given price* between 0 and 3 there are traders of type one who are willing to sell their automobiles at a price which traders of type two are willing to pay.

C. Symmetric Information

The foregoing is contrasted with the case of symmetric information. Suppose that the quality of all cars is uniformly distributed, $0 \leq x \leq 2$. Then the demand curves and supply curves can be written as follows:

Supply

$$S(p) = N \qquad p > 1$$

$$S(p) = 0 \qquad p < 1.$$

And the demand curves are

$$D(p) = (Y_2 + Y_1)/p \qquad p < 1$$

$$D(p) = (Y_2/p) \qquad 1 < p < 3/2$$

$$D(p) = 0 \qquad p > 3/2.$$

In equilibrium

$$p = 1 \qquad \text{if } Y_2 < N \tag{3}$$

$$p = Y_2/N \qquad \text{if } 2Y_2/3 < N < Y_2 \tag{4}$$

$$p = 3/2 \qquad \text{if } N < 2Y_2/3. \tag{5}$$

If $N < Y_2$ there is a gain in utility over the case of asymmetrical information of $N/2$. (If $N > Y_2$, in which case the income of type two traders is insufficient to buy all N automobiles, there is a gain in utility of $Y_2/2$ units.)

Finally, it should be mentioned that in this example, if trades of groups one and two have the same probabilistic estimates about the quality of individual automobiles – though these estimates may vary from automobile to automobile – (3), (4), and (5) will still describe equilibrium with one slight change: p will then represent the expected price of one quality unit.

III. EXAMPLES AND APPLICATIONS

A. Insurance

It is a well-known fact that people over 65 have great difficulty in buying medical insurance. The natural question arises: why doesn't the price rise to match the risk?

Our answer is that as the price level rises the people who insure themselves will be those who are increasingly certain that they will need the insurance; for error in medical check-ups, doctors' sympathy with older patients, and so on make it much easier for the applicant to assess the risks involved than the insurance company. The result is that the average medical condition of insurance applicants deteriorates as the price level rises – with the result that no insurance sales may take place at any price.[2] This is strictly analogous to our automobiles case, where the average quality of used cars supplied fell with a corresponding fall in price level. This agrees with the explanation in insurance textbooks:

> Generally speaking policies are not available at ages materially greater than sixty-five . . . The term premiums are too high for any but the most pessimistic (which is to say the least healthy) insureds to find attractive. Thus there is a severe problem of adverse selection at these ages.[3]

The statistics do not contradict this conclusion. While demands for health insurance rise with age, a 1956 national sample survey of 2809 families with 8898 persons shows that hospital insurance coverage drops from 63 percent of those aged 45 to 54, to 31 percent for those over 65. And surprisingly, this survey also finds average medical expenses for males aged 55 to 64 of $88, while males over 65 pay an average of $77.[4] While noninsured expenditure rises from $66 to $80 in these age groups, insured expenditure declines from $105 to $70. The conclusion is tempting that insurance companies are particularly wary of giving medical insurance to older people.

The principle of 'adverse selection' is potentially present in all lines of insurance. The following statement appears in an insurance textbook written at the Wharton School:

> There is potential adverse selection in the fact that healthy term insurance policy holders may decide to terminate their coverage when they become older and premiums mount. This action could leave an insurer with an undue proportion of below average risks and claims might be higher than anticipated. Adverse selection 'appears (or at least is possible) whenever the individual or group insured has freedom to buy or not to buy, to choose the amount or plan of insurance, and to persist or to discontinue as a policy holder.'[5]

Group insurance, which is the most common form of medical insurance in the United States, picks out the healthy, for generally adequate health is a precondition for employment. At the same time this means that medical insurance is least available to those who need it most, for the insurance companies do their own 'adverse selection.'

This adds one major argument in favor of medicare.[6] On a cost–benefit basis medicare may pay off: for it is quite possible that every individual in the market would be willing to pay the expected cost of his medicare and buy insurance, yet no insurance company can afford to sell him a policy – for at any price it will attract too many 'lemons.' The welfare economics of medicare, in this view, is *exactly* analogous to the usual classroom argument for public expenditure on roads.

B.   The Employment of Minorities

The Lemons Principle also casts light on the employment of minorities. Employers may refuse to hire members of minority groups for certain types of jobs. This decision may not reflect irrationality or prejudice – but profit maximization. For race may serve as a good *statistic* for the applicant's social background, quality of schooling, and general job capabilities.

Good-quality schooling could serve as a substitute for this statistic; by grading students the schooling system can give a better indicator of quality than other more superficial characteristics. As T.W. Schultz writes, 'The educational establishment *discovers* and cultivates potential talent. The capabilities of children and mature students can never be known until *found* and cultivated'[7] (italics added). An untrained worker may have valuable natural talents, but these talents must be certified by 'the educational establishment' before a company can afford to use them. The certifying establishment, however, must be credible; the unreliability of slum schools decreases the economic possibilities of their students.

This lack may be particularly disadvantageous to members of already disadvantaged minority groups. For an employer may make a rational decision not to hire any members of these groups in responsible positions – because it is difficult to distinguish those with good job qualifications from those with bad qualifications. This type of decision is clearly what George Stigler had in mind when he wrote, 'in a regime of ignorance Enrico Fermi would have been a gardener, Von Neumann a checkout clerk at the drugstore.'

As a result, however, the rewards for work in slum schools tend to accrue to the group as a whole – in raising its average quality – rather than to the individual. Only insofar as information in addition to race is used is there any incentive for training.

An additional worry is that the Office of Economic Opportunity is going to use cost–benefit analysis to evaluate its programs. For many benefits may be external. The benefit from training minority groups may arise as much from raising the average quality of the group as from raising the quality of the individual trainee; and, likewise, the returns may be distributed over the whole group rather than to the individual.

B.   The Costs of Dishonesty

The Lemons Model can be used to make some comments on the costs of dishonesty. Consider a market in which goods are sold honestly or dishonestly; quality may be represented, or it may be misrepresented. The purchaser's problem, of course, is to identify quality. The presence of people in the market who are willing to offer inferior goods tends to drive the market out of existence – as in the case of our automobile 'lemons.' It is this possibility that represents the major costs of dishonesty – for dishonest dealings tend to drive honest dealings out of the market. There may be potential buyers of good-quality products and there may be potential sellers of such products in the appropriate price range; however, the presence of people who wish to pawn bad wares as good wares tends to drive out the legitimate business. The cost of dishonesty, therefore, lies not only in the amount by which the purchaser is cheated; the cost also must include the loss incurred from driving legitimate business out of existence.

Dishonesty in business is a serious problem in underdeveloped countries. Our model gives a possible structure to this statement and delineates the nature of the 'external' economies involved. In particular, in the model economy described, dishonesty, or the misrepresentation of the quality of automobiles, costs Y_2 unit of utility per automobile; furthermore, it reduces the size of the used car market from N to 0. We can, consequently, directly evaluate the costs of dishonesty – at least in theory.

There is considerable evidence that quality variation is greater in underdeveloped than in developed areas. For instance, the need for quality control of exports and State Trading Corporations can be taken as one indicator. In India, for example, under the Export Quality Control and Inspection Act of 1963, 'about 85 per cent of Indian exports are covered under one or the other type of quality control.'[8] Indian housewives must carefully glean the rice of the local bazaar to sort out stones of the same color and shape which have been intentionally added to the rice. Any comparison of heterogeneity of quality in the street market and the canned qualities of the American supermarket suggests that quality variation is a greater problem in the East than in the West.

In one traditional pattern of development the merchants of the pre-industrial generation turn into the first entrepreneurs of the next. The best-documented case is Japan,[9] but this also may have been the pattern for Britain and America.[10] In *our* picture the important skill of the merchant is identifying the quality of merchandise; those who can identify used cars in our example and can guarantee the quality may profit by as much as the difference between type two traders' buying price and type one traders' selling price. These people are the merchants. In production these skills are equally necessary – both to be able to identify the quality of inputs and to certify the quality of outputs. And this is one (added) reason why the merchants may logically become the first entrepreneurs.

The problem, of course, is that entrepreneurship may be a scarce resource; no development text leaves entrepreneurship unemphasized. Some treat it as central.[11] Given, then, that entrepreneurship is scarce, there are two ways in which product variations impede development. First, the pay-off to trade is great for would-be entrepreneurs, and hence they are diverted from production; second, the amount of entrepreneurial time per unit output is greater, the greater are the quality variations.

C.   Credit Markets in Underdeveloped Countries

(1) Credit markets in underdeveloped countries often strongly reflect the operation of the Lemons Principle. In India a major fraction of industrial enterprise is controlled by managing agencies (according to a recent survey, these 'managing agencies' controlled 65.7 per cent of the net worth of public limited companies and 66 per cent of total assets).[12] Here is a historian's account of the function and genesis of the 'managing agency system':

> The management of the South Asian commercial scene remained the function of merchant houses, and a type of organization peculiar to South Asia known as the Managing Agency. When a new venture was promoted (such as a manufacturing plant, a plantation, or a trading venture), the promoters would approach an established managing agency. The promoters might be Indian or British, and they might have technical or financial resources or merely a concession. In any case they would turn to the agency because of its reputation, which would encourage confidence in the venture and stimulate investment.[13]

In turn, a second major feature of the Indian industrial scene has been the dominance of these managing agencies by caste (or, more accurately, communal) groups. Thus firms can usually be classified according to communal origin.[14] In this environment, in which outside investors are likely to be bilked of their holdings, either (1) firms establish a reputation for 'honest' dealing, which confers upon them a monopoly rent insofar as their services are limited in supply, or (2) the sources of finance are limited to local communal groups which can use communal – and possibly familial –

ties to encourage honest dealing within the community. It is, in Indian economic history, extraordinarily difficult to discern whether the savings of rich landlords failed to be invested in the industrial sector (1) because of a fear to invest in ventures controlled by other communities, (2) because of inflated propensities to consume, or (3) because of low rates of return.[15] At the very least, however, it is clear that the British owned managing agencies tended to have an equity holding whose communal origin was more heterogeneous than the Indian-controlled agency houses, and would usually include both Indian and British investors.

(2) A second example of the workings of the Lemons Principle concerns the extortionate rates which the local moneylender charges his clients. In India these high rates of interest have been the leading factor in landlessness; the so-called 'Cooperative Movement' was meant to counteract this growing landlessness by setting up banks to compete with the local moneylenders.[16] While the large banks in the central cities have prime interest rates of 6, 8, and 10 percent, the local moneylender charges 15, 25, and even 50 percent. The answer to this seeming paradox is that credit is granted only where the granter has (1) easy means of enforcing his contract or (2) personal knowledge of the character of the borrower. The middleman who tries to arbitrage between the rates of the moneylender and the central bank is apt to attract all the 'lemons' and thereby make a loss.

This interpretation can be seen in Sir Malcolm Darling's interpretation of the village moneylender's power:

> It is only fair to remember that in the Indian village the money-lender is often the one thrifty person amongst a generally thriftless people; and that his methods of business, though demoralizing under modern conditions, suit the happy-go-lucky ways of the peasant. He is always accessible, even at night; dispenses with troublesome formalities, asks no inconvenient questions, advances promptly, and if interest is paid, does not press for repayment of principal. He keeps in close personal touch with his clients, and in many villages shares their occasions of weal or woe. *With his intimate knowledge of those around him, he is able, without serious risk, to finance those who would otherwise get no loan at all.* [Italics added.][17]

Or look at Barbara Ward's account:

> A small shopkeeper in a Hong Kong fishing village told me: 'I give credit to anyone who anchors regularly in our bay; but if it is someone I don't know well, then I think twice about it unless I can find out all about him.'[18]

Or, a profitable sideline of cotton ginning in Iran is the loaning of money for the next season, since the ginning companies often have a line of credit from Teheran banks at the market rate of interest. But in the first years of operation large losses are expected from unpaid debts – due to poor knowledge of the local scene.[19]

IV.　COUNTERACTING INSTITUTIONS

Numerous institutions counteract the effects of quality uncertainty. One obvious institution is guarantees. Most consumer durables carry guarantees to ensure the buyer of some normal expected quality. One natural result of our model is that the risk is borne by the seller rather than the buyer.

A second example of an institution which counteracts the effects of quality uncertainty is the brand-name good. Brand names not only indicate quality but also give the consumer a means of retaliation if the quality does not meet expectations. For the consumer will then curtail future purchases. Often too, new products are associated with old brand names. This ensures the prospective consumer of the quality of the product.

Chains – such as hotel chains or restaurant chains – are similar to brand names. One observation consistent with our approach is the chain restaurant. These restaurants, at least in the United States, most often appear in interurban highways. The customers are seldom local. The reason is that these well-known chains offer a better hamburger than the *average* local restaurant; at the same time, the local customer, who knows his area, can usually choose a place he prefers.

Licensing practices also reduce quality uncertainty. For instance, there is the licensing of doctors, lawyers, and barbers. Most skilled labor carries some certification indicating the attainment of certain levels of proficiency. The high school diploma, the baccalaureate degree, the Ph.D., even the Nobel Prize, to some degree, serve this function of certification. And education and labor markets themselves have their own 'brand names.'

V.　CONCLUSION

We have been discussing economic models in which 'trust' is important. Informal unwritten guarantees are preconditions for trade and production. Where these guarantees are indefinite, business will suffer – as indicated by our generalized Gresham's law. This aspect of uncertainty has been explored by game theorists, as in the Prisoner's Dilemma, but usually it has not been incorporated in the more traditional Arrow–Debreu approach to uncertainty.[20] But the difficulty of distinguishing good quality from bad is inherent in the business world; this may indeed explain many economic institutions and may in fact be one of the more important aspects of uncertainty.

NOTES

1. The author would especially like to thank Thomas Rothenberg for invaluable comments and inspiration. In addition he is indebted to Roy Radner, Albert Fishlow, Bernard Saffran, William D. Nordhaus, Giorgio La Malfa, Charles C. Holt, John Letiche, and the referee for help and suggestions. He would also like to thank the Indian Statistical Institute and the Ford Foundation for financial support.
2. Arrow's fine article, 'Uncertainty and medical care' (*American Economic Review*, Vol. 53, 1963), does not make this point explicitly. He emphasizes 'moral hazard' rather than 'adverse selection.' In its strict sense, the presence of 'moral hazard' is equally disadvantageous for both governmental and private programs; in its broader sense, which includes 'adverse selection,' 'moral hazard' gives a decided advantage to government insurance programs.
3. O. D. Dickerson, *Health Insurance* (Homewood, Ill.: Irwin, 1959), p. 333.
4. O.W. Anderson (with J.J. Feldman), *Family Medical Costs and Insurance* (New York: McGraw-Hill, 1956).
5. H.S. Denenberg, R.D. Eilers, G.W. Hoffman, C.A. Kline, J.J. Melone, and H.W. Snider, *Risk and Insurance* (Englewood Cliffs, N.J.: Prentice Hall, 1964), p. 446.
6. The following quote, again taken from an insurance textbook, shows how far the medical insurance market is from perfect competition:

   'insurance companies must screen their applicants. Naturally it is true that many people will voluntarily seek adequate insurance on their own initiative. But in such lines as accident and health insurance, companies are likely to give a second look to persons who voluntarily seek insurance without being approached by an agent.' (F.J. Angell, *Insurance, Principles and Practices*, New York: The Ronald Press, 1957, pp. 8–9).

   This shows that insurance is *not* a commodity for sale on the open market.
7. T.W. Schultz, *The Economic Value of Education* (New York: Columbia University Press, 1964), p. 42.
8. *The Times of India*, Nov. 10, 1967, p.1.
9. See J.J. Levy, Jr., 'Contrasting factors in the modernization of China and Japan,' in *Economic Growth: Brazil, India, Japan*, ed. S. Kuznets, et al. (Durham, N.C.: Duke University Press, 1955).
10. C.P. Kindleberger, *Economic Development* (New York: McGraw-Hill, 1958), p. 86.
11. For example, see W. Arthur Lewis, *The Theory of Economic Growth* (Homewood, Ill.: Irwin, 1955), p. 196.
12. *Report of the Committee on the Distribution of Income and Levels of Living*, Part I, Government of India, Planning Commission, Feb. 1964, p. 44.
13. H. Tinker, *South Asia: A Short History* (New York: Praeger, 1966), p. 134.
14. The existence of the following table (and also the small percent of firms under mixed control) indicates the communalization of the control of firms. Source: M.M. Mehta, *Structure of Indian Industries* (Bombay: Popular Book Depot, 1955), p. 314.

Distribution of Industrial Control by Community			
	1911	1931 (number of firms)	1951
British	281	416	382
Parsis	15	25	19
Gujaratis	3	11	17
Jews	5	9	3
Muslims	–	10	3
Bengalis	8	5	20
Mrwaris	–	6	96
Mixed Control	28	28	79
Total	341	510	619

Also, for the cotton industry see H. Fukuzawa, 'Cotton Mill Industry,' in V.B. Singh, editor, *Economic History of India, 1857–1956* (Bombay: Allied Publishers, 1965).

15. For the mixed record of industrial profits, see D.H. Buchanan, *The Development of Capitalist Enterprise in India* (New York: Kelley, 1966, reprinted).

16. The leading authority on this is Sir Malcolm Darling. See his *Punjabi Peasant in Prosperity and Debt*. The following table may also prove instructive:

	Secured loans (per cent)	Commonest rates for – Unsecured loans (per cent)	Grain Loans (per cent)
Punjab	6 to 12	12 to 24 (18 3/4 commonest)	25
United Provinces	9 to 12	24 to $37\frac{1}{2}$	25 (50 in Oudh)
Bihar		$18\frac{3}{4}$	50
Orissa	12 to 18 3/4	25	25
Bengal	8 to 12	9 to 18 for 'respectable clients' $18\frac{3}{4}$ to $37\frac{1}{2}$ (the latter common to agriculturalists)	
Central Provinces	6 to 12	15 for proprietors 24 for occupancy tenants $37\frac{1}{2}$ for ryots with no right of transfer	25
Bombay	9 to 12	12 to 25 (18 commonest)	
Sind		36	
Madras	12	15 to 18 (in insecure tracts 24 not uncommon)	20 to 50

Source: Punjabi Peasant in Prosperity and Debt, 3rd ed. (Oxford University Press, 1932), p. 190.

17. Darling, *op. cit.*, p. 204.

18. B. Ward, 'Cash or credit crops,' *Economic Development and Cultural Change*, Vol. 8 (Jan. 1960), reprinted in *Peasant Society: A Reader*, ed. G. Foster et al. (Boston: Little Brown and Company, 1967). Quote on p. 142. In the same volume, see also G.W. Skinner, 'Marketing and social structure in rural China,' and S.W. Mintz, 'Pratik: Haitian Personal Economic Relations.'

19. Personal conversation with mill manager, April 1968.

20. R. Radner 'Equilibre de marchés à terme et au comptant en cas d'incertitude,' in *Cahiers d'Economietrie*, Vol. 12 (Nov. 1967), Centre National de la Recherche Scientifique, Paris.

5. Path dependence, its critics and the quest for 'historical economics'[1]

Paul A. David

1. INTRODUCTION

Contemporary research and writing being undertaken in the genre of evolutionary economics can be viewed as part of a broader, more catholic intellectual movement, one that I would characterize as a quest for *historical social science*. Yet, a decade after it began to be trendy among economists to say that 'history matters', some things remain less than entirely clear about the possible meanings attached to that phrase, if indeed it is taken to carry any substantive content at all. For me, at least, the expression 'history matters' does carry a quite precise set of connotations, namely those associated closely with the concept of *path dependence*. The latter refers to a property of contingent, non-reversible dynamic processes, including a wide array of processes that can properly be described as 'evolutionary'. The set of ideas associated with path dependence consquently must occupy a central place in the future, historical social science that economics should become.

However, by now you may well have begun to wonder whether the matter of history mattering really has been greatly clarified by my tying it to a second catchy expression that, unfortunately like the first, has come to be invoked more frequently than it is defined. What *is* 'path dependence' anyway? Does it have a meaning more precise than the slogan: 'history matters'? Is it about 'the Economics of QWERTY' or about something more general? If we were to conduct a systematic survey, even one confined to the academic economics profession, it probably would confirm my casual impression that the rising popularity of the term 'path dependence' has spawned a variety of usages, a perceptible measure of confusion, and even some outright misinformation.[2] If there are few who are prepared to dissent from the assertion that 'history matters', there are more who wonder whether history matters in ways that are important for economists to think about, and, there are many more who hold diverse and sometimes contradictory notions of how it comes about that history matters.

My immediate task on this occasion, therefore, is to try to clarify the

meaning and amplify the economic significance of 'path dependence'. My
hope is that the results of such an undertaking will enable others better to
appreciate some of the salient implications for our discipline of recovering a
conceptualization of change as a process that is *historical*, including implications for the way economic policy analysis is approached. A task so simple to
describe, however, is not necessarily so easy to perform. For one thing, much
of the training of the modern economist tends to weaken the receipients'
natural, intuitive understanding of historical causation. Consequently, some
remedial work is required in addressing an audience of academic economists,
many of whose members' advanced education will have left them severely
incapacitated in this particular regard.

To put this differently, most of us have been well schooled in working with
mathematical economic models whose dynamics admit perfect reversibility
and lack any strong sense of genetic causation. It strikes me that neither those
economists who asually assign to the influence of 'history' the things for
which their analysis does not adequately account, nor those sceptics who say
'Sure, history matters, but not for much', are adequately responding to the
challenges posed by the quite different class of dynamic processes that generate sequences of causally related *events*. One of the things about 'events' that
our everyday experience of change seems to confirm is that they happen – and
never 'un-happen'. By contrast with the realities of the world around us,
recognition of which forces itself implicitly and often only incompletely into
the consciousness of practicing economic advisors, much of the formal teach-
ing of economic analysis refers to a very different and special class of dynamic
processes in which all motion in the long run is 'continuous locomotion'. In
the context of analytical structures of that kind, which are familiar enough to
students of classical mechanics, 'change' may be said to occur without there
being any specific, individual 'events' that have causal significance.

To abandon the learned habits of peering at the world of economics automatically and exclusively from the peculiar vantage point afforded by a certain
and now certainly antiquated branch of physics, and to be able therefore to
take up another and contrary perspective, cannot be simply a matter of un-
learning. Something additional, and for many, something new has to be
learned. That 'something' can stand alongside neoclassical economic analysis,
and so enhance one's appreciation of the special features distinguishing that
paradigm from what may be called *historical economics*.

In asserting that 'history matters' I do not maintain that in economic
processes history always matters in the same ways. Nor would I contend that
economic processes have worked in the same way throughout history. The
issue of how much 'importance' should be attached to the particular category
of path dependent dynamical processes, in the sense of what proportion of the
changes occurring in the economy around us can best be understood in such

terms, remains for me one that must be addressed by empirical inquiries. But, like virtually all interesting empirical questions, this one cannot be resolved in an analytical vacuum. The very nature of the evidence that would be required to address it is prescribed by reference to alternative, analytical and statistical models that admit of historical changes that are path dependent, and changes that are path independent. Data acquire meaning only in the context of economic theory: as T.S. Ashton, the British economic historian, said long ago: 'the facts do not wear their hearts on their sleeves'.

To say that is not to diminish the value of 'mere facts', nor to dilute the force of the imperative to get details of the story straight. Examination of particular cases may serve to illustrate the phenomenon of path dependence, to exemplify one or another methodology of studying historical economics, and to identify and explore unresolved problems. The writing of a piece of economic history in this way may also be good fun, and, when it is well done it typically manages both to provide entertainment and to satisfy particular points of curiosity. To do it well, however, we must begin with some grasp of the conceptual issues and the theoretical framework that endows observations with meaning and import.

Therefore, on this occasion I am not going to delve into the details of selected historical cases, whether illustrative of the evolution of technologies, or of institutions and organizational forms, or of cultural beliefs. Historical economics needs greater investment in suitable theory, and the kind of theory that is required is harder than that upon which ahistorical economics has been able to rest. So I must ask that you forego for the present the enjoyment of another excursion into economic history, and, instead, attend more closely to the conceptual foundations that serve to underpin further research into path dependence in the economy. There will be an ancillary benefit in following this course: by anchoring our discussions firmly on these foundations with the aid of some precise definitions of path dependence (in section 2), it is quite straightforward to dispose of the misleading presentations of the concept by sceptics and critics.[3] I can then proceed (in section 3) to try clearing up the confusion that has developed in the literature over the connection between path dependence and economic inefficiency, before turning (in section 4) to take up the meaning and economic significance of the widely used term 'lock-in'.

After this necessary clearing of obscuring 'undergrowth' it will be seen (in section 5) that once we enter an explicitly dynamic framework, the questions of static welfare 'efficiency' and the meaning of 'market failure' become more complicated and involve subtle issues that the critics of path dependence have thus far failed to take on board. Moreover, the implications of path dependence for economic policy studies are in reality quite far reaching, in arguing for the abandonment of static welfare-analytic approaches to the problem of where government should intervene in the economy, and its replacement by explicitly dynamic analysis that asks whether 'now' is the time in this or that specific market. Moreover, the general thrust of the recommendations regarding issues of technology policy that emerge from considerations of path dependence, will more often than not turn out to be entirely opposite in nature to those that seem to be most worrisome to the concept's *laissez-faire* critics.

In sum, I am unable to find any compelling reasons why economic analysis should remain 'locked-in' to an ahistorical conceptual framework, apart from the unfortunate hysteresis effects of 'intellectual sunk costs'. But those effects are real, and must be countered. Therefore, drawing upon the analogy offered by field models of physical systems that have multiple basins of attraction, I suggest (in section 6) that some injection of further, intellectual 'energy' is likely to be necessary in order for our discipline to free itself from the local region of 'low potential' in which it has too long remained trapped.

2.   ALMOST EVERYTHING YOU WANTED TO KNOW ABOUT 'PATH DEPENDENCE' – BUT WERE ALWAYS AFRAID TO ASK

Path-dependence, as I wish to use the term, refers to a dynamic property of allocative processes. It may be defined either with regard to the relationship between the process dynamics and the outcome(s) to which it converges, or the limiting probability distribution of the stochastic process under consideration.

At the most intuitive level we may draw a distinction between dynamic processes that are path dependent, and the rest. The latter, path-*independent* processes, may be said to include those whose dynamics guarantee convergence to a unique, globally stable equilibrium configuration; or, in the case of stochastic systems, those for which there exists an invariant (stationary) asymptotic probability distribution that is continuous over the entire feasible space of outcomes – that is, a limiting distribution that is continuous over all the states that are compatible with the energy of the system.

Stochastic systems possessing the latter properties are said to be *ergodic*, and have the ability eventually to shake free from the influence of their past state(s). In physics, ergodic systems are said to be connected, in the sense that it is possible to transit directly or indirectly between any arbitrarily chosen pair of states, and hence, eventually, to reach all the states from any one of them.

Path dependent processes thus may be defined negatively, as belonging to the class of exceptions from the foregoing set of processes, in which the details of the history of the systems' motion do not matter – because they cannot affect its asymptotic distribution among the states. This leads us immediately to

*A **negative definition***: *Processes that are non-ergodic, and thus unable to shake free of their history, are said to yield path dependent outcomes.*

In this connection, it may be worthwhile to notice that the familiar homogeneous Markov chain invoked in many applications in economics – models of population migration and spatial distribution, of income and wealth, and occupational and social status distributions, firm size distribution, and so forth – is characterized by an invariant set of state-dependent transition probabilities that are finite (positive), and for convenience in many applications contexts, are specified so as to ensure that the process is *ergodic*. The distributions of the individuals or firms whose motions among the states are governed by Markov chains of this kind will each converge to their respective, invariant asymptotic probability distribution – a distribution that is continuous over the entire feasible state space. (This unique limiting distribution is the one that emerges as the transition matrix operator is repeatedly iterated.) When there is an absorbing state or subset of connected states (from which the probability of escape to the subset of transient states is zero), the system will converge weakly to that single attractor. Obviously, such a system's behaviour is not deterministic, but it may be said to be 'pre-destined', in the sense of being governed from the outset by a unique asymptotic probability distribution.

However, when a state-dependent process has two or more absorbing subsets (that is, distinct regions of equilibria that are locally stable), the homogeneous Markov process becomes *non-ergodic, and its outcomes can be said to be path dependent*. In the trivial case in which the initial condition of the system was one or the other of the absorbing states, it is plain that whatever governed that selection would fix the limiting position of the system. Further, it is no less self-evident that if there is at least one transient (non-absorbing) state from which the multiplicity of absorbing states can be reached, directly or indirectly, then the realization of the random process at that point in the system's history (on its path) will select one rather than the other outcome(s) to which the system eventually must converge.

For many purposes, however, we would like to say what a path dependent process *is*, rather than what it is not. Help from the probability theorists can be invoked in order to do so in a precise way. Focusing upon the limiting patterns generated by a random process (thus characterizing a dynamic system), we have

*A **positive definition***: *A path dependent stochastic process is one whose asymptotic distribution evolves as a consequence (function of) the process's own history.*

This broader definition explicitly takes in processes that possess a *multiplicity* of asymptotic distributions, as generally is the case for *branching processes* – where the prevailing probabilities of transitions among states are functions of the sequence of past transient states that the system has visited. Branching processes that are subject to local irreversibilities share the property of non-ergodicity. The latter therefore characterizes the processes of biological evolution, because speciation constitutes a non-reversible event.

Transition probabilities that are not invariant functions of the current state are also the characteristic feature of so-called non-homogeneous Markov chains. Rather confusingly, however, probability theorists sometimes refer to the latter as having *path dependent transition probabilities*, thereby contrasting them with the more familiar class of homogeneous (or first order) Markov chains whose transition probabilities are (current) *state* dependent.[4] But, as has been seen from the negative definition discussed above, path dependence of the transition probabilities is not a necessary condition for a process that generates path dependent outcomes.

The foregoing account of what the term 'path dependence' means may now be compared with the rather different ways in which it has come to be explicitly and implicitly defined in some parts of the economics literature. For the moment we may put aside all of the many instances in which the phrases 'history matters' and 'path dependence' are simply interchanged, so that some loose and general connotations are suggested without actually defining either term. Unfortunately much of the non-technical literature seems bent upon avoiding explicit definitions, resorting either to analogies, or to the description of a syndrome – the set of phenomena with whose occurrences the writers associate path dependence. Rather than telling you what path dependence *is*, they tell you some of the symptomology – things that may, or must happen when the condition is present. It is rather like saying that the common cold *is* sneezing, watering eyes and a runny nose. I can illustrate this with the following two passages:

> Path dependence is the application to economic systems of an intellectual movement that has lately come into fashion in several academic disciplines. In physics and mathematics, the related idea is called chaos – sensitive dependence on initial conditions. As chaos theory has it, a hurricane off the coast of Florida may be the fault of a butterfly flapping its wings in the Sahara. In biology the related idea is called contingency – the irreversible character of natural selection. Contingency implies that fitness is only a relative notion: survival is not of the fittest possible, but only of the fittest that happen to be around at the time. (Liebowitz and Margolis, 1995c, p. 33)

Elsewhere, the same authors propose a kindred explanation, albeit one that is slightly more formal:

> The use of path dependence in economics is, for the most part, loosely analogous to this mathematical construction: Allocations chosen today exhibit memory; they are

conditioned on past decisions. It is where such a mathematical process exhibits 'sensitive dependence on initial conditions', where past allocations exhibit a controlling influence, that it corresponds most closely to the concerns that economists and others have raised as problems of path dependency [sic]. In such a case, 'insignificant events' or very small differences among conditions are magnified, bringing about very different outcomes. It is that circumstance that yields both the 'non-predictability' and 'potential inefficiency' ... (Liebowitz and Margolis, 1995b, p. 210)

Much could be said about the inaccuracies in the texts just quoted. For the present, however, it will be sufficient to notice one thing that they do not say, and three things that they do say.

That path dependence is a property of *stochastic* sequential processes is *not* mentioned, and only the allusion to 'contingency' provides any hint of the subject's probabilistic context. Of course, in order to pick up this clue, one would need to suppress the extraneous and misleading surmise that 'contingency' has a meaning that is specific to (evolutionary) biology, where it 'implies' something about the nature of selections made on criteria of inclusive fitness.[5] Even that slender clue, however, is disguised by the statements that would have us associate path dependence with *deterministic* chaos, and the property of 'sensitive dependence on initial conditions' which characterizes that class of dynamic systems. The coupling of path dependence with chaos constitutes the first of the three positive assertions to which I previously referred, and it is incorrect. What it reflects is a too common predilection among mainstream economic writers for transposing concepts and arguments that are probabilistic in nature into simple deterministic models.[6] This habit is often seriously misleading, and must be especially so where neither certainty equivalence nor the operation of the central limit theorem of probability can legitimately be presupposed.

The second and third assertions disclose the authors' reasons why path dependence should be denounced as a problematic departure from the economic mainstream. They allege that a dynamic system in which there is 'memory' will be unpredictable, and worse, that it will be characterized by a potential for generating inefficient resource allocations. Like the first of the triad of assertions, these too are simply incorrect. There are some classes of non-ergodic stochastic processes whose outcomes are predictable, and I shall say more about these in due course. Further, it is vitally important to insist on logically distinguishing between systems that have the general property of path dependence, and that special sub-category of non-ergodic dynamic systems that may display (as an additional attribute) a susceptibility to one or another form of 'market failure'.

The latter condition, of course, is the one that adherents of strict neoclassical orthodoxy seem to find especially troublesome. Although I partake in the interest that most modern economists show regarding the efficiency of economic resource allocation, an obsession with the spectre of inefficiency was not what motivated me to inject the notion of path dependence into wide economic discourse, or to associate it with the application of insights from formal models of non-ergodic stochastic processes. This confession ought not to come as a surprise, especially to those who have encountered material that I have published before and since the pair of essays in which Clio, the muse of History, was coupled with the emergence of QWERTY as the *de facto* standard for typewriter keyboards (David 1985 and 1986).

The concept of path dependence and the associated framework of analysis is anchored in my long-standing quest to integrate *historicity* into economics. I think it important to distinguish between that peculiar aim, and the broader objectives of the 'new economic history' movement during the 1960s and 1970s, which saw the wholesale importation of the apparatus of modern economic analysis and econometric techniques into the study of economic history. Although the use of the economist's preferred methods of study of the past, undoubtedly has proved extremely illuminating in many contexts, it had become evident to some within the field that new constraints and analytical contradictions had been created by trying to understand economic history – which is to say 'economic dynamics' – through the assiduous application of *ahistorical* concepts and tools. It was the prospect of resolving those problems within the framework of path dependence that made the latter attractive from my vantage point. Imagine, then, my utter surprise to find this approach being attacked as a rival paradigm of economic analysis, whose only relevance consisted in the degree to which it could be held to represent a direct rejection of the normative, *laissez-faire* message of neoclassical microeconomics!

3. SIGNIFICANCE: DOES PATH DEPENDENCE MEAN THERE WILL BE INEXTRICABLE INEFFICIENCIES?

> Welcome to the world of path dependence, a world governed not by our stars, not by ourselves, but by insignificant accidents of history. In this unpredictable world, small seemingly inconsequential decisions lead inexorably to uncontrollable consequences. ... In the world of path dependence ... our expectations for market outcomes are turned upside down. The Invisible Hand does not work in the world of path dependence. (Liebowitz and Margolis 1995c, p. 33)

This passage, from the article 'Policy and path dependence – from QWERTY to Windows 95', published in the Cato Institute's journal *Regulation*, ironically describes what is purported to be the essential message of those propounding the concept of path dependence. It is the authors' general contention that path dependence really cannot hold much interest for economists, because the world of market economies does not conform to the one that they construe the concept to be describing; because *remedies* for unsatisfactory situations generally will be available, and found quickly by profit-hungry entrepreneurs attracted by the potential 'surplus' that is implicit in any seriously inefficient state of affairs. Hence, on this reasoning, the only sorts of path dependent phenomena which would warrant the attention of economists must be extremely rare occurrences.

But, as has been seen, the core content of the concept of path dependence as a dynamic property refers to the idea of history as an irreversible branching process. One must logically distinguish from this the idea that it is possible that some branchings are 'regrettable' because they created inextricable inefficiencies that, in some counter-factual but equally feasible world, could have been avoided. Moreover, it is plainly a mistake to impute to the economic theory of path dependence *as such* the set of propositions that underlie the second of these ideas, for the notion of market failure has been long established in the literature of welfare economics.

Actually, it is within the context of static general equilibrium analysis that economists developed the concept of 'market failure' – namely, that the Pareto optimality of allocations arrived at via atomistically competitive markets is not guaranteed *except* under a stringent set of convexity conditions on production and preference sets; and, further, it requires the existence of markets for all extant and contingent commodities. One may or may not accept the usefulness for pragmatic policy purposes of defining 'market failure' in a way that takes those conditions as a reference ideal. Analytically, however, it remains a total *non sequitur* to assert that the essence of path dependence – a property defined for analyses of dynamical and stochastic processes – consists in asserting propositions regarding the possibility of 'market failure' that were proved first in the context of purely static and deterministic models.

Quite the contrary proposition holds: under full convexity conditions a *non-tatonnement* general equilibrium process can be shown to converge in a strictly path dependent manner on one among the continuum of valid 'core' solutions which satisfy the criterion of Pareto optimality (see Fisher, 1983; and David, 1997b). This should be sufficient to expose the logical error of claiming that the essential difference between models of path dependence and standard neoclassical analysis must be the former's insistence on the presence of 'market failure'. To be sure, there are some underlying connections between the existence of conditions that give rise to path dependence in economic processes, and the possibility that the workings of competitive markets in those circumstances would result in allocations that are inefficient. But the circumstances in which competitive markets will not yield Pareto efficient outcomes are not in themselves either new, or arcane.

It might then be noticed that the taxonomy of path dependence proposed by

Liebowitz and Margolis (1995b), and curiously described as 'definitions of path dependence', embraces a classificatory principle that is based entirely on static optimality criteria. Inasmuch as such criteria remain conceptually orthogonal to the nature of the dynamical processes under consideration, it is perhaps not surprising to observe that the definitions offered by Liebowitz and Margolis for 'first-degree' and 'second-degree' path dependence do not actually serve to distinguish between dynamic systems that are path independent and those that are path dependent. The first-degree form describes a situation in which all the outcomes among which selections might be made are not Pareto-ranked, such as would exist for the Nash equilbria of in a pure coordination game; the second-degree situation is one in which the outcome realized is dominated by a feasible alternative, yet represents the unavoidable *ex post* consequence of having taken an action that *ex ante* represented the 'best' strategy.[7]

In discussing the conceptualization of third-degree path dependence in which there is market failure leading to inefficiencies of an 'irremediable' kind, Liebowitz and Margolis (1995b) make reference to the test of 'remediability' suggested by Oliver E. Williamson. But, they entirely omit mention of the important distinction that Williamson's (1993) work drew between remediability through 'private ordering' and through 'public ordering'. Nowhere in the literature dealing with theoretical and empirical aspects of path dependent economic phenomena have I found it said that this property leads to outcomes for which remediation via public ordering is wholly *infeasible*. For the state to undertake to 'correct' a market outcome might become socially inefficient. But that is a different proposition from its being simply infeasible. So, it is not open to the critics to claim that path dependence would have empirical or policy substance for economists if only it did not exclude the possibility of remediation by public ordering in those circumstances where private ordering was unworkable.[8]

One certainly must agree that among economists at large most of the interest in path dependence results from the possibilities that sub-optimal equilibria will be 'selected' by a dynamic process. So it is understandable (and certainly to be expected) that brief treatments of points of controversy concerning theoretical contentions and empirical 'evidence' would tend to focus upon that question to the exclusion of everything else. Nevertheless, there is more to economic life than the possibility of welfare losses due to static inefficiencies. The identities of winners and losers in market rivalries is of interest to the owners and employees of the enterprises involved. The structure of industry itself may be of significance for dynamic efficiency through innovation and entrepreneurship. Indeed, the intense recent interest of the business press (and the Justice Department) in the positions of Microsoft and its present and future rivals in the market for web-browsers and related software, makes it plain that something more is perceived to be at stake than the comparative social rates of return on further incremental investment in their respective product lines.

More generally, all manner of political and social sequelae, as well as questions of equity, are attached to the dynamics governing the evolution of income and wealth distributions, and processes of socio-economic stratification. If analysis of positive feedback mechanisms that affect those aspects of life would significantly enhance economists' abilities to understand and predict the path dependent phenomena arising therein, does that not warrant at least some notice in assessment of the conceptual framework's significance?

4.   THE MEANING OF 'LOCK-IN' IN THE HISTORICAL CONTEXT OF PATH DEPENDENCE

The current state of imprecision and confusion in discussions of the meaning and significance of the term 'lock-in' has not been alleviated by the use of 'lock-in' as one among the taxonomic criteria applied to classify path dependent processes in the recent work of Professors Liebowitz and Margolis. Quite the reverse. I must begin by reiterating some doubts as to the coherence of creating a taxonomy for path dependent economic processes that turns upon whether or not it is possible to imagine a system being inextricably 'locked in' to a state that is locally and globally dominated by other allocative arrangements. Yet the latter would appear to be the very condition that is indicated, when the term is taken by Liebowitz and Margolis (1994, 1995b, 1995c) to refer to a situation where all the participating agents know they would derive a *net* gain by arranging by whatever means were necessary, collectively to exchange the status quo for some other available configuration.

By 'net gain', in this definition, is meant a surplus over and above the full costs of organizing and implementing the move to another state. *Ex hypothesis* there will be sufficient surplus in the new state to compensate everyone and leave someone better off after absorbing all the costs of negotiation, mechanism design, and insuring credible commitment that may be required to implement a collective escape. Therefore, in the circumstances thus posited, one would be hard put indeed to see how, if the agents involved were economically rational individuals, the *status quo* could have persisted long enough to be of interest. What is there in the imagined situation that would serve to lock in anyone to so unstable an attractor? Either we accept that people behave rationally and that such situations will be as scarce as hens' teeth, or this is a rendering of the notion of lock-in that would oblige economists to acknowledge that sometimes history that really matters is a result of the workings of the mysterious, the irrational, or the wildly improbable forces in economic life – or possibly all three.

By contrast, as the term 'lock-in' has been used in my work and that of Arthur (1989), it simply is a vivid way to describe the entry of a system into a trapping region – the basin of attraction that surrounds a locally (or globally) stable equilibrium. When a dynamic economic system enters such a region, it cannot escape except through the intervention of some external force, or shock, that alters its configuration or transforms the underlying structural relationships among the agents. Path dependent systems – which have a multiplicity of possible equilibria among which event-contingent selections can occur – may thus become locked in to attractors that are optimal, or that are just as good as any others in the feasible set, or that take paths leading to places everyone would wish to have been able to avoid, once they have arrived there.

From this vantage point, Arthur's (1989) phrase 'lock-in by small historical events' is evidently a gloss that should not be read too literally; it is a convenient contraction of the foregoing reference to the way in which trapping regions may be entered – although somewhat unfortunate, in allowing a hasty reader to suppose that the antecedent events somehow have *created* the local stability, or locked-in state. To be more precise, albeit more cumbersome, one should say that such configurations are self-sustaining (Nash) equilibria; that in the case of a path dependent process some particular historical event caused – that is, initiated the sequence of transitions that effectively selected, one rather than another among such configurations to be realized as the system's emergent property.

In some circumstances, as in the case of pure coordination games (where there are strategic complementarities in the dynamic interactions among agents) there is no Pareto-ranking of a multiplicity of available equilibria from amongst which a path dependent, branching process can make a selection. *Which* coordination point is reached is a matter of welfare indifference to the parties involved. A coordination equilibrium, thus, provides us with the paradigmatic situation in which individuals are content to remain doing something, even though they would be happier doing something else if everybody would also do that other thing too. The reason they don't change what they are doing is, generically, that there are information imperfections that make it unlikely that a decentralized process can get everyone coordinated to move elsewhere, collectively.[9] Now notice that while incomplete information may be critical in blocking spontaneous escapes from dominated coordination equilibria, it is not a necessary condition for decentralized market processes to select such states. This is another reason why presenting 'lock-in' as a particular (pernicious, and supposedly uncommon) form of 'path dependence' is an invitation to further analytical confusions.

This last, important point can be elaborated on by observing that the generic problems of escaping from lock-in of the system to a globally inferior (but locally stable) attractor are rooted in 'pure' coordination costs. Such costs may be very high, however, especially if the individual agents are expected to act spontaneously under conditions of incomplete information. Hence, the nature of the *ex post* coordination problem generally is not the same as the problem of arranging coordination with agents who do not yet exist, or who have yet to recognize the complementaries between their interests and capabilities and those initiating the action. The sources of *ex ante* market failure that allow the system to be led into a globally inferior equilibrium are not necessarily the ones that make it very hard to get out.

Of course, if and when the structure of economic incentives and constraints bearing upon the process under study is altered by events that, for the purposes of the analysis may reasonably be regarded as 'exogenous innovations' (in the state of relevant knowledge, or in the regulatory institutional regime), the previous attractor(s) may be destroyed, freeing the system to endogenously begin to evolve some new configurations. Thus, the advent of microwave transmission technologies in the 1950s may be seen to have undermined the prevailing regulatory regime governing the US telecommunications industry (which had itself emerged through a path dependent process); and the denouement, in the event of the AT&T divestiture, brought into being a liberalized regulatory regime and new market structure that may be said to have formed new 'attractive paths', for the evolution of digital telecommunications technologies. But to claim that the evidence of change itself is sufficient to dispose of the notion of a persisting inefficient lock-in is tantamount to supposing that Schumpeter's gale of 'creative destruction' is blowing continuously at full force, through every niche, nook and cranny of the economy. Indeed, it is a way of losing one's sense of the variations in the flow of events through time that makes it interesting to read histories.

Strategic re-definitions, playing with words to avoid the force of the concepts with which they were originally associated, is a form of rhetoric that is essentially obscurantist. By the purely semantic trick of re-defining path dependence to come in various degrees of seriousness, and by associating the most 'serious' form to be, not a process, but a particular outcome state gauged in terms of allocational efficiency, it is possible to give superficial plausibility to the claim that no serious economic consequences are associated with the phenomenon of path dependence. This has been the taxonomic gambit tried by Professors Liebowitz and Margolis, who reserve their 'most serious' form of path dependence (third-degree) to be the state in which the *status quo* is Pareto-dominated *even after all transition and adjustment costs are considered*. They then can ask, rhetorically, why should one suppose that we would ever find a situation of 'serious path dependence', where people refused to make themselves individually and collectively better off, after paying all the bargaining, transactions and information costs of arranging their escape from a bad situation? Why indeed? If one insists that the only sort of sub-optimality worth worrying about is the kind so wasteful as to justify escaping at any finite cost, then one is implicitly accepting the actual or equivalent loss of all the remedial expenditures (the costs of undoing the effects of outcomes we collectively prefer not to live with). Yet, those remedial expenditures might not have been unavoidable *ex ante*. Is it not pertinent for economists advising private and public agencies to consider the likelihood that some substantial portion of those costs were consequences of the path dependence of the dynamic process through which 'regrettable' outcomes were 'selected'?

Suppose, for the moment, that the significant economic question to be addressed in regard to the possibility of 'lock-in' is this: how can we identify situations in which it is likely that at some future time individuals really would be better off had another equilibrium been selected *ab initio*? By that we must mean that an alternative outcome would be preferred in some collective sense (perhaps by application of a compensation test) to the one that they are now in, and that they also (collectively) should be ready to incur some substantial costs to rectify the situation – assuming it was feasible to do so. Were it possible to answer that question by saying that such conditions will never obtain, then economists could well afford not to bother with the distinction between dynamic processes whose outcomes were path dependent and those which were path independent. It would be a distinction that might interest students of history, but would otherwise be inconsequential for economic policy. But such would be true only if multiple equilibria could be shown never to exist outside the context of pure coordination games (that is, where none are Pareto-dominated), or if it could be shown that it would never be possible to identify the structural conditions that give rise to other multiple equilibrium situations. We have no impossibility theorems of this sort, and neither of these propositions is likely to be established empirically.

5.   PATH-CONSTRAINED MELIORATION, THE BURDENS OF COUNTERFACTUAL HISTORICAL ANALYSIS, AND SOME POLICY IMPLICATIONS

There is, however, another way to look at the question. It may be that the selection of Pareto-dominated equilibria in positive feedback systems is never allowed to become serious enough (in the Liebowitz–Margolis sense) to impress the contemporary observer who can imagine clever, if costly, mechanisms for organizing collective escapes from locally sub-optimal situations. This, indeed, is a cogent point, and deserves closer attention than it usually receives from economists who challenge the champions of historical economics to look around and find a 'really important' example – by which they seem to mean, a case of path dependent dynamics leading to a grossly inefficient equilibrium. Instead of imagining that history is played out without anybody noticing what is happening, and then, when an equilibrium appears to be reached people gather round and assess its optimality, we must allow for the process to encompass possibilities and consequences of incremental *path-constrained meliorating actions* being taken by observant, intelligent agents.

The static framework of welfare analysis within which too many economists are still being taught to do their thinking tends to suppress the natural disposition to conceptualize the whole flow of current economic life as contingent upon the results of antecedent choices. Seen in truly historical perspective, a great deal of human ingenuity, especially the sort that is said to be 'mothered by necessity', is devoted to trying to cope with 'mistakes' that are threatening to become 'serious' in their economic consequences; to assuring, somehow, that their more pernicious effects will be moderated, if not abated altogether. This is done *ex post*, by contriving technological 'fixes' and 'patches', by commandeering temporary task forces to handle emergencies that established organizational structures are discovered to be handling badly, by sustained efforts at 'reforming' (not reinventing) long-standing institutions, and, yes, by concerted educational campaigns to untrain people who have acquired dysfunctional habits of one sort or another.

We like to refer to all of that activity as 'progress' and, in a historically local sense, that is just what it is: melioration. But the meliorative options are more often than not quite tightly bounded by the existing critical situation: it is the existing software code that threatened to malfunction badly when the year 2000 dawned, not some other programs and data formats that were not implemented, although they might well have been trivial to modify. The resources spent in such perceived loss-avoidance activities are part of what we are happy to consider productive investments, adding to the net product, whereas some part of it could equally well be thought of as the deferred costs of regrettable decisions made in haste to be remedied at leisure, and sometimes for great profit. They might equally be called regrettable economic opportunities (see David, 1999).

Most of the situations in which the discomforts of remaining in a bad coordination equilibrium could be really large are those in which the institution, or technology, or behavioural norm has become highly elaborated and deeply embedded in numerous activities throughout the economy. One must then contemplate a counter-factual world in which the whole general equilibrium course of evolution would have been very different. Consideration of the implications of general purpose technologies is one of the ways in which economists today are coming to grips with this sort of systems analysis. Little wonder that economic historians have been and should be concerned primarily with such questions.

In considering the nature of the policy lessons that might be drawn from the foregoing view of the incremental evolutionary development of complex technological systems, some remarks on the putative role played by 'historical accidents' in path dependent processes are now very much in order. Unfortunately, the use of that phrase itself is prone to cause misunderstandings. It is quite misleading to take it to suggest that some original economic irrationality, or implementation error (accident) must be implicated whenever we find that positive network externalities have given rise to a sequence that turned out to be other than a globally optimal path. Indeed, only those who are hostile to the very idea of path dependence would repeatedly insist upon a literal interpretation of the phrase 'accidents of history'. Doing so suggests that the essential feature of such processes is that the original actors in the drama – whether as contributors to the design of a technical system, or an institutional rule structure, or a particular form of business organization, or as the initial adopters of such innovations – had to have been acting arbitrarily, or irrationally in the context of their economic circumstances. Such an interpretation is not only logically unwarranted; it obfuscates an important but widely overlooked feature common to the histories of many network technologies, and one that has some bearing upon the way public policy might be approached in that area.

The facts of all the technological instances recently under re-examination – QWERTY, 640K lower memory in the IMB PC, AC vs. DC electrical current, light-water reactors, and VCR formats too – are quite consistent with the view that the behaviour of the initiating actors of the drama, generally, was quite deliberate (not at all random in the sense of remaining inexplicable to the historian), and furthermore reasonably conformable to the urgings of the profit motive. Yet, generally, their actions were also bounded by a parochial and myopic conception of the process in which they were engaging – in the sense that these decision agents were not concerned with whether the larger system that might (and was) being built around what they were doing would be optimized by their choice.[10] In most cases they can be held to have failed entirely to foresee the complementary innovations and investments that would be influenced by their initial commitment to one rather than another course of action. In other words, their failure of imagination took the form of not thinking *systemically* about the technological and industrial structures that they were engaged in developing. Thomas Edison, of course, being a systems inventor *par excellence*, was an exception in that particular regard; yet, as has been shown by David (1991, 1992c), Edison's business strategy in the context of the 'Battle of the Systems' – including his sudden decision to withdraw from the flourishing electrical supply systems industry altogether – appears to have been driven by quite different, rather myopic, but nonetheless rational economic considerations.

In general, what were difficult for the pioneers in any area to foresee were the complementaries that would emerge subsequently, and in so doing open the possibilities of developing a more complex, distributed system whose components were not produced or purchased integrally. The Remington Co. engineers who put the finishing touches on the first commercially successful typewriters to carry QWERTY into the world did not dream of the possibility of touch-typing manuals; Edison had not anticipated that anyone would devise an efficient and economical converter to link DC electrical supply facilities with distant users by way of polyphase AC networks. Similarly, in more modern times, neither of the rival vendor groups behind the Sony Betamax and VHS cassette formats in the early VCR market had anticipated the commercial importance of pre-recorded movies and video rental stores.[11] Nor were the IBM engineers in Texas, as they rushed to create a readily producible personal computer, concerned with the amount of random access memory that would be needed to load a word-processing program like WordPerfect whilst keeping an Excel spreadsheet and a LAN-modem open and running in the background.

The point here is not that these folks ought to have seen the shape of the future. Rather it is that the shape of the larger systems that evolved was built upon their work, and thus in each case preserved, and was in some respects much constrained by it – even in the way that they coped with the legacies of those initial decisions, taken quite deliberately, but with quite other and in some measure more evanescent considerations in mind.

From the foregoing it may be seen that a proper understanding of path dependence, and of the possibilities of externalities leading to market failure, is not without interesting implications for economic policy. But those are not at all the sorts of glib conclusions that some critics have alleged must follow if one believes that history really matters – namely, that government should try to pick winners rather than let markets make mistakes. Quite the contrary, as I began trying to make clear more than a decade ago.[12] One thing that public policy could do is to try to delay the market from committing to the future inextricably, before enough information has been obtained about the likely technical or organizational and legal implications, of an early, precedent-setting decision.

In other words, preserving open options for a longer period than impatient market agents would wish is the generic wisdom that history has to offer to public policy makers, in all the applications areas where positive feedback processes are likely to be preponderant over negative feedbacks. Numerous dynamic strategies can and have been suggested as ways of implementing this approach in various, specific contexts where public sector action is readily feasible. Still more sensible and practical approaches will be found if economists cease their exclusive obsession with traditional questions of static welfare analysis and, instead of pronouncing on the issue of where state intervention would be justified in the economy, start to ask what kind of public actions would be most appropriate to take at different points in the evolution of a given market process.

The 'first best' public policy role in these matters, therefore, is not necessarily the making of positive choices, but instead the improvement of the informational state in which choices can be made by private parties and government agencies. In the context of the recent literature on sunk cost hysteresis and options theory, one may see that the more history matters – because complementaries create irreversibilities in resource commitments – the more worthwhile it is to invest in being better informed prior to leaping. There is an evident opportunity cost in giving priority to investments in further information acquisition; quite standard economics can be relied on to balance the expected value of waiting (searching) for further 'news', against the anticipated costs to the current generation(s) of not allowing markets to make choices on the basis of the knowledge that is presently available. Obviously, some assessment of the rate at which the relevant information states are capable of evolving will turn out to be of critical importance in determining when a stage has been reached where it no longer is best to defer irreversible resource commitments.

6. OVERCOMING 'INTELLECTUAL SUNK COST HYSTERESIS' AND ESCAPING FROM DISCIPLINARY 'LOCK-IN' TO AHISTORICISM

The cluster of ideas that are now identified with the concept of path dependence in economic and other social processes probably would not excite such attention, nor require so much explication, were it not for the extended prior investment of intellectual resources in developing economics as an ahistorical system of thought. For many economists, their own costs sunk in mastering that discipline have produced a facility for reasoning that suppresses natural, human intuitions about historical causation. They thus have a 'learned incapacity' (in Thorstein Veblen's apt phrase) to see how historical events could exert a causal influence upon subsequent outcomes that would be economically important. Perhaps unknowingly, such folk have fully internalized Aristotle's teleological principle of explanation, which rejected the method of reference to antecedents, and so escaped infinite explanatory regress by substituting forward-looking functionalism (as we would describe it). This was undoubtedly useful, even though it has had the intellectual side effect, in many disciplines, of encouraging the formal suppression of the intuitive impulse to refer to pre-existing states and intervening 'events' when asked to account for the way things are today.

Mainstream economics is not alone among the social sciences in providing a way to explain an existing state of the world by reference to the purpose or end (*telos*) that it serves, rather than to the conditions from which it may have evolved.[13] This has proved a source of deep insights into many matters, but not into all matters of concern to economists and students of broader cultural phenomena, such as the spread of languages and social communication norms.[14] Nor, for that matter, does it suffice to provide good accounts of biological phenomena. In modern Darwinian evolutionary theory there is a beautiful, productive tension between the teleological principle of natural selection according to inclusive fitness, and the antecedents principle, namely, that the possibilities of evolution are tightly constrained at every moment by the current contents of the gene pool, which is the product of species' history. Perhaps that is why we might be drawn towards evolutionary biology as 'the Mecca for economics'.

Modern economics in its ahistorical, convergence model formulation serves some intellectual purposes very well, and the perpetuation of the methodological *status quo* can be seen to serve still other rational private ends. Nevertheless, if that style of explanation was entirely satisfactory in account-ing for all economic and social phenomena without reference to legacies from the past, some of us would not presently be so exercised by trying to adjust contemporary economic thinking to the notion that history matters – nor would others be strenuously resisting that adjustment. Path dependence is a concept requiring explication for many today, simply because so much of economics committed itself to theories that would make the results of choice behaviours consistent in the sense of being path independent. But there is no compelling reason to regard that as an exclusive commitment.

Path dependence, at least to my way of thinking, is therefore about much more than the processes of technological change, or institutional evolution, or hysteresis effects and unit roots in macroeconomic growth. The concepts asso-ciated with this term have implications for epistemology, for the sociology of knowledge, and cognitive science as well.[15] Nevertheless, it would be quite wrong to imagine that positive feedback dominates all aspects of economic life (let alone 'life'), just as it is unwarranted to proceed on the supposition that economic dynamics everywhere are intrinsically characterized by the opera-tion of stabilizing, negative feedback systems. Considering the possibility that the former framework is the one most relevant in a particular context does not rule out the opposite conclusion, or preclude appropriate resort to the latter framework – the familiar convergence models of neoclassical economics. These really are not necessarily mutually exclusive tool-sets, or incompatible standards, that cannot be integrated into a larger intellectual system. Even though we should be aware of the workings of strong social processes, famil-iar in the sociology of knowledge, that can turn normal science procedures into exclusionary dogmas, it is not necessary for social and behavioural scientists to adopt positions that exacerbate and amplify those tendencies.

Once the concept and the ideas surrounding path dependence are properly understood, there can be no reason to construe them as necessarily corrupting the discipline of economics, or to fear that once admitted they would be subversive of all *laissez-faire* policies. There simply are no good grounds to go on actively resisting these ideas, which if accepted will lead us into previously little-explored regions of theoretical and empirical enquiry. Nor is there even a sound precautionary case for seeking to contain their spread until it can be determined what would become of the grand edifice of economic analysis as we know it, once the assumed global dominance of negative feedback processes were discarded. The logic of sunk cost hysteresis has a legitimate place in the conventional theory of optimal investment behaviour. Yet, when it is carried over and applied to the field of *intellectual* investments in new tools of economic analysis, the result is a self-defeating orthodoxy of thought and surely not the optimal progress of our discipline.

NOTES

1. This chapter has evolved from my 'Keynote Address' to the European Association for Evolutionary Political Economy, at their Meetings held in Athens, 7–9 November 1997. I am grateful for the pithy comments that I received on a related earlier paper (David, 1997b), from Avner Greif, Frank Hahn, Joel Mokyr, Robert Solow, Edward Steinmueller and Gavin Wright. Stavros Ioannides contributed very helpful editorial corrections. None among them should be held responsible for the deficiencies or excesses that remain in the present text.

2. I hesitate to write 'dis-information' at this point, as that connotes intentions rather than consequences. I prefer to proceed on the supposition that those who have repeatedly misrepresented the meaning of the term in the course of criticizing 'path dependence' as an erroneous economic theory, and those who have deemed it to be an empty concept (in the sense that it is essentially devoid of empirical relevance for economists), simply are confused about its meaning.

3. For this purpose it is best that I confront the critical treatment of path dependence by Professors Stanley Liebowitz and Stephen Margolis (1995b, 1995c). I therefore put to one side a rebuttal of the specific factual allegations that have been adduced in Liebowitz and Margolis's (1990) riposte to the story of QWERTY as related in David (1985, 1986). That attack has recently been cited by Ruttan (1997), who refers to the emblematic tale of QWERTY as 'the *founding myth* of the path dependence literature' (emphasis added). Although Liebowitz and Margolis fail to substantiate their contention that QWERTY simply is 'a fable', their rhetorical strategy of attacking that case as though it constituted the only economically interesting exemplar of path dependence, managed to raise a small cloud of doubt regarding the empirical significance of the more general phenomenon. On the latter issue, however, see David (1999) for another view.

4. Liebowitz and Margolis (1995b: pp. 209–10) fall into just this confusion on the one occasion on which they offer a formal definition of the meaning of 'path dependence'. They say, correctly: 'The meaning closest to current use in economics is that of stochastic processes that incorporate some concept of memory.' But, thereupon they draw from the *Encyclopedic Dictionary of Mathematics* (Cambridge, MA: MIT Press, 1987) the following definition of 'path dependence': Letting $P(n)$ be the probability of event $E(n) = A(1)$ on the n-th trial, and $(1 - P(n))$ be the probability of the mutual exclusive outcome $E(n) = A(2)$, then the general 'response probability' for the sequential process is: $P(n + 1) = f\{P(n), E(n), E(n - 1), \ldots, E(1)\}$. When the function $f = f\{P(n), E(n), E(n - 1), \ldots, E(n - d)\}$, the

response probability is said to be '*d*-trial path dependent'. In the special case where $d = 0$ it is 'path independent'.

The text in Liebowitz and Margolis (1995b: p. 210) then goes on to assert, quite erroneously: 'The use of path dependence in economics is, for the most part, loosely analogous to this mathematical construction: Allocations chosen today exhibit memory; they are conditioned on past decisions.' One should notice that if 'allocations' are associated with 'events', $E(i)$, and (probabilistic) decisions at moment n are characterized by the pairs $[P(n); 1 - P(n)]$, then the foregoing statement does not correspond to the mathematical construction of '*d*-trial path dependence', any more than the latter corresponds to the generic usage of the concept of path dependence by David (1985, 1986, 1988, 1989, et seq.), or by Arthur (1988, 1989, 1990, 1994), by Cowan (1991, 1996), by Durlauf (1990, 1996), Krugman (1991, 1994), and others contributing to the economics literature.

5.　The reference in the passage quoted to 'contingency' as the conceptual counterpart in biology of the idea of path dependence is followed by Liebowitz and Margolis's (1995b: p. 33) statement that 'In *Wonderful Life*, Stephen J. Gould applies this intellectual revolution to paleontology.' But, it should be shiningly clear from that work by Gould (1989: pp. 282ff, esp.), and really no less from his earlier writings, that he is not drawing upon a recent intellectual revolution: 'I regard Charles Darwin as the greatest of all historical scientists. Not only did he develop convincing evidence for evolution as the coordinating principle of life's history, but he also chose as a conscious theme for all his writings . . . the development of a different but equally rigorous methodology for historical science. Historical explanations take the form of narrative: E, the phenomenon to be explained, arose because D came before, preceded by C, B, and A. If any of these earlier stages had not occurred, or had transpired in a different way, then E would not exist (or would be present in a substantially altered form, E', requiring a different explanation. . . . I am not speaking of randomness (for E had to arise, as a consequence of A through D), but of the central principle of all history – *contingency*' (Gould, 1989: pp. 282–3). Further on, Gould (1989: pp. 283–4) writes of the universal psychological appeal of the notion of historical contingency, in terms that leave no doubt that this is not a concept specific to evolutionary biology: 'Historical explanations are endlessly fascinating in themselves, in many ways more intriguing to the human psyche than the inexorable consequences of nature's laws. . . . Contingency is the affirmation of control by immediate events over destiny. . . . Contingency is a license to participate in history, and our psyche responds. The theme of contingency, so poorly understood and explored by science, has long been a mainstay of literature. . . . Tolstoy's theme in all his great novels.' What Gould provides in *Wonderful Life* is a new interpretation of the record of life left in the Burgess Shale, but, as he takes pains to acknowledge, this interpretation 'is rooted in contingency' – a very old and far from revolutionary idea.

6.　The practice can be employed with potent rhetorical effect on an unsophisticated audience, because the deterministic reformulation may then be subjected to criticisms from which the original analysis would be immune. A striking instance of such a switch is to be found in Liebowitz and Margolis's (1995b: pp. 214–15) reproduction and critique of a deterministic payoff tableau, used by Arthur (1989) purely *as a heuristic device* – to convey the possibility that a sequence of myopic adoption decisions under increasing returns to adoption could result in the commitment of the ensemble of adopters to a dominated outcome. In the course of pointing out that the payoff tableau may be read in a way that is inconsistent with the results reported for Arthur's stochastic model, there appears the following commendably candid footnote (pp. 214–15, n. 15): 'Actually, Arthur states that this example does not exhibit any 'non-ergodicity', meaning that it is not path dependent in the sense that small differences in historical sequences play a role in the final equilibrium. In this example the end result is the same no matter the order of initial participants. But it illustrates lock-in very well.' I might note that this footnote is the only place I have found in Liebowitz and Margolis's publications on path dependence where the concept is explicitly defined with reference to non-ergodicity, and even so the passage omits explicit reference to probability.

7.　Furthermore, Liebowitz and Margolis (1995b) offer a description of 'third-degree' path dependence that would apply equally to deterministic chaos – which, as was noted above, the authors correctly acknowledged to be not really the same thing as path dependence.

8. This, however, would seem to leave Liebowitz and Margolis in the position of having to insist that economists should not attach real importance to path dependence because its 'third-degree' form ignores the reality that, even when remediation would not occur via 'private ordering', it would most likely be achievable through 'public ordering'. That is hardly what one expects from defenders of *laissez-faire*.
9. For discussion of this in the context of technical compatibility standards, see, for example, David and Greenstein (1990b); on social conventions, organizational routines and formal institutions, David (1994c), and David (1994d).
10. See, for example, David (1987, 1990); David and Bunn (1988), Cowan (1991).
11. Compare the detailed analyses of the VHS market in Baba and Imai (1990), Cusumano, Mylonadis and Rosenbloom (1992) and Grindley (1992), none among which are noticed in Liebowitz and Margolis (1994), or by the latter authors' subsequent references to this case.
12. Especially in David (1987), David and Bunn (1988), David and Greenstein (1990) and, most forthrightly in David (1992b).
13. See David (1993b) for more on the teleological mode of analysis in economics.
14. For further discussion of the latter topics, see, for example, David (1993a, 1994c), David and Foray (1993d, 1994d).
15. On these epistemological topics, see, for example, the stochastic models discussed in David and Sanderson (1997), and David (1998b, 2000).

REFERENCES

Works by Paul A. David

A chronological listing of publications dealing explicitly with conceptual and method-ological aspects of path dependence, macro-level irreversibilities and hysteresis in economic processes. (**Co-authors' names** appear in boldface).

(1969), 'Transport innovation and economic growth: Professor Fogel on and off the rails', *Economic History Review*, 22(3), December, pp. 506–25.

(1971), 'The landscape and the machine: technical interrelatedness, land tenure and the mechanization of the corn harvest in Victorian Britain', in D.N. McCloskey (ed.), *Essays on a Mature Economy*, London: Methuen, pp. 145–205.

(1975), *Technical Choice, Innovation and Economic Growth: Essays on American and British Experience in the Nineteenth Century*, Cambridge: Cambridge University Press.

(1985), 'Clio and the economics of QWERTY', *American Economic Review*, 75(2), May.

(1986), 'Understanding the economics of QWERTY: the necessity of history', in W.N. Parker (ed.), *Economic History and the Modern Economist*, London: Basil Blackwell.

(1987), 'Some new standards for the economics of standardization in the information age', in P. Dasgupta and P.L. Stoneman (eds), *The Economics of Technology Policy*, London: Cambridge University Press.

(1988a), 'Path dependence: putting the past into the future of economics, *Institute for Mathematical Studies in the Social Sciences Technical Report 533*, Stanford University, November.

(1988b), 'The economics of gateway technologies and network evolution: lessons from electricity supply history' (with **Julie A. Bunn**), *Information Economics and Policy*, Vol. 3, Winter, 165–202.

(1989), 'When and why does history really matter?', *A Presidential Address to the Economic History Association*, Delivered at the Smithsonian Museum of Science and Technology, Washington DC, September. (Department of Economics Working Paper, Stanford University, October 1989.)

(1990), 'The economics of compatibility standards: an introduction to recent research', (with **S. Greenstein**), in *Economics of Innovation and New Technology*, 1(1, 2), Fall: 3–42.

(1991), 'The hero and the herd: reflections on Thomas Edison and the "Battle of the Systems" ', in P. Higonnet, D.S. Landes and H. Rosovsky (eds), *Favorites of Fortune: Technology, Growth, and Economic Development Since the Industrial Revolution*, Cambridge, MA: Harvard University Press.

(1992a), 'Path dependence and economics', the 1991–1992 Marshall Lectures delivered at the University of Cambridge, April 28–29. Lecture I: 'The invisible hand in the grip of the past'; Lecture II: 'Models of non-ergodic economic dynamics, and their implications for policy'. (Center for Economic Policy Research Working Paper, Stanford University, August, 1992.)

(1992b), 'Path dependence in economic processes: implications for policy analysis in dynamical system contexts', *Background Paper – Rosselli Foundation Workshop on Path Dependence*, Torino, Italy, 29–30 May. (Center for Economic Policy Research Working Paper, Stanford University, August, 1992.)

(1992c), 'Heroes, herds and hysteresis in technological history', *Journal of Industrial and Corporate Change*, 1(1): pp. 129–80.

(1993a), 'Path dependence and predictability in dynamic systems with local network externalities: a paradigm for historical economics', in D. Foray and C. Freeman (eds), *Technology and the Wealth of Nations*, London: Pinter Publishers.

(1993b), 'Historical economics in the long run: some implications of path dependence', in G.D. Snooks (ed.), *Historical Analysis in Economics*, London: Routledge.

(1993c), 'Intellectual property institutions and the panda's thumb: patents, copyrights, and trade secrets in economic theory and history', in M. Wallerstein, et al. (eds), *Global Dimensions of Intellectual Property Protection in Science and Technology*, Washington, DC: National Academy Press.

(1993d), 'Percolation structures, Markov random fields and the economics of EDI standards diffusion', (with **Dominique Foray**), in G. Pogorel (ed.), *Global Telecommunication Strategies and Technological Change*, Amsterdam: Elsevier Science Publishers.

(1994a), 'Dynamics of technology diffusion through local network structures' (with **Dominique Foray**) in L. Leydesdorff (ed.), *Evolutionary Economics and Chaos Theory: New Developments in Technology Studies*, London: Pinter Publishers.

(1994b), 'Positive feedbacks and research productivity in science: reopening another black box', in O. Grandstrand (eds.), *Technology and Economic Change*, Amsterdam: Elsevier, chapter 8.

(1994c), 'Les standards des technologies de l'information, les normes de communication et l'état: un problème de biens publics', in A. Orleans (ed.), *L'analyse économique des conventions*, Paris: Presses Universitaires, chapter 10.

(1994d), 'Why are institutions the "carriers of history"? Path dependence and the evolution of conventions, organizations and institutions', *Structural Change and Economic Dynamics*, 5(2): pp. 205–20.

(1995), 'Dépendence du sentier et économie de l'innovation: Un rapide tour d'horizon' (with **Dominique Foray**), *Revue d'Economie Industrielle*: Special edition: 'Economie industrielle – développements récents, 1st trimester, 1995: pp. 27–51.

(1997a), 'Making use of treacherous advice: cognitive progress, Bayesian adaptation and the tenacity of unreliable knowledge', (with **Warren C. Sanderson**), in J.V. Nye and J. Drobak (eds), *Frontiers of the New Institutional Economics*, San Diego, CA: Academic Press, chapter 12.

(1997b), 'Path dependence and the quest for historical economics: one more chorus of the ballad of QWERTY', University of Oxford Discussion Papers in Economic and Social History, No. 20 (November).

[On-line as: <http://www.nuff.ox.ac.uk/economics/history/pap20>.]

(1998a), 'Marshallian externalities and the emergence and spatial stability of technological enclaves', (with **Dominique Foray and Jean-Michel Dalle**), *Economics of Innovation and New Technologies* (Special issue on Economics of Localized Technical Change, ed. C. Antonelli), 4(2, 3):147–82.

(1998b), 'Communication norms and the collective cognitive performance of "invisible colleges" ', in G. B. Navaretti, P. Dasgupta, K.-G. Maier and D. Siniscalco (eds), *Creation and Transfer of Knowledge: Institutions and Incentives*, Berlin-Heidelberg: Springer-Verlag.

(1998c), 'From the economics of QWERTY to the millennium bug', *Stanford University Economics Department Newsletter*, Stanford CA, Fall 1998/1999.

(1999), 'At last, a remedy for chronic QWERTY-skepticism!', Discussion Paper for the European Summer School in Industrial Dynamics (ESSID), held at l'Institute d'Etudes Scientifiques de CargPse (Corse), France, September.

(2000), 'Path dependence and varieties of learning in the evolution of technological practice', in John Ziman (ed.), *Technological Innovation as an Evolutionary Process*, Cambridge: Cambridge University Press, chapter 10.

Other Works Cited

Arthur, W.B. (1988), 'Self-reinforcing mechanisms in economics', in *The Economy as an Evolving Complex System*, (Santa Fe Institute Studies in the Science of Complexity, 5), Redwood City, CA: Addison-Wesley.

Arthur, W. Brian (1989), 'Competing technologies and lock-in by historical small events', *Economic Journal*, 99 (March): 116–31.

Arthur, W. Brian (1990), 'Industry location patterns and the importance of history', *Mathematical Social Sciences*, 19: 235–51.

Arthur, W. Brian (1994), *Increasing Returns and Path Dependence in the Economy*, Ann Arbor, MI: University of Michigan Press.

Arthur, W.B, Yu. M. Ermoliev and Yu. M. Kaniovski (1983), 'A generalized urn problem and its applications', *Kibernetika*, 19: 49–57 (in Russian). Translated in *Cybernetics*, 19: 61–71.

Arthur, W.B., Yu. M. Ermoliev and Yu. M. Kaniovski (1986), 'Strong laws for a class of path-dependent urn processes', *Proceedings of the International Conference on Stochastic Optimization, Kiev 1984*, Arkin, Shiryayev and Wets (eds), New York: Springer (Springer Lecture Notes in Control and Information Sciences), p. 81.

Baba, Y. and K. Imai (1990), 'Systemic innovation and cross-border networks: the case of the evolution of the VCR systems', Paper presented to the Schumpeter Society Conference on Entrepreneurship, Technological Innovation and Economic Growth, held at Airlie House, VA, June 3–5.

Basalla, G. (1988), *The Evolution of Technology*, Cambridge: Cambridge University Press.

Brown, L. (1993), *The New Shorter Oxford English Dictionary, On Historical Principles*, Oxford: Clarendon Press.

Cowan, R. (1990), 'Nuclear power reactors: a study in technological lock-in', *Journal of Economic History*, 50(3), September: 541–67.

Cowan, R. (1991), 'Tortoises and hares: choice among technologies of unknown merit', *Economic Journal*, **101**(407), July: 801–14.

Cowan, R. and P. Gunby (1996), 'Sprayed to death: path dependence, lock-in and pest control strategies', *Economic Journal*, 106(436), May: 521–42.

Cusumano, M.A., Y. Mylonadis and R.S. Rosenbloom (1992), 'Strategic maneuvering and mass-market dynamics: the triumph of VHS over Beta', *Business History Review*, 66 (Spring): 51–94.

David, P.A., R.C. Maude-Griffin and G.S. Rothwell (1996), 'Learning by accident? Reductions in the risk of unplanned outages in US nuclear power plants after Three Mile Island', *Journal of Risk and Uncertainty*, 12: 175–98.

Durlauf, S. (1990), 'Non-ergodic economic growth and fluctuations in aggregate output', *American Economic Review*, 80(3).

Durlauf, S. (1996), Neighborhood feedbacks, endogenous stratification, and income inequality', in *Dynamic Disequilibrium Modelling*, Cambridge: Cambridge University Press.

Eldridge, N. (1985), *Time Frames: The Rethinking of Darwinian Evolution and the Theory of Punctuated Equilibria*, New York: Simon and Schuster.

Fisher, F.M. (1983), *The Disequilibrium Foundations of Equilibrium Economics*, New York: Cambridge University Press.

Fogel, R.W. (1964), *Railroad and American Economic Growth*, Baltimore: Johns Hopkins Press.

Föllmer, H. (1974), 'Random economies with many interacting agents', *Journal of Mathematical Economics*, 1: 51–62.

Gould, S.J. (1989), *Wonderful Life: The Burgess Shale and the Nature of History*, New York: W.W. Norton and Company.

Grimmet, G. (1989), *Percolation*, New York: Springer-Verlag.

Grindley, P. (1992), *Standards, Business Strategy and Policy: A Casebook*, London: London Business School.

Koot, G.M. (1987), *English Historical Economics, 1870–1926*, Cambridge: Cambridge University Press.

Krugman, P. (1991), *Geography and Trade*, Cambridge, MA: MIT Press.

Krugman, P. (1994), *Peddling Prosperity*, New York: W.W. Norton and Company.

Liebowitz, S.J., and Stephen E. Margolis (1990), 'The fable of the keys', *Journal of Law and Economics,* 33(1), April: 1–25.

Liebowitz, S.J., and Stephen E. Margolis (1994), 'Network externality: an uncommon tragedy', *Journal of Economic Perspectives*, 8(2), Spring: 133–50.

Liebowitz, S.J., and Stephen E. Margolis (1995a), 'Are network externalities a new source of market failure? *Research in Law and Economics*, 17(0): 1–22.

Liebowitz, S.J., and Stephen E. Margolis (1995b), 'Path dependence, lock-in, and history', *Journal of Law, Economics, and Organization*, 11(1), April: 205–26.

Liebowitz, S. and Stephen E. Margolis (1995c), 'Policy and path dependence: from QWERTY to Windows 95', *Regulation: The Cato Review of Business & Government*, 1995, number 3: 33–41.

Liggett, T.M. (1985), *Interacting Particle Systems (Grundlehren der mathematischen Wissenschaftern 276)*, Berlin: Springer-Verlag.

McCloskey, D.N. (ed.) (1971), *Essays on a Mature Economy*, London: Methuen.

McCloskey, D.N. (1974), 'Victorian growth: a rejoinder to Aldcroft', *Economic History Review*, Second Series, 27(2), May: 275–7.

McCloskey, D.N. (1976), 'Does the past have useful economics?', *Journal of Economic Literature*, 14(2), June: 434–61.

Mokyr, J. (1990), *The Lever of Riches: Technological Creativity and Economic Progress*, New York: Oxford University Press.

North, D.N. (1990), *Institutions, Institutional Change and Economic Performance*, Cambridge: Cambridge University Press.

Ruelle, D. (1991), *Chance and Chaos*, Princeton: Princeton University Press.

Ruttan, V.W. (1997), 'Induced innovation, evolutionary theory and path dependence: sources of technical change', *Economic Journal*, 107(444), September: pp. 1520–47.

Solow, R.M. (1986), 'Economics: is something missing?', in William N. Parker (ed.) *Economic History and the Modern Economist*, Oxford: Basil Blackwell, pp. 21–9.

Steward, I. (1990), *Does God Play Dice? The New Mathematics of Chaos*, London: Penguin.

Teggart, F.J. (1977), *Theory and Processes of History* (second paperback printing of the 1941 Edition of *Theory of History* (1925) and *The Processes of History* (1918), published in one volume), Berkeley, CA: University of California Press.

Teggart, F.J. (1939), *Rome and China, a Study of Correlations in Historical Events*. Berkeley, CA: University of California Press.

Williamson, O.E. (1993), 'Transaction cost economics and organization theory', *Industrial and Corporate Change*, 2(2): pp. 107–56.

PART 2

Theoretical Responses

6. Information and efficiency: another viewpoint[1]

Harold Demsetz

The importance of bringing economic analysis to bear on the problems of efficient economic organization hardly requires comment, but there is a need to review the manner in which the notion of efficiency is used in these problems. The concept of efficiency has been abused frequently because of the particular approach used by many analysts. My aim is to examine the mistakes and the vagueness associated with this approach. I shall focus attention on the problem of efficiently allocating resources to the production of information because in this case the issues stand out clearly. Since Kenneth J. Arrow's paper 'Economic Welfare and the Allocation of Resources for Intervention'[2] has been most influential in establishing the dominant viewpoint about this subject, my commentary necessarily is a critique of Arrow's analysis.

The view that now pervades much public policy economics implicitly presents the relevant choice as between an ideal norm and an existing 'imperfect' institutional arrangement. This *nirvana* approach differs considerably from the *comparative institution* approach in which the relevant choice is between alternative real institutional arrangements. In practice, those who adopt the nirvana viewpoint seek to discover discrepancies between the ideal and the real and if discrepancies are found, they deduce that the real is inefficient. Users of the comparative institution approach attempt to assess which alternative real institutional arrangement seems best able to cope with the economic problem; practitioners of this approach may use an ideal norm to provide standards from which divergences are assessed for all practical alternatives of interest and select as efficient that alternative which seems most likely to minimize the divergence.[3]

The nirvana approach is much more susceptible than is the comparative institution approach to committing three logical fallacies – *the grass is always greener fallacy, the fallacy of the free lunch*, and *the people could be different fallacy*. The first two fallacies are illustrated in a general context in part I of what follows; in part II, they and the third fallacy arise in contexts more specific to the economics of knowledge. Part III is a discussion of Arrow's conclusion about the role of monopoly in the production of knowledge, and part IV offers a general criticism of the nirvana approach.

I

The grass is always greener fallacy can be illustrated by the following two quotations from Arrow's paper:

> To sum up, we expect a free enterprise economy to underinvest in invention and to research (as compared with an ideal) because it is risky, because the product can be appropriated only to a limited extent, and because of increasing returns in use. This underinvestment will be greater for more basic research. Further, to the extent that a firm succeeds in engrossing the economic value of its inventive activity, there will be an under-utilization of that information as compared with an ideal allocation.[4]
> . . .
> The previous discussion leads to the conclusion that for optimal allocation to invention it would be necessary for the government or some other agency not governed by profit-and-loss criteria to finance research and invention.[5]

An examination of the correctness of the premise is the main task of this chapter, but for present purposes the premise contained in the first quotation can be assumed to be correct. It is clear from both quotations and from the text in which these quotations are imbedded that Arrow is claiming that free enterprise does not result in an ideal allocation of resources to the production of knowledge. From this premise he draws the general conclusion, given in the second quotation, that optimal allocation requires that the government or other nonprofit agency should finance research and invention.

Whether the free enterprise solution can be improved upon by the substitution of the government or other nonprofit institutions in the financing of research cannot be ascertained solely by examining the free enterprise solution. The political or nonprofit forces that are substituted for free enterprise must be analyzed and the outcome of the workings of these forces must be compared to the market solution before any such conclusions can be drawn. Otherwise, words such as 'government' and 'nonprofit' are without analytical content and their use results in confusion. Since Arrow does not analyze the workings of the empirical counterparts of such words as 'government'[6] and 'nonprofit,' his conclusion can be clarified by restating it as follows: 'The previous discussion leads to the conclusion that for optimal allocation to invention it would be necessary to remove the nonoptimalities.' The same charge, of course, can be levied against those who derive in a similar way the opposite policy conclusion, one that calls for a reduction in the role played by government.[7]

Given the nirvana view of the problem, a deduced discrepancy between the ideal and the real is sufficient to call forth perfection by incantation, that is, by committing the grass is always greener fallacy. Thus usually accomplished by invoking an unexamined alternative. Closely associated in practice with this fallacy is the fallacy of the free lunch. An example of the latter is given in

Arrow's discussion of the difficulties posed for the competitive system by uncertainty:

> I will first sketch an ideal economy in which the allocation problem can be solved by competition and then indicate some of the devices in the real world which approximate this solution.
>
> Suppose for simplicity that uncertainty occurs only in production relations. Producers have to make a decision on inputs at the present moment, but the outputs are not completely predictable from inputs . . . [T]he outputs [are] determined by the inputs and the 'state of nature.' Let us define 'commodity-option' as a commodity in the ordinary sense labeled with a state of nature . . .
>
> Suppose – and this is the critical idealization of the economy – we have a market for all commodity-options. What is traded on each market are contracts in which buyers pay an agreed sum and the sellers agree to deliver prescribed quantities of a given commodity if a certain state of nature prevails and nothing if that state of nature does not occur. For any given set of inputs, the firm knows its output under each state of nature and sells a corresponding quantity of commodity options; its revenue is then completely determined. It may choose its inputs so as to maximize profits . . .
>
> An equilibrium is reached on all commodity-option markets, and this equilibrium has precisely the same Pareto-optimality properties as competitive equilibrium under uncertainty.
>
> In particular, the markets for commodity-options in this ideal model serve the function of achieving an optimal allocation of risk-bearing among the members of the economy . . .
>
> But the real economic system does not possess markets for commodity-options.[8]

Here I must raise an objection, for there is nothing in principle that prohibits the sale of commodity options. The real economic system does, in fact, allow exchange of commodity-options.[9] Arrow continues:

> [If commodity options are unavailable] the firm and its owners cannot relieve themselves of risk-bearing in this model. Hence any unwillingness or inability to bear risks will give rise to a nonoptimal allocation of resources, in that there will be discrimination against risky enterprises as compared with the optimum.[10]

Arrow here has slipped into the fallacy of the free lunch. The word 'nonoptimal' is misleading and ambiguous. Does it mean that free enterprise can be improved upon? Let me suppose that the cost of marketing commodity options exceeds the gain from adjustment to risk. This would account for their presumed absence. Can it then be said that free enterprise results in a nonoptimal adjustment to risk? To make this assertion is to deny that scarcity is relevant to optimality, a strange position for an economist. In suggesting that free enterprise generates incomplete adjustments to risk, the nirvana approach, by comparing these adjustments with the ideal, is led further to equate incomplete to nonoptimal. This would be correct only if commodity-options or other ways of adjusting to risk are free. In this way, the nirvana approach relies on an implicit assumption of nonscarcity, but since risk shifting or risk reduction cannot generally be accomplished freely the demonstration of nonoptimality is false.

II

Arrow calls attention to three problem areas in the production of knowledge and invention, risk aversion, indivisibilities, and inappropriability. These are discussed in this section. In his analysis of risk-aversion, Arrow recognizes three major substitutes for commodity-option contracts: insurance, common stock, and cost-plus contracts. He finds that each of these fails to completely eliminate the discrepancy between optimal allocation in his ideal norm and allocation in a free enterprise system:

> (1) the economic system has devices for shifting risks, but they are limited and imperfect; hence, one would expect an underinvestment in risky activities; (2) it is undoubtedly worthwhile to enlarge the variety of such devices, but the moral factor creates a limit to their potential.[11]

The route by which he reaches these conclusions is revealed by his discussion of the adjustment to risk provided by insurance.

> Suppose that each firm and individual in the economy could forecast perfectly what prices would be under each state of nature. Suppose further there were a lottery on the state of nature, so that before the state of nature is known any individual or firm may place bets. Then it can be seen that the effect . . . is the same as if there were markets for commodity-options of all types . . .
>
> References to lotteries and bets may smack of frivolity, but we need only think of insurance to appreciate that the shifting of risks through what are in effect bets on the state of nature is a highly significant phenomenon. If insurance were available against any conceivable event, it follows . . . that optimal allocation would be achieved. . . .
>
> Unfortunately, it is only too clear that the shifting of risks in the real world is incomplete. There are a number of reasons why this should be so, but I will confine myself to one, of special significance with regard to invention. In insurance practice, reference is made to the moral factor as a limit to the possibilities of insurance . . . The insurance policy changes the incentive of the insured [in the case of fire insurance], creating an incentive for arson or at the very least for carelessness . . . As a result, any insurance policy and in general any device for shifting risks can have the effect of dulling incentives . . .
>
> The moral factor [is] of special relevance in regard to highly risky business activities, including invention . . . [S]uch activities should be undertaken if the expected return exceeds the market rate of return, no matter what the variance is. The existence of common stocks would seem to solve the allocation problem; any individual stockholder can reduce his risk by buying only a small part of the stock and diversifying his portfolio to achieve his own preferred risk level. But then again

the actual managers no longer receive the full reward of their decisions; the shifting of risks is again accompanied by a weakening of incentives to efficiency. Substitute motivations whether pecuniary ... or nonpecuniary ... may be found, but the dilemma of the moral factor can never be completely resolved.[12]

My dissatisfaction with Arrow's approach can be explained by first referring to one sentence in the above quotation '[S]uch activities should be undertaken if the expected return exceeds the market rate of return, no matter what the variance is.'[13] This statement would certainly be false for a Robinson Crusoe economy. Suppose that the expected rate of return on one project equals the expected rate of return on a second project. If the variances of the expected returns differ, and if Crusoe is risk averse, there is good economic reason for Crusoe to prefer the less risky project. Reduction of risk is by hypothesis an economic good for Crusoe and he should be willing to pay a positive price, such as a lower expected return, in order to acquire this good. It is clear in this simple case that the economist has no more reason for saying that Crusoe should be indifferent between these projects than he has for saying that Crusoe should be risk neutral.

Once it is admitted that risk reduction is stipulated to be an economic good, the relevant question for society is what real institutional arrangements will be best suited to produce risk reduction or risk shifting. We no longer delude ourselves into thinking that the world would be a more efficient place if only people were not risk averse; the taste for risk reduction must be incorporated into the concept of efficiency.

Given the fact of scarcity, risk reduction is not achievable at zero cost, so that the risk averse efficient economy, as we have already noted, does not produce 'complete' shifting of risk but, instead, it reduces or shifts risk only when the economic gain exceeds the cost. Once we seek to compare different institutional arrangements for accomplishing this, it is difficult to keep scarcity from entering our calculations so that it becomes obviously misleading and incorrect to assert that an economy, free enterprise or otherwise, is inefficient if it fails to economize on risk as it would if it were costless to shift or reduce risk.

Two types of adjustment to risk seem possible: pooling independent activities so that the variance in expected return is reduced and facilitating the assumption of risk by those who are less risk averse. The market is an institutional arrangement that encourages both types of adjustment by rewarding those who successfully reduce or shift risk. Thus, future contracts provide a method whereby much risk is shifted to speculators.[14] Conditional contracts of the commodity-option type already discussed also can be purchased for a premium. And even with risk pooling, some risk remains to be borne by sellers of insurance, so that a payment for risk bearing is in order.

Moral hazard is identified by Arrow as a unique and irremedial cause of incomplete coverage of all risky activities by insurance. But in truth there is nothing at all unique about moral hazard and economizing on moral hazard provides no special problems not encountered elsewhere. Moral hazard is a relevant cost of producing insurance; it is not different from the cost that arises from the tendency of men to shirk when their employer is not watching them. And, just as man's preference for shirking and leisure are costs of production that must be economized, so moral hazard must be economized in shifting and reducing risk. A price can be and is attached to the sale of all insurance that includes the moral hazard cost imposed by the insured on insurance companies. And this price is individualized to the extent that other costs, mainly cost of contracting, allow. The moral hazard cost is present, although in differing amounts, no matter what percentage of the value of the good is insured.

The moral hazard problem is no different than the problem posed by any cost. Some iron ore is left unearthed because it is too costly to bring to the surface. But we do not claim ore mining is inefficient merely because mining is not 'complete.' Some risks are left uninsured because the cost of moral hazard is too great and this may mean that self-insurance is economic. There is no special dilemma associated with moral hazard, but Arrow's concentration on the divergence between risk shifting through insurance and risk shifting in the ideal norm, in which moral hazard presumably is absent, makes it appear as a special dilemma. While it may cost nothing to insure risky enterprises in the world of the ideal norm, it does in this world, if for no other reason than the proclivity of some to commit moral hazards. Arrow's approach to efficiency problems has led him directly to 'the people could be different' fallacy.

Payment through insurance premiums for the moral hazard cost imposed on insurance sellers brings into play the usual price mechanism for economizing. The fact that not everyone is insured is irrelevant to the question of efficiency. The absence of insurance, especially when moral hazard is important, merely is evidence of the unwillingness to shift all risk to others at premium levels that cover the cost imposed on sellers of insurance by these moral hazards.[15]

Clearly, efficiency requires that moral hazards be economized. Otherwise, we implicitly assert that the loss of assets that accompanies the realization of a moral hazard imposes no cost on society. One way of economizing on moral hazards is to allow self-insurance. If the size of the premium that is required to get others to accept moral hazard cost is higher than people wish to pay, it is appropriate to reduce the loss of assets that would accompany moral hazard by allowing prospective buyers of such insurance to self-insure.

Do we shift risk or reduce moral hazards efficiently through the marketplace? This question cannot be answered solely by observing that insurance is incomplete in coverage. Is there an alternative institutional arrangement that seems to offer superior economizing? There may well be such an arrangement, but Arrow has not demonstrated it and, therefore, his allegation of inefficiency may well be wrong and certainly is premature.

Turning now to the possibility of reducing risk through the device of pooling, we find that Arrow takes the following position:

> The central economic fact about the processes of invention and research is that they are devoted to the production of information. By the very definition of information, invention must be a risky process . . . Since it is a risky process, there is bound to be some discrimination against investment in inventive and research activities . . . The only way, within the private enterprise system, to minimize this [moral factor] problem is the conduct of research by large corporations with many projects going on, each small in scale compared with the net revenue of the corporation. Then the corporation acts as its own insurance company. But clearly this is only an imperfect solution.[16]

The centralization of research does provide a more diversified portfolio of investment projects that allows owners to reduce the variance of the outcome of their inventive efforts. To some extent firms do centralize research efforts. But a real social cost is borne if this procedure is pushed too far. The more centralized is the production or financing of invention, the smaller is the degree to which the advantages of specialization can be enjoyed and the less keen is the stimulus offered by competition. These costs must be taken into account in identifying the efficient institutional arrangement, and I suppose that these costs do play a major role in limiting the voluntary centralization of research by industry. The efficient arrangement generally will be one that falls between complete centralization and complete specialization.

It may be that government production or financing of invention is a superior arrangement, in which case extensive use of market arrangements can be criticized. Government *can* take a risk neutral attitude (although I doubt that this is a desirable attitude in the nuclear age). But I do not know what attitude actually will be taken toward risk by government. Government is a group of people, each of whom in the absence of compensation to do otherwise, presumably is risk averse. The psychological propensity to be risk averse, if it is present, is found in employees of government as well as in employees of private enterprise, and a government probably is averse to political risks.

I suspect that the government will be less risk averse in some of its activity. The attempt to place a man on the moon by 1970 probably never will be subjected to careful market measures of risk and rate of return, but if it were, it is unlikely that it would appear worthwhile even if it is successful in the technological sense. In some cases, a technological success carries great weight in achieving political success and here government will be less risk averse.

In other governmental activities, however, the government is likely to behave toward risk in a much more risk-averse fashion than is private enterprise. For example, inventing and innovating a superior postal service, although it has some risk associated with it, seems to be technologically possible and economically promising. But the adverse political developments that could follow from the laying off of many postal employees leads the government to hold back. It is very averse to the risk of being voted out of office.

Arrow's analysis of risk merely states that the market copes with risk differently than it would if risk could be shifted or reduced costlessly, or than it would if people were neither risk averse not susceptible to moral hazard. But a relevant notion of efficiency must refer to scarcity and people as they are, not as they could be.

In his discussion of the inappropriability of new knowledge, Arrow recognizes that if information is to be produced privately, its producers must be able to realize revenues from the use or sale of information. For this to be possible, information must be appropriable, and Arrow is not optimistic about the ease with which the value of information can be captured by its discoverer. Some part of Arrow's pessimism, I believe, is attributable to his tendency to see special and unique problems in establishing property rights to information when the problems are neither special nor unique.

Appropriability is largely a matter of legal arrangements and the enforcement of these arrangements by private or public means. The degree to which knowledge is privately appropriable can be increased by raising the penalties for patent violations and by increasing resources for policing patent violations.

It is true that all 'theft' of information cannot be eliminated at reasonable cost. But knowledge is not unique in this respect, since the same can be said of any valuable asset. The equilibrium price that is paid to producers of automobiles will in part reflect the fact that there is a positive probability that the purchaser will have his automobile stolen. The problem of theft is as pervasive as the problem of moral hazard, and although there may be differences in the cost of reducing the theft of different types of assets there is no difference in principle. It may be argued, as Arrow does, that the ease of theft of knowledge is heightened by the fact that knowledge once used becomes easily known by others. But the theft of an automobile also is made easier when it is removed from the home garage.

One characteristic of knowledge that increases the cost of enforcing private rights is the possibility of stealing information without thereby depriving its owner of the 'ability' to use the information, although, of course, the profitability to the owner of using the information may be reduced if the thief uses it. Compared with more tangible assets the detection of the theft of knowledge may need to rely to a greater extent on discovering its subsequent use by others. But if Arrow is correct in asserting that '[t]he very use of information in any productive way is bound to reveal it, at least in part,'[17] then detecting its subsequent use by nonowners may be relatively easy. In any case, the reduction in theft of knowledge can be accomplished, without increasing the probability of detection, by raising the penalties to the thief if he is apprehended. A harsher schedule of penalties always can be used to enhance the appropriability of knowledge.[18]

The truth of the matter is that I, at least, have no more than casual notions about the cost, per dollar value of knowledge, of establishing property rights in information. Given the appropriate legal apparatus and schedule of penalties it may be no more difficult to police property rights in many kinds of knowledge than it is to prevent the theft of automobiles and cash. And even if some kinds of information are more difficult to protect, I am not sure which institutions yield the better solution to the problem or what public policy deduction should be made.

We now turn to what Arrow identifies as the problems of indivisibility (or, in more current terminology, the problem of public goods).

> The cost of transmitting a given body of information is frequently very low. If it were zero, then optimal allocation would obviously call for unlimited distribution of the information without cost. In fact, a given piece of information is by definition an indivisible commodity, and the classical problems of allocation in the presence of indivisibilities appear here . . .[19]
>
> As we have seen, information is a commodity with peculiar attributes, particularly embarrassing for the achievement of optimal allocation . . . [A]ny information obtained . . . should, from the welfare point of view, be available free of charge (apart from the cost of transmitting information). This ensures optimal utilization of the information but of course provides no incentive for investment in research. In an ideal socialist economy, the reward for invention would be completely separated from any charge to the users of information. In a free enterprise economy, inventive activity is supported by using the invention to create property rights; precisely to the extent that it is successful, there is an underutilization of the information.[20]

The partitioning of economic activity into the act of producing knowledge and the act of disseminating already produced knowledge is bound to cause confusion when the attempt is made to judge efficiency. It is hardly useful to say that there is 'underutilization' of information if the method recommended to avoid 'underutilization' discourages the research required to produce the information. These two activities simply cannot be judged independently. Since one of the main functions of paying a positive price is to encourage others to invest the resources needed to sustain a continuing flow of production, the efficiency with which the existing stock of goods or information is used cannot be judged without examining the effects on production.

If, somehow, we knew how much and what types of information it would be desirable to produce, then we could administer production independently of the distribution of any given stock of information. But we do not know these things. Arrow's assertion that '[I]n an ideal socialist economy, the reward for invention would be completely separated from any charge to the users of information' begs this whole problem. How would such a system produce information on the desired directions of investment and on the quantities of resources that should be committed to invention? There are ways, of course. Surveys of scientists and managers could be taken and a weighting scheme could be applied to the opinions received; no doubt there are many other ways of making such decisions. But the practice of creating property rights in information and allowing its sale is not clearly inefficient in comparison with these real alternatives.

Arrow does acknowledge the adverse incentive effects that would obtain in a private enterprise economy if information were made freely available, but this does not deter him from asserting that the capitalistic method is inefficient in its distribution of information. This ambiguity and looseness in Arrow's analysis is attributable directly to his viewpoint and approach. If he were to compare a real socialist system with a real capitalistic system the advantages and disadvantages of each would stand out, and it would be possible to make some overall judgment as to which of the two is better. But Arrow compares the workings of a capitalistic system with a Pareto norm that lends itself to static analysis of allocation but, nonetheless, that is poorly designed for analyzing dynamic problems of production. He finds the capitalistic system defective. The socialist ideal, however, resolves static allocation problems rather neatly. But this is only because all the dynamic problems of production are ignored. The comparison of a real capitalistic system with an ideal socialist system that ignores important problems is not a promising way to shed light on how to design institutional arrangements for the production and distribution of knowledge.

Indivisibilities in the use of knowledge become important only when the costs of contracting are relatively large. This point generally has been ignored. If everyone is allowed the right to use already available knowledge because one person's use of existing knowledge does not reduce its availability to others, there will tend to be underinvestment in the production of knowledge because the discoverer of knowledge will not enjoy property rights in the knowledge. But this underinvestment works to the disadvantage of others who would have the output of any additional investment made available to them at no cost. If the cost of contracting were zero, these prospective 'freeloaders' would be willing to pay researchers to increase the investment being made. Research activity would be purchased just as any other good.

The relevance of contracting cost is most clearly seen by supposing that there are two prospective freeloaders and one inventor. If the freeloaders are allowed to use successful research without paying the inventor, he will reduce his research efforts. But then the two freeloaders will find it in their interest to buy additional research effort from the researcher. The only implication of indivisibilities in the use of information is that it will pay for the freeloaders to join forces in buying this additional research, for by doing so they can share the required payment. If the cost of arriving at such an agreement is negligible, the resources devoted to experimentation will be the same as if the freeloaders were required to pay a fee to the inventor for the use of his successful experiments.

The objective of bargaining between those who produce knowledge and those who use it, whether the researcher has rights to the knowledge he produces or whether this knowledge is freely made available to all, is the production of knowledge at efficient rates. For if knowledge is produced at efficient rates, the social value of the research effort will be maximized. The bargaining between the interested parties will determine how this value is shared. If the cost of contracting, broadly interpreted, is zero, it will be in everyone's interest to reach an agreement that maximizes the value of the research effort because all will have a larger pie to share.

If the cost of contracting is positive, the kind of property rights system that is established may change the allocation of resources in the production of knowledge. If freeloading is allowed, that is, if users of knowledge are given the right to knowledge without paying for it, some prospective users will be inclined to stay out of any cooperative agreement between users. There will be an incentive to users jointly to pay researchers to increase the resources being committed to research, but if some users can remain outside this cooperative effort, they stand to benefit from research paid for by other users. This may lead to an underinvestment (underpurchase?) in research.

It might seem that the tendency for a user to remain outside any cooperative purchasing effort is independent of contracting costs. But this is not so. Broadly interpreted, such costs will include not only the cost of striking a bargain but also the cost of enforcing any bargain that is made. The property rights system that makes produced information freely available to all increases the cost of enforcing agreements. Let the user's purchasing organization attempt to acquire members. What does it have to offer prospective members? It cannot guarantee that those who join will have exclusive rights to the research output purchased, for the law says that anyone can use knowledge. The cost of enforcing a contract that promises exclusivity in the use of whatever knowledge is purchased is raised inordinately by this public policy, and that is why there will be a strong inclination to remain outside the buyer's cooperative effort.

If the legal system is changed so that producers of research have property rights in their research output, they will be able to transfer legal title to purchasers who can then exclude nonpurchasers from the use of the research. The incentive to remain a nonpurchaser is diminished with private appropriation of knowledge precisely because the cost of enforcing exclusive contracts is reduced.

The last assertion in the above quotation from Arrow's paper, 'In a free enterprise economy, inventive activity is supported by using the invention to create property rights; precisely to the extent that it is successful, there is an underutilization of the information', does not constitute an argument against the creation of property rights. The indivisibility problem may very will be handled best by a private property system that reduces the cost of contracting and raises the cost of free-loading while, at the same time, it provides incentives and guidance for investment in producing information . . .

III

. . . The problem of efficiency and the possibilities of achieving efficiency through reform were associated historically with the grant of monopoly and tariff privileges by governments. In their historical settings, criticisms of inefficiency took on the characteristic of the comparative institution and not the nirvana approach. Critics of governmental policies who asked for reform were seeking to substitute an institutional arrangement that was both real and fairly well understood. They were confident of the beneficial results and of the practicality of allowing market enterprise to allocate resources. And, although the operation of political forces had not been subjected to the same careful study, the critics did know what they expected if governmentally created protection from those market forces were removed.

A process of refining the analytical concept of competition then set in, culminating in the currently accepted necessary conditions for perfect competition. These conditions, of course, can only be approximated by real institutions. On top of these are placed additional conditions on the nature of production, commodities, and preferences that are necessary if the equivalence of perfect competition and Pareto efficiency is to be established.

While the application of these conceptual refinements is an aid to solving some economic problems, especially in positive economics, their application to normative problems has led to serious errors. If an economy has no serious indivisibilities, if information is complete, etc., then the modern analysis can describe the characteristics of an efficient long-run equilibrium; this description is the main result of modern welfare analysis. But modern analysis has yet to describe efficiency in a world where indivisibilities are present and knowledge is costly to produce. To say that private enterprise is inefficient because indivisibilities and imperfect knowledge are part of life, or because people are susceptible to the human weaknesses subsumed in the term moral hazards, or because marketing commodity-options is not costless, or because persons are risk-averse, is to say little more than that the competitive equilibrium would be different if these were not the facts of life. But, if they are the facts of life, that is, they cannot be erased from life at zero cost, then truly efficient institutions will yield different long-run equilibrium conditions than those now used to describe the ideal norm.

It is one thing to suggest that wealth will increase with the removal of legal monopoly. It is quite another to suggest that indivisibilities and moral hazards should be handled through nonmarket arrangements. The first suggestion is based on two credible assumptions, that the monopoly can be eliminated and that the practical institutional arrangement for accomplishing this, market competition operates in fairly predictable ways. The second assertion cannot claim to have eliminated indivisibilities, risk-averse psychology, moral hazard, or costly negotiations, nor can it yet claim to predict the behavior of the governmental institutions that are suggested as replacements for the market.

I have stated elsewhere that I believe to be the basic problem facing public and private policy: the design of institutional arrangements that provide incentives to encourage experimentation (including the development of new products, new knowledge, new reputations, and new ways of organizing activities) without overly insulating these experiments from the ultimate test of survival. In the context of the problems discussed in Arrow's paper, these institutional arrangements must strive to balance three objectives. A wide variety of experimentation should be encouraged, investment should be channeled into promising varieties of experimentation and away from unpromising varieties, and the new knowledge that is acquired should be employed extensively. No known institutional arrangement can simultaneously maximize the degree to which each of these objectives is achieved. A difficult-to-achieve balance is sought between the returns that can be earned by additional experimentation, and by reducing the cost of producing goods through the use of existing knowledge. The concepts of perfect competition and Pareto optimality simply are unable at present to give much help in achieving this balance.

NOTES

1. The author wishes to thank the Lilly endowment for financial aid received through a grant of the University of California at Los Angeles for the study of property rights.
2. Kenneth J. Arrow, 'Economic welfare and the allocation of resources for invention', in *The Rate and Direction of Inventive Activity*, 609–25 (1962).
3. A practitioner of the nirvana approach sometimes discusses and compares alternative institutional arrangements. But if all are found wanting in comparison with the ideal, all are judged to be inefficient.
4. Kenneth J. Arrow, *supra* note 1, at 619.
5. *Id*. at 623.
6. This is a slight exaggeration. Arrow, in the last few paragraphs of this paper, does discuss some problems in substituting the government for the market. The important point, however, is that Arrow is not led to reconsider his allegation of inefficiency in the market place by his short discussion of some of the difficulties of resorting to government.

7. But for economists at least, the charge of committing the grass is always greener fallacy must be less severe in this case. The economist who suggests that we resort to the market because of unsatisfactory experience with government at least can claim professional knowledge of how the market can be expected to allocate resources. See pt. IV, pp. 19–20 *infra*.

8. Kenneth J. Arrow, *supra* note 1, at 610–11.

9. A labor contract with an adjustment for changes in the Consumer Price Index is a commodity-option. Such a contract specifies one wage rate if nature reveals one price level and another wage rate conditional upon the appearance of a different price level. Insurance premiums often contain deduction provisions if nature helps the driver avoid an accident. Firms often will sell products to other firms with the price conditional on delivery date, product quality, and prices that are being paid by other firms at the time of delivery. The American housewife is persistently offered a money back guarantee conditional on quality and sometimes independent of quality. Numerous other examples of commodity-options can be cited, such as limit orders to buy or sell that specify reservation prices, but there is no need here for a survey of the great variety of contractual relationships that exist.

10. Kenneth J. Arrow, *supra* note 1, at 611–12.

11. *Id.* at 614.

12. *Id.* at 612–14.

13. In the original text, Arrow places a footnote here: 'The validity of this statement depends on some unstated assumptions, but the point to be made is unaffected by minor qualifications.' The reader perhaps may be able to guess what is meant here and how it would affect my criticism.

14. It is not yet clear from available empirical studies whether speculators are in fact compensated, and it has been argued either that they are not risk averse or that they enjoy the sport so much that they are willing to bear risk without pay.

15. Arrow employs the moral hazard argument in his paper, 'Uncertainty and the welfare economics of medical care', *American Economic Review*, 53: 941–73 (1963). Mark V. Pauly criticized this use of the moral hazard argument and Arrow replied to the criticism, *American Economic Review*, 58: 531–38 (1968). My criticism of Arrow's argument is much the same as Pauly's. Two parts of Arrow's reply to Pauly should be noted. First, Arrow concedes 'that the optimality of complete insurance is no longer valid when the method of insurance influences the demand for the services provided by the insurance policy.' So far so good. However, secondly, Arrow states that 'If the amount of insurance payment is in any way dependent on a decision of the insured as well as on a state of nature, then optimality will not be achieved either by the competitive system or by an attempt by the government to simulate a perfectly competitive system.' The supporting argument given by Arrow in defense of this second statement leaves much to be desired since it assumes that contracts between the insurer and insured that ration the insurance service are somehow outside the competitive system, that the decision to consume more of the service is somehow a 'bad' even though the price of the insurance covers the full cost of the service, and, implicitly, that adherence to contractual agreements is not an important feature of the competitive system.

16. Kenneth J. Arrow, *supra* note 1 at 616.

17. *Id.* at 615. Arrow states this to support his notion that theft of knowledge is easy.

18. For a definitive analysis of the role of penalties in crime prevention (and of other aspects of the economics of crime), see Gary S. Becker, 'Crime and punishment: an economic approach', *Journal of Political Economy*, 76: 169–217 (1968).

19. Kenneth J. Arrow, *supra* note 1, at 614–15.

20. *Id.* at 616–17.

7. Efficiency wage models of unemployment: one view

H. Lorne Carmichael[1]

Persistent involuntary unemployment of workers is a recurrent problem in labor markets all over the world. Unemployed workers seem unable to find work even though they are willing to accept lower wages than those being paid employed workers with similar skills. What could be preventing wages from adjusting to clear these markets? Many recent papers, known collectively as the efficiency wage literature, now claim to have the answer. This chapter will survey the efficiency wage literature and critically evaluate some of its accomplishments.

Efficiency wage models have already been examined by Yellen (1984), Katz (1986) and Stiglitz (1987), and have received generally favorable reviews. This chapter is more critical. Its overall conclusion is that efficiency wage models provide some useful insights into the workings of the labor market, but they do not provide a satisfactory account of wage rigidity or involuntary unemployment.

There are at least five separate versions of 'the' efficiency wage model. They share a common structure, however, and this is outlined in the first section of the chapter. This section also attempts to relate efficiency wage models to other recent models of unemployment. Section II examines and criticizes the different approaches in detail. Section III evaluates the achievements of this approach and suggests some directions for future work.

I. A GENERAL EFFICIENCY WAGE MODEL

Efficiency wage models, as the name suggests, are first of all models of wages. They generate unemployment by showing that firms will sometimes want to set wages at non-market clearing levels. It is useful to begin, therefore, by reviewing how wages and employment are determined in some related models.

In a perfectly competitive labor market the wage for each type of labor is adjusted constantly to maintain equality of supply and demand. Overall employment fluctuates in response to demand changes as workers move up and down their labor supply curves. Unemployment is voluntary in that anyone who is not working prefers that state to employment at the going wage for people of his skills. As well, the value of a worker's marginal product is equal to the marginal value of his leisure, so there are no unexploited wage bargains between unemployed workers and firms. This model is successful in predicting the long-term response of wages to shifts in demand and supply, but it is clear that in the short run its depiction of voluntary unemployment and flexible wages is unrealistic.

A natural way to generate more realism is to assume that wages are inflexible in the short run. In this case a reduction in demand away from a long-run equilibrium will lead to rationing of jobs by employers as they attempt to stay on their labor demand curves. The unemployment here is involuntary, in that the unemployed would prefer to be working at the going wage, and is inefficient in that there are lost gains from trade between these workers and firms. The weakness of this model is that it is silent about the mechanism that keeps wages rigid. Unemployed workers who offer to work for less than the fixed wage ought to find work.

The early implicit contract models of Azariadis (1975), Baily (1974), and Gordon (1974) provide one explanation for wage rigidity. These models introduced the idea that wages can do more than just clear the market for labor. Wages in an implicit contract model are used to shift the risk generated by uncertain output market conditions from risk averse workers to the risk neutral firm. In good states a worker's wage will be less than his marginal product and in bad states it will be higher. It follows that workers cannot be trusted to go home when it is efficient for them to do so (i.e. when the marginal value of their time at home is higher than their marginal product). Employment reductions in bad states therefore take the form of involuntary layoffs.

Wage bargaining does not arise in bad states since there are no unexploited gains from trade. The value of a laid off worker's time at home is greater than his marginal product, even though it may be less than the wage being paid those workers who are retained. However the involuntary nature of the layoffs is an artificial result. It depends on the assumption that firms cannot pay workers while they are unemployed. When this constraint is relaxed, the model predicts that firms will set wages and benefits to equalize the worker's marginal utility of income across all states of nature. If this marginal utility is higher when workers have more leisure, then income and utility will be higher for laid off workers. Thus, if leisure is not strongly inferior, workers on layoff are predicted to be better off than those left working.

Efficiency wage models are similar to these older implicit contract models in that the wage is used for something other than the allocation of labor. The basic idea is that raising a worker's wages will directly increase his productivity.

Although the use of this idea to generate a model of unemployment is fairly new, the idea itself can be traced back at least as far as 1776. In the words of Adam Smith:[2]

> The liberal reward of labor, as it encourages the propagation, so it increases the industry of the common people. The wages of labor are the encouragement of industry, which, like every other human quality, improves in proportion to the encouragement it receives. A plentiful subsistence increases the bodily strength of the laborer, and the comfortable hope of bettering his position, and of ending his days perhaps in ease and plenty, animates him to exert that strength to the utmost. Where wages are high, accordingly, we shall always find the workmen more active, diligent, and expeditious, than where they are low[.]

In order to turn this observation into a model of unemployment, we can follow Solow (1979). Denote the relationship between wages and productivity as $p(w)$ and firm output by $F[p(w)N]$, where N is the number of workers. The firms will choose wages and employment to maximize

$$PF[p(w)N] - wN \qquad (1)$$

subject to

$$w \geq v \qquad (2)$$

where P is the price of output and v is the workers' alternative wage. The inequality constraint here is unusual, but recall that even in a competitive model the firm is allowed to set wages higher than the workers' alternative – it will simply never have a reason to do so. Here the firm may decide to pay a higher wage in order to make workers more productive. If we let $L = p(w)N$ and assume that the alternative wage constraint is not binding, routine manipulations of the first order conditions give us

$$p'(w^*)w^*/p(w^*) = 1 \qquad (3)$$

and

$$PF_L'p(w^*) - w^*. \qquad (4)$$

The firm's optimal strategy is to set an 'efficiency' wage w^*, and hire workers up to the point where the value of their marginal product at that wage equals the wage. Remarkably, the efficiency wage depends only on the characteristics of the relationship $p(w)$. It does not depend on demand or supply conditions in the market.[3] This solution is derived graphically in Figure 7.1.

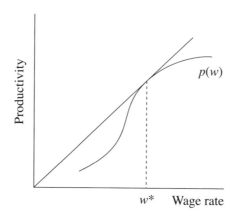

Figure 7.1

In Figure 7.1, for wages less than w^* increases in the wage will increase the productivity of workers by an even larger percentage amount. In this range the firm will actually increase its profits by increasing the wage. For wages greater than w^* productivity does not rise as fast, and the firm increases profits by lowering the wage. The optimal wage (assuming second order conditions are satisfied) therefore occurs where wage increases cause productivity increases of the same percentage amount – i.e. where the elasticity of $p(w)$ equals one.

In a competitive industry of identical firms, entry will occur until the price of output falls to reduce profits to zero. Each firm will want to hire a number of workers determined by condition (4). Aggregate labor demand therefore depends only on this number and the number of firms in the industry. If labor supply at the wage w^* exceeds labor demand there will be unemployment.

The unemployment is clearly involuntary in that unemployed workers earning v would prefer to be working at the wage w^*. As well, the value of an unemployed worker's time in his alternative is less than his marginal product were he to be hired at the current wage. Paradoxically, however, if an unemployed worker offered to work for less than the current wage, he would be refused. As the worker's wage falls, his marginal product falls by a larger percentage. At the efficiency wage the firm is breaking even on the marginal worker, so that at a lower wage the firm would make a loss. Thus there are no wage bargains, and the unemployment persists.

It appears that efficiency wage models might provide the elusive choice theoretic rationale for persistent fixed wage unemployment. Of course if unemployed workers can take low-wage jobs in other sectors of the economy, there will be no unemployment. However the model is then consistent with a 'dual' labor market and the existence of persistent, non-compensating wage differentials across firms.[4] As well, since the firm's wage is set at an interior maximum, changes in the wage have only a second order effect on profits. This means the lost profit from having wages set slightly wrong is small, and in particular may be less than the transactions cost of changing them. Akerlof and Yellen (1985) show that for plausible parameter values this rigidity can lead to first order losses for the whole economy. These results, as well as the very simple and intuitive nature of the models, are the major reasons why they are attracting so much attention.

Critics of efficiency wage theories do not dispute the idea that an increase in a worker's wages might increase his productivity. However, this assumption by itself is not sufficient to generate an efficiency wage. As should be clear from the diagram, there must also be a range of wages over which an increase in the wage increases productivity by an even larger percentage amount. Without this the firm will always increase profits by lowering wages, the alternative wage constraint will always be binding, and the firm will behave just like a perfect competitor. All of the models to be discussed below assume the strength of the wage productivity relationship is sufficient to generate an efficiency wage. We shall see, however, that there are other problems faced by this approach. In particular:

1) The strong wage rigidity result apparent in equation (3) does not survive in more detailed models. Thus while the models are consistent with non-market clearing wages, they do not predict that wages will be rigid as demand and supply conditions change. It is therefore not clear that these models are consistent with the large swings in unemployment rates observed over the business cycle.

2) In some of the models the assumptions that are used to justify the wage/productivity relationship are implausible or clearly at odds with reality.

3) In some cases efficiency wage models restrict the number of instruments that a firm can use to attract workers and keep them productive. When this constraint is relaxed, the models predict that other institutions will arise in response to the desire of unemployed workers to find jobs. These institutions are not observed. Thus the predictions of the models are not consistent with reality.

4) There are a few cases where an efficiency wage is only one of many possible outcomes of the model, so that the assumptions are not sufficient to support the conclusions claimed.

The main appeal of efficiency wage models is that they seem to provide a careful and rigorous theoretical explanation for non-market clearing wages and unemployment. Any serious attempt to evaluate these theories should therefore concentrate on the quality of this explanation. What do these models accomplish which could not have been achieved by the simple assumption that wages in some jobs are fixed in the short run? The major purpose of the next section, and of this paper, is to provide an answer to this question.

II.   EFFICIENCY WAGES IN MORE DETAIL

The five major styles of efficiency wage model differ from each other mainly in their justification for the wage/productivity relationship. This section examines four of the five in detail. The one left out is from the literature on economic development. It assumes that the nutritional gains made possible by higher incomes lead to increased productivity. While this literature is still active,[5] it has little relevance for developed economies, and it will not be reviewed here.

The first models covered are the gift-giving, or sociological, models. These papers assume that workers treat higher wages from the firm as a gift that must be repaid with the gift of extra effort. Next covered are the shirking models, which assume that higher wages increase the cost of dismissal to a worker who will then work harder to keep his job. This is followed by the turnover models, which assume that higher wages increase average worker productivity by reducing quits. Finally come the selection models, which assume that higher wages allow the firm to hire and retain better quality workers. The section ends with a discussion of some of the empirical work on efficiency wages.

It seems clear that there are many factors which can affect workers' productivity on the job. A 'good' foreman, army captain, or football coach, for example, can get his people to work harder without having to change their monetary rewards. One problem with trying to build models of phenomena like these is that these qualities or factors typically cannot be directly measured. The 'entrepreneurship' of a capitalist or the 'skill' of his managers must be defined as residuals, to account for differences in labor productivity across firms when everything measurable is held constant.

George Akerlof (1982, 1984) has explored the role of some of these 'non-economic' factors. He begins by arguing that people will work harder when they are paid more even when there is no implicit or explicit threat of dismissal. He interprets this as a 'gift exchange' between the firm and its workers, and draws upon evidence from other cultures to illustrate the ubiquity of this custom. The pay productivity relationship arises because as wages go up the workers feel that they are receiving a gift from the firm, and feel obligated to increase their effort in return. Similar models, such as Annable (1977), appeal to the effect of higher relative wages on worker 'morale' and thus their productivity.

It is easy to argue that this is no better an 'explanation' of wages in excess of market clearing than is the old fashioned assumption that 'workers resist wage cuts.' In each case unemployment arises because of restrictions that are placed on workers' utility functions. In fact there is the potential in the gift giving model for more than a simple explanation, but the model has not yet been pushed in this direction. When this is done the predictions of the model are not always consistent with the data.

Consider Figure 7.2. The worker has an alternative wage v and, following Akerlof (1982), suppose there is a minimal level of effort e^m that he will always exert. If the worker is paid his alternative and works at the minimal level, then the firm will make profits Π^* and the worker will get the utility level μ^m. Gift exchange models assume that when given a gift, people feel obligated to return a gift of equal value. One way to model this is to assume that when the firm pays the worker a wage higher than v the worker will respond with a level of effort which ensures that the firm remains on the isoprofit line through (v, e^m). 'Efficient gift giving' will therefore lead to the point (w^*, e^*), where the worker's indifference curve is tangent to the firm's isoprofit curve. If wages are set higher than this, the workers would prefer to give back some of the money (i.e., ask for a wage cut) rather than provide more effort.

The diagram makes it clear that gift giving allows the firm and the worker to achieve a more efficient outcome. In this example the worker gets all of the gains. However, there is a contract curve (not shown) of efficient points extending downwards from (w^*, e^*) to a point on the indifference curve through (v, e^m). A more general model might predict that the parties would achieve a point on this curve that left them with a fair division of the gains. If the firm can enforce any level of effort, it can do no better than to choose the

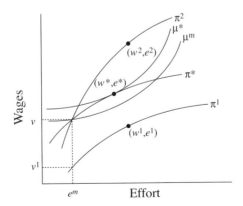

Figure 7.2

efficient point at the other end of the contract curve. However, if monitoring and enforcement of effort is costly, gift giving can be an effective tool for achieving an efficient outcome.

This model of efficient gift giving can generate some predictions about the response of effort and wages to changes in market conditions. If the value of workers' outside opportunities falls, wages might shift to a point like (w^1, e^1). On the other hand, if the value of workers' output rises, the isoprofit lines will become steeper and wages and effort might shift to a point like (w^2, e^2). (The worker's indifference curves for these cases are omitted from the diagram for clarity.) Wages in excess of market clearing can therefore be an outcome of this model, but these wages should not be rigid in the face of changing supply or demand conditions.[6]

This style of efficiency wage model will not be discussed in more detail because the theories have not, in fact, progressed very much further. Indeed, the most disappointing aspect of this approach is that there seems to be no interest among its proponents in working out precisely the implications of the model and the conditions under which it will perform most realistically. In general there is nothing wrong with adding something to a worker's utility function in an attempt to improve our understanding of the world. But surely this should be the point where the analysis begins, not the point where it ends.

Shirking Models

The basic idea behind the shirking efficiency wage model is that higher wages increase the cost to a worker of being dismissed. The worker will then work harder to make sure he keeps his job. There are two related problems with this approach. The first is that efficiency wages are not the unique equilibrium of the shirking model. The second is that when efficiency wages do arise as an equilibrium, other institutions, such as the posting of entrance fees by workers, should also arise. These issues will be treated after a discussion of the models themselves. But first the idea of a self-enforcing contract is introduced.

Self-enforcing contracts
The formal structure of the shirking efficiency wage model is an outgrowth of implicit contract theory begun by Azariadis (1975), Baily (1974) and Gordon (1974). These early implicit contracts, despite their name, were modeled as explicit, legally enforceable agreements between a firm and its workers. Both wage and employment levels could be prespecified as functions of the state of demand, usually indexed by the price of the firm's output. While it was argued that concern about its reputation could make a firm behave as if it were legally bound by an explicit contract there were no attempts to model reputations formally until much later (Holmstrom [1981], Carmichael [1984]).

These papers were followed by many more that modeled explicit contracts under asymmetric information: Hall and Lilien (1979), Grossman and Hart (1981), Green and Kahn (1983), Cooper (1983). In this approach it is assumed that realizations of the state of the world are observed by only one of the parties. Since explicit contracts can be written conditional only on variables that are publicly observed, contracts that are feasible may involve distortions. Unfortunately, Mookerjee (1986) has shown that with standard utility functions and technologies, these distortions seem to be in the direction of overemployment and involuntary retentions – i.e. workers preferring to be laid off rather than retained.

The latest variety of implicit contract is termed self-enforcing. In this literature some variables are observable to both the firm and the worker, but not to any third party such as the legal system. These variables are called non-verifiable. Other variables are observable to all parties, and are called verifiable. Explicit contracts can only be written conditional on verifiable variables. Nonetheless, both the firm and the worker can threaten to condition their future behavior on non-verifiable variables.

The importance of this distinction should become clear in the following example, which is the basic shirking efficiency wage model. Suppose a worker and a firm get together to form a relationship which may last for several future periods. The worker's role will be to provide effort which is costly to himself but useful in the production process. The firm will pay him in return. An explicit contract can be written specifying the wage to be paid (as certified by check stubs) and the times the worker is to be on the premises (as certified by a time clock). Wages and hours of work are therefore verifiable. Effort, on the other hand, is not verifiable. While both the firm and the worker may have a good idea as to how hard the worker has worked over a given period, this will be hard to establish in a court. The firm can, however, threaten to terminate the relationship if it determines that a certain standard of effort is not maintained.

The firm and the worker therefore sign an explicit contract which specifies the wage to be paid the worker for each period he is in attendance at the firm. The worker promises to provide effort on the job, and the firm promises to renew the arrangement next period if and only if this effort is forthcoming. The promises constitute a self-enforcing implicit contract if and only if it is in each party's interest to keep its promises. In the jargon of game theory, the requirement is simply that the announced strategies of the firm and the worker form a subgame perfect equilibrium.

The analysis of self-enforcing contracts is complicated because the problem cannot be set up as a compact constrained maximization problem. Instead, it must be specified as a game between the firm and its workers. However, its advantage is that it explicitly comes to terms with the idea of a contract which is implicit. Implicit contracts are collections of promises which, while they may not be written down, are nonetheless credible in that everyone knows that they will be upheld.

The central problem is to characterize the possible self-enforcing implicit contracts (the one outlined above might not be the only one) and in particular to determine whether wage rigidity and/or unemployment are necessarily a part of them. We will call a self-enforcing agreement 'non-trivial' if it speci- fies behavior which is not in the direct short-term interest of one or both of the parties. A preliminary result[7] is that such an agreement will exist only if a continuation of the relationship will generate a surplus for the two parties.

The reason is quite simple, and can be illustrated in the context of our example. The worker always has the short-run incentive to cheat. If the threat of contract nonrenewal is to prevent this, the worker must expect to earn more from a continuation of the relationship than he could if he were fired and had to go work elsewhere. Assume this is true and the worker does not cheat. The firm can also end the relationship by falsely claiming that cheating has occurred and firing the worker. The worker has no redress through the courts if this happens since the firm's promise not to do it is implicit in the contract. To prevent this 'firm cheating,' the contract must be designed so that the net benefits to the firm of a continuation of the relationship if no cheating has been detected are at least as great as what the firm can get by firing the worker. Since the worker must earn more than what he would get elsewhere if fired and the firm can earn no less, the total benefits to the two parties if their rela- tionship continues must exceed what they will get if it ends.

A surplus of this nature can be generated in many ways. The direct costs involved in changing jobs or in finding replacement workers will do it. So will training or talents which make a worker more productive at one firm than else- where. As well, if a worker is fired, other firms may conclude that he is dishonest and refuse to hire him, or hire him only at lower wages. Similarly, if a firm fires a worker without just cause and the other workers at the firm know this, the firm may have to pay them higher wages to prevent them from cheat- ing or quitting. A fifth possibility is for the two parties to explicitly contract with a third to pay him a penalty if a separation occurs. Yet a sixth potential source of a surplus, and the one which efficiency wage models emphasize, is unemployment. Here, while all firms pay the same wage and there are no mobility costs, there are fewer jobs than workers so that fired workers must spend some time unemployed before finding a new job. A final possibility, encouraged more by parents than economists perhaps, is the sense of guilt that some people may feel when they are unable to keep their promises.

The importance of the surplus and its source will become clear as we discuss the shirking efficiency wage models. The best known paper is Shapiro and Stiglitz (1984), although Calvo (1979), Malcolmson (1981) and Foster and Wan (1984) consider similar models. The basic Shapiro and Stiglitz story is already quite familiar. Consider a market with many indistinguishable firms and many indistinguishable workers. Firms live forever and workers die off at an exponential rate, so that the expected remaining lifetime of a worker is independent of his age. Effort is costly to workers, and is non-verifiable. There are no mobility costs, specific capital, reputations, third parties, or morals that could be used to generate the surplus required for a self-enforcing contract.

When all firms pay the same wage, workers will have no incentive to be honest, since if they are fired they can simply go to another firm and earn the same wage. An individual firm, by raising the wage it pays, can prevent this. However, if all firms try this, workers will again have no incentive to be honest because they can still move costlessly to another firm if they are fired. As wages rise, however, more workers are attracted to the industry and fewer jobs are available, creating (eventually) some unemployment. Equilibrium is attained when unemployment duration has reached the point where the relative cost of being unemployed is high enough to deter cheating.

In the language of self-enforcing contracts, the Shapiro–Stiglitz model is precisely the example we have been working with. The firm explicitly promises to pay the worker a fixed wage for every period he is employed. The worker implicitly promises to provide effort, and the firm implicitly promises to retain the worker if and only if it determines that this effort is forthcoming. Involuntary unemployment, according to Shapiro and Stiglitz, is necessary if there is to exist a self-enforcing contract which will elicit the effort of workers.

Multiple equilibria

The Shapiro–Stiglitz paper is truly seminal in that it has stimulated much controversy (Bull [1985], Carmichael [1985] and the replies by Shapiro and Stiglitz [1985a, 1985b]) as well as much further work (Strand [1987], Sparks [1986]). One of the more interesting critiques is due to MacLeod and Malcolmson (1987, 1989). These authors accept the basic framework of the Shapiro–Stiglitz model, including the infinite horizon and the absence of any source for a surplus other than unemployment, but show that with a slight expansion of the firm's set of possible promises there may be a multiplicity of self-enforcing contracts. All of these equilibira involve unemployment, but not all of them involve unemployment of workers.

MacLeod and Malcolmson begin by examining the problem faced by one risk neutral firm and one risk neutral worker, each with exogenous alternatives. The two agents are more productive when together than when apart, so there is a surplus available for the formation of a self-enforcing contract. The firm's explicit contract, as before, is to pay the worker a wage if he shows up for work. The worker promises to work and the firm promises to fire him if he doesn't, again as before. However, the firm can also promise to pay the worker an extra bonus if his effort is high. This bonus is like a piece rate, but remember that output is not observable to any third party. The worker further promises to quit if he has provided effort and the bonus is not forthcoming.

The main result of the paper is that contingent wage contracts of this kind can be self enforcing. To illustrate, consider the extreme case where the threat of firing plays no role in eliciting effort from workers. Assume that the total pay promised to honest workers (i.e. the guaranteed wage plus the bonus) is equal to the worker's alternative wage. The threat of firing therefore means nothing to the worker. To prevent worker cheating, the bonus must be large enough to outweigh the personal benefits of being lazy,[8] and the firm's promise to give this bonus to honest workers must be credible. If the firm cheats on the worker by refusing to pay, the most the worker can do is quit. This threat to quit will keep the firm honest if the threat is credible and if the firm expects to earn sufficient profits from a continuation of the relationship. The worker's threat to quit is credible, however, since he is indifferent between staying in this job and going to his alternative job. Thus the firm's promise to pay the bonus is credible so long as it expects to get a large enough surplus from the relationship. Wages contingent on effort can therefore be a part of a self-enforcing contract. It is not necessary that effort be observable by any third party.

A small expansion of the firm's set of promises introduces a large degree of indeterminacy into the outcome. In fact any contract in the range between full contingent wages and pure efficiency wages can be self enforcing so long as the surplus is shared correctly between the two parties. One way to eliminate the indeterminacy and generate some predictions is to extend the model to market equilibrium. The basic idea is that individual firms in designing their employment contracts will take the tightness of the labor market as given. The characteristics of the market, again in the absence of any other source for a surplus, will determine who gets the surplus and thus the form of any self-enforcing agreement.

To see this, consider the case where the labor market is very tight, so that there are more job openings than workers. A worker who gets fired will quickly find a new job at the same terms as his old one. Firms will have to wait for a time before their vacancies are filled, so that a quit will deprive them of future profits. Only firms with incumbent workers can get the surplus, and it follows that the only self-enforcing agreement is the contingent wage one. Similarly, if the labor market is very slack so that there are more workers than jobs, then employed workers get the surplus and the only self-enforcing agreement is the efficiency wage one.

None of this is unrealistic. Firms do seem to pay workers bonuses which are not enforced by any external contract, and it is an interesting prediction that this should be observed more often in tight labor markets. However the important (and unfortunate) conclusion is that the causality is running in the wrong direction. It is the existence of excess labor which leads to the efficiency wage contract equilibrium – not the uniqueness of the efficiency wage contract as a solution to an incentive problem which leads to unemployment. To emphasize – the unemployment in this more general shirking efficiency wage model is exogenous. It is the form of the contract (contingent wages or efficiency wages) which is determined within the model.

The bonding critique
Much of the debate about the shirking efficiency wage model has focused on the issue of bonding. (Bonds were first introduced in a shirking model by Becker and Stigler [1974].) An unemployed worker in the Shapiro–Stiglitz model should be willing to pay money up front for the opportunity to work at the efficiency wage. Since this entrance fee, or bond, is a sunk cost by the time the worker comes to make his effort decision, it should not affect his incentives and his promise to work should therefore be credible. In equilibrium the size of the up front payment should adjust so that the unemployed worker is indifferent about the prospect of taking a job.

The shirking style efficiency wage models appear to predict the emergence of entrance fees. These fees are very seldom observed in the labor market. It is therefore up to the proponents of this approach to demonstrate within the context of their models the reason why bonds are not observed. It is not legitimate, as several authors have done (Akerlof and Katz [1989], Strand [1987], Dickens and Katz [1987]) to appeal to this evidence in order to justify the assumption that bonds will not be paid.

Shapiro and Stiglitz, in their original paper, argue that bonds do not arise because unemployed workers can't afford to pay them, and because if a worker did pay one the firm would simply claim that he had cheated, fire him, and keep the bond. The first claim is countered by Carmichael (1985) who shows that with imperfect capital markets the size of the bond will be smaller, but it will not be zero. The market for new workers will clear when the expected utility of the contract (including the bond) equals that of the alternative. Thus, imperfect capital markets do not explain the absence of bonds.

A firm will only fire a worker to steal his bond if the value of the bond exceeds the extra profits the firm can expect to earn by continuing the relationship into the future. The claim that firms would steal workers' bonds, no matter how small, is therefore equivalent to the claim that firms earn no surplus from a continuation of the relationship. This claim is correct in the Shapiro–Stiglitz model. When unemployment is the only source of a surplus, and when firms can easily replace workers (i.e. when there is excess labor), the firm earns no surplus. However there are theoretical and empirical arguments which make it clear that in practice firms do earn a surplus from their workers.

The theoretical argument is due to Clive Bull (1987). He notes that in the Shapiro–Stiglitz model the firm and the worker do not know when their relationship is to end. This is quite unrealistic. Until just recently in the United States many firms and workers knew that their match would end with mandatory retirement when the worker reached age 65. This practice continues in many other countries. When there is a last period to the relationship, Bull shows that unemployment will not be sufficient to generate the surplus required for a self-enforcing contract.

Bull considers the incentive problem at the very last opportunity that the worker has to cheat. Since the worker will be going home to retire afterwards anyway, the threat of being fired is not effective unless the firm can retain some contingent payment which is paid after all the work is completed (perhaps a non-vested pension, for example). But it will never be in the firm's interest to pay such a pension once the worker has retired because there is no future relationship from which to earn a surplus by being honest. Bull suggests that reputations are the only way to solve this problem. The firm's actions must be monitored by other workers or prospective workers whose beliefs about the firm will change if it cheats in this way. Since mobility costs, specific training and unemployment are not important at retirement, the general result is that with a finite horizon and in the absence of explicit agreements with third parties, reputations are necessary for the existence of non-trivial self-enforcing implicit contracts. But if a firm is to care about its reputation, it must expect to earn a surplus in future periods (Klein and Leffler [1981], Shapiro [1982]). And if a firm can develop a reputation for treating its older workers honestly, then it should also be able to develop one for being honest with younger workers who have paid their entrance fees.

There is other, more direct evidence that firms earn a surplus from retaining their workers. Lazear (1979) suggests that the existence of mandatory retirement itself can be interpreted as direct evidence that older workers are getting paid more than they are worth. Firms are able to resist the temptation to fire these older workers at an earlier date even though it would increase short-term profits. Firms often report quits as 'regretted', and will institute programs to reduce turnover. Clarke (1973), Fair (1985), and Fay and Medoff (1985) note that firms hoard labor in recessions, presumably because they expect to earn more profits from them when business conditions return to normal. All of this evidence indicates that firms would like to keep their workers, other things equal, and should therefore be able to resist the temptation to fire a worker just in order to steal a small entrance fee.

There is also the theoretical possibility of designing a self-enforcing contract which implicitly uses the other workers at the firm to produce a surplus and allow the use of entrance fees. Papers which exploit this idea include Carmichael (1983a, 1983b), Malcolmson (1984, 1986) and

Bhattacharya (1987). For example, the entrance fees of all the workers could be placed into a pension fund and redistributed to the other workers if cheating occurs. Since the firm does not get to keep the bond if a worker is fired, it has no reason to fire him unjustly. Promotion tournaments and seniority rules for promotions also implicitly use the other workers at a firm as a third party.

That bonds are not observed in the labor market when there seems to be no theoretical way of ruling them out is evidence against the shirking models. However, other institutions might possibly perform the same function as bonds. Edward Lazear (1979, 1981) suggests that firms and workers can handle the shirking problem without the necessity of an up front fee. Workers pay their entrance fee when they are young by working for less than they are worth. However, Lazear's model is essentially an efficiency wage model since workers are paid more than their alternatives throughout their careers.

Akerlof and Katz (1989) investigate whether a rising wage profile of this kind can deter cheating in a model where the present value of a job to a newly hired worker is the same as his alternative. They argue that if the worker has any opportunities to cheat right after he has been hired he will do so since he has nothing to lose if he is caught and fired. The firm can concentrate its monitoring efforts on young workers, but if monitoring is costly at the margin (Dickens, Katz, Lang, and Summers [1986]) the firm will optimally trade off more intensive monitoring of young workers with a small efficiency wage premium.

Akerlof and Katz appeal to the absence of bonds in practice to justify their assumption that firms will not require them, and interpret their result as evidence that firms might pay efficiency wages. However it is clear from Bull's work that firms with rising wage profiles must be prevented from firing their older workers by a concern about their reputations. This concern should also be sufficient to allow them to charge bonds. It seems more compelling to interpret the Akerlof and Katz result as evidence against the shirking models, since even with rising wage profiles the shirking models predict the emergence of bonds and bonds are not observed.

To conclude this section, it is worth re-emphasizing the importance of the surplus in any self-enforcing agreement. Market forces will never eliminate this surplus if the market is to clear in non-trivial self-enforcing implicit contracts. Nonetheless market forces, in particular the desire of unemployed workers to find jobs, will lead to institutions minimizing the importance of unemployment as a source of this surplus. If mobility costs and the returns to firm specific training are already present in the market, nothing further is lost by using them to make an agreement self-enforcing. Clever design of tournament or pension schemes can also support these agreements while exploiting the gains from trade between unemployed workers and firms. Finally, the absence of bonding in practice seems to indicate either that these other sources are sufficient, or that the marginal effect of wage increases on worker performance is just not strong enough to justify high wage policies.[9] When one considers the ingenuity with which people are able to get around price controls in other markets (on rent controlled apartments, for example) it becomes very hard to believe that some form of bonding would not now be prevalent if the shirking models were true and if the distortions caused were as significant as they appear to be in the labor market.

Turnover Models

The turnover models by Stiglitz (1974) and Salop (1979) are very similar in structure to the shirking models. In the turnover approach firms bear costs if workers quit, so that a reduction in quits will increase average labor productivity. Increasing wages reduces quits, so the required wage productivity relationship can arise. Note that the worker's quit decision involves a comparison of the benefits of staying in his current job with those of leaving to an alternative, just as does his decision to cheat in the last section.

Unemployment can enter the model in a very familiar way. If there is no unemployment and all firms pay the same wage, turnover rates may be fairly high. By raising its wage, one firm can reduce its quit rate. However when all firms try this, the quit rate rises once again. As with the shirking model, equilibrium will obtain when the unemployment rate is high enough, and thus quits low enough, that further increase in the wage cease to be profitable.

Firms would not care about quits if they could make workers pay up front for all of their training and hiring costs. However, Stiglitz (1987) argues that imperfect capital markets and worker aversion to risk will prevent this. He also points to the fact that firms do regret quits as direct evidence that workers are not paying all of these costs.

As a theory of unemployment, this argument contains some serious flaws. The first is that imperfect capital markets, while they do prevent the worker from paying all of his training costs, are not sufficient to prevent the labor supply constraint from binding. The argument is essentially the same as was made in the last section and need not be repeated here. A more important problem is pointed out by Yellen (1984) and is understood by Salop (1979). Those factors which make turnover costly to the firm (training and hiring costs) are themselves sources of a surplus. It follows that a self-enforcing contract can always be designed to control worker turnover without the necessity of bringing in unemployment. This point is made quite easily given what we know already about self-enforcing contracts and the shirking model.

Suppose that hiring a worker consumes resources with the value C. Once hired, a worker will produce the amount P. The worker has an alternative wage v. Suppose that the worker pays a share of the hiring cost given by s. In a perfectly competitive labor market the wage w for joining this firm will be just enough to compensate the worker for leaving his alternative – i.e. $w - sC = v$. If there is free entry of firms, then profits will be bid to zero, so that $P - (1 - s)C = w$. These two conditions tell us simply that in equilibrium $P - C = v$. Net of the hiring cost, there is no surplus to the relationship.

If the worker pays the entire hiring cost, then he will be paid his productivity once he is hired. In this case the firm will not regret quits. If there is some reason why the worker cannot pay the entire fee, then he will be paid less than his productivity once he is hired. The firm will therefore regret it if he quits. But there is nothing here which requires unemployment in either the labor or the capital market.

It is clear that in the turnover model a firm would never fire a worker just to collect his share of the hiring cost. The firm expects to pay this worker less than he is worth if he stays, and to replace him would involve more hiring costs. Thus the 'bonding critique' is even more powerful when applied to this model. If unemployment were really a consequence of firms' concerns about reducing turnover, there is no doubt at all that unemployed workers would be offering to pay some portion of their hiring costs, and firms would be accepting these offers. This brings out the only major difference between the turnover and the shirking models. The existence of a hiring or training cost is itself the source of a surplus. In the shirking model a worker who has just arrived can cheat and impose on the firm a monetary loss. A bond can prevent this, but a contract can be designed to prevent the firm from stealing it. Hiring costs, however, create their own surplus so that no other source (such as unemployment) is ever necessary. As a model of unemployment, accordingly, this approach has little promise.

Adverse Selection Models

When workers have different alternatives or different tastes for a given job and the employer cannot pay them different wages, some employed workers will be earning rents. By the same token, if a firm advertises a job at a given wage, only those workers with alternatives which on net are less than the wage advertised will apply. All but the marginal applicant for any job will be involuntarily unemployed, in that they would prefer to be working at the offered wage to remaining in their alternatives. The question of interest is whether any of these applicants will remain unemployed. In other words, will firms set their wage offers higher than the level which will attract exactly the number of workers they need?

In practice it seems clear that they do. Barron, Black, and Lowenstein (1987) reveal that as reported on a survey of employers conducted by the US Department of Labor in 1982, firms on average screened nine candidates for each successful one, and spent an average of 2.44 hours recruiting and interviewing each one. Firms clearly take their hiring decisions seriously, and only a small proportion of applicants is successful.

In perhaps the best known paper in this area, Weiss (1980) considers a simple model where firms never learn their workers' productivity and the existence of some special form of capital insures that workers are in general more productive at the firm than elsewhere. Workers' productivities are perfectly correlated with their alternatives, so as the firm raises its offered wage it draws in applicants with higher alternatives and at the same time increases the average productivity of its pool of applicants. The firm hires randomly from this pool. If the wage/productivity relationship is strong enough, the firm will set its wage high enough to draw in an excess of applicants.

The result depends on some very special assumptions. For example, if access to this special capital is free, then as more firms enter this industry the problem of finding an equilibrium wage is not trivial. Firms which enter the market late face a higher quality labor pool since some of the lower quality workers have already been hired by the incumbent firms. As well, even in the one firm case if the correlation between productivity at the firm and elsewhere is less than perfect the wage/productivity relationship may not be strong enough to generate an efficiency wage.

One plausible extension suggested by the survey results is that firms might set the wage high enough to attract a large pool of applicants so that they can choose the best from among them. The average quality of the workers in the pool need not be an increasing function of the wage, but the average quality of those hired may be. If this relationship is strong enough, then it will be profitable for the firm to pay an efficiency wage.

Investigation of this possibility requires a model of worker testing. These models can get quite complicated. A problem with them was first identified in the extensive signaling and screening literature from the early 1970s (Spence [1974] and Stiglitz [1975] are two of the classic references). If worker talents are general (i.e. valuable at many firms), then workers must pay a fee up front covering the costs of their testing. If not, no firm will screen since another one will hire away the workers who are successful and save on the costs of testing them. Suppose now that a worker does not know his own ability. He has the option of working for a firm which does not screen and pays all its workers the average marginal product of all workers. This will always be more attractive than the option of going to a firm which does screen, paying the screening fee and then working for his actual marginal product. His expected wage is the same in each case, but in the first he pays no fee. Thus no firms will ever screen since in equilibrium they cannot get workers to pay for it.

In practice firms do not seem to be overly concerned about the possibility that other firms will immediately steal away the people they have just hired. Part of the reason is surely that there are information and mobility costs which make such 'raiding' costly, and that some of the skills being tested for are specific to the firm. Models of this kind may offer the most promising explanation for the willingness of firms to pay wages in excess of the minimum needed to bring forth the amount of labor they want to hire. Firms like to have a pool of applicants for their jobs so that they can pick and choose from among them. Rigorous modeling of this idea is an important task for future research.

One advantage of these models is that there appear to be no instruments the firm can use to solve its problem other than the value of its employment offer.[10] The requirement of an up front bond, for example, would have exactly the same effect as a reduction in the wage – i.e. it would discourage the best workers in the pool of applicants from applying.

Proponents of the shirking model, such as Shapiro and Stiglitz (1985b), when confronted with the 'bonding critique', sometimes point to this property of the selection models and argue that some combination of the two approaches may be consistent with the data. However there is a sense in which the two are incompatible. A firm which faced a pool of indistinguishable workers would prefer those with the lowest alternatives if it were worried about shirking. In this case the bonding critique says it should demand an up front payment, to 'select out' workers with high alternatives. If it wants workers with high alternatives because they are more productive, then a bond will select out exactly the workers it wants to hire.

While at a theoretical level the 'hiring pool' model may be the best of the efficiency wage models, it is important to note that, like the others, it is not really a model of fixed wages. In times of high unemployment offered wages will fall since the firm does not have to offer as high a wage in order to attract a given size pool of applicants. As a theory of unemployment it also has its limits. It is hard to believe, for example, that the dramatic increase in unemployment in a recession is due to an increase in the optimal queue length for those firms which are still hiring workers.

Empirical Work

Explicit empirical work on efficiency wage models is at an early stage, and few of the papers have yet been published. Nonetheless work is proceeding at a fast pace and it seems worthwhile to discuss briefly the directions being taken. Readers wanting more information are referred to the reply to this paper by Kevin Lang and Shulamit Kahn (1990).

Efficiency wage models were designed to account for unemployment, so it is not particularly compelling to point to the existence of unemployment as evidence for the approach. So far, research has concentrated on studies of occupational and industrial wage differentials.[11] These differentials remain even after correcting for the usual human capital variables of age, experience, and education, and often are not consistent with the usual compensating differences explanation. They have been quite stable over time, indicating that short-run adjustment costs are not likely to be the problem, and they seem consistent across occupational groups. The basic patterns seem clear over many studies – wages are generally higher in industries where firms are larger and more profitable, and where they have higher capital/labor ratios, relatively fewer women and blacks, higher layoff rates, and higher unionization rates. Several authors have looked only at occupation/industry changes in an attempt to control for unobserved worker quality, and here the results are mixed. Krueger and Summers (1988a) find the differentials persist while Murphy and Topel (1988) find that they largely disappear.

Proponents of efficiency wage theories have spent some time arguing that these results are inconsistent with the standard competitive human capital approach to wage differentials. However, the argument, 'Much of the pattern of inter-industry wage differentials is left unexplained by the competitive model so the efficiency wage model must be correct,' is hardly compelling. It would be more convincing if efficiency wage models could predict precisely which characteristics of a firm should be correlated with high wages. Then, if in the cross section these variables explained a large fraction of inter-firm wage differentials, there would be strong support for these models. In the absence of predictions like these, efficiency wage models from the purely empirical perspective are no stronger than a model which argues that wages in some industries are higher for 'historical' reasons.

Some authors, notably Oi (1983) and Dickens and Katz (1987), have attempted to work out the predictions of efficiency wage models for wage differentials in more detail, but for the most part this has not been done in a formal manner. It is perhaps easiest to appreciate the problems in a diagrammatic analysis.

In Figure 7.3 the curves labeled A and B represent the wage/productivity relationships at two firms. The efficiency wages at each are indicated on the diagram as w^{*A} and w^{*B}. The productivity curve for firm A is drawn to be steeper at all common values of the wage, so that the returns to increasing the wage are higher at firm A. As well, workers there are more productive at the same wage. Nonetheless the efficiency wage at firm A is lower! This is because the size of the efficiency wage depends on the proportional effects of wages on productivity. At firm A workers are more productive to start with, so that similar increases in productivity are lower in percentage terms.

Of course the curves for A and B could be redrawn to get any conclusion one wants consistent with the basic facts that workers are more productive at A and that increasing wages is also more effective at A. But this is precisely the problem. It is simply not obvious what (if anything) efficiency wage models predict about wage differentials in the cross section. The results

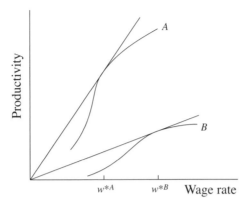

Figure 7.3

depend on the precise way in which a firm's size, capital labor ratio, and skill requirements, and other characteristics combine to affect the position and shape of the entire wage/productivity relationship.

A competitive model which is consistent with all of the observations on wage differentials, although it also has trouble predicting their character, is in Murphy and Topel (1988). They make the assumption that workers have different talents which match the requirements in different industries. Some talents are in short supply, so that workers with these talents can earn rents if they find jobs in the right industries. The search for good matches leads to movements between industries since industry characteristics matter as much as personal ones in determining the wage a worker receives. 'Luck' is important to a worker in the original distribution of talents and in finding a good match early.

The efficiency wage stories, with the exception of the selection models, minimize the effect of personal characteristics and emphasize the element of chance. Workers line up for high wage jobs and some are accepted, largely at random. Other workers end up in poorly paid jobs, again largely through no lack of talent or fault of their own. At a decidedly casual level of empiricism, one could choose between these models by considering the fates of those high school classmates who did not continue their educations. These people are largely indistinguishable to the econometrician, and yet go on to very diverse careers and levels of income. Choosing between the approaches is essentially equivalent to deciding whether it was luck or relative talents which had the greater influence on their relative successes.

Direct measurement of the wage/productivity relationship is not a useful way of testing efficiency wage models. At a firm paying an efficiency wage, an increase in that wage should increase productivity by the same relative amount. If the human capital model is true, an increase in productivity should be associated with an increase in the wage by the same relative amount.

It is just too early to say whether the empirical work done thus far will lead to any truly definitive tests of the theory. There is still some disagreement over the basic stylized facts about wage differentials, and the process of working out precisely the restrictions each model can put on observable quantities has only just begun. The same is true of the more recent firm/worker matching models. A great deal more work remains to be done.

III.   CONCLUSIONS

The basic puzzle that efficiency wage theory is designed to solve is why wages appear to be rigid in the face of apparently unexploited gains from trade between firms and unemployed workers. The major criterion for evaluating the success of the theory has therefore been its ability to provide a theoretical justification for rigid marginal wages. The theory's explanation is that lowering the wage would reduce worker productivity to such an extent that firm profits would fall.

The sociological theories might well be correct, but if so it means that the old idea that 'workers resist wage cuts' was right all along. The theory is dissatisfying because it has such a short distance between its assumptions and its conclusions. It might be interesting to analyze gift giving as an evolutionary cultural equilibrium, in which case this criticism will be mitigated and at the same time some predictions as to when gift giving will arise might be obtained. However, as it stands the approach seems to have stalled at the level of an explanation rather than a theory.

The shirking model argues that unemployment is necessary to generate a surplus from the relationship between a firm and its workers. However there seem to be many other sources for a surplus such as direct mobility costs, reputations, third parties, and specific human capital. In the presence of any of these the shirking model predicts that firms will start charging workers entrance fees. These fees are not observed, which casts doubt on the idea that firms will use high wage policies to reduce shirking. Even in the theoretical case where unemployment is the only potential source of a surplus, efficiency wages will arise only if there is excess labor to start with.

The turnover models argue that quits are costly to firms, so that an increase in wages can increase productivity by reducing quits. These models seem to have no hope of generating unemployment. The simple reason is that hiring costs and specific capital, which are factors which make firms want to reduce quits, are themselves the source of a surplus. Self-enforcing contracts to reduce turnover can therefore always be designed without the necessity of unemployment.

The selection models appear to have the most promise, particularly in a framework of matching specific talents and training. The emphasis that firms place on the selection of new employees indicates clearly that firms do have a selection problem – i.e. they do set wages at a level where the number of applicants exceeds the required number of workers. Even if increasing the offered wages does not increase the average quality of candidates, it may increase the average quality of those hired under the firm's selection procedures. It is encouraging that these models do not predict the emergence of bonding. On the other hand, they do predict flexible wages and it seems clear that they cannot account for large swings in the aggregate unemployment rate.

There are two aspects to the wage rigidity puzzle. The first concerns the reasons why the wages of those workers who are retained during recessions remain relatively constant. Differences in risk aversion, transactions costs, and efficiency wage considerations may all be part of the story. The wages of these workers play no allocative role, however. To understand involuntary unemployment we have to answer a harder question. Why are there no wage bargains between firms and those workers who are unemployed? These workers need not be hired at the same wage as incumbents. The basic conclusion of this chapter is that the efficiency wage models by themselves have not yet provided a convincing answer. The puzzle of wage rigidity as it relates to involuntary unemployment remains largely unsolved.

This survey has pointed out several directions for further research. Within the efficiency wage framework, the sociological models and the 'hiring pool' selection model are as yet relatively unexplored and may prove to be fruitful. The data on industrial wage differentials can be used to distinguish among the theories if they can only be pushed for more precise predictions. It may also be possible to combine ideas from efficiency wage models with ideas from outside this framework to generate entirely new approaches. There are a great many possibilities and a great deal of work remains to be done.

NOTES

1. Queen's University, Kingston, Ontario, K7L3N6, Canada. Comments from Kevin Lang have had a major influence on the direction of this chapter. I would also like to thank Bentley MacLeod, Steve Jones, and Andy Weiss. The comments and complaints of several anonymous referees have (I hope) led to substantial improvements in the exposition. The Social Sciences and Research Council of Canada provided research support.
2. Adam Smith (1937, 81). I am grateful to Bruce Shearer for bringing this passage to my attention.
3. Extensions of the model will relax this strong independence, but the general result that at the efficiency wage the supply of labor will exceed the demand is maintained.
4. This aspect of the theory has been the focus of most of the empirical work. See the section on empirical work later in the paper.

5. References to nutritional models include Liebenstein (1957), Stiglitz (1976), and Dasgupta and Ray (1986).
6. Akerlof (1982) claims that reduction in e^m will actually increase worker effort. He does not provide an explicit model, so it is not clear whether this one is an exact representation of his ideas. If so, however, Shearer (1988) shows that to get his result it is necessary to assume that leisure is inferior.
7. The importance of the surplus is brought out in Klein and Leffler (1981), Shapiro (1982), and MacLeod and Malcolmson (1978).
8. There is no theoretical reason why the guaranteed wage must be positive. (If it is negative, the worker is paying a bond.) When monitoring is imperfect, the size of the bonus may have to be very large, so if the overall value of the offer is to be equal to the worker's alternative, this may indeed be an outcome. In this case the size of the surplus needed to prevent firm cheating will also have to be large.
9. There seems to be no doubt that shirking by workers is a concern of firms, but this does not mean that at the margin wage increases are a profitable way to control it.
10. This is true so long as workers do not know more about their productivity than the firm. See the papers by Guasch and Weiss (1980, 1981, 1982).
11. I would like to thank Kevin Lang for sending me the recent papers on which this section is based. The ones I would recommend to an interested reader are the two by Dickens and Katz (1987, 1988) since they give the most comprehensive surveys of the recent literature, as well as the best attempt to determine explicitly the predictions of each of the models to be tested. The information in this paragraph is drawn from these papers as well as Murphy and Topel (1988), and Krueger and Summers (1988a, 1988b).

REFERENCES

Akerlof, George. 'Gift Exchange and Efficiency Wage Theory: Four Views.' *American Economic Review*, Papers and Proceedings, May 1984, 79–83.

Akerlof, George. 'Labor Contracts as a Partial Gift Exchange.' *Quarterly Journal of Economics*, November 1982, 543–69.

Akerlof, George and Lawrence Katz. 'Do Deferred Wages Eliminate the Need for Involuntary Unemployment as a Worker Discipline Device?' in *Advances in the Theory and Measurement of Unemployment*, edited by Y. Weiss and G. Fishelson. London: Macmillan, 1989, 172–203.

Akerlof, George and Janet Yellen. 'Can Small Deviations from Economic Rationality Make a Significant Difference to Economic Equilibria?' *American Economic Review*, September 1985, 708–20.

Annable, James E. 'A Theory of Downward Rigid Wages and Involuntary Unemployment.' *Economic Inquiry*, July 1977, 326–44.

Azariadis, Costas. 'Implicit Contracts and Underemployment Equilibria.' *Journal of Political Economy,* December 1975, 1183–202.

Baily, Martin. 'Wages and Employment Under Uncertain Demand.' *Review of Economic Studies*, January 1974, 37–50.

Barron, John, Dan Black and Mark Lowenstein, 'Employer Size: The Implications for Search, Training, Capital Investment, Starting Wages, and Wage Growth.' *Journal of Labor Economics*, January 1987, 13–27.

Becker, Gary and George Stigler. 'Law Enforcement, Malfeasance, and the Compensation of Enforcers.' *Journal of Legal Studies*, January 1974, 1–18.

Bhattacharya, Sudipto. 'Tournaments, Termination Schemes, and Forcing Contracts.' Mimeo, School of Business, University of California, Berkeley, 1987.

Bull, Clive. 'Equilibrium Unemployment as a Worker Discipline Device: Comment.' *American Economic Review*, September 1985, 890–91.

Bull, Clive. 'The Existence of Self-Enforcing Implicit Contracts.' *Quarterly Journal of Economics*, February 1987, 147–59.

Calvo, Guillermo. 'Quasi-Walrasian Theories of Unemployment,' *American Economic Review*, Papers and Proceedings, May 1979, 102–7.

Carmichael, H. Lorne. 'The Agent-Agents Problem: Payment by Relative Output.' *Journal of Labor Economics*, January 1983b, 37–50.

Carmichael, H. Lorne. 'Can Unemployment be Involuntary?' *American Economic Review*, December 1985, 1213–14.

Carmichael, H. Lorne. 'Firm Specific Human Capital and Promotion Ladders.' *Bell Journal*, Spring 1983a, 241–58.

Carmichael, H. Lorne. 'Reputations in the Labor Market.' *American Economic Review*, September 1984, 713–25.

Clarke, C. Scott. 'Labor Hoarding in Durable Goods Industries.' *American Economic Review*, December 1973, 811–23.

Cooper, Russel. 'A Note on Overemployment/Underemployment in Labor Contracts Under Asymmetric Information.' *Economics Letters*, January 1983, 81–7.

Dasgupta, Partha and Debraj Ray. 'Inequality as a Determinant of Malnutrition and Unemployment: Theory.' *Economic Journal*, December 1986, 1011–34.

Dickens, William and Lawrence Katz. 'Interindustry Wage Differences and Industry Characteristics,' in *Unemployment and the Structure of Labor Markets*, edited by Kevin Lang and Jonathan Leonard. Oxford: Basil Blackwell, 1988, 48–89.

Dickens, William and Lawrence Katz. 'Interindustry Wage Differences and Theories of Wage Determination.' National Bureau of Economic Research, Working Paper No. 2271, June 1987.

Dickens, William, Lawrence Katz, Kevin Lang and Lawrence Summers. 'Are Efficiency Wages Efficient?' National Bureau of Economic Research Working Paper No. 1935, June 1986.

Fair, Ray. 'Excess Labor and the Business Cycle.' *American Economic Review*, March 1985, 239–45.

Fay, John and James Medoff. 'Labor and Output over the Business Cycle: Some Direct Evidence.' *American Economic Review*, September 1985, 638–55.

Foster, James E. and Henry Y. Wan. 'Involuntary Unemployment as a Principal Agent Equilibrium.' *American Economic Review*, June 1984, 476–85.

Gordon, Donald F. 'A Neoclassical Theory of Keynesian Unemployment.' *Economic Inquiry*, December 1974, 431–59.

Green, Jerry and Charles Kahn. 'Wage Employment Contracts.' *Quarterly Journal of Economics*, Supplement, March 1983, 173–87.

Grossman, Sandford and Oliver Hart. 'Implicit Contracts, Moral Hazard, and Unemployment.' *American Economic Review*, Papers and Proceedings, May 1981, 301–7.

Guash, Luis and Andrew Weiss. 'An Equilibrium Analysis of Wage Productivity Gaps.' *Review of Economic Studies*, June 1982, 485–97.

Guash, Luis and Andrew Weiss. 'Self Selection in the Labor Market.' *American Economic Review*, June 1981, 275–84.

Guash, Luis and Andrew Weiss. 'Wages as Sorting Mechanisms in Competitive Markets with Asymmetric Information: A Theory of Testing.' *Review of Economic Studies*, September 1980, 653–64.

Hall, Robert and David Lilien. 'Efficient Wage Bargains under Uncertain Supply and Demand.' *American Economic Review*, December 1979, 868–79.

Halmstrom, Bengt. 'Contractual Models of the Labor Market.' *American Economic Review*, Papers and Proceedings, May 1981, 308–13.

Katz, Lawrence. 'Efficiency Wage Theories: a Partial Evaluation,' in *NBER Macroeconomics Annual*, edited by Stanley Fisher. Cambridge, MIT Press, 1986, 235–76.

Klein, Benjamin and Keith Leffler. 'The Role of Market Forces in Assuring Contractual Performance.' *Journal of Political Economy*, August 1981, 615–32.

Krueger, Alan B. and Lawrence H. Summers. 'Efficiency Wages and the Wage Structure.' *Econometrica*, March 1988b, 259–74.

Krueger, Alan B. and Lawrence H. Summers. 'Reflections on the Inter-industry Wage Structure,' in *Unemployment and the Structure of Labor Markets*, edited by Kevin Lang and Jonathan Leonard. Oxford: Basil Blackwell, 1988a.

Lang, K. and Kahn, S. 'Efficiency Wage Models of Unemployment: A Second View' *Economic Inquiry* 28 (April 1990), 296–306.

Lazear, Edward. 'Agency, Earnings, Profiles, Productivity and Hours Restrictions.' *American Economic Review*, September 1981, 606–20.

Lazear, Edward. 'Why is There Mandatory Retirement?' *Journal of Political Economy*, December 1979, 1261–84.

Leibenstein, Harvey. *Economic Backwardness and Economic Growth*. New York: Wiley, 1957.

Macleod, Bentley and James Malcolmson. 'Implicit Contracts, Incentive Compatibility, and Involuntary Unemployment.' *Econometrica*, March 1989, 312–22.

Macleod, Bentley and James Malcolmson. 'Involuntary Unemployment in Dynamic Contract Equilibria.' *European Economic Review* 31(1), 1987, 427–35.

Malcolmson, James. 'Rank Order Contracts for a Principal with Many Agents.' *Review of Economic Studies*, October 1986, 7–18.

Malcolmson, James. 'Unemployment and the Efficiency Wage Hypothesis.' *Economic Journal* 91(4), 1981, 848–66.

Malcolmson, James. 'Work Incentives, Hierarchy, and Internal Labor Markets.' *Journal of Political Economy*, June 1984, 486–507.

Mookherjee, Dilip. 'Involuntary Unemployment and Worker Moral Hazard.' *Review of Economic Studies*, December 1986, 739–54.

Murphy, Kevin and Robert Topel. 'Unemployment, Risk and Earnings: Testing for Equalizing Wage Differences in the Labor Market,' in *Unemployment and the Structure of Labor Markets,* edited by Kevin Lang and Jonathan Leonard. Oxford: Basil Blackwell, 1988, 103–40.

Oi, Walter. 'Heterogeneous Firms and the Organization of Production.' *Economic Inquiry*, April 1983, 147–71.

Salop, Steven. 'A Model of the Natural Rate of Unemployment.' *American Economic Review*, March 1979, 117–25.

Shapiro, Carl. 'Consumer Information, Product Quality, and Seller Reputation.' *Bell Journal*, Fall 1982, 20–35.

Shapiro, Carl and Joseph Stiglitz. 'Can Unemployment be Involuntary: Reply.' *American Economic Review*, December 1985b, 1215–17.

Shapiro, Carl and Joseph Stiglitz. 'Equilibrium Unemployment as a Discipline Device, Reply.' *American Economic Review*, September 1985a, 892–3.

Shapiro, Carl and Joseph Stiglitz. 'Equilibrium Unemployment as a Worker Discipline Device.' *American Economic Review*, June 1984, 433–44.

Shearer, Bruce. 'A Model of Gift Giving in the Labor Market.' Mimeo, Queen's University, Kingston, Ontario, July 1988.

Smith, Adam. *The Wealth of Nations.* New York: Random House, 1937.

Solow, Robert. 'Another Possible Source of Wage Stickiness.' *Journal of Macroeconomics*, Winter 1979, 79–82.

Sparks, Roger. 'A Model of Involuntary Unemployment and Wage Rigidity: Worker Incentives and the Threat of Dismissal.' *Journal of Labor Economics*, October 1986, 560–81.

Spence, Michael. 'Job Market Signaling.' *Quarterly Journal of Economics*, August 1974, 355–79.

Stiglitz, Joseph E. 'Alternative Theories of Wage Determination and Unemployment in DCS's: the Labor Turnover Model.' *Quarterly Journal of Economics*, March 1974, 194–227.

Stiglitz, Joseph E. 'The Economic Consequences of the Dependence of Quality on Price.' *Journal of Economic Literature*, March 1987, 1–48.

Stiglitz, Joseph E. 'The Efficiency Wage Hypothesis, Surplus Labor, and the Distribution of Income in LDC's.' *Oxford Economic Papers*, May 1976, 185–207.

Stiglitz, Joseph E. 'The Theory of Screening, Education, and the Distribution of Income.' *American Economic Review*, June 1975, 283–300.

Strand, Jon. 'Unemployment as a Discipline Device with Heterogeneous Labor.' *American Economic Review*, June 1987, 489–93.

Yellen, Janet. 'Efficiency Wage Models of Unemployment.' *American Economic Review*, Papers and Proceedings, May 1984, 200–205.

Weiss, Andrew. 'Job Queues and Layoffs in Labor Markets with Flexible Wages.' *Journal of Political Economy*, June 1980, 526–38.

8. Do informational frictions justify federal credit programs?[1]

Stephen D. Williamson

Through federal agencies, the US government administers a wide array of credit programs, which alter the allocation of credit (and the distribution of income) in the United States in important ways. In this chapter, we will consider the credit market effects of three types of federal credit programs. First, we examine direct government lending, which takes place in the United States through several federal agencies, including the Farmers Home Administration (FmHA) and the Small Business Administration (SBA). Second, we consider loan guarantees, which are an important form of federal government intervention in credit markets. Much of the activity of the SBA is accounted for by loan guarantees, and the mortgage insurance programs of the Federal Housing Administration (FHA) are essentially loan guarantees. Third, we study the promotion of secondary markets in private loans, an area in which the federal government has been active, especially in regard to the mortgage market. The Government National Mortgage Administration (GNMA) buys FHA-insured mortgages and packages these as 'pass-through securities.' GNMA pass-through securities are backed by the US government. The Federal National Mortgage Administration (FNMA) is a privately owned corporation which performs a role similar to GNMA. The mortgages backing FNMA pass-through securities are conventional rather than insured, and these securities have no explicit government backing. However, it is generally recognized that the liabilities of FNMA are implicitly backed by the US government; i.e. FNMA is 'too big to fail.'

When efficiency arguments are used to justify federal credit programs, there is usually some appeal to 'market failures' which, it is argued, arise because of informational frictions in credit markets. The following quote from Jaffee and Stiglitz (1990, p. 839) is instructive:

When credit is allocated poorly, poor investment projects are undertaken, and the nation's resources are squandered. Credit markets . . . may not function well . . . in allocating credit. The special nature of credit markets is most evident in the case of credit rationing, where borrowers are denied credit even though they are willing to pay the market interest rate (or more), while apparently similar borrowers do obtain credit.

Jaffee and Stiglitz stop short of advocating specific types of government intervention in credit markets, but it would seem that an implication of the above passage is that the 'special nature of credit markets' creates problems that need to be addressed.

The literature on the effects of government credit programs in environments with imperfect information is perhaps smaller than one would expect. A set of related papers, in which adverse selection models are used to analyze federal credit programs, includes Smith and Stutzer (1989), Gale (1990a, 1990b, 1991), and Lacker (1993b). The more specialized topic of government-provided deposit insurance programs has also received some attention (for example, Kareken and Wallace, 1978 and Diamond and Dybvig, 1983).

The purpose of this chapter is modest. We will confine attention here to two particular private information models of the credit market, and the effects of some government credit programs in those models. Without being all-encompassing, the models incorporate many features of credit markets on which the literature in this area has focused, including moral hazard, adverse selection, the incentive role of debt contracts, and credit rationing.

We first study a costly state verification model, which is similar to models in Williamson (1986, 1987). Those models in turn built on earlier work by Townsend (1979) and Diamond (1984). Other closely related work is Gale and Hellwig (1985). The setup here is a two-period model of a credit market, where the optimal financial contracts written by lenders and borrowers are debt contracts. Given costly verification of the return on borrowers' investment projects, debt contracts act to give borrowers the incentive to correctly report investment outcomes, while minimizing the deadweight losses from costly verification.[2] The costly state verification model has the property that an equilibrium can exhibit credit rationing. That is, in equilibrium it may be the case that some would-be borrowers do not receive loans while other identical agents do. Credit rationing arises because an increase in the loan interest rate not only increases the expected payment from the borrower to the lender, but also increases the probability that the borrower defaults, thus increasing expected verification costs. This second effect may outweigh the first at the equilibrium interest rate, so that there is no contract an agent who is rationed out of the market can offer which will yield a higher expected return to the lender.

Given the possibility of a credit rationing 'problem' in the credit market, is there any role for government credit programs to improve the allocation of credit? For the particular programs we consider, the answer is no. Direct government lending on the same terms offered by the private sector will only displace an equal quantity of private lending, and does not relieve any of the rationing that exists in the absence of government intervention.[3] The effects of government loan guarantees are perverse; these act to distort private contracts in such a way that, if rationing exists without the government loan guarantee, the program lowers the interest rate faced by lenders, increases the interest rate faced by borrowers, and increases the probability that a borrower is rationed. Therefore, all credit market participants are worse off with intervention.

The second modeling framework we consider is a new one, from Wang and Williamson (1993). In this model, there is costly screening of borrowers in a credit market with adverse selection.[4] There are two types of borrowers, g and b, who differ according to the distribution of investment returns that they face, and type is private information. A lender can learn a borrower's type by incurring a fixed screening cost. This type of model is similar to the costly state verification setup, in that there can be costly revelation of private information. However, an important difference is that information costs are incurred before investment takes place, rather than ex post, as in the costly state verification model.

Some features of the equilibrium in this model are similar to those of the standard Rothschild–Stiglitz (1977) adverse selection model. If an equilibrium exists, then it is a separating equilibrium where types g and b are offered different incentive-compatible contracts, and there are conditions under which an equilibrium will not exist.

In equilibrium a type g borrower (whose investment return distribution is superior to that of a type b borrower, in the sense of first-order stochastic dominance) is screened with positive probability, while a type b borrower is not screened. An important feature of the model is that debt contracts are equilibrium contracts, as they act to induce self-selection while minimizing expected screening costs.

In the costly screening model, we consider two types of government credit programs, direct loans to would-be borrowers who are denied private credit, and direct subsidized loans. The offering of loans to borrowers who have been denied private credit alters incentives to borrowers who consider misrepresenting their type, as the denial of credit is a penalty that is used by private lenders to induce self-selection. If the interest rate on government loans is set sufficiently high, then the agents who bear the necessarily higher screening costs are worse off, and no agents are better off.[5] However, if the interest rate on government loans is sufficiently low, then the welfare of type g borrowers falls, the welfare of type b agents rises (if an equilibrium existed in the absence of the government credit program), and an equilibrium may exist with government intervention where it did not exist without it. Thus, this type of program can act to alter incentives in possibly useful ways.

Direct subsidized lending in the costly screening model can act to reduce interest rates faced by all agents, including those who are not directly targeted by the program. Here, if type b agents can receive a subsidized loan from the government, then type *g* agents can be screened less intensively. The costs of subsidization, which may include screening costs (if subsidized loans are sufficiently attractive), must be borne by someone, which implies that subsidized lending programs are not a Pareto improvement.

It is straightforward to extend the costly state verification and costly screening models studied here, following Williamson (1986) and Wang and Williamson (1993), to the case where a financial intermediary structure is an equilibrium phenomenon. Thus, these models can be used to address problems related to the repackaging of private loans into tradeable securities, a form of financial intermediation. Here, there is no role for the government to play in promoting financial intermediation, as there are no unrealized intermediation opportunities in equilibrium. However, in the US regulatory environment, where there are various restrictions (including branching regulations) which tend to limit diversification by banks, institutions like GNMA and FNMA may have a welfare-improving role to play. Here, we suggest that a first-best solution would involve eliminating restrictions that limit the size of US banks and their ability to branch.

The remainder of the paper proceeds as follows. In section 1, we set up a model of a credit market with costly state verification, and study the effects of two government credit programs in this environment. We follow a similar approach for the costly screening model in section 2, while in section 3 we study financial intermediation and the role of pass-through securities. Section 4 is a summary and conclusion.

1.   CREDIT WITH COSTLY STATE VERIFICATION

The model studied in this section is similar to the costly state verification models in Williamson (1986) and Williamson (1987). This type of model is useful for our purposes, as it has informational frictions capable of generating equilibrium credit rationing, an apparent 'inefficiency.'

1.1 The Model

Consider the following partial equilibrium model of a credit market. There are two periods, 1 and 2, and the population consists of a continuum of agents with unit mass, uniformly distributed on the interval [0, 1]. Letting *i* index agents, if $i \in [0, \alpha]$, then *i* is a *lender*, and if $i \in [\alpha, 1]$, then *i* is an *entrepreneur*. Thus, the fraction of the population who are lenders is α, where we assume that $\frac{1}{2} < \alpha < 1$. Each lender has one unit of time in period 1, which can be used either to produce one unit of the investment good, or consumed as leisure. A given lender *i* has preferences given by

$$u^i(c, \ell, e) = c - \ell \left[r_\ell + \left(\frac{i}{\alpha} \right) (r_u - r_\ell) \right] - e,$$

where c is consumption in period 2, ℓ is leisure in period 1, e is effort expended in monitoring borrowers, and $0 < r_\ell < r_u$. Note that different lenders have different marginal utilities of leisure, so as to generate a supply function for credit which is increasing in the return on credit instruments. Each lender can potentially supply an unlimited quantity of effort in period 2.

Each entrepreneur has access to a technology that takes one unit of the investment good as input in period 1, and yields a stochastic quantity of consumption, x, in period 2, where x is distributed according to the probability distribution function $F(x)$, with the corresponding probability density function $f(x)$. Assume that $f(x) > 0$ for $x \in [0, 1]$, $f(x) = 0$ otherwise, and that $f(x)$ is continuously differentiable on $[0, 1]$. There is costly state verification (Townsend, 1979; Gale and Hellwig, 1985; Williamson, 1986, 1987), in that the return x is observable only to the entrepreneur. Any other agent must incur a fixed cost of γ units of effort to observe x in period 2. Entrepreneurs maximize the expected value of consumption in period 2.

1.2 Equilibrium

Optimal contracts between lenders and entrepreneurs are determined as by Williamson (1987), to maximize the expected utility of an entrepreneur, subject to the constraint that the lender receive an expected return from the contract that is at least the credit market expected return, r. Assuming that verification strategies are deterministic,[6] the optimal contract is a debt contract. That is, suppose a loan is made from a lender to an entrepreneur, and let $R(x)$ denote the payment from the entrepreneur to the lender in period 2. Then the optimal contract is $R(x) = x$, $x \in [0, R]$, and $R(x) = R$, $x \in [R, 1]$ for some constant $R \in [0, 1]$. Verification takes place for $x \in [0, R]$, and does not take place otherwise. Thus, the states where $x < R$ correspond to bankruptcy states, R is the promised payment on the debt, and γ is a bankruptcy cost. Here, R satisfies

$$\pi^\ell(R, \gamma) = \int_0^R (x - \gamma) \, dF(x) + R[1 - F(R)] = r. \tag{1}$$

A debt contract acts here to minimize the deadweight losses with verification costs. It is necessary for verification to occur in some states of the world, otherwise the entrepreneur would always report to the lender that the return on the investment project was $x = 0$, implying a payment of zero. A debt contract induces the entrepreneur to report the investment outcome truthfully, and payments are as high as possible in verification states so as to minimize expected verification costs.

In (1), $\pi^\ell(R, \gamma)$ is the expected return to the lender, which can be rewritten, using integration by parts, as

$$\pi^\ell(R, \gamma) = R - \int_0^R F(x)\, dx - \gamma F(R). \tag{2}$$

We will assume restrictions on $F(x)$ which guarantee that $\pi^\ell(R, \gamma)$ has the following property.

$$\pi^\ell_{11}(R, \gamma) = -f(R) - \gamma f'(R) < 0. \tag{3}$$

Given condition (3), $\pi^\ell(R, \gamma)$ is a concave function of R for fixed γ, as in Figure 8.1, and there exists some R^* such that $\pi^\ell(R, \gamma)$ achieves a unique maximum for fixed γ with $R = R^*$. Let r^* denote the maximum possible expected return to the lender, where $r^* = \pi^\ell(R, \gamma)$.

Assuming that $r^* > r_\ell$, so that the credit market does not shut down entirely, there can be two possible outcomes, as in Williamson (1987). First, there may exist an equilibrium where every entrepreneur receives a loan. Here, we have $r \le r^*$ and the quantity of loans is $1 - \alpha$, where

$$r = r_\ell + \left(\frac{1 - \alpha}{\alpha}\right)(r_u - r_\ell)$$

and R is determined by $\pi^\ell(R, \gamma) = r$. This equilibrium exists if and only if

$$r_\ell + \left(\frac{1 - \alpha}{\alpha}\right)(r_u - r_\ell) \le r^*.$$

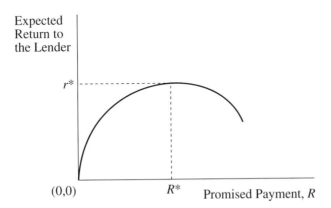

Figure 8.1   *Expected return to the lender as a function of the promised payment*

Alternatively, the equilibrium may exhibit credit rationing. Here, in equilibrium each entrepreneur offers a loan contract on the market with a promised payment of R^*, and each lender accepts a contract at random. We have $r = r^*$, and the loan quantity is q, which is the solution to

$$r^* = r_\ell + \left(\frac{q}{\alpha}\right)(r_u - r_\ell). \tag{4}$$

This equilibrium exists if and only if the solution to (4), $q < 1 - \alpha$, that is,

$$r_\ell + \left(\frac{1-\alpha}{\alpha}\right)(r_u - r_\ell) > r^*.$$

Thus, the equilibrium is unique, and either displays rationing or does not. All borrowers here are identical, but in equilibrium some may not receive loans while others do. In a rationing equilibrium, the entrepreneurs who do not receive loans are worse off than the entrepreneurs who do, but would-be borrowers cannot bid loans away from those who receive them, as any alternative to the equilibrium loan contract will only yield a lower expected return to the lender.[7]

The rationing equilibrium represents a situation that some government credit programs seem designed to 'correct'. A group of similar (identical in this case) would-be borrowers is treated asymmetrically by the credit market, which might lead to the inference that the market is not working efficiently, and that matters can be improved with government help. Furthermore, note that in any credit rationing equilibrium the market return, r, is less than the social return from investment.[8] Investment projects that go unfunded would yield a return higher than r if funded, as entrepreneurs always receive some of the surplus. We will consider two types of government credit programs in turn. The first is a program of direct loans, like those administered by the Farmers Home Administration (FmHA) and (to some extent) the Small Business Administration (SBA). The second is a program of loan guarantees, similar to much of the activity carried out by the SBA, and also to the mortgage insurance programs of the Federal Housing Administration (FHA).

1.3 Direct Government Loans

Suppose that the government makes direct loans at the market loan interest rate, R, financing these loans by borrowing from lenders at the risk free interest rate r. The government is assumed to have access to the same verification technology as the private sector, and faces the same prohibition on the use of randomised verification strategies. Now, whether or not there is credit rationing in equilibrium, it is an immediate result that the equilibrium will be invariant to the quantity of government lending, g. Here, the government has no advantage in lending over the private sector, and acts in the same way as would a private lender.[9] Acting in this way, therefore, the government simply displaces a quantity of private lending equal to g. Gale (1990a) obtains a similar result in an adverse selection credit rationing model where debt contracts are imposed.

The only way the government can alter the allocation of resources in this framework is through tax and subsidy schemes. For example, if the government has access to lump sum taxes and transfers on lenders and entrepreneurs, then resources could be transferred directly from lenders to borrowers in period 1, and back again in period 2. The government would need to incur verification costs in taxing borrowers, but an appropriate set of taxes and transfers would imply that the quantity of projects financed would correctly reflect the social return from investment. A scheme like this would seem to assume too great an advantage for the government. Also, such a scheme would not result in a Pareto improvement over the case with no government involvement, as some borrowers would necessarily be worse off.

1.4 Government Loan Guarantees

Suppose now that the government guarantees to each lender some fixed fraction of the promised payment on a loan. That is, the government guarantees that the lender will receive no less than vR, where $0 < v < 1$ and R is the promised payment. Lenders pay an insurance premium, P, which is constant across states of the world, and is treated as fixed by lenders. The premium is set so as to make the loan guarantee program self-financing. Assume here that verification is publicly observable, so that the government knows if a lender verifies the return on an entrepreneur's project, and what the return is if verification takes place.[10] Here, the government will never make a payment to a private lender unless the borrower fails to meet the promised payment, verification takes place, and $x < vR$.

The expected return to the lender is now

$$\pi^\ell(R, \gamma, v) = \int_0^{vR} (vR - \gamma) \, dF(x) + \int_{vR}^R (x - \gamma) \, dF(x) \qquad (5)$$
$$+ R[1 - F(R)] - P,$$

Which can be rewritten using integration by parts as

$$\pi^\ell(R, \gamma, v) = R - \int_{vR}^R F(x) \, dx - \gamma F(R) - P. \qquad (6)$$

Again, the lender treats the premium, P, as fixed, but the government sets P so that the loan guarantee program breaks even, that is,

$$P = \int_0^{vR} (vR - x)\, dF(x). \tag{7}$$

From equation (6), we have

$$\pi_1^{\ell}(R, \gamma, v) = 1 - F(R) + vF(vR) - \gamma f(R),$$

so that

$$\pi_{13}^{\ell}(R, \gamma, v) = F(vR) + v^2 f(vR) > 0.$$

Therefore, for given P, each lender perceives that the first partial derivative of their expected return function with respect to the loan interest rate is higher for each loan interest rate. In Figure 8.2, we show a typical expected return function with $P = v = 0$, and, holding constant the probability distribution of the return on the investment project, $F(x)$, and the verification cost, γ, the lender's perceived expected return function with $P > 0$ and $v > 0$.

Now, suppose that there is no credit rationing in an equilibrium without loan guarantees, that is $P = v = 0$, and the loan quantity is $q = 1 - \alpha$. The equilibrium loan payment, $\hat{R}$, and the equilibrium risk-free market return, $\hat{r}$, are determined as in Figure 8.3. If the government implements a loan guarantee program with $v > 0$ and P determined by (7), then equilibrium interest rates are invariant to the loan guarantee program, as in Figure 8.3. We obtain this result

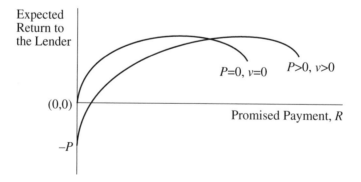

Figure 8.2   Effect of a loan guarantee on the lender's expected return function

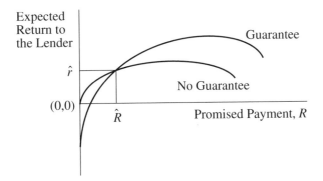

Figure 8.3   Effects of a loan guarantee when there is no credit rationing

by substituting for P in (5) using (7), and given that $\hat{R} < R^*$ since, with the loan guarantee, $\pi^{\ell}_{13}(R, \gamma, v) > 0$.

In this case where, in the absence of loan guarantees, there is initially a credit rationing equilibrium, as in Figure 8.4, we have an initial equilibrium loan payment R_1, and an equilibrium risk free market return r_1. Here, when loan guarantees are introduced, the equilibrium will now be one with a higher payment, R_2, and a lower risk free market return, r_2. The equilibrium with a loan guarantee must be at a point where the perceived expected return function for the lender with a loan guarantee intersects the expected return function with no guarantee (that is, the loan guarantee program is self-financing). Therefore, with a loan guarantee, we must have $r_2 \leq r_1$, so that there will be

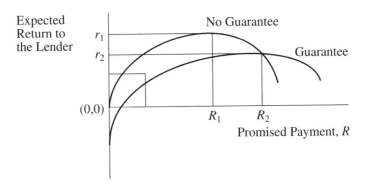

Figure 8.4   Effects of a loan guarantee in a credit rationing equilibrium

rationing in equilibrium. Since $\pi^{\ell}_{13}(R, \gamma, v) > 0$, we get $R_2 > R_1$ and $r_2 > r_1$. As there must be rationing, the equilibrium occurs at the maximum of the perceived expected return function for the lender.

With a loan guarantee, the lower market return to lenders implies that the supply of loanable funds will be lower, and more borrowers will be rationed than without the loan guarantee program. In this case, the effect of loan guarantees is perverse. Such programs are typically intended to promote more lending, which should make all credit market participants better off. Here, all agents are worse off in terms of expected utility. Lenders face lower interest rates, borrowers face higher interest rates, and the probability of receiving a loan for each entrepreneur is lower.

Here, the reason that loan guarantees have at best no effect, and at worst reduce welfare for everyone, is that they distort an otherwise optimal contractual arrangement between borrowers and lenders. One way to correct the harmful effects of the loan guarantee program is to face lenders with a premium schedule that reflects the higher risk inherent in higher loan interest rates. In fact, if lenders face a premium schedule given by (7) then, substituting in (6), the expected return function faced by a lender is independent of v, and the loan guarantee program is neutral, which is optimal.

2. CREDIT WITH COSTLY SCREENING

In this section, we consider a credit market model with adverse selection and costly screening of loan applicants. This model is similar to the one studied in Wang and Williamson (1993).[11] It is related to the costly state verification approach in the previous section, in that there exists private information that can be revealed at a cost, and debt contracts will prove to be the optimal contractual arrangement. However, there are two important differences between this type of model and the costly state verification approach. First, in this model there is a cost of screening borrowers *ex ante*, rather than a cost of verifying the *ex post* return. Arguably, screening costs are more important to the operation of real-world credit markets than *ex post* auditing costs. Second, debt contracts in this context are in some ways more robust. For example, debt contracts survive here even with randomization, which is not the case in costly state verification models.

2.1   The Model

There are two periods, 1 and 2, and a continuum of agents. The agents are of three types: lenders, type b borrowers, and type g borrowers. The fraction of borrowers who are type g is δ, where $0 < \delta < 1$, and the fraction of all agents who are lenders is strictly greater than the fraction who are borrowers.

In period 1, each lender has one unit of an investment good, which can either be exchanged with a borrower for some promise to pay consumption goods in period 2, or invested for one period at the risk free return r, which we treat here as fixed. Lenders maximize the expected value of $u^{\ell}(c, e) = c - e$, where c is consumption in period 2, and e is effort in screening borrowers in period 1.

Borrowers have no endowment in period 1, and maximize the expected value of period 2 consumption. Each borrower has access to an investment project which requires 1 unit of the investment good to fund in period 1, and yields a random quantity of the consumption good, x, in period 2 if the project is funded. Here, x is public information, in contrast to the costly state verification model studied in the previous section. The return on the investment project of a borrower of type i is distributed according to the probability distribution function $F_i(\cdot)$, where $i = g, b$. The associated probability density function is $f_i(\cdot)$. Assume that $f_i(x) > 0$ for $x \in [0, 1]$, $f_i(x) = 0$ otherwise, that $f_i(x)$ is continuous on $[0, 1]$, and that

$$\frac{f_g(x)}{f_b(x)} < \frac{f_g(y)}{f_b(y)}; \, x, y \in [0, 1]; \, x < y. \tag{8}$$

Condition (8) is essentially identical to the monotone likelihood ratio property often assumed in principal agent problems with moral hazard, and it implies first-order stochastic dominance of $F_b(\cdot)$ by $F_g(\cdot)$, that is $F_b(x) > F_g(x)$, $x \in (0, 1)$. Letting μ_i denote the mean investment return for a type i borrower, we assume that $\mu_i > r$, for $i = g, b$.

If borrowers are not screened, then type is private information. However, each lender has access to a technology with which to observe a borrower's type at a cost of γ units of effort in period 1, where $\gamma \geq 0$. A given borrower can contact at most one lender in period 1, but a lender may contact as many borrowers as she wishes.

2.2 Equilibrium

The equilibrium concept used here is similar to the one in Rothschild and Stiglitz (1977). Contracts offered by lenders to borrowers in period 1 consist of payment schedule/screening probability pairs $[R_i(x), \pi_i]$, $i = g, b$, where $R_i(x)$ denotes the period 2 payment from a type i borrower to the lender, and π_i is the probability that the lender uses the screening technology to verify the type of an agent claiming to be type i when that agent applies for a loan.[12]

Equilibrium contracts must satisfy five conditions. First, they must be feasible. That is,

$$0 \le R_i(x) \le x, x \in [0, 1], i = g, b.$$

Second, the contracts are constrained to be monotonic.

$$x \le y \Rightarrow R_i(x) \le R_i(y); x, y \in [0, 1], i = g, b. \tag{9}$$

This monotonicity restriction can be justified if it is possible for borrowers to fake higher levels of output. For example, suppose that borrowers can borrow temporarily in period 2 before their output quantity is publicly observed. If the payment schedule did not satisfy (9), then for some realizations the borrower could do better by borrowing temporarily in period 2 (at a zero interest rate) so as to make a lower payment to the lender. Third, the contracts should be incentive compatible, or

$$\int_0^1 R_i(x) \, dF_i(x) \le (1 - \pi_j) \int_0^1 R_j(x) \, dF_i(x) + \pi_j \mu_i; \, i, j = g, b. \tag{10}$$

On the left side of (10) is the expected cost to a type i borrower of applying for and receiving a loan when reporting her true type, while the right side is the expected cost when the borrower applies and misreports her type as j. Here, the borrower is screened with probability π_j. If screening does not take place, then the borrower's expected cost is the expected payment for a type j agent, and if the borrower is screened and found to be lying, then she is denied a loan and the expected cost is μ_i. Fourth, a contract should earn zero expected profits given the agents who accept it. Fifth, there should exist no alternative contract that some agent type strictly prefers to the equilibrium contract offered to their type, and that earns nonnegative expected profits given the agents who accept it.

As is shown in Wang and Williamson (1993), the equilibrium has some features in common with the equilibrium in the Rothschild-Stiglitz (1977) insurance model. In particular, if an equilibrium exists, it is a separating equilibrium where different contracts are offered to each type of borrower, and an equilibrium does not exist for some parameter values. Three important properties of the equilibrium are:

1. Type g borrowers are screened with positive probability, while type b borrowers are not screened. That is, $\pi_g > 0$ and $\pi_b = 0$.
2. The unique equilibrium contract for a type g borrower is a debt contract, that is $R_g(x) = x$ for $x \in [0, \bar{R}_g]$, and $R_g(x) = \bar{R}_g$ for $x \in [\bar{R}_g, 1]$ for some constant $\bar{R}_g \in [0, 1]$.

3. There exists a continuum of equilibrium contracts for a type b borrower, and one of these contracts is a debt contract, characterized by the promised payment $\bar{R}_b \in [0, 1]$.

We can determine π_g, $\bar{R}_g$, and $\bar{R}_b$ as the solution to the following three equations.

$$\bar{R}_b - \int_0^{\bar{R}_b} F_b(x) = r, \tag{11}$$

$$\bar{R}_g - \int_0^{\bar{R}_g} F_g(x)\, dx = \pi_g \gamma + r, \tag{12}$$

$$r = (1 - \pi_g) \left[\bar{R}_g - \int_0^{\bar{R}_g} F_b(x)\, dx \right] + \pi_g \mu_b. \tag{13}$$

Here, equations (11) and (12) are zero expected profit conditions for the contracts offered to type b and type g agents, respectively. That is, the expected payment to the lender must equal the expected screening cost plus the opportunity return which could be earned elsewhere by the lender. Equation (13) is the incentive constraint (10) for $i = b$ and $j = g$. That is, the incentive constraint is binding for a type b agent. It is straightforward to show that the solution to (11), (12), and (13) satisfies the incentive constraint for a type g agent, that is, (10) for $i = g$ and $j = b$, with strict inequality, or $\bar{R}_b > \bar{R}_g$.

In equilibrium, type b borrowers are faced with higher interest rates than are type g borrowers. To induce borrowers to self select, type g borrowers must be screened with positive probability. Since screening is costly, lenders wish to minimize the screening cost so as to offer the best possible contract to type g borrowers. This is accomplished by offering debt contracts to type g borrowers. Condition (8) implies that a type g borrower tends to have more probability mass in the upper end of her return distribution than does the type b borrower. Therefore, if the type g agent is offered a debt contract, this does as much as possible to manipulate payment schedules in a way that the type g agent likes and the type b agent does not. This induces self-selection at the lowest possible expected screening cost.

An equilibrium does not exist in the case where there is a pooling contract which both agents prefer to the contracts which solve (11), (12), and (13). In Wang and Williamson (1993), it is shown that an equilibrium exists if and only if $\bar{R} \geq \bar{R}_g$, where $\bar{R}$ is the solution to

$$\delta \left[\bar{R} - \int_0^{\bar{R}} F_g(x)_{dx} \right] + (1 - \delta) \left[\bar{R} - \int_0^{\bar{R}} F_b(x)_{dx} \right] = r, \tag{14}$$

and $\bar{R}_g$ is determined by (11), (12), and (13). Here, $\bar{R}$ characterizes a pooling debt contract offered to both types with no screening of either type, and this pooling contract earns zero expected profits if it attracts both types in the relative proportions that exist in the population. It is shown in Wang and Williamson (1993) that, for fixed γ and r, an equilibrium exists for $\delta \leq \delta^*$ for some $\delta^* > 0$, and does not exist otherwise. Also, for fixed r and δ, an equilibrium exists for $\gamma \leq \gamma^*$ for some $\gamma^* > 0$, and does not exist otherwise. An increase in γ leads to an increase in the loan interest rate faced by a type g borrower, and to a decrease in the screening probability.

2.3 Government Credit Programs

In this model, the government credit programs considered in the previous section will have no effect. Direct government loans that have contractual arrangements identical to private loans, for type g and b borrowers, will not alter equilibrium interest rates, and neither will government loan guarantees for either borrower type. These two types of programs do not affect incentives for borrowers, and therefore self-selection is achieved in the same manner with the government program as without it. We will therefore consider two alternative government credit programs which will have important incentive effects here: (1) government lending to those denied private credit, and (2) government lending at subsidized interest rates. Many federal credit programs for housing, agriculture, and small business contain restrictions of lending to those without access to private credit, and much of this lending activity would not be profitable for a private intermediary, and therefore involves subsidization.

Government lending to borrowers denied private credit

Thus far, we have assumed that a borrower can contact at most one lender in period 1. Here, we will assume that a borrower can contact one private lender, and can then contact the government. Borrowers are only potentially denied credit in a separating equilibrium, where a type b borrower claiming to be a type g borrower is caught cheating with probability π_g, in which case the borrower does not receive a loan. In the separating equilibrium discussed above, no one is ever denied credit in equilibrium, as the incentive constraint (13) implies that type b agents weakly prefer to accept the contract offered to their own type. Suppose, however, that the government implements a credit program offering a debt contract with a promised payment of R_p, to any borrower who is denied credit. Assume that, if the government makes a loss or profit on this lending, the required taxes or transfers fall on agents other than lenders and borrowers in the credit market. Effectively, government credit will only go to agents who apply for credit under a separating contract, misreport their type, and upon screening are found to have cheated.

Suppose first that, in the absence of this government credit program, there exists an equilibrium π_g, $\bar{R}_g$, and $\bar{R}_b$, the solutions to (11), (12), and (13). With the government credit program in place, the incentive constraint for a type b agent is altered from (13) to

$$r = (1 - \pi_g)\left[\bar{R}_g - \int_0^{\bar{R}_g} F_b(x)\, dx\right] + \pi_g\left[R_p - \int_0^{R_p} F_b(x)\, dx\right]. \qquad (15)$$

A separating equilibrium is now the solution to (11), (12), and (15). It is straightforward to show that a solution exists, and that this solution is unique, if and only if $R_p \geq R_b$, where R_b is the solution to (11). Substituting for π_g in (12) using (15), we get an equation which solves for $\bar{R}_g$.

$$\bar{R}_g - \int_0^{\bar{R}_g} F_g(x)\, dx = r + \gamma\left[\frac{r - \bar{R}_g + \int_0^{\bar{R}_g} F_b(x)\, dx}{R_p - \int_0^{R_p} F_b(x)\, dx - \bar{R}_g + \int_0^{\bar{R}_g} F_b(x)\, dx}\right] \qquad (16)$$

Supposing that $R_p \geq \bar{R}_b$, and letting $\bar{R}_g^*$ denote the solution to (16), $\bar{R}_g^*$ decreases as R_p increases. Here, we get the noninterventionist solution for $R_p = 1$, which implies that, with $\bar{R}_b \leq R_p < 1$, type g borrowers face higher interest rates with the government credit program than without it. Also note, from (12) that, since $\bar{R}_g^* > \bar{R}_g$ we also have $\pi_g^* > \pi_g$, so that type g agents are screened with higher probability when the government credit program is in place. As the government credit program causes the loan interest rate faced by a type g agent to rise, it is now possible that an equilibrium will not exist, where existence was obtained without the government credit program. That is, we could have $\bar{R}_g^* > \bar{R} \geq \bar{R}_g$, where $\bar{R}$ solves (14).

Here, offering loans to agents who are denied private credit simply increases the incentive for type b agents to misrepresent their type, which in turn implies that lenders must put more effort into screening in order to induce self-selection. As expected screening costs are higher in making loans to type g agents, these agents must bear higher interest rates. Type b agents are no better off, as they face the same interest rate, given by the solution to (11). Thus, in this case the government credit program simply exacerbates incentive problems in the credit market, making some agents worse off without making anyone better off, or causing a problem of non-existence of equilibrium.

In the case where $\bar{R} < R_p \leq \bar{R}_b$, where $\bar{R}$ solves (14), an equilibrium does not exist. Here, from (15), there exists no verification probability that will force self-selection. That is, the loan contract offered by the government to those denied credit is sufficiently attractive that a type b borrower posing as a type g borrower is not penalized enough if caught cheating and denied a private loan. There does not exist a pooling equilibrium as, given that $\bar{R} < R_p$, a

contract can always be offered that type g borrowers strictly prefer to a pooling contract, and that does not attract any type b borrowers, even given the
favourable loan contract offered by the government.

If $\bar{R} > R_p$, then an equilibrium always exists, but it is a pooling equilibrium,
with the loan contract $\bar{R}$ satisfying (14). Here, R_p is sufficiently low that, in the
pooling equilibrium, there is no contract that could be offered that would make
type g agents better off while earning nonnegative expected profits and not
attracting any type b agents. That is, the government loan contract offered to
those denied private credit is so attractive that it is impossible to induce
borrowers to self-select. If an equilibrium exists in the absence of the government credit program, then it must be the case that $\bar{R} > \bar{R}_g$, that is, type g
borrowers are worse off with the government program than without, while $\bar{R} <
\bar{R}_b$, so that type b agents are better off. An equilibrium may not exist without
the government credit program, in which case all agents are clearly better off
with government intervention than without it.[13]

Here, offers of government loans to borrowers denied private credit alter
the pay-offs to type b agents claiming to be type g agents, in a way that encourages cheating. If the offered interest rate on government loans is set too high,
then the incentive effect causes a decrease in expected utility for some agents
and no change for others, or it leads to non-existence of equilibrium. If the
interest rate on government loans is set sufficiently low, then the equilibrium
is not Pareto comparable to the equilibrium without government intervention.
Type g agents are worse off with government intervention, while type b agents
are better off.[14] In this case, government intervention can yield existence of
equilibrium when an equilibrium would not exist otherwise. Thus, this type of
government loan program in a credit market with adverse selection need not
be a bad thing. Note also that, in equilibrium, there is no direct cost to government lending activity, as the government only makes offers to lend that are
never accepted, but that agents take into account in making their decisions.

Subsidized government lending

Now, consider a government loan program of direct lending, whereby the
government writes debt contracts with private agents with a promised payment
R_p. We will assume that a borrower can contact the government and then
contact one private lender in period 1. Any subsidy in this program is financed
by taxes that fall on agents other than the lenders and borrowers in the credit
market.

Suppose first that an equilibrium exists in the absence of government intervention, characterized by the interest rates $\bar{R}_g$ and $\bar{R}_b$, and the screening probability π_g which solve (11), (12), and (13). If the interest rate on government loans
is set such that $\bar{R}_g \leq R_p < \bar{R}_b$, then the equilibrium depends on the quantity of
government lending which takes place. If the government offers a quantity of

loans which is less than the number of type *b* borrowers, then equilibrium interest rates are unaffected by government intervention. Type *b* borrowers prefer a government loan, and so apply to the government first, but the government must ration credit. Some type *b* borrowers are then forced to borrow at the higher private loan rate, and type *g* borrowers face the same interest rate as without intervention. Thus, the type *b* agents who receive subsidized loans are better off, but all other agents are indifferent to the government intervention. In the case where the government serves all type *b* borrowers, let $\bar{R}_g^*$ and π_g^* denote, respectively, the promised payment and the screening probability for a type *g* agent. Here, $\bar{R}_g^*$ and π_g^* solve the following two equations.

$$\bar{R}_g^* - \int_0^{\bar{R}_g^*} F_g(x)\, dx = \pi_g^* \gamma + r; \tag{17}$$

$$R_p - \int_0^{R_p} F_b(x)\, dx = (1 - \pi_g^*)\left[\bar{R}_g^* - \int_0^{\bar{R}_g^*} F_b(x)\, dx\right] + \pi_g^* \mu_b. \tag{18}$$

Here, since $R_p < \bar{R}_b$ the solution we obtain has the property that $\bar{R}_g^* < \bar{R}_g$ and $\pi_g^* < \pi_g$. That is, since the government loan interest rate is more attractive to type *g* borrowers than the interest rate they would receive on private loans in the absence of government intervention, the government loan program acts to mitigate the incentive problem in the credit market. Thus, type *g* borrowers are screened less intensively, so that lenders face lower costs and therefore offer type *g* borrowers a lower interest rate. In this case, the subsidy makes all borrowers better off.

In cases where an equilibrium does not exist without government intervention, the introduction of this subsidized government loan program could produce existence. That is, since $\bar{R}_g^* < \bar{R}_g$, it could be the case that $\bar{R}_g^* < \bar{R} < \bar{R}_g$, where $\bar{R}$ solves (14). Here, lenders are indifferent to government intervention, and all borrowers are strictly better off with intervention.

The final case we need to consider is one where $R_p < \bar{R}_g$. First suppose, at the extreme, that the government lends to all borrowers at the gross interest rate R_p. This would clearly make all borrowers better off than they would be without government intervention. Second, suppose the government rations funds, allocating loans at random, but makes no attempt to discriminate among borrowers according to type. Here, the credit market equilibrium will be identical with and without government intervention, but the quantity of private lending will be smaller. Both borrower types strictly prefer government loans to private loans, so the fraction of borrowers receiving government loans who are type *g* will be δ, the population fraction. Those getting government loans are better off than they would be without the government lending program, and others are indifferent. Third, suppose that the government wishes to target type *b* borrowers for government lending, and attempts to produce self-selection by screening borrowers. This scheme will not work here, as borrowers have the option of borrowing from a private lender if denied credit by the government.

A more interesting setup to consider here (and one that eliminates the criticism that the government is treated differently in this section from the private sector) is one in which borrowers can contact a most one lender during the period; that is, if a borrower contacts the government, then the borrower does not have the option of obtaining private credit. Given this assumption, there is the potential that the government could successfully screen borrowers by (1) modifying the contract offered to those receiving government loans; (2) rationing government loans; (3) using the costly screening technology.

Exploring this fully is outside the scope of this paper, but we can make the following conjectures about results. Given that the objective is to confine government lending to type *b* agents, a contract that would be most desirable for type *b* agents relative to type *g* agents is an all-or-nothing contract where the payment by the borrower is zero if $x < s$, and x for $x \geq s$, for some constant $s \in [0, 1]$. Rationing schemes also aid in generating the correct incentives, as type *g* agents have more to lose from being denied a loan. Finally, costly screening works as previously, except that type *b* borrowers are screened rather than type *g* borrowers. With any of these schemes, the equilibrium will be identical to the one with no government intervention unless a scheme is imposed where all type *b* agents apply for a government loan in equilibrium. In this case, there need not be any screening of loan applicants in the market for private credit. As a result, type *g* agents do not bear any screening costs, and they must then be better off than without government intervention. Type *b* agents will also be better off.

In this type of model, subsidized government lending programs typically make all credit market participants at least as well off as in the absence of intervention. We get this result because subsidized lending generally introduces slack into incentive constraints, and therefore the expected costs of screening private loan applicants can fall. However, subsidized lending is clearly not a Pareto improvement here, as the subsidies need to be financed through taxes on some agents, and if the government sets its interest rates sufficiently low, then it may also need to incur the costs of screening out groups of borrowers that it does not wish to target.

3.   FINANCIAL INTERMEDIATION AND PASS-THROUGH SECURITIES

In studying some types of government loan programs, it is necessary to consider the financial intermediation process in more detail than in sections 1 and 2, where there was direct lending from ultimate borrowers to ultimate lenders. The US government, through its agencies, engages in the promotion of forms of financial intermediation that seem designed to correct for perceived deficiencies in the private financial intermediation process. Principal among these schemes are programs to ensure a secondary market in private loans, through the trading of 'pass-through' securities. These pass-through securities are assets backed by a portfolio of loans, most typically mortgage loans, some with guarantees from federal agencies. The pass-through securities of the Government National Mortgage Administration (GNMA), for example, are backed by mortgages insured by the Federal Housing Administration (FHA) or guaranteed by the Veterans Administration (VA), and the pass-through securities themselves are backed by the US government. Pass-through securities issued by the Federal National Mortgage Administration, a private corporation, have no explicit government backing, but are implicitly backed by the federal government.

Each of the models in sections 1 and 2 is capable, with minor modification, of generating a financial intermediary structure endogenously. In the costly state verification model in Section 2, we can simply follow Williamson (1986), and assume that investment projects each require k units of the investment good in period 1 in order to operate, where $k > 1$. An optimal financial structure then has all lending done by large financial intermediaries, which lend to a large number of borrowers, and borrow from a large number of depositors. An intermediary writes debt contracts with borrowers, and makes risk-free payments of r units of consumption to each depositor in period 2, by exploiting the law of large numbers. The monitoring of borrowers is delegated to the financial intermediary (Diamond, 1984) which would have an incentive to misreport its portfolio returns to depositors (and would therefore need to be monitored) if it were not fully diversified. Thus, financial intermediation serves here to economize on verification costs; if there were direct lending, each of the k lenders who lent to an entrepreneur would have to verify the investment project's return in the event of default.

In the model of section 2, we can obtain a similar 'delegated screening' result (see Wang and Williamson, 1993 for more details). Suppose, as with the costly state verification model, that each borrower's investment project requires k units of the investment good to operate, where $k > 1$. Again, a perfectly diversified intermediary writes debt contracts with borrowers and offers depositors a certain return. Here, only loans made to type g borrowers are intermediated in equilibrium, as loans to type b borrowers do not require costly screening. In this model, intermediation economizes on screening costs, in that direct lending requires that each lender screen the borrower, but with intermediation each borrower is screened only once.

If we consider either the costly state verification model with financial intermediation, or the costly screening model with financial intermediation, there is no role for the government to play in promoting pass-through securities. In these models, securitization is simply a form of financial intermediation, but these models contain no unrealized gains to intermediation activity in equilibrium. Therefore, in these models the issuance of pass-through securities would not be profitable for a private lender, and it would not be welfare-improving for the government to promote this activity.

To gain some perspective on mortgage-backed (and related) securities, and their role in a US context, it is useful to examine experience in other countries. In Canada, for example, loan sales are virtually nonexistent in the mortgage market. Mortgage loans are negotiated by chartered banks and other depository institutions and are then held in the asset portfolios of those institutions. An important difference between Canada and the United States is Canada's branch banking system, which permits banks and other mortgage lenders to diversify broadly. In the United States, a patchwork of branch banking restrictions and other regulatory constraints tends to limit the diversification that an individual institution is able to achieve. Therefore, given existing banking regulations, government intervention to promote a market in mortgage-backed securities may well be welfare improving. This government-promoted intermediation activity simply provides the diversification that the private sector is unable to supply because of regulatory impediments. However, the form that intermediation takes in the United States is second best, in that there is a replication of screening and monitoring costs. For example, borrowers in the mortgage market are screened first by a particular lending institution or mortgage broker, and may later be screened (possibly at random) when the mortgages are sold to FNMA for packaging. If the loans are negotiated and held by the same financial intermediary, the screening costs are only incurred once. Therefore, it would seem that the first best solution would be to eliminate regulations that promote unit banking. This would likely do away with the need for markets in securities backed by private loans.

4. SUMMARY AND CONCLUSION

Here, we have studied the effects of some government credit programs in two private information models of credit markets. The first of these models is a setup with costly state verification, where a borrower's investment project return is observable by a lender at a cost. The second model is an adverse selection environment, where a borrower's type is private information, but where there exists a costly screening technology that reveals type. Together, these models exhibit many of the important characteristics useful in determining what role for government credit programs, if any, arises because of informational frictions. In particular, the two models have elements of moral hazard, adverse selection, costly information acquisition, incentive problems as determinants of optimal contractual arrangements, and equilibrium credit rationing.

In the costly state verification model, a program of direct government loans (at market interest rates and with the same contractual arrangements as private loans) has no effect, even if there is credit rationing without the government program. Government lending simply displaces an equal quantity of private lending. Government loan guarantees have no effect on the quantity of lending or interest rates, if there is no credit rationing prior to government intervention. If an equilibrium without intervention exhibits credit rationing, then a loan guarantee program has perverse effects. Interest rates faced by lenders (borrowers) fall (rise), and credit rationing becomes more severe.

The costly screening model has the property that, in general, government loan programs will have no effect unless they alter the incentives of borrowers or are subsidized. Government loans to borrowers denied private credit tend to increase screening costs for lenders and to increase interest rates for some groups of borrowers. If government loan interest rates are set appropriately, then the welfare of targeted groups may increase. Subsidized government loans make the targeted recipients of the loans better off, but they can also make other borrowers better off by reducing incentive problems. If government lending becomes more attractive, then misrepresenting type becomes less attractive for some borrowers, screening costs fall for lenders, and interest rates decrease.

An important form of government intervention in credit markets in the United States is the promotion of secondary markets for private loans. Given the current regulatory environment, this type of intervention may be welfare improving, but in a world with no regulatory impediments to diversification by private financial intermediaries, intervention is most likely suboptimal. It can be argued that markets in 'pass-through' securities are an inefficient form of financial intermediation, which can thrive only because of the unit banking restrictions which make private financial intermediation inefficient.

Many types of government credit market interventions which are potentially important have not been considered here. In particular, we have ignored government deposit insurance and its interaction with financial regulations, mainly because we feel that there are not ready-made models that deal with deposit insurance in a satisfactory way. Also, we have only touched on issues associated with the structure of financial intermediaries. As both models studied here can deliver intermediary structures endogenously, this is an area where this work can be extended.

NOTES

1. The comments of William Gale, Joseph Haubrich, Jeff Lacker, Bruce Smith, and Cheng Wang were helpful in revising this chapter. The author is grateful for financial support from the National Science Foundation, award no. SBR 93-08819.
2. Another model of optimal debt contracting is Lacker (1993a).
3. This is similar to a result in Gale (1990a).
4. A related model with costly screening is in De Meza and Webb (1988).
5. The flavor of this result is similar to those in Smith and Stutzer (1989) and Gale (1990b). In their setups, loan subsidies to the wrong type can worsen adverse selection problems.
6. In Townsend (1979, 1988), and Mookherjee and Png (1989), it is shown that a random verification strategy can in general improve on any deterministic verification strategy. However, Boyd and Smith (1993) show that the quantitative improvement is small for plausible parameter values.
7. It is not clear whether or not rationing equilibria can exist with random verification. Rationing equilibria are possible in this case if expected verification costs increase as the expected return to the lender increases. This might occur since there would be a greater incentive to cheat with a higher expected return to the lender, requiring that verification probabilities increase in at least some states.
8. This is also true in an equilibrium with no rationing.
9. Note here that there is no role for financial intermediation as, for example, in Williamson (1986). Here, lending is just as efficient when carried out through individuals as through well-diversified intermediaries.
10. It would not make any qualitative difference for the results if verification were not observable. The government would then have to verify the return to the entrepreneur when a lender makes a claim to a government payment. This then makes the government loan program even less efficient than with the assumptions we make but, as will be shown, loan guarantees are inefficient even without replication of verification costs.
11. A related model is De Meza and Webb (1988), in which there is a similar screening technology. De Meza and Webb do not have random screening, as is the case here, and they ignore the role of debt contracts in minimizing screening costs.
12. Note that the payment schedule faced by a borrower is independent of whether or not screening takes place. This contract structure would arise if we assumed a technology that allows the lender to commit to a particular screening strategy, but third parties could not observe whether or not screening takes place.
13. With 'nonexistence,' all lenders invest at the certain return r, and no borrower gets a loan. Thus, lenders are indifferent with respect to cases where credit market equilibria do and do not exist, and all borrowers are strictly worse off with nonexistence.
14. Smith and Stutzer (1989) and Gale (1990b) obtain results similar in flavor to some of the ones here. In their models, rationing of low-risk types achieves self-selection, and any government program that acts to relieve this credit rationing will exacerbate incentive problems.

REFERENCES

Boyd, John and Bruce D. Smith. 'The Welfare Costs of Absolute Priority Rules: Stochastic versus Nonstochastic Monitoring in a Costly State Verification Environment.' Working paper, Federal Reserve Bank of Minneapolis and Cornell University, 1993.

De Meza, David and David C. Webb. 'Credit Market Efficiency and Tax Policy in the Presence of Screening Costs.' *Journal of Public Economics* 36 (1988), 1–22.

Diamond, Douglas. 'Financial Intermediation and Delegated Monitoring.' *Review of Economic Studies* 51 (1984), 393–414.

Diamond, Douglas and Philip Dybvig. 'Bank Runs, Liquidity, and Deposit Insurance,' *Journal of Political Economy* 91 (June 1983), 401–19.

Gale, Douglas and Martin Hellwig. 'Incentive-Compatible Debt Contracts: The One-Period Problem.' *Review of Economic Studies* 52 (1985), 647–64.

Gale, William G. 'Federal Lending and the Market for Credit.' *Journal of Public Economics* 42 (1990a), 177–93.

Gale, William G. 'Collateral, Rationing, and Government Intervention in Credit Markets.' In *Asymmetric Information, Corporate Finance, and Investment*, edited by R. Glenn Hubbard, pp. 41–61, Chicago: University of Chicago Press (1990b).

Gale, William G. 'Economic Effects of Federal Credit Programs.' *American Economic Review* 81 (March 1991), 133–52.

Jaffee, Dwight and Joseph Stiglitz. 'Credit Rationing.' In *Handbook of Monetary Economics*, edited by Benjamin Friedman and Frank Hahn, pp. 838–5. Amsterdam: North-Holland, 1990.

Kareken, John and Neil Wallace. 'Deposit Insurance and Bank Regulation: A Partial Equilibrium Exposition.' *Journal of Business* 51 (1978), 413–38.

Lacker, Jeffry. 'Collateralized Debt as the Optimal Contract.' Working paper, Federal Reserve Bank of Richmond (1993a).

Lacker, Jeffry. 'Does Adverse Selection Justify Government Intervention in Loan Markets?' Working paper, Federal Reserve Bank of Richmond (1993b).

Mookherjee, Dilip and Ivan Png. 'Optimal Auditing, Insurance, and Redistribution.' *Quarterly Journal of Economics* 104 (May 1989), 399–416.

Rothschild, Michael and Joseph Stiglitz. 'Equilibrium in Competitive Insurance Markets: An Essay on the Economics of Imperfect Information.' *Quarterly Journal of Economics* 90 (1977), 629–50.

Smith, Bruce D. and Michael Stutzer. 'Credit Rationing and Government Loan Programs: A Welfare Analysis.' *American Real Estate and Urban Economics Association Journal* 17 (1989), 177–93.

Townsend, Robert. 'Optimal Contracts and Competitive Markets with Costly State Verification.' *Journal of Economic Theory* 21 (1979), 265–93.

Townsend, Robert. 'Information Constrained Insurance: The Revelation Principle Extended.' *Journal of Monetary Economics* 21 (May 1988), 411–50.

Wang, Cheng and Stephen D. Williamson. 'Adverse Selection in Credit Markets with Costly Screening.' Working Paper (1993), University of Iowa.

Williamson, Stephen D. 'Costly Monitoring, Financial Intermediation, and Equilibrium Credit Rationing,' *Journal of Monetary Economics* 18 (September 1986), 159–79.

Williamson, Stephen D. 'Costly Monitoring, Loan Contracts, and Equilibrium Credit Rationing.' *Quarterly Journal of Economics* 102 (February 1987), 135–46.

9. The demand for and supply of assurance[1]

Daniel B. Klein

QUALITY AND SAFETY RESTRICTIONS

Many agree that the consumption and production of bread are best left to voluntary processes. But many who favor free enterprise for such tangible goods oppose it for matters of quality and safety. The economist Jerome Rothenberg (1993) says: 'The market's myriad decentralized actions do not themselves ensure adequate safety. Centralized controls of various sorts are needed. These have been instituted in the form of regulations, constraints, information programs, licensing and certification' (172). Sometimes economists and others espouse quality and safety restrictions such as housing codes, occupational licensing, pharmaceutical approval, consumer product recalls, financial exchange regulations, and workplace safety regulations. I will offer a formulation of these matters that suggests that the broad reasons we favor free enterprise in bread carry over to quality and safety issues.

TRUSTERS AND PROMISERS

Many transactions involve promises of quality and safety that cannot be fully verified before the fact. One party decides whether to trust the other to deliver what is promised. A consumer decides whether to trust the grocer or pharmacist or mechanic to deliver the quality promised. A merchant decides whether to trust a prospective employee. A landlord decides whether to trust a prospective tenant.

The canonical example is a creditor deciding whether to trust a borrower who promises to repay the loan. The trust relationship is clarified by Figure 9.1. Truster (the creditor) decides either to trust or not trust Promiser (the prospective borrower). If Truster decides to trust, then Promiser decides whether to keep his promise or to cheat. If he keeps his promise, then both parties achieve a happy outcome – each receives a payoff of 1. If Promiser cheats, he gets a payoff of W and leaves Truster with a payoff of −1. But if

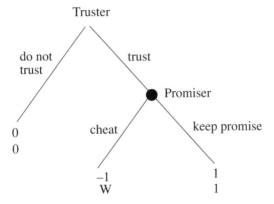

Figure 9.1   Truster decides whether to trust Promiser

Truster initially suspects that W is greater than 1, then she suspects that Promiser will cheat, and she decides not to trust in the first place. Deciding not to trust results in a payoff of zero for both players. A lack of trust is a social tragedy because it prevents society from achieving outcomes in which everyone is better off.

I employ the following analytic scheme:

- Promiser communicates the content of the promise.
- Truster heeds any of a variety of *assurances* of Promiser's trustworthiness.
- Truster thereby forms a level of *confidence* in Promiser's trustworthiness.
- The parties make the decisions as depicted in the Figure 9.1.

The parties may deviate from this scheme in many ways. They may negotiate the promise or restructure the relationship. They may make fulfillment incremental rather than all-at-once, withhold payment until the promise is fulfilled, demand a security deposit, commit collateral, or attach a warranty or guarantee. But with suitable interpretation, every transaction that entails an element of trust may be viewed in the manner suggested above.

THE DEMAND FOR ASSURANCE

Truster owns a car and the muffler is falling off. A local auto shop promises to do repairs honestly according to estimates. Truster seeks to produce for herself confidence in the promise, enough confidence to trust Promiser and to feel she has trusted responsibly. The inputs to her confidence production are any of the variety of assurances of trustworthiness. Thus, the entertaining of a promise ushers in a *demand for assurance.*

In the free enterprise system the demand for X tends to create opportunities for entrepreneurs to profit by supplying X.[2] When X is bread or toothpaste, we put a lot of stock in this dialectic. But when it comes to assurance, some academic economists suggest that information asymmetries and externalities cause free markets to 'fail.' The Nobel economist Kenneth Arrow (1974) says: 'Trust and similar values, loyalty or truthtelling, are examples of what the economist would call "externalities" . . . They are not commodities for which trade on the open market is technically possible or even meaningful' (23).

Too often, economists conceive of demand and supply in narrow terms – as the exchange or delivery of something the quantity of which can be measured along a horizontal axis. Equilibrium models (such as textbook supply-and-demand) blinker our understand of that intangible and highly particularistic transaction cost, assurance.[3] As noted, the demand for assurance corresponds to particular promises, so in making the final decision about auto repairs, Truster assesses the combination:

(Thing-promised and its price, Confidence (Assurance), Other transaction costs)

Economists have neglected the corresponding demand for assurance. They have neglected the range of entrepreneurs (including the truster and the promiser themselves) who may find profit in supplying assurance.[4] My contention is that the free enterprise system mobilizes an impressive, complex array of techniques to supply assurance, techniques which in one fashion or another overcome or circumvent any of the particular pitfalls stressed by market-failure theorists and other pessimists. Even for assurance, the essential dialectic holds up well, and restrictions, which are often very costly,[5] are typically unredeemed.

The supply of assurance uses many methods and takes many forms. I attempt to catalog the more important methods.

POINTED KNOWLEDGE CAN OBVIATE THE ROLE OF TRUST, OR PROVIDE A WARRANT FOR IT

The woman with the broken muffler seeks pointed knowledge about how to restore her vehicle to road-worthiness. In inquiring about her broken muffler, the woman may come to apprehend the technical measures required; she may even find that she is able to fix it herself. If she can trace a good information path, information is less asymmetric, and she might circumvent the need for trust.

But information that does nothing, in the narrow sense, to reduce asymmetry may be precisely what the woman needs. The woman may seek to discover not what is wrong with her muffler, but simply *who is an honest serviceman*. Her pointed knowledge may not provide a direct demonstration of quality, but rather an assurance of quality. Similarly, in rhetoric, our warrant for an idea may be, not a direct demonstration of its validity, but its endorsement by a trusted authority. The information she obtains may tell her, not about how her automobile operates, but how the serviceman operates. Assurance itself becomes a valued input to the transaction, and those who can provide it will tend to prosper.

In any sort of personalized service, an important factor is face-to-face contact. By talking we may get a clearer understanding of the content of promises. Clarity, repetition, and publicness reinforce accountability. Often personal rapport is a part of the experience characteristics or necessary to informed treatment.

Even when trusters have little technical knowledge of the trouble, they can get an impression as to whether the promiser is trustworthy. It is always a good sign when the promiser takes pains to explain why the trouble is occurring and what the various options for remedy are. An understanding of the trouble usually comes down to a few basic relationships. Explaining the situation helps to inform the truster and creates a measure of accountability for the promiser.[6] In a wide range of contexts the Internet is making it easy to probe the content of promises and integrity of promisers. Broadband technologies enable virtual face-to-face interaction.

INFORMAL CHANNELS OF INFORMATION SHARING

The housing development where I used to live has a home-owners association that issues a monthly newsletter. In one issue there appeared recommendations for a plumber, a painter, an electrician, a Volvo mechanic, a window cleaner, a carpet cleaner, a piano tuner, a woodworker, a brick-layer, a cabinet builder, a nanny, a handyman, a house cleaner, a furniture transporter, a floorer, two garage door servicemen, and seven house cleaners. My neighbors provided the recommendations, acting individually and giving their own phone numbers for details. People in the neighborhood know each other well enough to doubt that anyone would take a bribe to recommend a lousy nanny or handyman. The recommended individual is quite likely to be an illegal practitioner, even an illegal alien.

The newsletter serves as a sort of community concierge that directs members down happy information paths. The newsletter column exists because there are information problems to be solved. No one would get good-neighbor points or that pleasant helping feeling for helping to solve a non-existent problem.

The newsletter is a kind of local gossip. Gossip arises among family, friends, acquaintances, neighbors, and coworkers. It takes the forms of chatting, group meetings, correspondence, leaflets, bulletin boards, newsletters, local newspapers, Internet websites and e-mail. Anthropologist Sally Merry writes, 'gossip can be viewed as a means of storing and retrieving information.' 'It forms dossiers on each member of one's community: who is a good curer, who can be approached for loans . . . who is a good worker, and who is a thief.' In consequence, 'the individual seeks to manage and control the information spread about him or her through gossip' (pp. 275, 279). In the marketplace, promisers do likewise by maintaining quality. A study of consumer complaints against Coca-Cola products found that, of complainers unsatisfied with the company's response, the median told nine other people about her unsatisfactory experience (TARP, 1981, 14).

EXTENDED DEALINGS

Continuance, repetition, or information sharing – any of which are what I call *extended dealings* – open up vast institutional possibilities and provide fertile ground for trust. Our power to damage a promiser's reputation or to withdraw from dealings serves as a hostage that we hold against his promises.[7] Career promisers build and protect their reputation, sensing the truth in the saying, 'Time wounds all heels.'

Gossip, letters of recommendation, newsletters, data banks, consumer survey literature, information reporting bureaus, and referral agencies all make for extended dealings. These practices serve not only those trusters who make use of them, but also those who do not. Although a promiser often knows whether a particular truster has frequent dealings, he rarely knows whether the truster has extended dealings. The promiser does not see the truster gossip, and therefore, except in rare cases like the hapless motorist who pulls off the interstate for sudden repairs, the promiser must treat every truster as one who might be extending information to others. Lackadaisical trusters gain by the presence of pernickety trusters (except when they are being pernickety while we are waiting in line). Extended dealing exhibits positive externalities among the set of trusters, and there is an argument for government facilitation or performance of such services (Beales and Salop, 1980). But even though this sort of free-riding among the trusters does occur, the informed portion of the clientele does create a margin of punishment and reward, a margin that favors the trustworthy in the contest for commercial prosperity.

Extended dealings might benefit even trusters known to have isolated dealings. In the marketing of a standardized product, promisers cannot deal with trusters selectively. Even for services, protocol and the force of habit – including moral habits – usually keep the promiser honorable even when he knows that cheating would go unpunished (other than by his conscience, that is).

TRUSTWORTHY PROMISERS CULTIVATE EXTENDED DEALINGS

Wary trusters share information, but the practice is unwelcome only by the promisers who are not trustworthy. Trustworthy promisers welcome information sharing and, where permitted by law, tend to organize themselves to facilitate and expand the extension of dealings.

There are two ways in which a trustworthy promiser gains reputation by having a large base of trusters with extended dealings. First, when extended trusters are satisfied, they increase their own patronage and spread the good word. In his book *Industry and Trade*, Alfred Marshall (1927, 297) referred to 'that highest form of advertisement, which comes from the recommendations of one customer to another; and from the inducements which dealings with one department offer to dealings with another.' Second, promisers who enjoy a large extended base attract new, nondiscriminating trusters merely by the fact. Less pernickety trusters are attracted to a promiser with a large extended base because they know that such a promiser has strong reputational incentives to make good, and that trustworthiness has probably been a means by which he achieved his standing.

THE UMBRELLA OF THE BRAND NAME

In the late 19th century, as transportation systems and mass production created a national market in America, consumers confronted 'a profusion of unstandardized packaged goods . . . [and] unfamiliar selling and processing techniques,' making it hard for them to judge such qualities as 'the freshness of food or the durability of clothing.' The consumer historian Norman Silber continues:

> To ease the minds of customers about problems of quality, reliability, and safety, manufacturers and advertisers appealed to consumers to buy according to brand names. National Biscuit, Heinz Soup, Armour Meat, Standard Oil, and other companies placed one banner on many different products. The consumer who found one product of a brand to be satisfactory, those companies suggested, could assume that all other products also would be suitable. (Silber 1983, 3)

A brand name is a way of gathering together an array of services that make for frequent dealings. The array will be shaped by finding a fit with the tastes of the clientele (as well as by scope economies). Game theorists tell us that repetition makes for good offices; hence promisers try to enhance repetition.

A machine-tool company such as Black & Decker makes hundreds of different products, but its customers will generalize to some extent about all of them based on their experience with only a few (see Goodman, Broetzmann, and Ward 1993 on customer satisfaction and brand loyalty). By enlarging its product base the company creates frequent dealings with many of its customers, giving them a better opportunity to evaluate its trustworthiness. In this way, Black & Decker becomes a provider of assurance, as well as tools. The inventor-genius may create, *de novo*, in his basement workshop a fantastic new tool, but it is not a great *product* until it is combined with assurance. The inventor may find it advantageous to sell his invention to Black & Decker and let the firm offer it under the umbrella of its brand name. In a sense, Black & Decker is the expert that tells the truster that the new gizmo is trustworthy. Black & Decker is not merely a manufacturer, distributor, and advertiser, it is also a *knower* that grants its own seal of approval. A 'knower' is anyone who knows valuable information about the promiser's trustworthiness (in this case, the inventor's).

DEALERS MAKE FOR EXTENDED DEALINGS

Besides generating extended dealings with consumers, Black & Decker is at the center of a starlike pattern of dealings with scattered inventors. Consider the similar case of the used car dealer. The used car dealer might have only isolated dealings with the sellers of used cars (like Black & Decker has with some inventors). But, unlike ordinary individuals, he knows all about cars and deals on an equal information footing with the seller. By gathering up a stock of used cars from an array of isolated sellers, the dealer produces a fixed lot of cars and a basis for extended dealings with buyers. Although he does not have many frequent customers, the dealer is a fixture in the community and a subject of gossip. A buyer gets to know her car intimately, and if it disappoints her she will gossip. Also, the dealer can offer guarantees and warranties. The dealer, then, besides reducing transaction costs and upgrading the commodity, transforms a series of isolated dealings – many dyadic matchings between a buyer and a seller – into the starlike pattern shown in Figure 9.2.[8]

Dealers often have credentials that enhance credibility. The infrequent buyer feels that she can trust the credentialed dealer because the credential is a costly, irreversible investment. The truster is assured that the dealer has an incentive to protect his reputation, because he has the option of reaping the

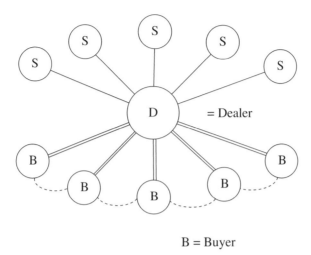

Figure 9.2 The dealer has a star-like pattern of dealings. With sellers he deals on an equal informational footing. Once he has gathered the goods he has extended dealings with buyers.

returns of honest and competent dealings (Marshall, 1927, 270; Klein and Leffler, 1981; De Long, 1991; Nichols, 1998). Economist Gary Biglaiser (1993, 221) says: 'Coin and stamp dealers display to the public that they belong to dues-paying professional societies and are certified numismatists and philatelists . . . Many used-car dealers train mechanics to check and maintain car quality. If the dealers cheat customers and go out of business, then the investment in their employees' human capital is lost.'

REPUTATIONAL NEXUS AND THE MIDDLEMAN

My confidence in a house cleaner is strengthened by a neighbor's recommendation. My confidence is made still stronger by my neighbor's continued dealings with the house cleaner. Our relationships form a *reputational nexus*, a constellation of extended dealings. By acting discreditably, the house cleaner would damage her relationships both with me and with the neighbor.

Reputational nexuses exist in the family, the church, the social club, the neighborhood, the workplace, and the marketplace, creating a vast netting between the social patchwork. Social network theorists figure that any pair of

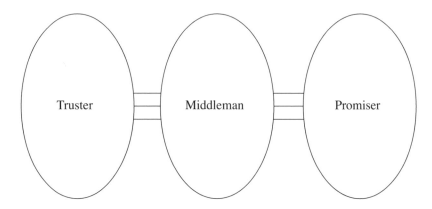

Figure 9.3   The middleman creates a bridge of trust between two traders

adult Americans can be linked by three or fewer intermediary acquaintances (Pool and Kochen, 1989, 16).

The ordinary retailer, who serves as the link between the consumer and the producer, demonstrates the reputational bridge. Many of the matches between consumers and producers are irregular – as when a consumer purchases an ulcer medication – but the consumer has extended dealings with the pharmacy, which in turn has extended dealings with the producer. As the economist Janet Landa (1994, 125) says, 'the middleman . . . mediates between traders . . . who do not trust each other but mutually trust the middleman.' The middleman creates a bridge of trust between two traders (see Figure 9.3).

The private, liberal-arts college is a middleman. It contracts with the ultimate promiser – the professor – and tries to build a reputation for general quality with trusters – students and parents. The firm, the chain-store, and the trade association are all different species of contract nexus. Simple contracting can produce assurance in much the same way that a chain-store does. The health care organization contracts with physicians and hospitals: the patient has extended dealings with the HMO, and the HMO has extended dealings with the physician. The reputational role of the HMO ranges over a contractual continuum, from employment within the firm (the staff model), through intermediate stages (group practice, individual practice associations), to selective contracting with health care providers (Wagner, 1989).

THE MIDDLEMAN ALSO ACTS AS KNOWER

Besides straddling two extended relationships, the middleman also acts as a knower. The retailer specializes in knowing good products from bad – by recognizing brand names and seals of approval, studying the information on labels and packaging, keeping track of customer complaints and returns, conducting his own tests and investigations, hiring testing services, following trade or consumer literature, observing whether other retailers carry the product, and chatting with industry colleagues.

In his role as knower, the middleman works in information that is often too costly for the consumer to gather and judge herself (Pashigian and Bowen, 1994). In a sense, the premium she pays to the middleman, whether he is an established retailer, a brand-name manufacturer, or a contracting organization like an HMO, is a fee for the luxury of being uninformed yet assured.

No commodity is entitled to a strong market; it must concede its dependence on the services and institutions that produce recognition and assurance. Effective middlemen, such as Nordstrom's clothing stores, sell more of the product and at higher prices. Manufacturers respond by seeking to have their products carried by such middlemen. (Notice that, like Landa [1994], I am using the term 'middleman' in a sense that is much broader than the common usage, of one in between the manufactuer and the retailer.)

The two end points of the reputational link, the manufacturer and the consumer, both have an incentive to avoid the prisoner's dilemma outcome. Among the diverse, complex, and imperfect institutional experiments that take place in a free and open field, trusters and promisers will favor and sustain those experiments that produce assurance. Middlemen and knowers strive to produce it, because their cut comes from happy trusting outcomes.

KNOWER SERVICES: FEE FOR INFORMATION

We might view gossiping as a sort of exchange. Exchanging information with acquaintances is one basis for our personal relationships. Information provision by gossip comes to be seen as a trade and as a source of profit. But the economist Hayne Leland (1980, 268) says, 'information on quality has many aspects of a public good: a consumer can give it away and still have it. Under such circumstances, inadequate resources will be channeled to providing information.'

Information provision can be divided into generation and conveyance. Information generation takes the forms of testing, inspecting, researching, evaluating, or interpreting. Consumers Union does all of these when generating product ratings in *Consumer Reports*. Consumers Union makes profits by selling its magazine to trusters. Is its information a public good? Once one person has the ratings, she can indeed share them with her friends and acquaintances – she may even sell her expertise in some manner. But the law forbids her from reproducing or selling the information. The information is proprietary and to a good extent excludable.[9] If you can protect information at the conveyance stage, then you can appropriate its value at the generation stage.

Excludability is often achieved in large measure by legal sanctions. Yet often excludability is simply a matter of technical limitations on the part of would-be free-riders. Information conveyance requires information receiving, organization, storage, retrieval, and transmission. Credit bureaus such as Experian, TransUnion, and Equifax sell credit reports to trusters. They make profits by facilitating dealing, just as Manhattan parking entrepreneurs make profits by facilitating shopping. Experian releases valuable information to millions of parties every month, but that does not mean that they can appropriate the value of the information by reselling it. Experian provides highly individualized information. It makes information complete, speedy, and precise. For someone to free-ride on Experian by entering and competing, she would have to invest in vast data-processing systems. Kenneth Arrow jumps to conclusions when he says that in the absence of special legal protection, entrepreneurs cannot profit by selling information.[10] Like the private parking garage, the service performed by Experian is largely excludable.

Consumers Union reports on standardized products, and its conveyance of information is uniform, not individualized. In consequence, it would be damaged by free-riding if its information were not protected by law. Experian deals in information of a more particularistic nature, namely credit records, and its conveyance is individualized. Its information is protected by the technical limitations of whoever might think of reselling the information, as well as by contractual protections and federal law. Whenever quality information is individualized, the opportunities for *re*conveying it are limited. Thus knowers can make money by being hired by trusters to inspect customized security equipment, manufacturing plants, and used automobiles; to give second opinions on medical matters; and to evaluate prospective employees (Rees, 1966). And the beloved kibitzer can keep up a steady trade in local gossip because others cannot receive, interpret, organize, retrieve, and transmit information nearly as well as he can.

Kenneth Arrow has pointed out that trade in information is often hobbled by the fact that the 'value of information is frequently not known in any meaningful sense to the buyer; if, indeed, he knew enough to measure the value of information, he would know the information itself' (1963, 946). In the case of *Consumer Reports* or Experian, however, the buyer does have a good idea of the value of the information she is purchasing, even though she does not know the information itself. Granted, the consumer cannot measure the value *perfectly* without in fact having the information, but she might know the range of the value, or the expected value. In this respect, *Consumer Reports* is like the *New York Times* or a Stephen King novel or a movie ticket.

SEALS OF APPROVAL AND SELF-DISCLOSURE BY PROMISERS

When a knower generates basic quality information on a standardized product of interest to a wide class of trusters, reconveying the information might be easy, and he may go broke trying to sell information to trusters. In that case he goes to work for the promisers (Beales and Salop, 1980). If a lack of parking spaces would prevent customers from coming to buy, and an independent parking entrepreneur could not exclude nonpayers, then the retailer would himself provide space for customer parking, at no charge. Similarly, if a lack of information would prevent trusters from entering into deals, the promiser provides the information. If his quality is high, he has every incentive to self-disclose far and wide.

Pauline Ippolito (1986, 23) remarks on how sellers self-disclose:

> Low tar and nicotine cigarette sellers have been vigorous in distinguishing themselves from the higher tar brands (going far beyond the mandated disclosures in advertisements). High mileage automobiles often feature this fact in their advertisements. Lower calorie foods (especially in the diet soda and frozen food categories) have been very successful in conveying their superiority to higher calorie counterparts. The same is true for high fiber foods.[11]

Sellers strive to demonstrate or indicate the uses, conveniences, durability, or special pleasures of their products or services.[12] They set up displays, employ salespeople to demonstrate and describe the product, advertise product characteristics, recruit referral agencies, and offer guarantees and warranties (which in Grossman's model [1981] lead to perfect disclosure). Assurance is a necessary input to the consumer's own production of confidence.

That the provision of information may exhibit public-goods characteristics is not a curse to promisers but a blessing. An independent knower often evaluates quality or safety. If the word is favorable, the promiser broadcasts it. Computer and automotive advertisements tout 'editor's choice' accolades, household products display the *Good Housekeeping* seal of approval, movie ads reproduce favorable excerpts from the critics, restaurants display favorable dining reviews. Gerald O'Driscoll (1976) argues that the American Express sticker on a merchant's window is a seal of approval.

Electronics manufacturers hire Underwriters' Laboratories to test and inspect their products and grant a UL mark upon approval. Companies and governments hire Moody's to rate their securities and use the ratings to market their securities.[13] Promisers assure trusters by advertising in media that police integrity – a strategy first employed against the quackery of patent medicine by *Ladies' Home Journal* (Calkins 1928, 49). Another class of knowers paid by promisers, particularly relevant to the issue of occupational licensing, is made up of professional schools, technical schools, institutes, and training programs that grant degrees and certificates. These credentials are then prominently displayed on office walls and listed in *curriculum vitae*. Transcripts and honors give a sort of rating system. Each of these organizations grants its own seal of approval.

Research on seals of approval has suggested that seals like the UL mark are not really understood by consumers and do not significantly enhance the consumers' confidence in the product (Parkinson, 1975; Beltramini and Stafford, 1993). Researchers show test subjects advertisements with and without seals of approval, and see if subjects have greater confidence in the ads with seals of approval. Such research is flawed for several reasons. First, assurances might gain meaning only to consumers genuinely interested in the promise. Unlike genuine prospective buyers, test subjects do not have an interest in the particular products advertised, and hence do not have the incentive to gain pointed knowledge about relevant signals of quality. The research also says that consumers poorly understand seals of approval, because they do not know on what basis the seal is awarded. But again, pointed knowledge for the consumer is knowledge of whether products with the seals are more likely to be satisfactory, not formal knowledge of how seals are awarded. Knowledge of how seals are awarded might be known to only a few, but those few may provide the base upon which an inverted pyramid of divided knowledge is sustained, making the seal an effective signal to those farther up the pyramid who use only very limited pointed knowledge. In other words, advertising credibility may not be the relevant test of a seal's value: the seal may be most important to the distributors, retailers and other middlemen who decide whether to carry the product.

FRANCHISES AS A SYSTEM OF SEALS OF APPROVAL

When a motorist pulls off the interstate and into Joe's Garage for sudden repairs, she will have isolated dealings with Joe and feel vulnerable. The motorist would do better to pull into Midas, Shell, or Mobil, because if the local Midas franchisee cheats her, it faces the prospect of punishment. Punishment would come, not from her (the motorist), but from the franchisor, who polices the service and probity of their franchisees using 'mystery shoppers,' audits, inspections, and complaint investigation. They *do* have to fear that the customer will harm them by not returning or by injuring the franchise's reputation.

The franchisor is a knower that provides a seal of approval. When the serviceman wearing the Midas shirt and cap approaches us, he is not our connection to Midas. Midas is our connection to him. Midas is like a friend, and the serviceman is the friend of a friend. Although it is mutually understood that the motorist and the Midas franchisee will be interacting only once, the motorist has extended dealings (of an indirect sort) with the franchisor, who in turn has extended dealings with the franchisee. A franchise operation succeeds partly by capitalizing on product familiarity and low-cost replication of a successful formula, but also by producing that intangible input to mutual gains, assurance.

A CLASSIFICATION OF INDEPENDENT KNOWER ORGANIZATIONS

Two distinctions aid us in thinking about knower organizations: first, whether the knower is engaged in information generation or conveyance (or both); and second, whether the knower is remunerated by trusters or by promisers. Using the two distinctions we get a classification scheme as shown in Figure 9.4.[14]

WAYS OF APPREHENDING UNTRUSTWORTHINESS

Trustworthy promisers have every incentive to self-disclose. But the untrustworthy do not strive to self-disclose; in fact, they have a special incentive to deceive. How do trusters apprehend the untrustworthy?

One way is to ask for a public elucidation of the content of the promise. If they fudge and prevaricate, suspicions arise. Perhaps even more telling are the accolades, coveted seals of approval, and glowing endorsements that are not. When we view a *curriculum vitae*, a meagerness of distinctions will make itself evident and lead us to doubt outstanding ability. Similarly, trusters remain wary when they do not hear any of the wide variety of horns that trustworthy promisers blow in self-disclosing. It is precisely because the horns are unavailable to untrustworthy promisers that they are effective signals of quality.

One sort of evidence is the demonstration of traits distinctive to trustworthiness, such as announcing, 'Established in 1924,' or promotional efforts lucrative only for a worthy promise (Klein and Leffler, 1981). Before the Federal Deposit Insurance Corporation was created to bail out banks, banks had traditionally used large pillars and heavy marble in their architecture to signal permanence. Another way to apprehend untrustworthiness is to hire knower services. Hired inspectors, *Consumer Reports*, Dun & Bradstreet, Experian, Roger Ebert, and the neighborhood gossip all report on the trustworthy and untrustworthy alike.

A third way of apprehending untrustworthiness is forged by competitors.

Knower is remunerated by

	Trusters	Promisers
Generation	Hired inspectors (for buildings, automobiles) Letters of recommendation Doctors Financial advisors Hired investigators American Automobile Association	Credential givers (universities, institutes, training programs) Underwriters' Laboratories American Dental Association *US Pharmacopoeia* Good Housekeeping Security ratings (Moody's, Standard & Poor's) Securities underwriters Financial and accounting audits Notary public Letters of recommendation Orthodox Union (kosher foods) Internet seals of approval (TrustE, Cyber Patrol, Safesurf, Verisign, BBB Online)
Generation and conveyance	*Consumer Reports* Dun & Bradstreet Industry newsletters Hobby, product, and news publications Restaurant and movie reviews Employment agencies Brokers Internet chat groups (eBay)	Franchises Better Business Bureau Medical data banks Employment agencies Brokers (securities, real estate, produce, art, collectables)
Conveyance	Gossip, e-mail Consumer credit bureaus	Referral services Advertising firms Signs, labels, packaging, displays, sales help Web pages

Knower engages in information

Figure 9.4   Classification of knower services

Promisers expose the poor characteristics of competitors' products, if only by insinuation, in advertisements, sales demonstrations, and marketing literature. Before the imposition in 1971 of restrictions on cigarette advertising, advertisements for low-tar brands sometimes pictured rival brands and listed the tar content beside each. Many researchers think that the restrictions have inhibited the market for low-tar cigarettes.[15] Competitive advertising is a great service to trusters, as it helps them discover product differences and the validity of product claims.

In his 1928 book titled *Business the Civilizer*, advertising executive E.E. Calkins wrote of an early case of competitive exposé:

> Dr. Lyon's Tooth Powder and Colgate's Dental Cream are both using their advertising space to offset undue claims instead of stretching them further. That is one of the values of advertising. It will correct itself. The lying advertisements will find themselves surrounded by truth and will be forced back in line by the weight of public opinion. (284)

Of the 65 advertising challenges resolved by the Better Business Bureau's National Advertising Division in 1992, almost all of which dealt with the truth and accuracy of advertising claims, 72 percent were brought by competitors.[16]

In the areas of health care and pharmaceuticals, competitive exposé is restricted – drug manufacturers are not permitted to report findings about their own products, much less their rivals'. A robust arena of self-disclosure and competitive exposé, also known as free speech, would help trusters gain the opportune, pointed knowledge they can really use (Ippolito and Mathios 1990, 479; Russo *et al.* 1986). In his famous paper on the market for lemons, George Akerlof (1970, 495) suggested that sometimes 'dishonest dealings tend to drive honest dealings out of the market.' Freedoms to engage in self-disclosure and competitive exposé – and, first of all, to enter and exist as a trustworthy alternative to the lemon – are what best ensure that honest dealings drive dishonest dealings out of the market.

INTEGRITY AND HAYEKIAN DIALECTICS

Economists have explained the coordination of promises but have done much less to explain the integrity of promises. The integrity issue looms larger as society becomes more complex. 'The more civilized we become, the more relatively ignorant must each individual be of the facts on which the working of his civilization depends. The very division of knowledge increases the necessary ignorance of the individual' (Hayek 1960, 26). Increases in the division of knowledge imply the growth of our dependence on things unknown to us and of the role of trust in economic affairs.

But the answer to our question *What explains promise integrity?* turns out to be, excepting the tort-enforcement explanation, a special instance of the answer to the original question *What explains promise coordination?* People truck, barter, and exchange, utilizing their local knowledge. To assure that promises will be kept, other promises are made. There is a demand for and supply of assurance:

> In actual life the fact that our inadequate knowledge of the available commodities or services is made up for by our experience with the persons or firms supplying them – that competition is in a large measure competition for reputation or good will – is one of the most important facts which enables us to solve our daily problems. The function of competition is here precisely to teach us *who* will serve us well: which grocer or travel agency, which department store or hotel, which doctor or solicitor, we can expect to provide the most satisfactory solution for whatever particular personal problem we may have to face. (Hayek, 1948, 97)

But doesn't the 'assurance industry,' while supposedly solving one trust problem, simply create other trust problems? The manufacturer, wanting retailers to trust his microwave oven, contracts with Underwriters Laboratories, but how do we know we can trust UL? UL would stand to lose much if, by compromising integrity, its reputation were injured. Hence it would be incorrect to say that the division of knowledge implies a constant amount of vulnerability, or constant amount of doubt. No such conservation principle holds, because in the competitive processes of voluntary affairs, assurances tend to be shifted to the ground where they are strongest.

The Internet is vastly expanding all forms of information exchange and assurance. When critics find some fault in e-commerce, such as doubts about privacy, security, or trustworthiness, entrepreneurs invent an e-solution, usually taking the form of a middleman service or a knower service.

Intellectuals, commentators, and regulators working on quality and safety regulation should seriously consider how resourceful middlemen, expert knowers, trustworthy promisers, and wary trusters find ways to overcome virtually any of the supposed failures of the free enterprise system. The demand for assurance brings forth a supply of assurance.

NOTES

1. This chapter is a revised and expanded version of the paper bearing the same title that appeared in *Economic Affairs*, March 2001, pp. 4–11.
2. The terms 'demand,' 'entrepreneur,' 'profit,' and 'supply' are being used in broad senses.
3. Whether we ought to regard assurance as a transaction cost depends on how exactly we define transaction cost. If transaction costs are simply costs (other than price paid to the seller) of completing a transaction, assurance is not a transaction cost. But if transaction

costs are costs (other than price) of coming to, assessing and completing an *ex-ante*-worthwhile transaction, then assurance is a transaction cost.

4. The neglected has been by no means entire. Many types of research may be credited here, but five come especially to mind: (1) empirical studies of reputation and its value, (2) game-theoretic models of reputation, (3) consumer and marketing research on various certifiers and 'knower' organizations, (4) studies of customs and norms elicited and sustained without (or even in the face of) governmental legal authority, and (5) libertarian explorations of how assurance has been, is, or would be provided in the absence of government intervention. For a Schematic Bibliography see Klein (1997).

5. Large literatures exist on each of the quality-and-safety interventions noted above. I read the bulk of this research as indicating that these policies have high costs with few corresponding benefits. For a review of the literature on occupational licensing, for example, see Svorny (1998), on workplace safety see Magat and Viscusi (1992), on the Food and Drug Administration, see Klein and Tabarrok (2001).

6. However, chatting might reveal to a cunning promiser that the truster is naive, ignorant, or powerless.

7. Common usage of the term 'reputation' is sometimes at variance with my usage. In my usage, someone recognized for faithfully delivering the quality promised has a good reputation, even if that quality is regarded as low. My usage focuses on keeping the promise, not on what is promised. But the content of the promise is formed in large part by the quality that people come to expect, so my usage, in fact, addresses the broad notion of 'reputation for quality' better than it might at first seem. Attached to every Nike product is the implicit statement: 'and we promise that it is of Nike quality.'

8. Economist Eric Bond (1982, this volume) studied the market for used pick-up trucks, looking for lemons-market results, and found none. He reports (p. 839): Pick-up 'trucks that were purchased used required no more maintenance than trucks of similar age and lifetime mileage that had not been traded.' It would be interesting to learn whether used vehicles purchased from dealers require less maintenance than those purchased from isolated individuals.

9. *Consumer Reports* states its position in each issue: 'Neither the Ratings nor the reports may be used in advertising or for any other commercial purpose. Consumers Union will take all steps open to it to prevent commercial use of its materials, its name, or the name of *Consumer Reports*.' Silber (1983, 31) notes that in the 1950s '[a]ttorneys successfully protected the ratings of the magazine from unauthorized use by commercial interests.'

10. 'In the absence of special legal protection, the owner [of information] cannot, however, simply sell information in the open market. Any one purchaser can destroy the monopoly, since he can reproduce the information at little or no cost' (Arrow, 1962, 151).

11. Ippolito and Mathios (1990, 479) examine the effect of the removal in 1984 of a ban on health claims in the cereal market: 'The evidence clearly demonstrates that fiber cereal consumption increased once the ban on health-claims advertising was removed. The development of fiber cereals also increased when producers were given the ability to advertise the health features of the products. Moreover, advertising appeared to reduce some of the differences across the population [of cereals], suggesting that advertising may have had its effects by reducing the costs of acquiring information.'

12. Beales, Craswell and Salop (1981, 502f) offer a good discussion of self-disclosure, as well as of imperfections in the quality-information market generally.

13. Viscusi (1978) provides a model of quality certification which yields a happy outcome, in explicit contrast to the unhappy outcome of Akerlof's model (1970).

14. The classification raises questions for research. Here is a list any of which might make a good dissertation topic: What sorts of dealings have depended historically on the existence of independent knower organizations? How much is a seal of approval worth to a promiser? Do trusters come to recognize credentials and seals of approval? Is competition among seals of approval desirable, or does it create bewildering cacophony? Do trumpeted seals of approval always signify satisfactory quality? Do seals of approval act as barriers to entry? Do knower organizations foster collusion? What leads members of the Better Business Bureau and similar organizations to join and cooperate? How do organizations that develop standards interface with the legal system? Do these organizations remain impartial? What

keeps them honest? Where information is based on past dealings, what damage is done to privacy? What can we learn from knower organizations about undercover tactics as a way to monitor and control behavior? What types of knower organizations tend to act as rent-seekers for their promiser-supporters (for example, the A.M.A.)? What types of organizations tend to act as rent-seekers, or mere political crusaders, for their truster-supporters (for example, consumer-interest lobbyists)? Will encryption and the Internet enable everyone to pursue detailed and interactive information paths about product safety while sitting at their personal computers?

15. '[T]he ban substantially increased the cost to firms of introducing new low-tar brands and the cost to consumers of obtaining information about these newer brands, thus slowing down the movement to these lower-tar cigarettes' (Schneider et al., 1981, 610).

16. BBB 1992 Annual report, p. 2.

REFERENCES

Akerlof, George A. 1970. 'The Market for "Lemons": Quality Uncertainty and the Market Mechanism.' *Quarterly Journal of Economics* 84, August: 488–500.

Arrow, Kenneth J. 1962. 'Economic Welfare and the Allocation of Resources for Invention.' Reprinted in Kenneth J. Arrow, *Essays in the Theory of Risk-Bearing*: 144–63. Chicago: Markham Publishing Co., 1971.

Arrow, Kenneth J. 1974. *The Limits of Organization*. New York: W.W. Norton.

Beales, Howard, Richard Craswell, and Steven C. Salop. 1981. 'The Efficient Regulation of Consumer Information.' *Journal of Law and Economics* 24, December: 491–539.

Beales, Howard and Steven Salop. 1980. 'Selling Consumer Information.' *Advances in Consumer Research* 7: 238–41.

Beltramini, Richard F. and Edwin R. Stafford. 1993. 'Comprehension and Perceived Believability of Seals of Approval Information in Advertising.' *Journal of Advertising* 12(3), September: 3–13.

Biglaiser, Gary. 1993. 'Middlemen as Experts.' *Rand Journal of Economics* 24, Summer: 212–23.

Bond, Eric W. 1982. 'A Direct Test of the "Lemons" Model: The Market for Used Pickup Trucks.' *American Economic Review* 72, September: 836–40.

Calkins, Earnest Elmo. 1928. *Business the Civilizer*. Boston: Little, Brown and Co.

De Long, J. Bradford. 1991. 'Did J.P. Morgan's Men Add Value? An Economist's Perspective on Financial Capitalism.' In *Inside the Business Enterprise: Historical Perspectives on the Use of Information*, edited by Peter Temin: 205–36. Chicago: University of Chicago Press.

De Alessi, Louis and R.J. Staaf. 1992. 'What Does Reputation Really Assure? The Relationship of Trademarks to Expectations and Legal Remedies.' *Economic Inquiry* 32, July: 477–85.

Grossman, Sanford J. 1981. 'The Informational Role of Warranties and Private Disclosure about Product Quality.' *Journal of Law and Economics* 24, December: 461–83.

Hayek, Friedrich A. 1948. *Individualism and Economic Order*. Chicago: University of Chicago Press.

Hayek, Friedrich A. 1960. *The Constitution of Liberty*. Chicago: University of Chicago Press.

Ippolito, Pauline M. and Alan D. Mathios. 1990. 'Information, Advertising and Health

Choices: A Study of the Cereal Market.' *Rand Journal of Economics* 21, Autumn: 459–80.

Ippolito, Pauline M. 1986. 'Consumer Protection Economics: A Selected Survey.' In *Empirical Approaches to Consumer Protection Economics*, edited by Pauline M. Ippolito and David T. Scheffman: 1–33. Washington, DC: Federal Trade Commission.

Klein, Daniel B., editor. *Reputation: Studies in the Voluntary Elicitation of Good Conduct*. Ann Arbor: University of Michigan Press, 1997.

Klein, Daniel B. and Alexander Tabarrok. 2001. www.FDAReview.org (An extensive review and evaluation of FDA policy available online.)

Landa, Janet T. 1994. *Trust, Ethnicity, and Identity: Beyond the New Institutional Economics of Ethnic Trading Networks, Contract Law, and Gift-Exchange*. Ann Arbor: University of Michigan Press.

Leland, Hayne E. 1980. 'Minimum-Quality Standards and Licensing in Markets with Asymmetric Information.' In Occupational Licensure and Regulation, edited by Simon Rottenberg: 265–84. Washington, DC: American Enterprise Institute.

Magat, Wesley A. and W. Kip Viscusi. 1992. *Informational Approaches to Regulation*. Cambridge: MIT Press.

Marshall, Alfred. 1927. *Industry and Trade*. Third edition. London: Macmillan and Co.

Merry, Sally Engle. 1984. 'Rethinking Gossip and Scandal.' In *Towards a General Theory of Social Control*, Vol. 1, *Fundamentals*, edited by Donald Black: 271–302. New York: Academic Press.

Nichols, Mark W. 1998. 'Advertising and Quality in the US Market for Automobiles.' *Southern Economic Journal* 64(4): 922–39.

O'Driscoll, Gerald P. 'The American Express Case: Public Good or Monopoly?' *Journal of Law and Economics*. 19(1) (April 1976): 163–75.

Parkinson, Thomas L. 1975. 'The Role of Seals and Certifications of Approval in Consumer Decision-Making.' *Journal of Consumer Affairs* 9, summer: 1–14.

Pashigian, B. Peter and Brian Bowen. 1994. 'The Rising Cost of Time of Females, the Growth of National Brands and the Supply of Retail Services.' *Economic Inquiry* 32, January: 33–65.

Pool, Ithiel de Sola and Manfred Kochen. 1978. 'Contacts and Influence.' Reprinted in *The Small World*, edited by Manfred Kochen: 3–51. Norwood, New Jersey: Ablex Publishing.

Rees, Albert. 1966. 'Information Networks in Labor Markets.' *American Economic Review* 56 (May): 559–66.

Rothenberg, Jerome. 1993. 'Social Strategy and the Tactics in the Search for Safety.' *Critical Review* 7: 159–80.

Russo, J. Edward, Richard Staelin, Catherine A. Nolan, Gary J. Russell and Barbara L. Metcalf. 1986. 'Nutrition Information in the Supermarket.' *Journal of Consumer Research* 13 (June): 48–70.

Schneider, Lynne, Benjamin Klein and Kevin M. Murphy. 1981. 'Government Regulation of Cigarette Health Information.' *Journal of Law and Economics* 24, December: 575–612.

Silber, Norman Isaac. 1983. *Test and Protest: The Influence of Consumers Union*. New York: Holmes and Meier.

Svorny, Shirley. 1998. 'Licensing: Market Entry Restriction.' In *Encyclopedia of Law and Economics*, ed. B. Bouckhaert and G. De Geest. Cheltenham: Edward Elgar.

TARP, Inc. 1981. 'Measuring the Grapevine – Consumer Response and Word-of

Mouth.' Study Conducted for the Corporate Consumer Affairs Department of the Coca-Cola Company by Technical Assistance Research Programs Inc.

Viscusi, W. Kip. 1978. 'A Note on "Lemons" Markets with Quality Certification.' *Bell Journal of Economics* 9: 277–9.

Wagner, Eric R. 1989. 'Types of Managed Health Care Organizations.' In *Managed Health Care Handbook*, edited by Peter R. Kongstvedt: 11–18. Rockville, MD: Aspen Publishers.

PART 3

Empirical and Experimental Responses

10. Beta, Macintosh and other fabulous tales

Stan J. Liebowitz and Stephen E. Margolis

In this chapter we examine a number of the standards or technology battles that are often cited as examples of lock in. Of course, the most prominent of these claimed failures is the QWERTY keyboard, which we discussed at length in Liebowitz and Margolis (2001). In this chapter we present the VHS–Beta history at some length, then consider several other cases.

Readers familiar with scholarly empirical work in economics may find our attention to case histories a bit out of the ordinary. Economists don't usually concern themselves much with individual cases: We tend to look at time-series of aggregate data – GNP and unemployment, the money supply or consumer expenditure – or at large data sets based on hundreds, thousands, or even larger numbers of companies, individuals, and products. This is because economists are usually looking for a pattern of behavior, a test for a theory that is held to apply *in general*. But theories of path dependence are different from such generalizing theories. In contrast, theories of third-degree path dependence and lock-in do not allege that these outcomes are the norm, or even that they are particularly common. Rather, they allege only that such path dependence is possible and perhaps that it is sufficiently likely to be important. Adherents of path dependence go somewhat further than this, arguing that it is likely to be common. But this argument does not come from the theory. Given that the theoretical result is a theorem about the possibility of lock-in, the empirical support, naturally enough, is a demonstration that the possible phenomenon has occurred. And also naturally enough, the empirical counterclaim involves calling into question these alleged demonstrations.

VHS VERSUS BETA

After the typewriter keyboard, the VHS–Beta battle is the most often mentioned of alleged path-dependent market failures.[1] In our discussions in the previous chapters, we have used the names VHS and Beta in simple hypothetical examples of how the standards traps operate and how escapes are possible.[2] We turn now to the actual history of this standards battle, a history that is significant for several reasons. First, it incorporates structural features found in some of the models discussed here: in particular, it incorporates both economies of scale and ownership. Second, the actual history of the battle fails to support the claim that an inferior format dominated as a result of technological interrelatedness and economies of scale. Finally, it is a wonderful example of the foresight of the parties involved, and the tactics and strategies used to try to establish their standards.

The Ampex Corporation publicly demonstrated the first commercially viable videorecorder in 1956. These machines were sold for several years only to professional broadcasters. Eventually, Ampex concluded that transistors would replace tubes, and, having no experience with transistors, entered into an agreement with Sony to transistorize the videorecorder. In return, Sony received the rights to use Ampex-owned patents in machines designed for the home-use (nonprofessional) market, which Ampex was willing to cede.

The Ampex–Sony relationship quickly soured, however, and Ampex decided that it needed a Japanese partner to sell its recorders to the Japanese broadcast market. This time Ampex entered a partnership agreement with Toshiba. Other Japanese electronics producers that wanted to manufacture videorecorders then became Ampex's licensees. Eventually, various incompatible models of videorecorders coexisted in the marketplace, but none of these early machines proved successful in the home-use market.

In 1969 Sony developed a cartridge-based system called the U-matic for the home-use market. Because Matsushita, JVC (an independent subsidiary of Matsushita), Toshiba, and Hitachi all had such products in the works, Sony sought to bring in some partners to share the format in order to establish it as a standard. After Sony promised to make a few suggested changes to the machine, Matsushita, JVC, and Sony agreed to produce machines based on the U-matic specification (although Sony was to get the bulk of the eventual sales). The three companies also agreed to share technology and patents. Production of the U-matic began in 1971. Although it enjoyed some success in educational and industrial markets, high costs and excessive bulk led to its failure in the home-use market.

Attempts to break into the home-use market continued. In 1972 an American company came out with a product called Cartrivision that did many of the things that a Betamax was later to do (although it traded off picture quality for a longer playing time). Cartrivision was sold with a library of prerecorded programs. It failed when several technical problems arose, including the decomposition of the prerecorded tapes in a warehouse, which led to negative publicity. Phillips produced a home recorder in 1972, but it never achieved much success. Sanyo and Toshiba joined forces to launch a machine known as the V-Cord, which also did poorly. Matsushita produced a machine called the AutoVision – a dismal failure. Of note for our story, Matsushita's management attributed this failure to the AutoVision's short, 30-minute tape capacity, a lesson that would later prove important. A Matsushita subsidiary, Kotobuki, introduced the VX-100 to the home-use market.

When Sony began selling Betamax in April 1975, it had a tape capacity of one hour. At the same time, JVC was also working on a machine known as the Video Home System, or VHS. As it had done earlier with the Umatic, Sony sought to cut through the clutter of competing formats and make Betamax the standard. Before introducing Betamax to the market, it once again offered its format to Matsushita and JVC, providing technical details of the Betamax, including an advance in azimuth recording that helped eliminate the problem of crosstalk. After lengthy discussions, dragging on for over a year, the three finally agreed to have a meeting to compare the Betamax, VHS, and VX machines. This meeting took place in April 1976 (a year after Sony had put Betamax on the market). Lardner (1987) describes the meeting as follows:

> The first item on the agenda was the simultaneous playing, through all three [machines], of a 'Sesame Street' type of children's program. . . . The Sony contingent's eyes were on the JVC machine. . . . What they saw was a considerably smaller machine than the Betamax. . . . Mechanically, too, VHS had a notable distinction: the use of a loading system called M-loading. . . . The basic concept had been tried in some of the early U-matic prototypes. . . . In other respects, JVC's and Sony's machines were strikingly similar. Both were two-head, helical-scanning machines using half-inch tape in a U-matic type of cassette. Both – unlike the V-cord, the VX, and indeed all the color video recorders to date – used azimuth recording and countered the problem of cross talk by juggling the phase of the color signal. So the Betamax and the VHS were in a class by themselves as far as tape efficiency went.
>
> The real difference between them lay in how the two companies had chosen to exploit that advantage: Sony to make the cassette paperback size, and JVC to achieve a two-hour recording capacity. . . . Eventually one of [the Sony people] said what all of the Sony representatives were thinking: 'It's a copy of Betamax.' (151–2)

Needless to say, this apparent usurping of Sony's technological advances by JVC created bitterness between the one-time allies. Sony and Matsushita-JVC decided to go their separate ways.

The only real technical differences between Beta and VHS were the manner in which the tape was threaded and the size of the cassettes. The Beta format's threading offered some advantages for editing and special effects. But the larger cassette in the VHS format allowed more tape to be used, and for any given speed of tape, this implied a longer recording or playing time. For any given recording technique, slowing the tape increases recording time, but it also decreases picture quality. Because of its larger cassette size, VHS always offered an advantageous combination of picture quality and playing time. Otherwise, the differences between Beta and VHS were fairly trivial from a technical point of view. Our current perception of the differences is likely magnified by the advertising claims of each camp, the passage of time, and possibly by the fact that Beta still survives, reincarnated as a high-end broadcasting and videophile device.

The different choices of cassette size were based on different perceptions of consumer desires: Sony's managers, perhaps as a result of problems with the bulky U-matic, perhaps as a result of their many successes with portable devices, believed that a paperback-sized cassette, allowing easy carrying, was paramount. In contrast, Matsushita's managers, responding to the failure of the 30-minute Autovision machine, believed that a two-hour recording time, allowing the taping of full-length feature movies, was essential.

This difference was to prove crucial. Sony was first to the market and enjoyed a virtual monopoly for almost two years. In an attempt to solidify its dominance of the US market, Sony allowed its Beta machines to be sold under Zenith's brand name (Zenith being one of the major US television manufacturers). To counter this move, Matsushita set up a meeting with RCA, which had previously concluded and publicly stated that a two-hour recording time was essential for a successful home videorecorder. By the time the meeting between Matsushita and RCA took place, however, Sony had announced a two-hour Betamax, Beta II. RCA proposed to Matsushita that it produce a machine that could record a football game, which implied a three-hour recording time. Six weeks later Matsushita had a working four-hour machine that used the same techniques to increase recording time that Sony had used in the Beta II.

RCA began selling VHS machines in summer 1977 (two years after Sony's introduction of the Betamax), dubbing its machine SelectaVision. The advertising copy was simple: 'Four hours. $1000. SelectaVision.' Zenith responded by lowering the price of its Beta machine to $996. But within months VHS was outselling Beta in the United States. A Zenith marketing executive is quoted as saying, 'The longer playing time turned out to be very important, and RCA's product was better styled.'

The battle escalated. Sony recruited Toshiba and Sanyo to the Beta format, and Matsushita brought Hitachi, Sharp, and Mitsubishi into its camp. Any improvement in one format was soon followed by a similar improvement in the other. The similarity of the two machines made it unlikely that one format would be able to deliver a technological knockout punch. When one group lowered its price, the other soon followed. The two formats proved equally matched in almost all respects save one: VHS's longer playing time. When Beta went to two hours, VHS went to four. When Beta increased to five hours,

VHS increased to eight. Of course, a consumer who wanted better picture quality could set either machine to a higher tape speed.

The market's referendum on playing time versus tape compactness was decisive and immediate, not just in the United States, but in Europe and Japan as well. By mid-1979 VHS was outselling Beta by more than two to one in the United States. By 1983 Beta's world share was down to 12 percent. By 1984 every VCR manufacturer except Sony had adopted VHS. Klopfenstein summarizes (our italics):

> Although many held the perception that the Beta VCR produced a better picture than VHS, technical experts such as Weinstein (1984) and Prentis (1981) have concluded that this was, in fact, not the case; periodic reviews in Consumers Reports found VHS picture quality superior twice, found Beta superior once, and found no difference in a fourth review. In conclusion, *the Beta format appeared to hold no advantages over VHS other than being the first on the market, and this may be a lesson for future marketers of new media products* (1989: 28).

How does this history address the theory and empiricism around path dependence? First, and most obviously, it contradicts the claim that the Beta format was better and that its demise constitutes evidence of the pernicious workings of decentralized decision making or sensitive dependence on initial conditions. Regarding the one aspect that clearly differentiated the two formats, tape length, consumers preferred VHS.

Second, even though the technical differences between the two formats were small, the advantage of longer recording times was sufficient to allow VHS to overcome Beta's initial lead. There might not have been any great harm had the market stayed with Beta, inasmuch as its recording time was up to five hours by the early 1980s. But consumers were not willing to wait those few extra years, and the market was responsive enough to make the switch to the better path.

Third, the history illustrates the role of ownership, strategy, and adopters' foresight in facilitating a change in paths. The formats were each owned, and both Sony and JVC-Matsushita expended considerable effort to establish their standards, indicating that they expected to capture some of the benefits of doing so. The ability of VHS to attract partners such as RCA and Matsushita indicates the market participants' ability to recognize the large potential gains from promoting a superior standard.

Although it is sometimes argued that the dominance of VHS resulted from the random association of VHS with a more aggressive licensing and pricing strategy, the pricing and promotion of the two formats were in fact closely matched. Sony was certainly no babe in the woods with regard to marketing consumer electronics. But consumers were apparently quick to identify a standard that they preferred and were confident that many others would do the same. Not only was the switch to VHS rapid, but it was also repeated in separate national markets. Thus, there is no evidence that the market choice was due to blunders, unlucky promotional choices, or insufficient investment by the owners of the Beta format.[3]

An additional aspect of this standards battle further illustrates the richness of market behavior. Although the Beta format's advantages in editing and special effects were apparently relatively unimportant for home users, they were important for broadcasters. And the Beta format does survive in broadcasting, where editing and special effects are relatively more important. Broadcasters and home users do interact, of course, but mostly over the airwaves or cable. Their interaction does not generally involve much exchange of the cassettes themselves, and for those occasions when it does, broadcasters can keep some VHS equipment. But the high-performance, high-cost broadcasting machines that use the Beta format are one reason that many people assume that the Beta format offers higher quality.

The importance of Beta's survival in broadcasting is that there were really two standards battles, not one, and two different outcomes. Consumers got the format that they preferred, and broadcasters got the standard they preferred. This is really a story of coexisting standards, much along the line of the possibilities discussed in chapter 5 of Liebowitz and Margolis (2001).

The Beta-VHS standards war is a rich example of a standards battle. It is *not*, however, a story of lock-in of the first product to market. Instead, it is a story of competing formats, consumers' switching when something better for them became available, and the coexistence of a minority standard that offers special benefits to a specialized group of users.

A final postscript on the Beta–VHS rivalry: one that indicates the dangers of lock-in stories. If a standard with a better picture were to come along but not be adopted, it might be tempting to suspect a potential case of lock-in. DVD might seem to fit this description, except that DVD is still thought likely to replace VHS. But if DVD should fail, we are likely to hear choruses of lock-in from the usual places. We should be slow to accept such a conclusion, however, since the market has already rejected a system with a higher quality picture that suffers no compatibility problems with VHS.

We are talking about SuperVHS, a system that, using special tape, can record and play back a picture with much higher resolution than ordinary VHS. SuperVHS machines can be purchased for about $350, which is somewhat higher than the price of a regular VHS machine with the same set of features normally found on SuperVHS (hi-fi, cable box control, and so forth). SuperVHS machines can play back regular VHS tapes, so there is no compatibility issue, and can even record regular VHS on regular tapes. With the special tapes, however, it has a picture that has 30–40 percent greater resolution. SuperVHS has been around for most, if not all, of this decade, so it has had plenty of time to generate market share, yet it clearly has failed to catch on.

Why has it failed? It can not be due to lock-in, for there is no compatibility issue and no differential network effects. SuperVHS machines are part of the same network as regular VHS. Thus we must conclude that consumers are not willing to pay an extra $150 for SuperVHS. Improved picture quality is not, apparently, worth that difference. The difference in picture quality may be large in terms of technical specifications, but the typical consumer may not be able to see it. On ordinary television screens of 27 inches or less, the fast speed of a regular VHS tape displays a picture that is about as good as the ordinary viewer can detect. Furthermore, regular VHS has a better picture than standard broadcast quality, which eliminates the value of SuperVHS for taping off the air. This is important because it tells us that even if Beta had a better picture than VHS, it might not have mattered as long as VHS's picture was good enough. After all, any difference between Beta and VHS is dwarfed by the difference between VHS and SuperVHS.

This story has implications beyond video recording. Just as the movement to a graphical operating system in computers did not take place until sufficiently powerful hardware became readily available and affordable (as we show in the next section of this chapter), the movement to a higher quality video format (tape or broadcast HDTV) is likely to require affordable large-screen televisions that will make the enhanced picture quality worthwhile. Should DVD or HDTV, currently in their embryonic phase, fail in the market, that failure can be taken as a failure of markets or standards only if cheap large-screen televisions are readily available.

COMPUTER OPERATING SYSTEMS: MAC VERSUS IBM

Among the popular examples of economic things that go bump in the night is the success of the DOS computer operating system. Macintosh, it is alleged, was far superior to command-line DOS, and even to DOS-based Windows, at least in its earlier versions. Yet Macintosh has garnered only a small share of the computer market and appeared, until quite recently, to be on the brink of extinction.

Because users clearly prefer a graphical user interface to a command-line interface, how did the DOS command-line interface manage to dominate personal computing when it and the Macintosh graphical user interface were competing head on? The usual story is that DOS was successful because DOS was successful. DOS had a large market share because there was a lot of software available for it, and there was a lot of software available for it because there were a lot of DOS-based machines in use. But it is also possible that DOS succeeded on its own merits.

First, DOS had a cost advantage over Macintosh. A graphical user interface requires considerably more computing power to get most jobs done, which significantly increased costs when that power was hard to come by. Furthermore, although Macintosh owners could see italics and boldface on screen, to print the screen as they saw it required a PostScript printer, and such printers cost in the vicinity of $1000 more than ordinary laser printers. Second, command-line DOS was faster than Macintosh.[4] Macintosh owners had to wait for their screen displays to change, whereas PCs owners had almost instantaneous updates.[5] Third, although the graphical user interface allowed users to access and learn programs more easily, in many business settings a computer was used for only a single application. Only one program could run at a time, and hard drives were small or nonexistent at first. Many programs were copy-protected, usually requiring that the floppy disk be kept in the drive, so it was awkward to change programs. In that environment, the operator had very little interaction with the operating system interface, and once the operator had learned the application, there were few advantages of the graphical user interface. Finally, it was easier to create software for DOS machines, which is one reason that many applications packages became available so quickly in the DOS world.

The case for DOS in the 1980s, therefore, was much stronger than it appears from the vantage of the 1990s, with our multimegabyte memories and multigigabyte hard drives. Now that we routinely use computers that run 30 times faster than the old DOS machines, with 50 times the memory and 100 times the hard-drive capacity, the requirements of a graphical operating system seem rather puny. But they were enormous back in the 1980s.

As processors became faster, memory cheaper, and hard drives larger, the advantages of command-line DOS diminished. If we were still using DOS, we would certainly have an example of being stuck with an inferior product, one that offers smaller net benefits to consumers. But we are not still using DOS. Instead we are using a Mac-like graphical user interface. If someone went to sleep in 1983 and awoke in 1999 to see a modern PC, he most likely would think that the Macintosh graphical user interface had been colorized and updated, with a second button added to the mouse.[6] This modern Rip van Winkle might be surprised to learn, however, that the owner of the graphical user interface was not Apple, but Microsoft.

Although the movement from DOS to Windows was costly, it occurred quite rapidly. As in the other examples, the evidence is quite the opposite of lock-in: It demonstrates that markets, far from getting stuck in ruts, make rapid changes when there is a clear advantage in doing so. Because Windows also ran DOS programs, it lowered the transition cost.[7]

The competition between DOS and Macintosh demonstrates the importance of the distinction between a fixed standard and flexible standard. A fixed standard at least allows for the hypothetical possibility that we get stuck – everyone would like to move but no one would like to go first. With a flexible standard, however, getting stuck is difficult to imagine. A flexible standard can evolve over time: It can add a new feature, or increase capacity, or adjust a parameter.

One important element in the success of the DOS-Windows platforms may well have been Microsoft's commitment to backward compatibility – evolution rather than revolution. In contrast, Macintosh computers were not compatible with earlier successful Apple products. This meant that the Macintosh did not have a base of carry-over users as early customers. Whether they stayed with Apple products or moved on to DOS, Apple customers faced an inevitable task of converting or abandoning files and applications.

Furthermore, Apple's behavior signaled customers that the company would not seek continuity in its operating systems in the future. In fact, Apple implemented, in fairly short order, two generations of incompatible operating systems – first the Lisa, and then the Macintosh.[8] Computer users, particularly commercial users, who found such abrupt changes to be disruptive took note of these policies. Commodore and Atari, which also were also early adopters of graphical user interface operating systems, took approaches similar to Apple's.

The Windows system is often criticized for continuing to carry the vestiges of the dated DOS system. But, as in all interesting economic problems, benefits are usually accompanied by a cost. The benefit of continuity from DOS to the various versions of Windows was unavoidably accompanied by the cost of carrying over certain DOS features.

METRIC VERSUS ENGLISH MEASUREMENT

George Washington, while president, spoke against the evils of metric. Did he know something we don't?

Washington was aware that the French had gone overboard in their adoption of metric. The switch to metric time in France after the revolution is a fascinating example of a case where the costs of switching were far greater than the benefits. The reason that metric time makes no sense is that is makes obsolete all clocks and provides no particular additional value. People do not often make calculations in time units, so having a system based on decimal units is of limited value. Metric time is rather like driving on the left or right side of the street – the choice is arbitrary, with little advantage for one over the other.

The costs of switching to metric measuring systems are nontrivial, and most Americans do not think that they outweigh the benefits. Tasks for which consumers most commonly use a measuring system, such as finding out how hot or cold it is outside, purchasing meat at the supermarket, or determining the speed of your automobile, do not benefit from metric. Thus, the failure to establish the metric system in the United States is a rational response to individual choices – not an indicator of a problem. This response contrasts sharply with the costly measures that have been implemented in Canada.

The metric system was adopted in Canada by government fiat in the 1970s. The change in standard happened only after considerable debate, and it is a high irony that one of the most persuasive arguments in this debate was that Canada needed to move quickly to stay on the same standard as the United States – where, at the time, there was some talk about a move to metric. In Canada, metric regulators went so far as to ban measurements in English units after the adoption of metric. Chaos in supermarkets and voter discontent quickly led regulators to allow the listing of both measurement systems, but metric continues to be the official measurement system in Canada. Nevertheless, to this day, English measurement is the de facto standard for many kinds of common measurement.

On the other hand, for many groups in the United States, such as scientists, metric is the standard. This is another example where the total number of people using a standard is less important than the particular individuals with whom one most closely interacts, and where two standards can coexist.

BUREAUCRACY AND THE MYTH OF MITI

All of these examples – keyboards, VCRs, computers, and the metric system – are fables that circulate as evidence of a kind of after-the-fact Murphy's law of markets. If something happened, it probably went wrong. But there is an opposite myth that may be even more costly. It is the myth that we could have avoided these 'disasters' by naming an omniscient, benevolent standards-dictator as an alternative to markets. Sometimes this savior is no more omniscient than a Monday morning quarterback: When he compares actual outcomes with a hypothetical ideal, it's obvious what should have happened. Often in these discussions, the wished-for arbiter of perfection is the government.

This is not to say that people don't harbor a good deal of cynicism about politics. But discussions of industrial policy often seem to incorporate a view that government, or the experts that it might draw upon, could figure out what technologies and standards are the best, even in the circumstances in which private parties are unable to sort these things out for themselves. It seems reasonable, however, to keep things even. There's no use in comparing real markets with a hypothetical, benevolent, and perfect government. Let's at least discipline ourselves to compare real markets with real government.

Now, governments are human institutions, and they are not omniscient. They can, however, do some very important things that private parties cannot manage. Even free-market types are usually willing to concede the utility of having a government that can record and enforce property rights, adjudicate contracts, and provide for the common defense. But governments can also fail. Even liberals acknowledge waste and fraud and misdirection of some government programs. For a better understanding of technology policy, what is required is not a litany of all the things that could happen, but some discussion of what has happened. For this, we do have a very good example: the Japanese Ministry of International Trade and Industry (MITI).

Only a few years ago, when the Japanese economy seemed to be a power-house that never made a misstep, MITI was often held up as an example of what the US government needed to do, an example of successful industrial policy. Now, with Japan in recession, and the repercussions of underpriced capital and subsidized industry being sharply felt, we do not hear so much about MITI. In fact, MITI is a story of substantial misdirection, of damaging commitments to particular technologies, and damaging restraints on entrepreneurs who were thought not to be doing the right things. MITI's gaffes are now well known – wrong on transistors, which succeeded; wrong on supercomputers, which did not; wrong on the buildup of the steel industry; wrong on synthetic fuels; wrong on Honda; and wrong on HDTV.[9] Very simply MITI, which may well have had the best shot of any government agency at steering an economy toward the best bets, was no substitute for the interplay of multitudes of profit-seeking rivals competing with each other to find the best mousetrap.

SOME OTHER EXAMPLES

Path-dependence advocates have sometimes claimed that the continued use of FORTRAN by academics and scientists is an example of getting stuck on the wrong standard.[10] But one doesn't have to peruse too many computer magazines to realize that FORTRAN has long ago been superseded by languages such as Pascal, C, C++, and now, perhaps, Java. Individuals continuing to use FORTRAN do so not because they want to be like everyone else, but because their cost of switching is too high. This is the opposite of the typical network-effects story. Network effects, as normally modeled, should have induced them to switch to mainstream programming languages years ago. This is a story of ordinary sunk costs, not of network 'externality' or other market failure. This is another story where, network effects, if of consequence, are not related to the total size of the networks as much as they are to the small group of individuals who interact in their work.

Path-dependence proponents have also sometimes claimed that the gasoline-powered engine might have been a mistake, and that steam or electricity might have been a superior choice for vehicle propulsion. They advance this argument in spite of the fact that in the century since automobiles became common, with all of the applications of motors and batteries in other endeavors, and with all the advantages of digital electronic power management systems, the most advanced electric automobiles that anyone has been able to make do not yet equal the state of the art in internal-combustion automobiles as of the late 1920s.

A number of scholars have begun to examine other instances that have, at one time or another, been alleged to illustrate lock-in to inferior standards. For many years, economic historians argued that the small coal cars that were used in England were an example of what was called 'technical backwardness.' The mechanism for this backwardness was much the same as other lock-in stories. The stock of cars led to certain adaptations around the cars, which led to renewal of the stock of cars, and so on. Recently, however, Va Nee Van Vleck (1997) reconsidered this case. She found that the small coal car was in fact well suited to Britain's geography and coal-distribution systems. In a very different subject area, Larry Ribstein and Bruce Kobayashi have examined the possibility that the adoption of state laws locks in the features of the statutes that are adopted by the first states to pass legislation. They find very little persistence of these initial statutory forms.

Finally, software applications offer many instances in which one product replaces another. Those histories are presented in detail in Liebowitz and Margolis (2001).

NOTES

1. The example is most prominent in Arthur (1990).
2. This history draws on Lardner (1987), chapters 3, 4, and 10.
3. In the economics literature of lock-in, the Beta–VHS story, very casually told, is often used to support the lock-in claim. Here, for example, is how Brian Arthur (1990) tells the story: 'The history of the videocassette recorder furnishes a simple example of positive feedback. The VCR market started out with two competing formats selling at about the same price: VHS and Beta. . . . Both systems were introduced at about the same time and so began with roughly equal market shares; those shares fluctuated early on because of external circumstance, 'luck' and corporate maneuvering. Increasing returns on early gains eventually tilted the competition toward VHS: it accumulated enough of an advantage to take virtually the entire VCR market. Yet it would have been impossible at the outset of the competition to say which system would win, which of the two possible equilibria would be selected. Furthermore, if the claim that Beta was technically superior is true, then the market's choice did not represent the best outcome' (p. 92).

4. See the discussion of a graphical spreadsheet (Excel) *vis-à-vis* text-based spreadsheets in chapter 7 of Liebowitz and Margolis (2001), where the speed penalty of the graphical product was rated as a fatal handicap.
5. The screen display on the PC required only 5 or 10 percent of the computer memory that was required by the Macintosh screen. Because this was constantly being updated when the screen changed, DOS screens tended to update instantaneously, whereas Macintosh screens had a noticeable lag and scrolling was much slower.
6. The original graphical user interface, developed at the Xerox PARC research center, had a mouse with three buttons. The PC has two. The use of but a single button appears to be a matter of pride in the Macintosh community and is sometimes defended as optimal. Another point that rabid Macintosh users often made when pointing to the superiority of their operating system has to do with whether menus drop down automatically, or require a mouse click. To most users, these are minor differences compared with the chasms that separated graphical and text based operating systems.
7. If Apple had been interested in converting DOS users, they could have incorporated DOS compatibility in their operating system (purchasing or licensing a DOS clone such as DR DOS, for example) and porting their operating system to the Intel platform so as not to render obsolete a user's hardware. Apple apparently thought of themselves as a hardware company and did not actively pursue this strategy.
8. This difference still separates the two companies. Apple, when it was switching to its recent Macintosh operating system (8.0), initially announced that it would not run software applications that were made to run under its older operating system (7.x). Microsoft, on the other hand, has been very careful about making Windows NT compatible with its Windows 95/98 operating system before it begins a serious migration of users, allowing five or six years for the process to be finished (assuming that Windows 2000 is delivered on time).
9. For a general discussion of the MITI, see Zinsmeister (1993).
10. In case you think we are making this up in order to create a ridiculous straw man, see Arthur (1990). A recent Stanford economics Ph.D. dissertation (Kirsch 1998) was also devoted to examining this issue. Kirsch reports to us that he went into the project hoping to find great inefficiency in the use of the internal combustion engine, but his research forced him to conclude otherwise.

REFERENCES

Arthur, W.B. 1990. 'Positive feedbacks in the economy.' *Scientific American* 262: 92–9.

Kirsch, David A. 1998. 'From competing technologies to systems rivalry: the electric motor vehicle in America, 1895–1915.' Ph.D. dissertation, Stanford University.

Klopfenstein, B.C. 1989. 'The diffusion of the VCR in the United States.' In M.R. Levy (ed.), *The VCR Age*. Newbury Park, Calif.: Sage Publications.

Lardner, J. 1987. *Fast Forward*. New York: W.W. Norton.

Liebowitz, Stan J. and Stephen E. Margolis. 2001. *Winners, Losers & Microsoft: Competition and Antitrust in High Technology*. Oakland, CA.: Independent Institute.

van Vleck, V.N. 1997. 'Delivering coal by road and rail in Great Britain: The efficiency of the "Silly Little Bobtailed Coal Wagons." ' *Journal of Economic History* 57: 139–60.

Zinsmeister, K. 1993. 'Japan's MITI Mouse.' *Policy Review* 64: 28–35.

11. Some evidence on the empirical significance of credit rationing[1]

Allen N. Berger and Gregory F. Udell

I. INTRODUCTION

The subject of credit rationing is the focus of a considerable body of theoretical analysis. One reason for this interest is the potentially important role that credit rationing may play in the transmission of monetary policy. Advocates of the availability doctrine in the 1950s suggested that monetary policy may operate in part through a rationing channel rather than an interest rate channel (e.g., Kareken, 1957; Scott, 1957). This early work on credit rationing depended on *ad hoc* price rigidity arguments for its motivation. Later work by Jaffee and Russell (1976) and Stiglitz and Weiss (1981) demonstrated that credit rationing may persist in equilibrium using information-based models. These papers spawned an entire generation of work on credit rationing based on an information-theoretic approach (e.g., Blinder and Stiglitz, 1983; Wette, 1983; Besanko and Thakor, 1987a, 1987b; Williamson, 1987).

Despite these theoretical efforts, there remains little consensus about whether credit rationing is an economically significant phenomenon. Riley (1987) argued that credit rationing in a Stiglitz–Weiss environment would be limited to the marginal class of observably distinct risk pools. Stiglitz and Weiss (1987) countered that Riley's result was model-specific rather than general. Others have argued that contractual mechanisms may be available that mitigate the rationing problem. These mechanisms include loan commitments (see Boot and Thakor, 1989; Sofianos, Wachtel, and Melnik, 1990) and collateral (see Bester, 1985; Chan and Kanatas, 1985; Besanko and Thakor, 1987b). Given the reasoned arguments on all sides of this issue, it is clear that the significance or insignificance of credit rationing will have to be established empirically.

Unfortunately, empirical tests of the extant theories of equilibrium credit rationing have been difficult to conduct because of the paucity of micro data on the contractual terms of commercial bank loans. Nevertheless, some evidence has been generated on this issue using macro data. Most of this research has exploited the fact that a key testable implication of credit rationing is that the commercial loan rate is 'sticky'; that is, it does not fully respond to changes in open-market rates. Often this research has focused on the speed with which the loan rate adjusts to market rates. Goldfeld (1966) and Jaffee (1971) found that the commercial loan rate was slow to adjust to open-market rate changes. Slovin and Sushka (1983) later found that the commercial loan rate was less 'sticky' than in Goldfeld's or Jaffee's results and took this as evidence against the credit rationing hypothesis, although their result may be subject to an alternative interpretation.[2] Using a different approach, King (1986, p. 298) found 'mixed support' for the credit rationing hypothesis. Sofianos et al. (1990) used time-series techniques and found evidence consistent with credit rationing, but only for loans funded without commitments. As discussed below, however, their results may also be subject to an alternative interpretation.

This chapter differs from previous empirical work on credit rationing of commercial loans in that individual loan data, rather than macro data, are employed. The micro data approach permits us to analyze the empirical implications of rationing models that relate to specific features of bank loan contracts and to examine the behavior of the commercial loan market at the individual loan level. The Federal Reserve's Survey of Terms of Bank Lending data set contains contract information on over 1 000 000 commercial loans made from 1977 to 1988.[3]

Consistent with previous studies, we find evidence of loan rate stickiness. In contrast to previous studies, however, we do not assume that this necessarily reflects credit rationing. While sticky loan pricing is consistent with the rationing hypothesis, it is not by itself sufficient evidence of it. One alternative explanation is that banks may offer implicit interest rate insurance to risk-averse repeat borrowers in the form of below-market rates during periods of high market rates, for which the banks are later compensated when market rates are low (see Fried and Howitt, 1980). Another possibility is that stickiness may be the result of loan recontracting between banks and companies experiencing financial distress when market interest rates are high. To avoid bankruptcy costs, banks may be willing to renegotiate and grant new loans at concessionary rates to such companies at these times (see Sharpe, 1991).

In this chapter, we develop a number of empirical tests that are capable of differentiating credit rationing from alternative explanations of price stickiness in commercial lending. We examine how loan rate stickiness varies across several loan contract features that may be related to rationing behavior. In addition, a more direct and definitive test of the quantitative effects of rationing focuses on the proportion of *new* loans that are issued under commitment. If rationing were widespread, this proportion would necessarily increase when credit markets are tight because borrowers without commitments can be rationed whereas commitment borrowers are contractually insulated from rationing.

The chapter proceeds as follows. Section II describes the data and the tests to be performed, and Section III gives the empirical results of those tests. Section IV presents conclusions.

II. DATA AND TEST DESCRIPTIONS

Our primary data source is the Federal Reserve's Survey of Terms of Bank Lending. Each quarter from 1977:1 to 1988:2, approximately 340 banks listed the individual characteristics of every domestic commercial and industrial loan and construction and land development loan made during one or more days of the first week of the second month of the quarter. The sample includes the 48 largest banks in the nation of terms of commercial and industrial lending plus 292 other banks chosen to represent the strata of smaller banks. Banks that withdrew from the sample were replaced with banks of similar size and other characteristics. In all, 460 different banks are represented in the sample.

Table 11.1 gives a description of each variable, as well as its sample mean, standard deviation, and number of independent observations.[4] The data set is quite large, with 1 103 933 independent observations on the terms of individual loans taken from 460 different banks and 46 time periods. The bank and macro variables, which have fewer independent observations, were allocated to their corresponding loan observations.

Tests of Loan Rate Stickiness

The 'stickiness tests' involve regressing the loan rate premium (PREM) against measures of real or nominal rates, the key loan contract variables, and a number of control variables for characteristics of the loan contract, the issuing bank, and the macro environment. For fixed-rate loans, PREM is the annualised (nominal) loan interest rate less the (nominal) rate on a Treasury security of comparable duration. For floating-rate loans, we ideally would subtract the Treasury rate with duration equal to the expected repricing interval, but this cannot be precisely determined from the data. As an approximation, we assume that all floating rate loans are expected to be repriced within four weeks and use the Treasury rate with duration equal to the minimum of the loan duration and four weeks.[5]

The primary exogenous variables are the comparable Treasury rate for each loan (TRATE) and its square (TRATE2), which measure open-market rates and summarize credit market conditions relevant to rationing. Note that the use of PREM and the TRATE variables allows for nonlinearities in the term

Table 11.1 Data used in regressions

	Mean	Standard Deviation	Number of Independent Observations
PREM	Annualized loan interest rate minus the rate for a Treasury security of equal duration, except that floating-rate loans over 4 weeks use the 4-week Treasury rate	0.0419	0.0217	1 103 933
TRATER	Real interest rate on a comparable Treasury security for the individual loan (as in PREM), calculated using the Livingstone Survey of inflationary expectations	0.0247	0.0259	1 103 933
TRATEN	Nominal interest rate on a comparable Treasury security for the individual loan (as in PREM)	0.0861	0.0332	1 103 933
CRUNCH	Equals one for quarters in which a credit crunch was operative, using Eckstein and Sinai (1986): 1978:2–1980:1, 1981:1–1982:4	0.2524	0.4344	46
COMMIT	Equals one if the loan is under commitment	0.5305	0.4991	1 103 993
FLOAT	Equals one if the loan is floating-rate	0.6152	0.4866	1 103 933
COLLAT	Equals one if the loan is secured (collateralized)	0.5760	0.4941	1 103 933
SIZE	Real size of the loan (LNSIZE = log[SIZE] used in regressions)	559.4 E3	369.1 E4	1 103 933
DURATION	Duration of the loan in years; the present-value weights use the initial loan interest rate (LNDURATION = log[DURATION] used in the regressions)	0.4106	0.6785	1 103 933

Variable	Description			
DEMAND	Equals one if the loan has no stated maturity (i.e., a demand note)	0.2618	0.4396	1 103 933
OVERNIGHT	Equals one if the loan is a 1-day (i.e., overnight) loan; set to zero prior to August 1982, when day of month maturities became available	0.0126	0.1113	599 387
SINGFAM	Equals one for a single-family construction and development loan	0.0455	0.2084	1 103 933
MULTIFAM	Equals one for a multifamily construction and development loan	0.0070	0.0831	1 103 933
NONRES	Equals one for a nonresidential construction and development loan	0.0270	0.1622	1 103 933
LNBANKASSETS	Natural logarithm of the total assets of the bank	15.1198	1.6985	6 293
GNPGROWTH	Real GNP growth over the previous quarter (%)	0.7630	1.0120	46
UNEMPLOY	Unemployment rate (%)	7.2077	1.2826	46
TIME	Time trend for the 46 dates (1, . . ., 46)	24.3343	13.6733	46
BANKDUMMIES	Dummies for all sample banks were included in every regression	. . .	. . .	460

Note: All dollar figures are constant 1987 dollars except as noted.

structure of interest rates, which would not be the case if the loan rate were used instead as the dependent variable and a single representative Treasury rate and the loan duration were included as regressors. A second measure of credit market tightness is the dummy variable CRUNCH, which takes on the value one for quarters in which Eckstein and Sinai (1986) determined that a credit crunch was operative. This variable allows for additional nonlinear effects of credit market conditions and allows us to focus particularly on the time periods in which rationing may have been most likely to occur.[6]

The analysis was conducted using both real and nominal interest rates as exogenous variables, denoted by TRATER and TRATEN, respectively. This represents a break from the empirical literature, which generally considers only nominal rates. Note that the dependent variable PREM does not depend on real versus nominal considerations, since it is the difference between two rates of the same duration. The use of the real rate (TRATER) more closely corresponds with the theoretical literature on credit rationing, which essentially describes a real phenomenon. Unfortunately, use of the real rate suffers in practice because inflationary expectations are unknown. In estimating inflationary expectations, we tried models of both rational and adaptive expectations as well as the Livingston Survey data. Since the results were similar across approaches, we simply report the results from using the Livingston data here. Use of the nominal rate (TRATEN) has the virtue of largely avoiding mismeasurement problems, but it may fail to capture effectively the changes in credit market tightness. However, to the extent that some economic agents react to changes in nominal prices because of nominal price stickiness in output or factor markets or because of difficulties in contracting in real rates, nominal rate stickiness may still be indicative of credit rationing.

In contrast to some of the empirical literature (e.g. Goldfeld, 1966; Jaffee, 1971; Slovin and Sushka, 1983), we use only contemporaneous open-market interest rates and do not include lags. In our opinion, this provides a cleaner test of the Jaffee and Russell (1976) and Stiglitz and Weiss (1981) models of *equilibrium* credit rationing. These are one-period models of lender responses to current credit market conditions. Therefore, the current comparable Treasury rate for the loan and its square seem to be good summary statistics for the conditions relevant to the setting of rates and rationing policies on *newly issued* loans. Thus the model tests whether, in equilibrium, banks raise loan rates equally with increases in risk-free open-market rates or whether they ration loan funds, *not* how long it takes to reach equilibrium.

In some of the regression models, the credit market tightness variables TRATE and CRUNCH are interacted with three key contract variables, COMMIT, COLLAT, and FLOAT, in order to determine whether loans with different contract terms exhibit different degrees of stickiness. Under a loan commitment contract, the lender agrees to extend credit at the borrower's request up to some prespecified amount over a given time period. Commitments explicitly provide insurance against credit rationing because they preclude the bank from denying a funding request on the basis of general market conditions (see Melnik and Plaut, 1986; Sofianos et al., 1990).[7] Indeed, a recent loan officer survey (Board of Governors, 1988) indicated that 'protection against credit crunches' ranked only behind minimizing transactions costs as a motivation for commitments. Therefore, any observed stickiness on commitment loans cannot reflect credit rationing of commitment borrowers, since they are contractually insulated from rationing.

The difference in stickiness between commitment and noncommitment loan rates may also reflect the difference in relative magnitudes of information problems between commitment and noncommitment borrowers and in the power of micro contracting to solve these problems. A study of loan commitments found commitment loans to be safer on average than noncommitment loans, suggesting that commitment borrowers may have fewer than average information problems (see Avery and Berger, 1991), although in some tangentially related research, commitments are not negatively related to all the risk measures (see Berger and Udell, 1990, 1992). The nature of the commitment contract or the commitment selection process might also attenuate the kinds of information problems that have typically been associated with credit rationing (see Boot, Thakor, and Udell, 1987; Kanatas, 1987; Thakor and Udell, 1987; Berkovitch and Greenbaum, 1991). Thus if information problems are creating the stickiness, it is likely that commitment loan rates would be less sticky, reflecting fewer information problems for commitment borrowers or the attenuation of these problems by the commitments.

Collateral has been found to be associated with higher risk and therefore may be associated with more information problems and loan rate stickiness (see Berger and Udell, 1990). However, the pledging of collateral can also mitigate information problems, reducing the associated stickiness (see Bester, 1985; Chan and Kanatas, 1985; Besanko and Thakor, 1987a, 1987b). Thus rates on secured loans may be more or less sticky than unsecured loans. Finally, floating-rate loans may have a different degree of stickiness than fixed-rate loans because of any sorting associated with the degree of fixity in rate repricing or differences related to the sharing of interest rate risk.

Tests of Proportions of Loans with Different Contract Features

The 'proportions tests' examine the testable implications of credit rationing that relate to how the proportions of new loans with different contract features vary with credit market tightness. The methodology is to form logit models of the probabilities that one dollar being lent for 1 year will (i) be under commitment, (ii) be secured, or (iii) be floating rate. Computing limitations rule out the possibility of using observation-by-observation logit estimations, so grouped logit models were formed by combining the loans made by a given bank at a given time. For every variable for which data were available by individual loan, a weighted average across all the loans for the bank-date combination was formed, with the weights being proportional to the size and duration of the individual loans. In this way, each loan is represented in proportion to its contribution to the bank's future loan portfolio.[8] The dependent variables were also transformed into log-odds ratio form $\ln[Y/(1 - Y)]$, where Y is the size-duration weighted proportion of new loans with the characteristic being examined (e.g., COMMIT). This form preserves the functional relationship of the observation-by-observation logit form but loses some information by averaging. Each regression was estimated by weighted least squares to avoid heteroskedasticity problems.[9]

The COMMIT proportions test provides a relatively direct and definitive test of the quantitative significance of credit rationing. If credit rationing is economically important, then the proportion of new bank loans made under commitment must increase substantially with open-market rates and credit market tightness. Simply put, rationing decreases the quantity of noncommitment lending from what it otherwise would have been but cannot reduce the quantity of commitment lending because of contractual constraints.[10] Two other factors related to information problems may also induce a positive relationship between open-market rates and the commitment proportion *even if no rationing actually occurs*: (i) borrowers may avoid rationing by switching funding from noncommitment sources to existing commitment lines (if not deterred by commitment covenants) or (ii) more borrowers may purchase commitment contracts when the probability of being rationed is increased.[11] It follows that a virtual necessary, but not sufficient, condition for rationing to be an important macro-economic phenomenon is that the proportion of new loans made under commitment increases substantially when open-market interest rates rise.

The COLLAT and FLOAT proportions tests are intended to reveal the extent to which rationing, if it occurs, affects borrowers with different contract terms differently. For instance, how the COLLAT proportion reacts to changes in open-market interest rates may reveal the net effect of (i) the difference in information problems for secured versus unsecured borrowers, (ii) the extent to which collateral arrangements solve these problems, and (iii) the extent to which borrowers who do not pledge collateral when rates are low may pledge collateral when rates are high to avoid rationing.

Both the stickiness and the proportions regressions include a number of additional loan-specific, macro, and bank variables as control variables. The loan-specific contract variable LNSIZE accounts for the possibility of scale economies in lending and the possibility that loan size may also be associated with credit risk; LNDURATION accounts for the possibility of a nonrisk term premium component of the dependent variable or another scale economy in lending; DEMAND accounts for differences in risk created by the bank's option to call a loan and any sorting effects related to this option. The OVERNIGHT, SINGFAM, MULTIFAM, and NONRES variables are exogenous factors that may provide information about the type of borrower or loan. The macro variables, GNPGROWTH, UNEMPLOY, TIME, and the square of TIME, are included to control for the effects of non-credit market cycles, changes in aggregate risk, and other trends that may be correlated with credit market conditions. The bank variable LNBANKASSETS is included to account for the possibility of segmented markets in which different-sized banks have access to different types of borrowers. Finally, every regression contains dummy variables for every bank in the sample to control for systematic differences in pricing caused by the presence of other pricing elements (e.g., up-front fees or compensating balances), as well as differences in regulatory and competitive environments across banks. The use of the individual bank dummies essentially provides the strongest set of controls for any type of stable bank differences that can be specified.

III.　EMPIRICAL RESULTS

Stickiness Test Results

Tables 11.2 and 11.3 show the results of the stickiness tests. The loan rate premia (PREM) are regressed on real and nominal rates, respectively, as well as loan contract terms and macro and bank control variables, although the coefficients of the control variables are not shown here (see Berger and Udell [1989] for these coefficients). All coefficients and derived statistics (including the coefficients of the control variables) are statistically significant because of the unusually large number of observations. The regression shown in column 1 of Table 11.2 has as regressors the real Treasury rate appropriate for the individual loan (TRATER) and its square (TRATER2), but excludes CRUNCH and any interaction terms. The individual coefficients of TRATER and TRATER2 are difficult to interpret because the variables move together, but their coefficients have opposite signs. To obtain a more meaningful summary statistic that measures the effects of a tightening of the credit market, we computed the predicted change in PREM that would be caused by a doubling of TRATER from its mean (i.e., from 2.472 percent to 4.944 percent). The predicted change and its t-statistic are shown in column 1 of the bottom section of the table. The –0.0059 predicted change suggests that when real rates double, the premium over the risk-free rate drops 59 basis points.[12] This represents a substantial degree of

Table 11.2 Regressions of loan-rate premia (PREM) on real interest rates, loan contract terms and control variables

Variable	(1) Coefficient	t-Statistic	(2) Coefficient	t-Statistic	(3) Coefficient	t-Statistic	(4) Coefficient	t-Statistic	(5) Coefficient	t-Statistic
TRATER	−0.4912**	−239.3	−0.5973**	−249.0	−0.6452**	−259.8	−0.5392**	−220.5	−0.5930**	−234.9
TRATER 2	3.4176**	150.7	3.6801**	161.5	3.8687**	169.4	3.6795**	162.0	3.8555**	169.5
CRUNCH					−2.2E − 4*	−2.5			0.0044***	−46.2
TR-COM-FLOAT			0.1289**	76.7	0.1089**	64.2				
TR-COM-FIXED			0.0379**	17.2	0.0288**	13.1				
TR-NOCOM-FLOAT			0.1436**	75.9	0.1292**	67.9				
TR-COL-FLOAT							0.0740**	41.6	0.0694**	38.7
TR-COL-FIXED							−0.1062**	−52.9	−0.0971**	−48.5
TR-NOCOL-FLOAT							0.0842**	43.1	0.0633**	32.1
CR-COM-FLOAT					0.0112**	107.8				
CR-COM-FIXED					0.0060**	46.9				
CR-NOCOM-FLOAT					0.0085**	73.5				
CR-COL-FLOAT									0.0043**	39.1
CR-COL-FIXED									−0.0066**	−57.2
CR-NOCOL-FLOAT									0.0074**	60.9
COMMIT	−0.0030**	−71.1					−0.0032**	−76.1	−0.0031**	−74.1
COLLAT	9.9E − 4**	25.0	0.0011**	27.8	0.0010**	25.9				
FLOAT	0.0081**	178.1								
COM-FLOAT			0.0015**	20.8	−0.0016**	−20.6				
COM-FIXED			−0.0043**	−50.7	−0.0062**	−68.4				
NOCOM-FLOAT			0.0040**	53.0	0.0012**	15.4				
COL-FLOAT							0.0064**	86.3	0.0051**	64.5
COL-FIXED							6.7E − 4**	8.8	0.0026**	31.0
NOCOL-FLOAT							0.0030**	38.0	0.0014**	16.5
R^2	0.28		0.28		0.29		0.29		0.30	

Simulated Effects of an Increase in Credit Market Tightness:

Predicted Change in PREM and *t*-Statistic from a Doubling of TRATER from Its Mean (0.02472) for Different Categories of Loans

COM- OR COL-FLOAT LOANS	-0.0059**	-249.6	-0.0048**	-149.8	-0.0062**	-182.3	-0.0048**	-145.2	-0.0059**	-171.7
COM- OR COL-FIXED LOANS			-0.0071**	-142.0	-0.0081**	-160.4	-0.0092**	-218.2	-0.0100**	-230.3
NOCOM- OR NOCOL-FLOAT LNS			-0.0045**	-116.2	-0.0057**	-140.9	-0.0045**	-120.8	-0.0060**	-153.7
NOCOM- OR NOCOL-FIXED LNS			-0.0080**	-228.1	-0.0089**	-240.9	-0.0066**	-173.6	-0.0076**	-192.8

Predicted Change in PREM and *t*-Statistic from a Credit Crunch (CRUNCH) for Different Categories of Loans

COM- OR COL-FLOAT LOANS					0.0109**	117.4			0.0086**	93.5
COM- OR COL-FIXED LOANS					0.0058**	48.1			-0.0023**	-22.8
NOCOM- OR NOCOL-FLOAT LNS					0.0082**	77.5			0.0117**	110.5
NOCOM- OR NOCOL-FIXED LNS					$-2.2E-4$*	-2.5			0.0044**	46.2

Note: Each observation represents the terms of an individual loan contract. Number of observations is 1 103 933. Intercepts were included for each bank in the sample, and the R^2's reflect the proportion of variance explained after these intercepts. Also included but not shown are the control variables LNSIZE, LNDURATION, DEMAND, OVERNIGHT, SINGFAM, MULTIFAM, NONRES, LNBANKASSETS, GNPGROWTH, UNEMPLOY, TIME, and TIME2.
* Statistically significant at the 5 percent level, two-sided.
** Statistically significant at the 1 percent level, two-sided.

Table 11.3 Regressions of loan-rate premia (PREM) on nominal interest rates, loan contract terms and control variables

Variable	(1) Coefficient	(1) t-Statistic	(2) Coefficient	(2) t-Statistic	(3) Coefficient	(3) t-Statistic	(4) Coefficient	(4) t-Statistic	(5) Coefficient	(5) t-Statistic
TRATEN	−0.2649**	−55.1	−0.4486**	−90.7	−0.4262**	−85.9	−0.3437**	−69.8	−0.3399**	−68.7
TRATEN 2	0.5819**	29.8	0.8520**	43.9	0.7787**	40.0	0.7624**	39.4	0.6945**	35.8
CRUNCH					−0.0012**	−12.6			0.0016**	16.0
TR-COM-FLOAT			0.1834**	131.8	0.1429**	89.3				
TR-COM-FIXED			0.0946**	51.2	0.0699**	33.8				
TR-NOCOM-FLOAT			0.1778**	113.9	0.1550**	86.0				
TR-COL-FLOAT							0.0865**	59.1	0.0775**	46.1
TR-COL-FIXED							−0.1296**	−76.8	−0.1046**	−55.4
TR-NOCOL-FLOAT							0.1167**	73.3	0.0898**	48.4
CR-COM-FLOAT					0.0065**	53.5				
CR-COM-FIXED					0.0040**	26.9				
CR-NOCOM-FLOAT					0.0037**	27.5				
CR-COL-FLOAT									0.0015**	11.7
CR-COL-FIXED									−0.0039**	−29.2
CR-NOCOL-FLOAT									0.0040**	28.0
COMMIT		−67.8					−0.0031**	−72.6	−0.0030**	−71.1
COLLAT	9.1E − 4**	22.4	9.6E − 4**	23.8	8.9E − 4**	22.2				
FLOAT	0.0088**	186.9								
COM-FLOAT			0.013**	−80.5	−0.0096**	−66.1				
COM-FIXED			−0.0123**	−68.5	−0.0114**	−62.5				
NOCOM-FLOAT			0.0082**	−53.0	0.0075**	−46.7				
COL-FLOAT							9.8E − 4**	6.7	0.0013**	8.8
COL-FIXED							0.0094**	57.1	0.0084**	50.2
NOCOL-FLOAT							−0.0049**	−30.8	−0.0035**	−21.3
R^2	0.24		0.25		0.26		0.26		0.26	

Simulated Effects of an Increase in Credit Market Tightness:
Predicted Change in PREM and *t*-Statistic from Increasing TRATEN from Its Mean (0.08608)
by 0.02472 for Different Categories of Loans

	PREM	*t*	PREM	*t*	PREM	*t*	PREM	*t*	PREM	*t*
COM- OR COL-FLOAT LOANS	-0.0037**	-120.1	-0.0024**	-68.7	-0.0032**	-84.0	-0.0026**	-75.6	-0.0031**	-81.2
COM- OR COL-FIXED LOANS			-0.0046**	-96.6	-0.0050**	-97.2	-0.0080**	-185.5	-0.0076**	-165.6
NOCOM- OR NOCOL-FLOAT LNS			-0.0025**	-65.8	-0.0029**	-67.3	-0.0019**	-49.8	-0.0028**	-65.5
NOCOM- OR NOCOL-FIXED LNS			-0.0069**	-179.4	-0.0067**	-165.4	-0.0048**	-119.7	-0.0050**	-118.1

Predicted Change in PREM and *t*-Statistic from a Credit Crunch (CRUNCH) for Different Categories of Loans

	PREM	*t*	PREM	*t*
COM- OR COL-FLOAT LOANS	0.0053**	50.9	0.0031**	30.6
COM- OR COL-FIXED LOANS	0.0028**	20.6	-0.0022**	-20.2
NOCOM- OR NOCOL-FLOAT LNS	0.0025**	20.8	0.0056**	46.3
NOCOM- OR NOCOL-FIXED LNS	-0.0012**	-12.6	0.0016**	16.0

Note: See note to Table 11.2.
** Statistically significant at the 1 percent level, two-sided.

stickiness in loan rates when compared to the historical average bank return on assets, which is less than 100 basis points. The elasticity of PREM with respect to TRATER evaluated at the sample mean is also substantial, –0.19.

The regression shown in column 1 of table 3 repeats the experiment using nominal Treasury rates (TRATEN, TRATEN2) in place of the real rates. When nominal rates are increased by the same amount as the real rates (2.472 percent), the measured stickiness is somewhat less, 37 basis points. This becomes much larger, 99 basis points (not shown), if nominal rates are instead doubled from their relatively large sample mean value (8.608 percent). We consider the lesser of these two increases to be more reliable, since twice the mean nominal rate is well above the dense part of the TRATEN distribution. The elasticity of PREM with respect to the nominal rate evaluated at the mean is –0.34, which exceeds (in absolute value) the real rate elasticity because of the larger mean of TRATEN.[13]

Figure 11.1 illustrates the relationships between the loan rate premia and Treasury rates over time. The solid lines in the figure connect the size-dura-tion weighted averages of PREM across all loans for each time period; the broken lines connect the weighted averages of TRATER in Figure 11.1a and TRATEN in Figure 11.1b. As shown, PREM is very highly negatively corre-lated with both real and nominal rates over the period from about 1979:4 to 1982:4 but is not highly related for the remainder of the sample. During this period, rates were at highs relative to the recent past, then fell and rose again to their sample peaks. The strong negative relationship during this period is consistent with credit rationing but is also consistent with the alternative theo-ries of rate stickiness.

By construction, the stickiness illustrated thus far is the same for all types of loans since TRATE was not interacted with any other variables in the regressions. However, as discussed above, most of the interesting testable implications apply to *relative* stickiness, which we turn to next. The regression shown in column 2 of Table 11.2 reproduces the regression in column 1 but allows stickiness to differ across loans in four categories of commitment and floating-rate status. The dummy variables COMMIT and FLOAT are replaced by three interaction terms, COM-FLOAT, COM-FIXED, and NOCOM-FLOAT, and these variables are interacted with TRATE, denoted by TR-COM-FLOAT, TR-COM-FIXED, and TR-NOCOM-FLOAT. This allows the four commitment-rate type combinations (including the unspecified category NOCOM-FIXED) to have independent degrees of stickiness. The results in column 2 suggest that all four categories of loans have sticky rates. When real rates are doubled, commitment loans have roughly the same stickiness as noncommitment loans for a given rate type (48 vs. 45 basis points for floating-rate and 71 vs. 80 basis points for fixed-rate), but floating-rate loans are substantially less sticky than fixed-rate loans for a given commitment status

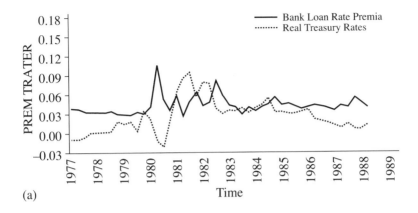

(a)

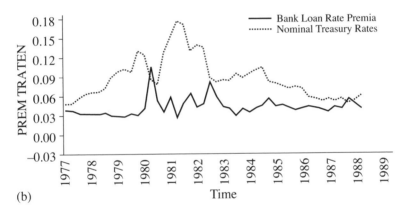

(b)

Figure 11.1 *Bank loan premia and Treasury rates of the same duration*
(1977: 1–1988: 2); (a) real Treasury rates; (b) nominal
Treasury rates

(48 vs. 71 basis points for commitment and 45 vs. 80 basis points for noncommitment). Column 3 replicates column 2 but adds the variable CRUNCH and its interactions with the other variables as well. The results show that during periods designated as credit crunches, the PREM actually *increased* for three of the four categories, contrary to the expectation under credit rationing that premia would be lower during credit crunches. In addition, an interaction term between TRATER and CRUNCH added to the regression (not shown) had a positive coefficient, suggesting that the responsiveness of loan rates to open-market rates is greater during credit crunches, again contrary to expectations if borrowers are rationed during crunches. These findings suggest either that the observed stickiness in the other regressions is largely unrelated to credit

rationing or that the Eckstein-Sinai credit crunches do not correspond well with rationing periods.[14] The results for nominal rates shown in the corresponding columns in Table 11.3 largely replicate those in Table 11.2, with the exception that commitment loans display somewhat less stickiness than noncommitment loans.

The finding that stickiness on commitment loans is substantial and is nearly the same as that on noncommitment loans of the same rate type suggests that the empirical literature that equated stickiness with credit rationing may be misleading. A large portion of all rate stickiness is accounted for by commitment loans and cannot be associated with credit rationing because commitment contracts preclude rationing. In addition, *if* the stickiness is caused by Stiglitz and Weiss-type information problems, we would expect rates on commitment loans to be less sticky than those on noncommitment loans, given the empirical results cited earlier and corroborated here that commitments are associated with higher than average quality borrowers who likely have relatively few information problems.[15] Therefore, the finding of near-equality of stickiness between commitment and noncommitment loan rates suggests that information problems are not the dominant reasons for rate stickiness.

The finding that stickiness is much more prevalent on fixed-rate than floating-rate loans has no direct implications for credit rationing but may be consistent with an alternative hypothesis. If lenders provide implicit interest rate insurance, this result suggests that they do so through fixed-rate loan contracts that insulate the borrowers from rate variation over the life of the contract.[16]

The results shown in columns 4 and 5 of Tables 11.2 and 11.3 replicate the models shown in columns 2 and 3, respectively, except that COLLAT replaces COMMIT in all the interaction terms. The results again show that rates on fixed-rate loans are stickier that those on floating-rate loans. They also again show that stickiness is generally less during CRUNCH periods, contrary to the predictions of the extant theories of credit rationing. The new result is that secured loans exhibit more rate stickiness than other loans with the same floating- or fixed-rate status in most cases, although the difference is often slight.[17] *If* information problems are driving the rate stickiness, then the slightly greater stickiness of secured loan rates suggests that borrowers who pledge collateral have more information problems than other borrowers (consistent with their greater risk discussed above) and that the process of pledging collateral does not fully offset these problems.

We also reran the main regressions using rates of growth of aggregate loans in place of the TRATE variables as alternative measures of credit market tightness (not shown). The results suggested that increasing credit tightness by reducing loan growth from its mean to zero actually results in slightly *higher* loan rate premia, contrary to the implications of credit rationing. The fact that loan rate premia do not consistently decline with alternative measures of credit market tightness (CRUNCH and reduced loan growth) suggests that rationing does not play an important role during periods of overall credit market tightness. This makes it more difficult to argue that credit rationing is an important macroeconomic phenomenon.

The stickiness data may also be used to examine Riley's (1987) version of credit rationing, which suggests that rationing would be substantial only for the marginal class of observably distinct risk pools. If differences across rate premia at a given time largely reflect risk differentials, then the stickiness results shown in Tables 11.2 and 11.3 would hold primarily for the loans with the highest premia (i.e., highest risk) under Riley's hypothesis. To examine this possibility, the data were ordered by PREM for each time period, separated into quintiles, and grouped with data from the same quintiles from all the other time periods. Rerunning the regressions separately for each quintile group showed that the stickiness prevailed over all five quintiles. When a difference appeared, the most stickiness was observed in the lowest-premium (i.e., safest) quintile and the least stickiness in the highest (i.e., riskiest) quintile. These results run contrary to the predictions of Riley's model. They also provide a robustness check of the main stickiness results, which prevail across different premia levels.

One final insight from the stickiness analysis comes from examination of the raw data on PREM. The data reveal that banks at times extend loans with interest rates below the comparable risk-free rate. To investigate this, we identify loans for which the rate is at least 1 percent below the comparable risk-free (i.e., PREM < –0.01) to guard against overmeasuring negative premia lending. While these negative loans are only 1 percent of the entire sample, their proportion varies directly with the interest rate cycle. They peaked at 7 percent of the sample when open-market rates were at their peak in 1982:2, more than 70 times as high as in the mid to late 1980s when open-market rates were substantially lower. The incidence of negative-premia loans is also more than 10 times as great on fixed-rate loans as on floating-rate loans, 2.3 percent versus 0.2 percent, respectively. These data are not consistent with extant theories of credit rationing, which require that banks earn a nonnegative expected economic profit on *each* loan by charging a rate sufficiently above the risk-free rate to compensate for expected credit losses. However, lending at a negative premium *is* consistent with other explanations of stickiness that recognize long-term lending relationships, such as implicit interest rate insurance or recontracting with financially distressed borrowers.

Overall, the stickiness results suggest that the empirical literature that equated stickiness with credit rationing may have been misleading because of the lack of available information on specific loan contract terms. With the notable exception of some of the collateral results, the data generally do not support the currently available theories of credit rationing as the dominant explanations of the stickiness. Nearly half of the observed stickiness occurs on commitment loans that cannot be symptomatic of rationing of this pool of borrowers, since they are contractually protected from rationing. Similarly, the portion of stickiness that is due to negative rate premia cannot reflect equilibrium credit rationing, which requires a nonnegative expected profit on each loan. The near-equality of stickiness on commitment and noncommitment loans casts additional doubt on whether information problems are major causes of stickiness, given the evidence in the literature that commitment loans are relatively safe and are likely associated with relatively few information problems. In addition, the finding that loan rate premia generally do not decrease in response to alternative measures of credit market tightness also casts doubts on whether the observed stickiness is symptomatic of credit rationing.[18]

Proportions Test Results

Tables 11.4 and 11.5 give the results for the proportions tests using real and nominal Treasury rates, respectively. The dependent variables are log-odds ratios ($\ln[Y/(1 - Y)]$) for the three important loan characteristics, COMMIT, COLLAT, and FLOAT. The exogenous variables are the same as those in the stickiness tests, except that all loan variables are size-duration weighted and no interaction terms are specified. Column 1 of Tables 11.4 and 11.5 shows the regressions for the probabilities that a dollar-year of loans will be made under commitment as functions of real and nominal rates, respectively; column 2 of both tables adds the CRUNCH variable. As discussed above, if credit rationing is an important macroeconomic phenomenon, then it is a virtual necessary condition that the proportion of new loans issued under commitment be substantially higher when rates are high. As shown in the bottom section of column 1 in Table 11.4 a doubling of real rates yields a 0.069 increase in the log-odds ratio $\ln[\text{COMMIT}/(1 - \text{COMMIT})]$. As also shown, this translates into an increase in the probability of COMMIT of 1.7 percent when evaluated at the mean probability of COMMIT of 49.7 percent.[19] Note that this 1.7 percent is effectively an estimate of the maximum effect of a doubling of real rates, since the logit specification yields the maximum derivatives at a 50 percent probability, with smaller effects toward the limiting probabilities of zero and 100 percent. The CRUNCH variable in column 2 of Table 11.4 again goes in the opposite direction of that predicted by rationing and actually has a larger absolute effect (−3.5 percent) than the doubling of real rates. Similarly, when the rate of real or nominal aggregate loan growth was substituted for TRATER, the predicted effect from decreasing loan growth from the mean to zero actually *reduced* the probability of COMMIT, contrary to the implications of credit rationing (not shown). The effects of nominal rates shown in columns

Table 11.4 *Grouped logit regressions of the probabilities of different loan contract terms on real interest rates and control variables*

Variable	ln[COMMIT/(1 – COMMIT)] (1) Coefficient	t-Statistic	ln[COMMIT/(1 – COMMIT)] (2) Coefficient	t-Statistic	ln[COLLAT/(1 – COLLAT)] (3) Coefficient	t-Statistic	ln[COLLAT/(1 – COLLAT)] (4) Coefficient	t-Statistic	ln[FLOAT/(1 – FLOAT)] (5) Coefficient	t-Statistic	ln[FLOAT/(1 – FLOAT)] (6) Coefficient	t-Statistic
TRATER	-2.1449*	-2.04	-0.9288	-0.85	-4.2401**	-3.76	-6.1881**	-5.36	-10.2090**	-8.23	-11.2191**	-8.83
TRATER2	65.5894**	5.90	61.3072**	5.49	15.3677	1.31	19.8048	1.69	83.9995**	6.59	86.4415**	6.78
CRUNCH			-0.1393**	-4.28			0.2553**	7.70			0.1323**	3.64
COMMIT	0.0464	1.05	0.0741	1.66	0.1131**	2.97	0.1195**	3.15	0.0826*	2.05	0.0818*	2.03
COLLAT	0.2896**	7.55	0.3019**	7.85					0.8240**	17.59	0.7988**	16.87
FLOAT					0.4397**	13.38	0.4093**	12.40				
R^2	0.12		0.12		0.17		0.18		0.09		0.09	

Simulated Effects of an Increase in Credit Market Tightness:

Predicted Change in Dependent Variable and *t*-Statistic from a Doubling of TRATER from Its mean (from 0.0250 to 0.0500)

	(1) Coefficient	t-Statistic	(2) Coefficient	t-Statistic	(3) Coefficient	t-Statistic	(4) Coefficient	t-Statistic	(5) Coefficient	t-Statistic	(6) Coefficient	t-Statistic
	0.0694**	6.19	0.0917	7.43	-0.0772**	-6.50	-0.1176**	-9.08	-0.0977**	-7.56	-0.1184**	-8.39

Change in the Probability of the Category at Its Mean from a Doubling of TRATER

	(1)	(2)	(3)	(4)	(5)	(6)
	0.0173	0.0229	-0.0193	-0.0293	-0.0244	-0.0296

Predicted Change in Dependent Variable and *t*-Statistic from a Credit Crunch (CRUNCH)

	(2) Coefficient	t-Statistic	(4) Coefficient	t-Statistic	(6) Coefficient	t-Statistic
	-0.1393**	-4.28	0.2553**	7.70	0.1323**	3.64

Change in the Probability of the Category at Its Mean from a Credit Crunch

	(2)	(4)	(6)
	-0.0348	0.0627	0.0330

Note: Each observation represents the size–duration weighted terms for a bank-date combination. Each dependent variable is $\ln[1/(1 – Y)]$, where Y is the size–duration weighted proportion of loans with the specified contract terms. Number of observations is 12,678. Intercepts were included for each bank in the sample, and the R^2's reflect the proportion of variance explained after these intercepts. Also included but not shown are the control variables LNSIZE, LNDURATION, DEMAND, OVERNIGHT, SINGFAM, MULTIFAM, NONRES, LNBANKASSETS, GNPGROWTH, UNEMPLOY, TIME, and TIME2.

* Statistically significant at the 5 percent level, two-sided.

** Statistically significant at the 1 percent level, two-sided.

227

Table 11.5 Grouped logit regressions of the probabilities of different loan contract terms on nominal interest rates and control variables

Variable	ln[COMMIT/(1 − COMMIT)] (1)		ln[COMMIT/(1 − COMMIT)] (2)		ln[COLLAT/(1 − COLLAT)] (3)		ln[COLLAT/(1 − COLLAT)] (4)		ln[FLOAT/(1 − FLOAT)] (5)		ln[FLOAT/(1 − FLOAT)] (6)	
	Coefficient	t-Statistic	Coefficient	t-Statistic	Coefficient	t-Statistic	Coefficient	t-Statistic	Coefficient	t-Statistic	Coefficient	t-Statistic
TRATEN	−12.4111**	−6.03	−12.1075**	−5.87	2.0088	1.03	1.7832	0.92	−9.3174**	−4.25	−9.2991**	−4.24
TRATEN2	53.8996**	6.58	54.9265**	6.70	−17.6635*	−2.25	−24.7333**	−3.14	40.6003**	4.64	40.9712**	4.67
CRUNCH			−0.0857*	−2.55			0.3005***	8.59			−0.0169**	−0.44
COMMIT					0.1119**	2.94	0.1153***	3.04	0.0894*	2.21	0.0900*	2.22
COLLAT	0.0814	1.83	0.0955*	2.13					0.8828**	18.81	0.8858**	18.68
FLOAT	0.2832**	7.38	0.2864**	7.47	0.4663**	14.28	0.4486**	13.75				
R^2	0.12		0.12		0.17		0.18		0.09		0.09	

Simulated Effects of an Increase in Credit Market Tightness:

Predicted Change in Dependent Variable and t-Statistic from Increasing TRATEN from Its mean (from 0.0859 to 0.0250)

	−0.0451**	−3.13	−0.0324*	−2.13	−0.0332*	−2.16	−0.0309	−1.91	−0.0365**	−2.74	−0.0771**	−5.46

Change in the Probability of the Category at Its Mean from Increasing TRATEN by 0.250

	−0.0113		−0.0081		−0.0083		−0.0077		−0.0091		−0.0193	

Predicted Change in Dependent Variable and t-Statistic from a Credit Crunch (CRUNCH)

			−0.0857*	−2.55			0.3005**	8.59			−0.0169**	−0.44

Change in the Probability of the Category at Its Mean from a Credit Crunch

			−0.0214				0.0735				0.0042	

Note: See note to Table 11.4.
* Statistically significant at the 5 percent level, two-sided.
** Statistically significant at the 1 percent level, two-sided.

1 and 2 of Table 11.5 show a decrease in the probability of COMMIT of about 1 percent, with both CRUNCH and nominal loan growth (not shown) also predicting a decrease in COMMIT when markets are tight. Thus in all but one of six cases, the COMMIT probability moves in the opposite direction of that predicted by rationing theory, and the one exception is a very small increase.

Figure 11.2 illustrates the relationships between the COMMIT/NONCOM-MIT ratio and Treasury rates over time. The solid lines in the figure connect the size-duration weighted averages of the COMMIT/NONCOMMIT ratio for each time period, and the broken lines connect the weighted averages of TRATER and TRATEN. The ratio is negatively correlated with both real and nominal rates over the 1979:4–1982:4 period and is either positively correlated

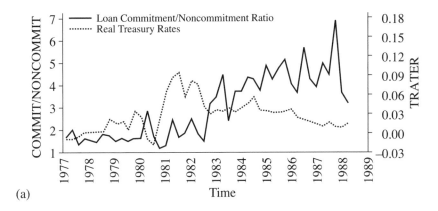

(a)

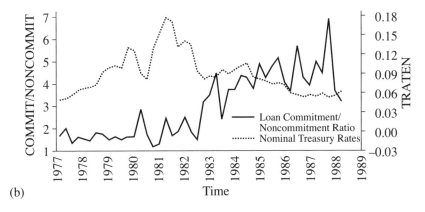

(b)

Figure 11.2   Ratio of commitment to noncommitment bank loans and Treasury rates of the same duration (1977: 1–1988: 2); (a) real Treasury rates; (b) nominal Treasury rates

or uncorrelated with open-market rates for the remainder of the sample. This runs counter to the empirical predictions of the credit rationing hypothesis since cyclical rationing would be most likely to appear during the volatile period in which real interest rates went up and down from their sample maximum levels. However, it should be noted that when the sample was split into early and late subsamples and the regressions were rerun (not shown), the computed effects of TRATE on COMMIT/NONCOMMIT remained about the same as those reported in Tables 11.4 and 11.5, apparently because of changes in the control variables.[20]

For additional evidence, the COMMIT regressions in Tables 11.4 and 11.5 were also rerun using as dependent variables the *quantities* of commitment and noncommitment loans in place of the log-odds ratios (not reported in the tables). Both types of loans were found to be increasing in the interest rate, suggesting that both commitment and noncommitment borrowers are able to obtain funding when rates are high. Thus even if some noncommitment borrower pools are subject to rationing, these data suggest that other noncommitment borrower pools increase their borrowing, more than offsetting any rationing effect in the aggregate.[21]

The log-odds and quantity COMMIT regressions together suggest that information-based, equilibrium credit rationing, if it exists, may be relatively small and economically insignificant. The one small increase in the commitment proportion from a doubling of real interest rates is counteracted by the opposite findings when nominal interest rates, CRUNCH, or loan growth is specified and by the finding that the quantity of noncommitment loans actually increases with both real and nominal rates. In addition, as discussed above, there are two other related explanations that are just as likely to account for the single small commitment proportion increase. First, when market rates are high, borrowers who have both commitment and noncommitment funding capacities may switch from noncommitment to commitment sources to avoid rationing. Second, borrowers may take out more commitment contracts when rates are rising to avoid rationing. Thus the one small increase in the commitment proportion when real open-market rates increase may indicate that Stiglitz and Weiss-type information problems are operative, but the extent to which they result in rationing or just more commitment protection from rationing is not identified.

The results and conclusions drawn here are somewhat in conflict with those of Sofianos et al. (1990), but this conflict is likely due to methodological differences and the fact that they used only aggregate data. Sofianos et al. ran vector autoregressive models of the dollar stocks (as opposed to new flows) of commitment and noncommitment loans aggregated from a sample of banks. They found that with lags of the interest rate included in the regressions, the coefficients of the lagged money stock were statistically significant in predicting (i.e., Granger-caused) noncommitment loans but were not statistically significant in predicting (i.e., did not Granger-cause) commitment loans. Sofianos et al. took this as evidence that a rationing channel acts on noncommitment loans but not on commitment loans. In subsequent runs provided by those authors, however, the sum of the lagged coefficients of the money stock was positive and statistically significant for commitment loans and negative and insignificant for noncommitment loans. These additional results conflict with a conclusion of credit rationing since it is noncommitment loans rather than commitment loans that should increase with the money stock for a given interest rate under rationing. To investigate these implications further, we reran our log-odds COMMIT models, adding lagged changes in the real money stock as exogenous variables (not shown in the tables). The sums of the money lags were positive and significant when real interest rates were included as regressors (positive and insignificant when nominal rates were included), again running contrary to the predictions of credit rationing.

Columns 3 and 4 of Tables 11.4 and 11.5 show that the probability of collateralized borrowing decreases by about 1–2 percent when open-market rates increase by 2.5 percent. Again, CRUNCH has the opposite effect of market rates. These findings are consistent with the stickiness results, which suggested that even after the pledging process, the remaining information problems are greater than average for the pools of borrowers in which collateral is pledged. These results also suggest that to the extent that rationing occurs, secured borrowers are more often rationed than unsecured borrowers. However, rerunning the regressions using the quantities of secured and unsecured loans as the dependent variables in place of the log-odds ratio (not shown in the tables) indicated that both secured and unsecured loans tend to increase when rates are high. This suggests that the rationing of secured borrowers, if it occurs, may not have much macroeconomic significance since other secured borrowers apparently make up the difference by increasing their borrowing.

The final columns in Table 11.4 and 11.5 show the regressions for the probability of FLOAT. The results show a small decrease in the FLOAT proportion of about 1–3 percent when open-market rates increase by 2.5 percent. This provides some weak evidence for the implicit interest rate insurance hypothesis to the extent that a fixed-rate loan is a superior vehicle to a floating-rate loan for providing this insurance. Rerunning the regressions using the quantities of floating-rate and fixed-rate loans as dependent variables (not shown in the tables) yielded a prediction that both types of loans increase with open-market rates.

Overall, the proportions tests suggest that credit rationing of commercial bank loan customers is not likely to be an important macro-economic phenomenon. The proportion of new loans issued under commitment does not increase substantially when real rates rise and actually decreases when most of the measures of credit market tightness increase, despite the fact that rationing can occur only by decreasing noncommitment loans. Moreover, the slight increase in the commitment proportion in the real rate regression appears to come about not because of a decrease in noncommitment loans, but simply because noncommitment loans increase by less than commitment loans do when interest rates increase. Increases in the money stock for a given interest rate also tend to increase commitment loans more than noncommitment loans, again contrary to the predictions of credit rationing.

Finally, we note that both the stickiness and proportions tests were subjected to a number of robustness checks beyond those reported above. The regressions were rerun using data from 1977 through 1983, leaving off the 1984–88 period, when it is generally agreed that rationing would be less severe or nonexistent. The results were qualitatively unaffected by this data omission. The stickiness regressions were rerun using the three-month Treasury rate for every loan rather than the comparable Treasury rate for the loan, and most of the results were similar. The stickiness regressions were also rerun with the TRATE variable interacted with LNSIZE, and with dummy variables for whether rates were increasing or decreasing. These interactions did not change the results qualitatively.[22] The proportions regressions for the three key contract terms were also rerun with each of the other two contract terms excluded as regressors, with no qualitative change in results.

IV.   CONCLUSIONS

This chapter has examined the empirical significance of information-based, equilibrium credit rationing of commercial bank loan customers by focusing on specific elements of the commercial loan contract. Such an analysis is suggested by the extant theories of credit rationing, which offer a variety of testable implications *vis-à-vis* specific loan contract features, particularly commitments. Earlier empirical studies have been unable to examine these implications because information on loan contract features has generally been unavailable.

Our major empirical results and their implications are summarized in Table 11.6. As in earlier studies, our results suggest that the commercial loan rate is sticky with respect to open-market rates, consistent with rationing. In contrast to other studies, however, use of the data on the key loan contract terms suggests that most of the stickiness does not reflect credit rationing. Nearly half of the observed loan rate stickiness occurs on loans made to commitment borrowers, who are contractually protected from rationing.

Table 11.6 Summary of major empirical results and their implications

Result	Implication
A. Stickiness Tests	
1. General stickiness. Loan rate premia over Treasury rates of equal duration decrease substantially with open-market rates	Consistent with credit rationing, implicit interest rate insurance, or recontracting with troubled borrowers
2. Commitment loan rates nearly as sticky as noncommitment rates. Also, some of the observed stickiness occurs on loans with negative premia over risk-free rates	Much of the stickiness cannot be explained by credit rationing since commitment borrowers cannot be rationed, and negative premia are inconsistent with equilibrium rationing theories
3. Fixed-rate loans have much stickier rates than floating-rate loans	Consistent with implicit interest rate insurance hypothesis
4. Secured loans have slightly stickier rates than unsecured loans	Consistent with credit rationing since collateral is more often required from riskier, more information-problematic borrower pools
5. Loan rate premia generally do *not* decrease with other measures of credit market tightness (CRUNCH or reduced aggregate loan growth)	Credit rationing, if it occurs, does *not* play an important role during periods of overall credit market tightness
6. Loan rate stickiness prevails over all risk class quintiles (as measured by rate premia)	Inconsistent with Riley (1987) version of of credit rationing, in which only the observably riskiest pools are rationed
B. Proportions Tests	
1. Commitment proportion of new loans does not increase substantially with real open-market rates and other measures of market tightness	Inconsistent with credit rationing having macroeconomic significance because only noncommitment borrowers can be rationed
2. The quantities of *both* new commitment loans and new noncommitment loans increase with open-market rates	Inconsistent with credit rationing having macroeconomic significance. If some noncommitment borrowers are rationed, others increase borrowing and make up for it
3. Commitment proportion of new loans increases with lagged money stock, given interest rates	Inconsistent with credit rationing, which predicts that money channel (i.e., rationing) affects only noncommitment loans
4. Collateral proportion of new loans decreases slightly with open-market rates, but quantities of both new secured and new unsecured loans increase	Consistent with greater relative rationing of riskier borrowers, but others increase borrowing, and make up for it
5. Fixed-rate proportion of new loans increases slightly with market rates	Consistent with implicit interest rate insurance hypothesis

Some of the remaining stickiness involves loans whose rate premia actually become negative when open-market rates are high, which also cannot be symptomatic of equilibrium credit rationing. Also in contrast to other studies, we are able to verify the robustness of our results using alternative measures of credit market tightness.

The most compelling evidence on rationing concerns the proportion of new loans made under commitment. Rationing requires that the fraction of new loans under commitment rise when open-market rates are high, since noncommitment borrowers are rationed and commitment borrowers are not. Our results suggest that this phenomenon does not occur to any great extent, and, in fact, the commitment ratio decreases with most of our measures of credit market tightness. The data also indicate that all types of commercial loans, including noncommitment loans, tend to increase in quantity during periods of high interest rates. This suggests that to the extent that some borrowers may be rationed, others take their places and receive bank loans. Taken together, the results in this paper do not rule out the existence of information-based equilibrium credit rationing of commercial bank borrowers, but they make it difficult to argue that such rationing constitutes an important macroeconomic phenomenon.

NOTES

1. Most of the work on this chapter was completed while Udell was a visiting economist at the Federal Reserve Board. The opinions expressed do not necessarily reflect those of the Board of Governors or its staff. We would like to thank the editors and the anonymous referee for guidance in rewriting the paper; Bob Avery, Mitch Berlin, Charles Calomiris, Mark Carey, Lee Crabbe, Jean Dermine, Doug Diamond, John Duca, George Fenn, Bruce Greenwald, Takeo Hoshi, Dick Ippolito, Jarl Kallberg, Anil Kashyap, Loretta Mester, Don Morgan, Len Nakamura, Rich Rosen, Tony Saunders, Steve Sharpe, Joe Stiglitz, Anjan Thakor, Paul Wachtel, and Arthur Warga for helpful comments; and John Leusner, Peter Zemsky, and Bill Glahn for invaluable research assistance.
2. Slovin and Sushka regressed the average commercial loan interest rate on the contemporaneous value and two quarterly lags of the commercial paper rate, using nine different specifications of other variables (their table 1, p. 1590). The coefficient of the second lag term was statistically significant at the 1 percent level in six of nine cases. They concluded that 'movements in interest rates are fully and quickly transmitted to commercial loan customers' (p. 1595), but an alternative conclusion is that the transmission mechanism takes at least two quarters and perhaps more.
3. There have also been a number of studies of credit rationing in the mortgage market. Duca and Rosenthal (1991) examined the behavior of the ratio of Federal Housing Administration (FHA) mortgages to total mortgages in the 'post-disintermediation era,' arguing that FHA mortgages are less vulnerable to rationing because they are government guaranteed. They found evidence of 'default-risk induced' rationing in the form of a positive relationship between FHA market share and the spread of AAA- over A-rated corporate bonds. See also Jaffee and Rosen (1979), Hendershott (1980), and Rosen and Rosen (1980).
4. A small number of loans (fewer than 1 percent) were deleted because of data problems. See Berger and Udell (1989) for details.

5. For the 4-week rate, we used the average of the bid-asked spread in the secondary Treasury bill market. The other Treasury data used were new issue (when available) or secondary market quotes of 3-, 6-, and 12-month bills and 2-, 3-, 5-, 7-, 10-, and 30-year bonds and notes. Durations were computed for these maturities, and the rates for all other durations were determined by interpolation and extrapolation. A number of other methods of computing the risk premia on floating-rate loans were tried, but the reported results were not qualitatively altered.

6. Eckstein and Sinai defined credit crunches as 'periods when financial distress produces sharp discontinuities in flow of funds and spending and when the financial strains include tight monetary policy, much lessened availability of money and credit, sharp rises of interest rates, and deteriorating balance sheets for households, businesses, and financial institutions' (p. 41).

7. Many commitments have escape clauses that permit the lender to abrogate the contract in the event that the borrower's condition has suffered 'material adverse change.' These clauses by necessity are triggered by changes in the *observable* quality of the borrower. Therefore, commitments with escape clauses still provide insurance against Stiglitz and Weiss-type rationing, which is driven by *unobservable* differences in borrower quality.

8. For example, a $5000 loan with two years' duration received ten times the weight of a $1000, one-year loan.

9. Each observation was divided by the estimated standard deviation of its error term, $(\{(1/Y) + [1/(1 - Y)]\}/n)^{1/2}$, where n is the sum of the size-duration weights for all the loans embodied in the bank-date observation.

10. The only case in which rationing would not be reflected in the proportion of loans made under commitment would occur if rationing were demand-induced and the increased demand came only from noncommitment borrowers. In this case, there would be excess demand for noncommitment loans, but the quantities of both commitment and noncommitment loans would remain constant. Although possible, this case seems quite unlikely. Increases in aggregate demand are generally associated with increased funding under working capital commitment lines to finance inventory replenishment, so that, if anything, the commitment proportion would increase.

11. This latter argument assumes that there are some fixed costs associated with issuing commitments that do not generally increase with the probability of takedown. An example might be the expected costs associated with the difficulty of writing a 'material adverse change clause' that adequately protects the bank against borrower credit deterioration. Without fixed costs, risk-averse borrowers would always purchase commitments from risk-neutral banks.

12. The formula for this change is $(2\mu - \mu)\beta_1 + [(2\mu)^2 - \mu^2]\beta_2$, where μ is the sample mean of TRATE and β_1 and β_2 are the coefficients of TRATE and TRATE2, respectively.

13. Note that the stickiness results would be essentially unchanged if the second-order terms (TRATE2) were not included in the regressions. Excluding these terms gives measured drops in PREM from changing TRATE of 53, 31, and 107 basis points in place of the reported 59, 37, and 99 basis points, respectively.

14. One possible nonrationing explanation for the positive relationship between loan rate premia and CRUNCH is that CRUNCH may be coincident with periods of increased aggregate risk and, therefore, higher risk premia on bank loans.

15. The rate premium is lower on commitment loans, ceteris paribus, by 30 basis points when the regression in col. 1 of Table 11.2 is used, suggesting less compensation for risk on commitment loans, consistent with Avery and Berger (1991). Similar results hold when the other regressions are used.

16. Some of the observed stickiness on fixed-rate loans may occur because the rates have been locked in by fixed-rate commitment contracts issued in the past. Unfortunately, this cannot be determined from the data, which have information on whether the *loan* is fixed-rate, but not on whether the *commitment* is fixed-rate.

17. This comes from comparing the effects of COL-FLOAT with NOCOL-FLOAT and COL-FIXED with NOCOL-FIXED.

18. It is interesting to note that the type of stickiness found here does not appear to carry over to corporate bond rates, suggesting that bank loan rates may be special in this regard. Lamy and Thompson (1988) found that the rate premium on primary issue corporate bonds

increased rather than decreased with Treasury rates in a model in which risk (as measured by bond ratings) was controlled for and interacted with changes in Treasury rates. Their procedure is similar to our interactions between loan contract features and TRATE.

19.   The change in probability from changing exogenous variables in a logit equation is given by

$$P_1 - P_0 = \frac{\exp(L_0 + \Delta L)}{1 + \exp(L_0 + \Delta L)} - P_0,$$

where P_1 and P_0 are the new and initial probabilities, L_0 is the log-odds ratio $\ln[P_0/(1 - P_0)]$, and ΔL is the predicted change in the log-odds ratio from changing the exogenous variables.

20.   The fact that the results hold up by subsample also lessens concern over the possible nonstationarity of the COMMIT ratio over the late subsample.

21.   The log-odds logit formulation is still preferred to using the quantities as dependent variables because the logit form automatically controls for any variables that affect the *overall level* of lending by the bank.

22.   The TR-LNSIZE interaction had a positive coefficient, consistent with the hypothesis that smaller loans may have more information problems that are reflected in a larger degree of rate stickiness.

REFERENCES

Avery, Robert B., and Berger, Allen N. 'Loan Commitments and Bank Risk Exposure.' *J. Banking and Finance* 15 (February 1991): 173–92.

Berger, Allen N., and Udell, Gregory F. 'Some Evidence on the Empirical Significance of Credit Rationing.' *Finance and Economics Discussion Series*, no. 105. Washington: Bd. Governors, Fed. Reserve System, December 1989.

Berger, Allen N., and Udell, Gregory F. 'Collateral, Loan Quality, and Bank Risk.' *J. Monetary Econ.* 25 (January 1990): 21–42.

Berger, Allen N., and Udell, Gregory F. 'Securitization, Risk, and the Liquidity Problem in Banking.' In *Structural Change in Banking*, edited by Michael Klausner and Lawrence J. White. Homewood, Ill.: Irwin, 1992, in press.

Berkovitch, Elazar, and Greenbaum, Stuart I. 'The Loan Commitment as an Optimal Financing Contract.' *J. Financial and Quantitative Analysis* 26 (March 1991): 83–95.

Besanko, David, and Thakor, Anjan V. 'Collateral and Rationing: Sorting Equilibria in Monopolistic and Competitive Credit Markets.' *Internat. Econ. Rev.* 28 (October 1987): 671–89. (*a*)

Besanko, David, and Thakor, Anjan V. 'Competitive Equilibrium in the Credit Market under Asymmetric Information.' *J. Econ. Theory* 42 (June 1987): 167–82. (*b*)

Bester, Helmut. 'Screening vs. Rationing in Credit Markets with Imperfect Information.' *A.E.R.* 75 (September 1985): 850–55.

Blinder, Alan S., and Stiglitz, Joseph E. 'Money, Credit Constraints, and Economic Activity.' *A.E.R. Papers and Proc.* 73 (May 1983): 297–302.

Board of Governors of the Federal Reserve System. 'Senior Loan Officer Opinion Survey on Bank Lending Practices.' Washington: Bd. Governors, Fed. Reserve System, May 1988.

Boot, Arnoud W.A., and Thakor, Anjan V. 'Dynamic Equilibrium in a Competitive Credit Market: Intertemporal Contracting as Insurance against Rationing.' Working paper. Bloomington: Indiana Univ., August 1989.

Boot, Arnoud W.A.; Thakor, Anjan V.; and Udell, Gregory F. 'Competition, Risk Neutrality and Loan Commitments.' *J. Banking and Finance* 11 (September 1987): 449–71.

Chan, Yuk-Shee, and Kanatas, George. 'Asymmetric Valuations and the Role of Collateral in Loan Agreements.' *J. Money, Credit and Banking* 17 (February 1985): 84–95.

Duca, John V., and Rosenthal, Stuart S. 'An Empirical Test of Credit Rationing in the Mortgage Market.' *J. Urban Econ.* 29 (March 1991): 218–34.

Eckstein, Otto, and Sinai, Alan. 'The Mechanisms of the Business Cycle in the Postwar Era.' In *The American Business: Continuity and Change*, edited by Robert J. Gordon. Chicago: Univ. Chicago Press (for NBER), 1986.

Fried, Joel, and Howitt, Peter. 'Credit Rationing and Implicit Contract Theory.' *J. Money, Credit and Banking* 12 (August 1980): 471–87.

Goldfeld, Steven M. *Commercial Bank Behavior and Economic Activity: A Structural Study of Monetary Policy in the Postwar United States.* Amsterdam: North-Holland, 1966.

Hendershott, Patric H. 'Real User Costs and the Demand for Single-Family Housing.' *Brookings Papers Econ. Activity*, no. 2 (1980), pp. 401–44.

Jaffee, Dwight M. *Credit Rationing and the Commercial Loan Market.* New York: Wiley, 1971.

Jaffee, Dwight M., and Rosen, Kenneth T. 'Mortgage Credit Availability and Residential Construction.' *Brookings Papers Econ. Activity*, no. 2 (1979), pp. 333–76.

Jaffee, Dwight M., and Russell, Thomas. 'Imperfect Information, Uncertainty, and Credit Rationing.' *Q.J.E.* 90 (November 1976): 651–66.

Kanatas, George, 'Commercial Paper, Bank Reserve Requirements, and the Informational Role of Loan Commitments.' *J. Banking and Finance* 11 (September 1987): 425–48.

Kareken, John H. 'Lenders' Preferences, Credit Rationing, and the Effectiveness of Monetary Policy.' *Rev. Econ. and Statis.* 39 (August 1957): 292–302.

King, Stephen R. 'Monetary Transmission: Through Bank Loans or Bank Liabilities?' *J. Money, Credit and Banking* 18 (August 1986): 290-303.

Lamy, Robert E., and Thompson, G. Rodney. 'Risk Premia and the Pricing of Primary Issue Bonds.' *J. Banking and Finance* 12 (December 1988): 585–601.

Melnik, Arie, and Plaut, Steven E. 'Loan Commitment Contracts, Terms of Lending, and Credit Allocation.' *J. Finance* 41 (June 1986): 425–35.

Riley, John G. 'Credit Rationing: A Further Remark.' *A.E.R.* 77 (March 1987): 224–7.

Rosen, Harvey S., and Rosen, Kenneth T. 'Federal Taxes and Homeownership: Evidence from Time Series.' *J.P.E.* 88 (February 1980): 59-75.

Scott, Ira O., Jr. 'The Availability Doctrine: Theoretical Underpinnings.' *Rev. Econ. Studies* 25 (October 1957): 41–8.

Sharpe, Steven A. 'Credit Rationing, Concessionary Lending, and Debt Maturity.' *J. Banking and Finance* 15 (June 1991): 581–604.

Slovin, Myron B., and Sushka, Marie E. 'A Model of the Commercial Loan Rate.' *J. Finance* 38 (December 1983): 1583–96.

Sofianos, George, Wachtel, Paul A., and Melnik, Arie. 'Loan Commitments and Monetary Policy.' *J. Banking and Finance* 14 (October 1990): 677–89.

Stiglitz, Joseph E., and Weiss, Andrew. 'Credit Rationing in Markets with Imperfect Information.' *A.E.R.* 71 (June 1981): 393–410.

Stiglitz, Joseph E., and Weiss, Andrew. 'Credit Rationing: Reply.' *A.E.R.* 77 (March 1987): 228–31.

Thakor, Anjan V., and Udell, Gregory F. 'An Economic Rationale for the Pricing Structure of Bank Loan Commitments.' *J. Banking and Finance* 11 (June 1987): 271–89.

Wette, Hildegard C. 'Collateral in Credit Rationing in Markets with Imperfect Information: Note.' *A.E.R.* 73 (June 1983): 442–5.

Williamson, Stephen D. 'Costly Monitoring, Loan Contracts, and Equilibrium Credit Rationing.' *Q.J.E.* 102 (February 1987): 135–45.

12. An empirical examination of information barriers to trade in insurance

John Cawley and Tomas Philipson[1]

Economists have long studied the market distortions that result from the asymmetry of information between well-informed demanders and poorly informed suppliers of insurance. Government regulation and sponsorship of insurance (e.g., Social Security in the United States) is often justified with the claim that such asymmetric information results in adverse selection and underprovision or lack of trade in insurance. Despite the important influence such arguments have had on how economists perceive and analyze insurance markets, there exists little direct evidence on the degree to which asymmetric information limits or affects trade in insurance markets or whether insurers can protect themselves against these problems by underwriting.

This chapter attempts to provide such direct evidence for the largest private individual insurance market in the world: life insurance. Of the roughly $2.1 trillion paid in premia for all types of insurance in 1995, more than half (58 percent) was for life insurance. Life-insurance premia constitute 3.6 percent of GDP in the United States in which it is the most widely held financial product, including bank savings accounts; it is estimated that 90 percent of two-adult households have life-insurance coverage.[2] Besides its large size, another reason that life insurance is an important market to study is that it has been presented as a prime example of a market saddled with the inefficiency associated with adverse selection.[3] In addition, the life-insurance market is particularly useful to analyze because the potentially private information crucial in that market (i.e., with regard to health and mortality) is also crucial to government-sponsored annuity and health insurance, such as Social Security and Medicare in the United States, which economists often justify with the claim that it is inefficiently provided in private markets due to information barriers to trade.[4]

This chapter derives and tests implications of the model of insurance under asymmetric information. An important feature of this study is that we use direct evidence on both the self-perceived and actual mortality risk of demanders of life insurance as well as the price schedules offered to them. More precisely, our data include consumers' beliefs about their mortality risk during the period covered by their life-insurance contract, who among them actually dies, the price schedules they face, and their demand for coverage. These data allow us to test not only predictions about price and quantity, but also predictions on how risk, whether experienced or as perceived by insurers or the insured, relates to price and quantity. Our main finding is that it is very difficult to interpret these data as generated by models of insurance markets that resemble conventional models of trade under asymmetric information.

In competitive insurance markets with asymmetric information,[5] a central implication is that, conditional on all observables to the insurer, high-risk individuals end up purchasing larger quantities of insurance than do low-risk individuals. This occurs because the low-risk individuals are quantity-constrained in order to make their contracts undesirable to those of higher risk. Since the high-risk consumers buy larger quantities, an insurer can break even in a competitive market only if marginal prices rise with quantity – the opposite of a bulk discount. Consequently, the total price is convex in the quantity of coverage. In technical jargon, such nonlinear prices are crucial for the risk-sorting across contracts to be incentive-compatible. However, because unit prices rise, arbitrage must be prevented, since multiple small contracts are cheaper than a single big one.

In order to test whether unit prices rise with quantity of insurance, we first checked the prices of the company that serves many academic economists in the United States: Teachers Insurance and Annuity Association (TIAA). Figure 12.1 depicts unit price charged by policy size. It shows that TIAA offers bulk discounts in its coverage; the cents per dollar of award falls with the size of the award.

Not surprisingly, TIAA charges higher premia to insure older individuals and smokers.[6] However, within each consumer group, the bulk discount (relative to the unit price of a policy smaller than $250 000) is 25 percent for an award between $250 000 and $499 000, and 30 percent for an award between $500 000 and $999 000.[7] As unit prices are constant across quantity only when equal to marginal price, such a decreasing step function implies that *marginal* prices look the same way except at the jumps.

The bulk discounts shown in Figure 12.1 are *not* the kind of nonlinear pricing that is predicted by the conventional models of insurance under asymmetric information. Bulk discounts violate the incentive-compatibility constraint of the separating equilibrium described in the conventional model of insurance under asymmetric information.

We also examine the covariance between contract size and risk. Risk is measured two ways: as perceived by consumers and as actually experienced through death. Conventional arguments about insurance under asymmetric

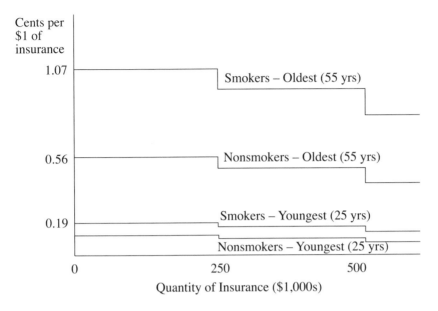

Source: Official Life Insurance Handbook (TIAA, Life Insurance Planning Center, 1977).

Figure 12.1   *Price as a function of quantity for Teachers Insurance and
Annuity Association (TIAA)*

information predict that the high-risk consumers purchase a larger quantity of
insurance than the low-risk consumers because the latter are quantity-
constrained. However, our data suggest the opposite: low-risk individuals hold
more coverage. Figure 12.2 illustrates this point unconditionally and on the
extensive margin for males, who constitute the bulk of the life insurance
market. The figure displays the ratio of the mortality risk of insured males to
the mortality risk of the overall population of males in 1970 and 1975, by age.[8]
The mortality of insured males is measured by the 1980 Commissioners
Standard Ordinary Table (CSO), which reflects the mortality of the insured
during 1970–1975.

If the insured had the same mortality risk as the general population, one
would expect the ratio to equal 1. Instead, Figure 12.2 indicates that men with
life insurance are of lower mortality risk than the overall population. Although
this unconditional result may of course be attributable to unobservables, such
as income effects on mortality and the likelihood of holding insurance, this
evidence is consistent with our more disaggregate analysis which controls for
many factors such as income yet still indicates a negative association between
insurance coverage and risk.

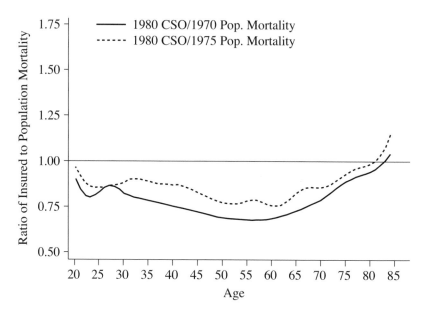

Figure 12.2   Mortality of males, 1970–1975

The two findings illustrated in Figures 12.1 and 12.2, bulk discounts and a negative covariation between risk and quantity, are remarkably robust across several data sources. Moreover, they are not coincidentally related. In a competitive insurance market, if unit prices fall with quantity, then risk and quantity must be negatively related. If the high-risk individuals could obtain larger contracts at lower unit prices, insurers could not break even.

The outline of this chapter is as follows. Section I lays out the predictions of interest from the theory of insurance under asymmetric information. In Section II, we analyze data from four sources: (i) a random sample of policies collected by LIMRA International, which is a consortium of life-insurance providers, (ii) price data from CompuLife, which is the main price quotation software for life-insurance agents in the United States, (iii) the Health and Retirement Study (HRS), and (iv) the Asset and Health Dynamics Among the Oldest Old (AHEAD). HRS and AHEAD are household surveys that not only contain data on the quantity and price of life insurance, but also record the actual and self-perceived mortality risk of the sample households. The first two data sources provide prices conditional on the observables used by insurers to price out risk. The last two data sources allow us to assess directly how risk (whether self-perceived or actual mortality) covaries with the quantity of insurance coverage. The two patterns we have described, bulk discounts and negative covariance between risk and quantity, are strikingly robust across these sources of data. In Section III, we offer our conclusions.

Our chapter relates to several papers that attempt to assess empirically the impact of asymmetric information on economic activity (see e.g., Eric W. Bond, 1982; David Genesove, 1993; Andrew D. Foster and Mark R. Rosenzweig, 1994). Our work also relates to previous studies on the predictive content of subjective mortality beliefs (see e.g., Daniel S. Hamermesh and F.W. Hamermesh, 1983; Hamermesh, 1985; W. Kip Viscusi, 1990, 1992; Michael Hurd et al., 1996) although our focus is on the relative beliefs of sellers and buyers, regardless of their absolute accuracy. Our analysis builds on this previous work in that we have direct data on what has many times been unobserved: the joint distribution of self-perceived risk, actual risk, and prices. These data allow us to better test the predictions of the model of insurance under asymmetric information.

I. INSURANCE UNDER ASYMMETRIC INFORMATION AND UNDERWRITING

This section outlines the predictions of the standard theory of insurance under asymmetric information, specifically, nonlinearity of prices and the covariance between risk and insurance quantity. The theory makes no predictions across risk classes observable to the insurer. The restrictions we describe apply only within observed risk classes.

Let q and $1 - q$ be the population proportions of high and low risks c_1 and c_0, with the unconditional risk thus being $c \equiv qc_1 + (1 - q)c_0$. For example, for life insurance, $(q, 1 - q)$ may be the fractions of smokers and nonsmokers and therefore (c_1, c_0) the mortality risks of the two groups. In the case of life insurance, let Y and $\bar{Y}$ be the income of the individual or benefitor when dead or alive and $U(\cdot)$ and $\bar{U}(\cdot)$ be the (possibly state-dependent) Von Neumann-Morgenstern utility functions. A consumer of risk c who faces the unit price p has a demand for insurance coverage denoted $D(p, c)$ defined by

$$D(p, c) = \underset{D}{\text{Argmax}} \; cU(Y + D - pD) + (1 - c)\bar{U}(\bar{Y} - pD). \tag{1}$$

This implies that risk raises demand, $D_c \geq 0$; people of higher risk value insurance more than do those of lower risk. This is necessary for the separating equilibrium in which the high-risk individuals choose a larger policy at a higher unit price. The case of life insurance does not require that utility is state-independent, as when altruistic bequest motives are present, or that individuals insure fully, as when the loss is hard to observe. The expected profits of the insurer are

$$\Pi \equiv E[D(p, c)(p - c)] \tag{2}$$

where the expectation is over consumer pairs (D, c) of coverage and risk. Unlike in other product markets, the cost of production in insurance markets is determined by buyers, and therefore has a direct effect on demand, beyond its indirect effect through pricing. It is useful to rewrite these profits as

$$\Pi = E[D(p - c)] = E[D](E[p] - E[c]) + \text{Cov}(D, p) - \text{Cov}(D, c). \tag{3}$$

Thus profits are decomposed into three parts. The first is the pricing above claim expenditures, sometimes referred to as 'loadings,' which may be due to alternative costs of production or markups in a noncompetitive industry. The second is positively related to the covariance between quantity and price, and the third is negatively dependent on the covariance of quantity and risk. The nonlinearity is needed because when more risky individuals demand larger contracts but all face the same unit price, the insurer cannot cover claims with premia. To illustrate, consider a Taylor-expanded quadratic form of total price and quantity to be estimated in the empirical section:

$$p_T(D) \equiv p(D)D = \alpha + \beta_1 D + \beta_2 D^2. \tag{4}$$

It implies the following profits:

$$\Pi = \alpha + E[D](\beta_1 - E[c]) + \beta_2 E[D^2] - \text{Cov}(D, c). \tag{5}$$

In this case, if there is fair pricing on average, $\alpha = 0$ and $\beta_1 = E[c]$, the first two terms vanish so that convexity in prices, $\beta_2 \geq 0$, must cover for any positive covariance between demand and risk. If one finds evidence of bulk discounts, therefore, it limits the amount of positive covariance between risk and quantity that can exist in a competitive market. Alternatively, if in a competitive market marginal prices fall with quantity, then negative risk-sorting must prevail to ensure profitability.

Figure 12.3 depicts such a separating equilibrium for two risk classes: high risk (c_1) and low risk (c_0). As insurers are predicted to offer only small contracts to, or not cover, the low-risk individuals in order to ensure that these contracts are undesirable to high-risk individuals, the equilibrium distribution of total price and quantity involves rising marginal prices, $dp_T/dD^2 \geq 0$. Hence average prices rise with quantity.[9] This is the opposite of a bulk discount. If bulk discounts exist, the separating equilibrium cannot occur; the pricing

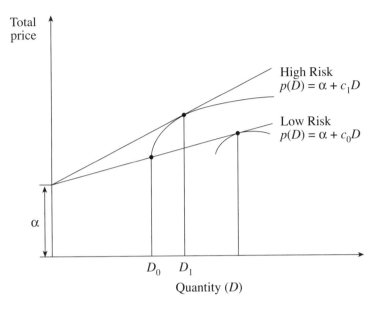

Figure 12.3   Equilibrium relation between risk and quantity under asymmetric information

schedule is not compatible with the incentives of risks to sort themselves out across contracts.[10]

It is important to stress that this schedule of convex total prices is feasible only if there is a prohibition on multiple contracts; several small contracts would be cheaper than a large one under convex pricing. However, bulk discounts, which may occur when firms pay fixed costs to underwrite, are feasible as long as insurance contracts are consumer-specific so that it is not feasible to arbitrage. Arbitrage under bulk discounts would take the form of dividing a large policy into several smaller ones for resale which is infeasible with consumer-specific products. Holding several small contracts may be consistent with utility-maximization under bulk discounts; in order to lower the default risk on their coverage, consumers may forgo the bulk discount available on a single contract and hold multiple, smaller policies.[11]

When insurers face an initial information disadvantage, they may underwrite rather than forgo mutually beneficial trades, and this underwriting may break the positive covariance between risk and quantity. For life insurance, where risk concerns mortality, this fixed underwriting cost may include the cost of physicians, medical exams, or diagnostic tests. In our framework, underwriting consists of the insurer paying a cost α to learn whether the consumer is of risk type c_0 or c_1, after which prices p_0 or p_1 are charged. If $\Pi(c, p)$ denotes the profit given cost and price, insurers underwrite when

$$\Pi(c, p) \leq q\Pi(c_1, p_1) + (1 - q)\Pi(c_0, p_0) - \alpha. \tag{6}$$

Whether underwriting occurs depends on the nonstandard direct effect of cost on demand. For example, when underwriting is costless and there is no state-dependence in consumption, all risks are priced out fairly, and everyone fully insures after underwriting. This implies a zero covariance between quantity and risk; $D(c, c) = L$ implies $\text{Cov}(D, c) = 0$. More generally, underwriting raises prices (and hence lowers demand) for high-risk consumers but lowers prices (and hence raises demand) for low-risk consumers. The allocation of information typically assumed to be present in insurance markets, that consumers know more than producers, is inconsistent with the assumption of profit maximization when gains from insurance trade dominate underwriting costs.[12]

II.   EMPIRICAL ANALYSIS

Because the theory to be tested concerns individual spot markets, our empirical analysis is concerned with the individual spot market in life insurance. Specifically, we restrict our analysis to term life insurance. For a term life policy, as opposed to a whole life policy, the annual premia are structured to cover annual outlays; that is, a term policy does not build cash value.[13] All of our analysis concerns individual policies; we excluded group policies because their premia reflect the risk of the entire group, and group term premia are often subsidized by employers or governments.

A.   Assessing the Nonlinearity in Prices

Perhaps the simplest evidence we have on the nonlinearity of prices is the extent to which people are allowed to hold multiple life insurance contracts. Under the price schedules predicted in the theory of insurance under asymmetric information, it would be cheaper to buy two small contracts rather than a large one. The prediction relies on multiple contracting being infeasible.

We found that multiple contracting is highly prevalent. Roughly one-quarter of the people in our HRS and AHEAD samples who hold any term life insurance hold multiple term life policies.[14]

The high prevalence of multiple contracting suggests that unit prices do not rise with quantity. If multiple contracts are permissible, consumers or insurance agents could easily circumvent the insurers' rising unit prices; instead of paying a high unit price on a single large policy, consumers could contract for smaller policies with multiple firms and pay a lower unit price. In contrast, multiple contracting with falling unit price is arbitrage-free because policies are person-specific, making it impossible for someone to buy a single large policy with a low unit price, divide it, and resell it.

We next directly assess the nonlinearity in prices using the price schedules offered to consumers. Let the total price be Taylor-expanded as before:

$$p_T(D) = \alpha + \beta_1 D + \beta_2 D^2. \tag{7}$$

Total price consists of a fixed underwriting component and a marginal price schedule that may depend on the size of the claim. The theory of insurance under asymmetric information predicts that $\beta_2 > 0$.[15]

We test for the nonlinearity of prices using three data sources with successively lower levels of aggregation: data from LIMRA International, which is a consortium of life-insurance providers; data from CompuLife, which is a price-quotation service for life-insurance agents in the United States; and data from HRS and AHEAD, which are individual household surveys.

Our first and most aggregate price data are from the 1994 *Buyer's Study* by LIMRA, which examined a random sample of the 28 000 new policies issued in the United States that year by 47 companies.[16] This sample has many disjoint companies not contained in the firm-specific price quotes of the price-quotation software CompuLife, which is considered later. It also contains a limited set of the demographic characteristics of the buyers, as well as features of policies including award size and premia. Figure 12.4 plots the unit price as a function of the award size by age categories (Figure 12.4a) and income (Figure 12.4b). Figure 12.4 shows that unit price falls dramatically with quantity, even for policies so large that fixed costs are a negligible proportion of the total costs.[17]

The predictions of the conventional theory of insurance under asymmetric information apply conditional on all observables to the insurer. The LIMRA data do not allow us to condition on these observables, but our next set of data does. The second set of data we consider is CompuLife, which is the price-quotation software for US life-insurance agents. CompuLife provides firm-specific price quotes for individual term insurance stratified by consumer characteristics (e.g., gender or smoking) and type of policies (e.g., length of term or award size) for a large proportion of US insurance companies. The purpose of the software is to help agents search for contracts among the roughly 2 000 active firms. The price quotes analyzed here are for one-year individual term contracts – the spot market for life insurance. These price data are useful for our purposes because they contain *offered* price schedules, as opposed to prices traded on; we observe the price schedule facing a given consumer, which maps directly into price schedule P_T discussed in the theoretical section.

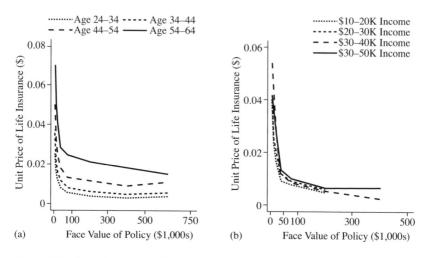

Note: Unit price is the cost per dollar of coverage.

Figure 12.4   LIMRA unit prices: (a) *Unit price by age of insured;* (b) *Unit price by income of insured*

The important aspect of the CompuLife price data is that they allow us to assess the distribution of prices and quantity conditional on observables of the sellers. Table 12.1 summarizes unit prices across quantity in these data for the covariate combinations used by the software: age, smoking status, gender, and preferred health status. Each row of this table considers a particular combination of these observables of consumers. Each cell in the table describes the average change in unit price between two policy sizes. For example, in the first row, a 30-year-old nonsmoking female of preferred heath status would pay, on average, $49.90 less per $100 000 of insurance if she bought a $500 000 policy instead of a $100 000 policy. If she instead purchased a policy for $1 million, she would receive an additional discount of $7.80 per $100 000 of coverage.

The table shows that, conditional on all combinations of covariates and quantities, unit prices fall with quantity. Unit prices do not rise even at the largest quantities, and thus marginal prices do not increase. Table 12.2, which reports the coefficient estimates from price regressions within risk groups, further describes the pattern of pricing.

The results in Table 12.2 reflect regressions of total price on quantity and quantity squared and thus are direct estimates of the quadratic price schedule $p_T(D)$. The coefficients on quantity represent risk (the magnitude varies across the risk groups accordingly), and the constant term reflects fixed costs. The

Table 12.1 Unit price and quantity: mean change in unit price across firms in CompuLife

Risk group	Change in policy size				
	$100–500K	$500–1,000K	$1,000–1,500K	$1,500–2,000K	$2,000–2,500K
30-year-old nonsmoking preferred females	-49.90 (-25.86)	-7.88 (-5.27)	-1.96 (-1.59)	-0.98 (-0.68)	-0.59 (-0.38)
30-year-old nonsmoking nonpreferred females	-46.18 (-21.63)	-8.03 (-4.69)	-1.76 (-0.91)	-0.88 (-0.45)	-0.53 (-0.27)
30-year-old smoking preferred females	-45.00 (-7.65)	-5.25 (-0.90)	-1.81 (-0.30)	-0.90 (-0.15)	-0.87 (-0.15)
30-year-old smoking nonpreferred females	-51.69 (-13.18)	-6.63 (-1.44)	-1.43 (-0.30)	-0.72 (-0.15)	-0.43 (-0.09)
30-year-old nonsmoking preferred males	-51.03 (-12.42)	-8.22 (-2.45)	-1.76 (-0.76)	-0.91 (-0.44)	-0.55 (-0.28)
30-year-old nonsmoking nonpreferred males	-46.08 (-16.90)	-8.07 (-2.89)	-1.65 (-0.55)	-0.83 (-0.27)	-0.50 (-0.16)
30-year-old smoking preferred males	-57.83 (-15.60)	-6.92 (-1.62)	-1.47 (-0.39)	-0.74 (-0.19)	-0.44 (-0.11)
30-year-old smoking nonpreferred males	-57.02 (-9.14)	-6.46 (-1.10)	-1.47 (-0.25)	-0.73 (-0.13)	-0.44 (-0.08)
40-year-old nonsmoking preferred females	-49.50 (-20.31)	-8.33 (-5.93)	-2.11 (-1.68)	-1.06 (-0.84)	-0.63 (-0.50)
40-year-old nonsmoking nonpreferred females	-51.33 (-15.52)	-9.28 (-4.57)	-1.85 (-0.94)	-0.93 (-0.47)	-0.56 (-0.28)
40-year-old smoking preferred females	-57.67 (-5.27)	-5.75 (-0.53)	-1.81 (-0.17)	-0.90 (-0.08)	-0.54 (-0.05)
40-year-old smoking nonpreferred females	-55.74 (-7.53)	-6.88 (-1.00)	-1.63 (-0.24)	-0.81 (-0.12)	-0.49 (-0.07)
40-year-old nonsmoking preferred males	-52.33 (-14.53)	-8.00 (-3.92)	-2.00 (-0.94)	-1.08 (-0.48)	-0.65 (-0.28)

Table 12.1   continued

Risk group	Change in policy size				
	$100–500K	$500–1,000K	$1,000–1,500K	$1,500–2,000K	$2,000–2,500K
40-year-old nonsmoking nonpreferred males	-50.22	-9.06	-1.93	-0.96	-0.58
	(-17.33)	(-3.27)	(-0.70)	(-0.34)	(-0.20)
40-year-old smoking preferred males	-51.67	-6.5	-2.11	-1.06	-0.63
	(-4.72)	(-0.57)	(-0.19)	(-0.09)	(-0.06)
40-year-old smoking nonpreferred males	-55.69	-6.46	-1.56	-0.78	-0.47
	(-6.34)	(-0.74)	(-0.18)	(-0.09)	(-0.05)
50-year-old nonsmoking preferred females	-55.00	-8.33	-2.00	-1.00	-0.60
	(-20.14)	(-3.66)	(-0.95)	(-1.00)	(-0.29)
50-year-old nonsmoking nonpreferred females	-58.67	-9.17	-1.76	-0.88	-0.64
	(-15.94)	(-3.68)	(-0.66)	(-0.33)	(-0.23)
50-year-old smoking preferred females	-54.67	-6.83	-2.17	-1.08	-1.15
	(-4.01)	(-0.47)	(-0.15)	(-0.08)	(-0.08)
50-year-old smoking nonpreferred females	-59.39	-10.28	-1.70	-0.85	-0.51
	(-5.69)	(-1.02)	(-0.18)	(-0.09)	(-0.05)
50-year-old nonsmoking preferred males	-58.33	-7.50	-2.06	-1.11	-0.67
	(-19.65)	(-2.52)	(-0.70)	(-0.37)	(-0.22)
50-year-old nonsmoking nonpreferred males	-59.00	-8.83	-1.81	-0.91	-0.79
	(-14.45)	(-2.27)	(-0.42)	(-0.21)	(-0.18)
50-year-old smoking preferred males	-59.83	-7.50	-1.78	-0.89	-0.53
	(-3.59)	(-0.46)	(-0.11)	(-0.06)	(-0.03)
50-year-old smoking nonpreferred males	-67.50	-8.92	-1.58	-0.79	-0.48
	(-3.76)	(-0.51)	(-0.09)	(-0.05)	(-0.03)

Notes: Each table entry gives the average change in unit price (here defined as the annual cost, in dollars, for $100 000 of coverage) between two policy sizes. For example, the first entry in the first row indicates that a 30-year-old nonsmoking female of preferred health would pay, on average, $49.90 less per $100 000 of insurance if she bought a $500 000 policy instead of a $100 000 policy. Numbers in parentheses are t-statistics.

250

Table 12.2 Total prices and quantity covariance in CompuLife data (dependent variable: total premium of term insurance)

	Preferred				Not preferred			
	Females		Males		Females		Males	
Independent variable	Smoking	Nonsmoking	Smoking	Nonsmoking	Smoking	Nonsmoking	Smoking	Nonsmoking
A. 30-Year-Olds:								
Intercept	47.6	70.37	91.98	76.69	81.11	68.62	89.14	71.04
	(0.32)	(1.84)	(0.95)	(1.47)	(0.66)	(1.35)	(0.59)	(0.91)
Award	87.08	36.45	101.22	44.90	84.07	50.92	105.06	59.30
	(7.44)	(12.27)	(13.36)	(11.05)	(8.76)	(12.87)	(8.93)	(9.72)
Award squared (about mean)	−0.03	0.02	0.09	0.04	0.07	0.02	0.09	0.03
	(−0.06)	(0.14)	(0.32)	(0.23)	(0.20)	(0.14)	(0.20)	(0.14)
R^2:	0.96	0.99	0.99	0.98	0.92	0.96	0.92	0.93
Number of observations:	36	36	36	36	108	108	108	108
B. 50-Year-Olds:								
Intercept	57.35	79.96	90.66	78.93	100.6	91.48	113.1	86.17
	(0.16)	(1.51)	(0.22)	(1.04)	(0.40)	(1.30)	(0.25)	(0.77)
Award	171.83	76.53	244.12	105.29	184.13	96.32	280.15	134.72
	(6.24)	(18.51)	(7.70)	(17.77)	(9.46)	(17.56)	(7.98)	(15.38)
Award squared (about mean)	−0.04	0.03	0.07	0.03	0.08	0.06	0.12	0.04
	(−0.04)	(0.21)	(0.06)	(0.12)	(0.11)	(0.29)	(0.09)	(0.13)
R^2:	0.95	0.99	0.97	0.99	0.93	0.98	0.90	0.97
Number of observations:	36	36	36	36	108	108	108	108

Notes: Unit price (multiplied by 1000) is regressed on term insurance award and its square separately for each CompuLife risk group. Table entries are regression coefficients (with t-statistics in parentheses).

251

sign of the coefficient associated with quantity squared is of particular interest. The theory of insurance under asymmetric information predicts that marginal costs rise, and so the coefficient should be positive and statistically significant. The table indicates that quantity has a linear effect but no quadratic nonlinear effect. The linear specification with a fixed production cost and constant marginal cost explains almost all risk adjusted variation in the prices; R^2 values are close to 1.[18]

The third set of data we utilize to assess the nonlinearity of prices is the public release data from the Health and Retirement Study (HRS) and the Asset and Health Dynamics Among the Oldest Old (AHEAD).[19] Both studies examine health, retirement, and economic status, but the HRS sample is drawn from persons who are between ages 51 and 61, while the AHEAD sample is from persons above age 70. These data complement the price data above because they provide individual level controls for determinants of mortality and demand for insurance.[20]

There were 12 652 respondents from 7 702 households in HRS and 8,223 respondents from 6 052 households in AHEAD:[21] 2 230 respondents in HRS reported owning individual term life insurance; 1 305 AHEAD respondents report paying premia for any term life insurance (they were not asked whether their policies are individual or group). However, we believe that they are mainly individual policies; group life insurance is generally offered through employment, and the vast majority of individuals in the AHEAD sample are retired. Evidence from the non-age-eligible spouses in HRS who resemble our AHEAD sample supports this hypothesis; of HRS respondents age 70 or over who pay premia for some term insurance, 75 percent have individual policies.

HRS and AHEAD respondents reported their perceived mortality risk. This is of particular value to our topic; it reflects the (possibly private) information of those who demand insurance.[22] AHEAD respondents were asked: 'Using a number from 0 to 100, what do you think are the chances that you will live to be at least [90, 95, or 100, depending on the age of the respondent]?' HRS respondents were asked: 'Using a number from 0 to 10, where 0 equals absolutely no chance and 10 equals absolutely certain, what do you think are the chances that you will live to be 75 or more? And how about the chances that you will live to be 85 or more?'[23]

HRS and AHEAD respondents were asked to report their expectation of survival over a varying number of years. The forecast period ranged from 14 to 24 years in HRS, and from 11 to 15 years in AHEAD. Ideally, we would analyze separately the reports for each forecast length, but in practice this would leave us with insufficient sample sizes to conduct meaningful analyses. We analyze the self-reported risk of HRS respondents in three groups: ages 51–55, 56–58, and 59–61, whose forecasts were over 20–24 years, 17–19 years, and 14–16 years, respectively. We analyze the self-reported risk of

AHEAD respondents in two groups: Group A, whose beliefs are associated with a forecast period of 11–13 years, and Group B, whose forecast was over 14–15 years.

In order for us to compare these self-perceived risks to annual premia, we also had to convert the belief about survival after many years to a belief about mortality after one year. We decided to use the ten categories reported as representing short-run self-perceived risk. In other words, we assume that those who report themselves as more likely to die within ten years would also have reported themselves as more likely to die within one year. This assumes that the order of risk is preserved across time, that is, the subjective survival functions of different individuals do not cross. The main benefit of this approach is that it avoids choosing a parametric form of survival to convert its level at ten years into a level at one year.[24]

The unit price of a policy was computed by dividing the reported annual term insurance premium by the term insurance award.[25] We are not able to estimate actual risk for AHEAD because only one wave of that study is currently available. However, we were able to estimate actual risk for HRS. We computed actual mortality risk as the fitted value of a logit regression of experienced mortality between the two waves of HRS on demographic and health characteristics.[26] Because there was sample attrition and it is not known whether the attrited members are still alive, we computed two measures of fitted risk: an upper bound on mortality for which attrited sample members were assumed to be dead, and a lower bound on mortality for which attrited sample members were assumed to be alive.

Table 12.3 reports results for several regressions of unit price on quantity. We estimate the models for the entire HRS and AHEAD samples, controlling for three of the risk correlates used to price insurance: age, gender, and smoking. We are unable to condition on 'preferred' status, the fourth risk category used to price insurance in CompuLife. The major result reported in Table 12.3 is a negative and significant covariance between unit price and quantity consistent with the CompuLife findings.

We recognize two scenarios in which the negative covariance between unit prices and quantities may be spurious. The first is the possibility that higher unobserved wealth or income leads to better health and larger insurance purchases. The second possibility is that those who have a greater unobservable bequest motive may live longer.

With respect to both of these possible confounding problems, HRS and AHEAD represent the best available data source, containing information about mortality risk, income, and wealth, detailed life-insurance data, and a census of family members who could receive bequests. Little income and wealth is left unrecorded in HRS and AHEAD relative to other surveys; detailed measurement of assets and income was one of the major objectives of

Table 12.3 Unit prices and quantity covariance in HRS and AHEAD data (dependent variable: unit price of term insurance)

Independent variable	HRS				AHEAD			
	Females		Males		Females		Males	
	Nonsmokers	Smokers	Nonsmokers	Smokers	Nonsmokers	Smokers	Nonsmokers	Smokers
Intercept	70.79	31.36	13.97	76.66	-3.51	39.76	-123.69	-294.38
	(1.44)	(0.57)	(0.77)	(1.53)	(-0.04)	(0.13)	(-1.17)	(-2.02)
Award	-0.65	-0.75	-0.08	-0.23	-6.82	11.56	-0.92	-5.22
	(-7.08)	(-5.3)	(-7.46)	(-4.69)	(-5.00)	(1.31)	(-4.39)	(-3.16)
Award squared (about mean)	0.00	0.00	0.00	0.00	0.11	-0.82	0.00	0.05
	(4.06)	(3.34)	(3.94)	(3.59)	(4.38)	(-1.43)	(2.93)	(2.98)
R^2:	0.10	0.15	0.10	0.12	0.22	0.46	0.13	0.41
Number of observations:	650	183	894	315	262	24	230	45

Notes: Insurance unit price (multiplied by 1000) is regressed on term insurance award, its square, age, wealth, and the following proxies for bequest motives: number of grandchildren, number of children, age of youngest child, average age of children, number of siblings, age of spouse, and an indicator variable for married. Table entries are regression coefficients (with t-statistics in parentheses).

the surveys. We include wealth as a regressor in the regressions reported in Table 12.3. We also control for bequest motive using the following proxies: married, spouse present; age of spouse; number of siblings; number of children; age of youngest child; average age of children; and number of grandchildren. We believe that unobserved income, wealth, and bequest motives are less of a problem for these data than for any other available data with comparable mortality information.[27]

To test whether this negative covariance is driven by a correlation between longevity and unobserved income or wealth, we regressed the log of the quantity of term insurance on instrumented unit price.[28] The negative correlation between unit price and quantity was robust to the use of instruments in the HRS sample, but instrumented price was not statistically significant in the AHEAD regressions; this may be due to the increased inefficiency caused by the weak explanatory power of our instruments. We find no support, however, for the theory of insurance under asymmetric information, which predicts a positive correlation between unit price and quantity.

We also test whether the negative covariance we observe between unit prices and quantities is a result of those who place more value on leaving bequests (and therefore buy larger quantities of insurance) tending to live longer. Besides controlling extensively for bequest motives in the regressions, we investigated whether proxies for bequest motives are correlated with actual mortality between waves or mortality beliefs. The only bequest proxy significantly correlated with risk (whether actual or perceived) was marital status.[29] There is little or no correlation between longevity and the motive to leave bequests in these data.

This section demonstrates unambiguously that there are bulk discounts in the pricing of term life insurance. This finding does not seem to be attributable to confounding effects of unobserved income or bequest motives.

B. Assessing the Covariance Between Risk and Quantity

Using the self-perceived and actual risk measures available in HRS and AHEAD, we next assess the predicted covariance between risk and quantity on both the extensive and intensive margins; that is, whether one holds life insurance and, if so, how much.

1. Risk and quantity covariation on the extensive margin

To assess the risk and quantity covariation on the extensive margin, we first return to Figure 12.2, which plots the mortality risk of those with life insurance compared to the general population. Figure 12.2 plots the ratio of the 1980 Commissioners Standard Ordinary (CSO) life-table mortality (based on mortality among those covered by life insurance between 1970 and 1975) to the mortality experienced by the US population in 1970 and 1975.[30] For most adult years, the mortality of men with life insurance turns out to be below that of the general population; the insurers are covering lower-than-average risks. The relative risk of the insured is actually lower than depicted in the figure; the 1980 CSO table reports mortality rates that are higher than were actually observed during 1970–1975, because the 1980 CSO is used for establishing reserve requirements, and the creators of the table wished to be conservative.[31]

Going beyond these aggregate patterns, we also examined the relationship between risk and the likelihood of holding life insurance using individual data from HRS and AHEAD. First, we estimated a logit regression of whether one holds term life insurance on indicator variables for self-perceived risk (the omitted category is a self-reported risk of zero – a certainty of surviving). We also control for the potential loss caused by the death of the insured, wealth, and bequest motives.

The results, contained in Table 12.4, show that in HRS, respondents with the highest self-perceived risk are the least likely to have insurance. However, in AHEAD, the most risky are no more or less likely than the least risky to have insurance. In AHEAD, it is the middle categories of self-reported risk that are more likely to purchase insurance.

Table 12.5 contains estimates of the same logit regression as was used for Table 12.4, with the exception that instead of using self-perceived risk, we now use actual risk, measured as the predicted probability of dying between the first and second wave. The upper bound of actual risk assumes that those who attrite from the sample have died, while the lower bound of actual risk assumes that attritors are still alive. The results for actual risk are similar to those for self-reported risk: while the coefficient on actual risk is not always statistically significant, the point estimates suggest that the relatively risky are less likely to have insurance.

2. Risk and quantity covariation on the intensive margin

We next examine the relationship between risk and demand on the intensive margin. We regressed the log of the quantity of term insurance on indicator variables for self-perceived risk, controlling for the potential loss caused by the death of the insured, wealth, and bequest motives. The results appear in Table 12.6.

The correlation between self-perceived risk and quantity of insurance is in many cases statistically insignificant. However, the point estimates suggest that high-risk individuals hold a lower quantity of insurance.

We next regressed the log of the quantity of insurance on our measures of actual risk, with the same additional controls as in Table 12.6. The results are contained in Table 12.7; we find no statistically significant relationship between actual risk and quantity.

Table 12.4 *Equilibrium demand and self-perceived risk in the HRS and AHEAD data (dependent variable: have term insurance = 1)*

Self-perceived risk (SPR)	HRS — Age 51–54 Model 1	Model 2	HRS — Age 55–58 Model 1	Model 2	HRS — Age 59–61 Model 1	Model 2	AHEAD — Group A Model 1	Model 2	AHEAD — Group B Model 1	Model 2
0.0 < SPR ≤ 0.1	0.35 (2.11)	0.38 (2.28)	0.09 (0.55)	0.09 (0.57)	0.36 (1.81)	0.39 (1.92)	−0.22 (−0.77)	−0.24 (−0.84)	0.15 (0.5)	0.16 (0.51)
0.1 < SPR ≤ 0.2	0.17 (1.32)	0.19 (1.46)	0.27 (2.18)	0.29 (2.29)	0.14 (0.90)	0.14 (0.86)	0.05 (0.19)	0.06 (0.23)	0.38 (1.31)	0.41 (1.38)
0.2 < SPR ≤ 0.3	0.24 (1.66)	0.25 (1.72)	0.32 (2.15)	0.32 (2.14)	0.25 (1.35)	0.22 (1.20)	0.44 (1.93)	0.44 (1.93)	0.32 (1.19)	0.39 (1.42)
0.3 < SPR ≤ 0.4	0.04 (0.20)	0.06 (0.31)	0.19 (1.04)	0.21 (1.12)	0.03 (0.12)	0.06 (0.25)	−0.12 (−0.33)	−0.10 (−0.29)	−0.32 (−0.72)	−0.36 (−0.79)
0.4 < SPR ≤ 0.5	0.15 (1.30)	0.18 (1.55)	0.32 (2.75)	0.31 (2.71)	0.13 (0.95)	0.11 (0.82)	0.12 (0.73)	0.12 (0.71)	0.45 (2.18)	0.48 (2.28)
0.5 < SPR ≤ 0.6	−0.33 (−1.52)	−0.32 (−1.50)	0.53 (2.41)	0.54 (2.50)	−0.11 (−0.40)	−0.15 (−0.55)	0.19 (0.56)	0.16 (0.45)	1.01 (2.66)	1.02 (2.68)
0.6 < SPR ≤ 0.7	−0.14 (−0.63)	−0.16 (−0.74)	−0.15 (−0.70)	−0.16 (−0.73)	0.26 (1.04)	0.21 (0.86)	−0.04 (−0.13)	−0.09 (−0.27)	0.32 (0.94)	0.33 (0.95)
0.7 < SPR ≤ 0.8	−0.25 (−1.15)	−0.29 (−1.30)	0.13 (0.61)	0.18 (0.83)	0.65 (2.28)	0.63 (2.17)	0.48 (2.23)	0.49 (2.28)	0.20 (0.72)	0.24 (0.86)
0.8 < SPR ≤ 0.9	−0.02 (−0.07)	−0.02 (−0.07)	0.61 (1.79)	0.54 (1.63)	−0.09 (−0.21)	−0.16 (−0.38)	0.27 (1.23)	0.23 (1.04)	0.53 (2.14)	0.59 (2.36)
0.9 < SPR ≤ 1.0	−0.42 (−2.30)	−0.47 (−2.56)	−0.34 (−1.99)	−0.35 (−2.02)	0.00 (−0.02)	−0.02 (−0.10)	0.00 (0.02)	0.05 (0.30)	0.39 (1.89)	0.49 (2.35)
Number of observations:	3318	3318	3280	3280	2181	2181	2354	2354	1876	1876

Notes: Table entries are regression coefficients from logit regressions (with t-statistics in parentheses). In Model 1, an indicator variable for 'have term insurance' is regressed on loss of income insured, wealth, indicator variables for self-reported risk, and the following proxies for bequest motives: number of grand-children, number of children, age of youngest child, average age of children, number of siblings, age of spouse, and an indicator variable for married. Model 2 is the same as Model 1 but with age and indicator variables for female and smoker added as regressors. In HRS, self-perceived risk was reported as an integer between 0 and 10. In AHEAD, self-perceived risk was reported as an integer between 0 and 100. In AHEAD, Group A reports self-perceived risk over a range of 11–13 years. For Group B, the range is 14–15 years. The omitted category is reported mortality risk of zero.

257

Table 12.5   Equilibrium demand and actual risk in HRS (dependent variable: have term insurance = 1)

Independent variable	Model 1	Model 2	Model 1	Model 2
Actual risk (upper bound)	−0.49	−1.28		
	(−1.71)	(−4.19)		
Actual risk (lower bound)			−0.1	−0.4
			(−0.42)	(−1.59)
Number of observations:	6644	6644	6644	6644

Notes: Table entries are regression coefficients from logit regressions (with *t*-statistics in parentheses). In Model 1, an indicator variable for 'have term insurance' is regressed on loss of income insured, wealth, actual risk, and the following proxies for bequest motives: number of grandchildren, number of children, age of youngest child, average age of children, number of siblings, age of spouse, and an indicator variable for married. Model 2 is the same as Model 1 but with age and indicator variables for female and smoker added as regressors. Actual risk is the likelihood of death, estimated from a logit regression of mortality on demographic characteristics. Attrited sample members are assumed to be dead in the upper bound of mortality and alive in the lower bound.

Overall, our results are hard to interpret in terms of conventional models of insurance under asymmetric information; we find a neutral or negative, as opposed to a positive, covariance between risk and quantity of insurance.

C.   The Relative versus Absolute Risk Knowledge of Consumers and Producers

As the pattern of pricing and risk depend on the allocation of information between the demanders and suppliers, we conclude by assessing this allocation using direct evidence contained in HRS and AHEAD. This relates to previous work showing that individuals are relatively well informed about their own mortality prospects (see e.g., Hamermesh and Hamermesh, 1983; Hamermesh, 1985; Viscusi, 1990, 1992; Hurd et al., 1996). However, an important distinction here should be made between absolute versus relative information on risk. Information barriers in markets concern the relative beliefs of buyers and sellers, whether or not these beliefs are accurate.

We first compare self-perceived and actual risk in our data; this measures the accuracy of consumers' beliefs. Figure 12.5 is a whisker plot of self-perceived risk and the upper bound of actual risk for those aged 51–54 in the HRS.

Figure 12.5 indicates a rather weak dependence between self-perceived and actual risk.[32] The pattern is similar for those aged 55–58 and 59–61, and if we

Table 12.6   Equilibrium demand and self-perceived risk in the HRS and AHEAD data (dependent variable: log of term insurance award)

Self-perceived risk (SPR)	HRS Age 51–54		HRS Age 55–58		HRS Age 59–61		AHEAD Group A		AHEAD Group B	
	Model 1	Model 2	Model 1	Model 2	Model 1	Model 2	Model 1	Model 2	Model 1	Model 2
0.0 < SPR ≤ 0.1	0.27 (1.60)	0.28 (1.69)	0.53 (3.39)	0.52 (3.41)	0.18 (0.96)	0.20 (1.02)	0.23 (0.88)	0.11 (0.47)	−0.48 (−1.52)	−0.37 (−1.26)
0.1 < SPR ≤ 0.2	0.21 (1.82)	0.23 (2.05)	0.29 (2.58)	0.30 (2.71)	0.04 (0.26)	0.07 (0.47)	−0.08 (−0.38)	0.02 (0.13)	0.21 (0.76)	0.19 (0.72)
0.2 < SPR ≤ 0.3	0.31 (2.38)	0.28 (2.30)	0.08 (0.58)	0.07 (0.55)	0.16 (0.94)	0.14 (0.82)	−0.04 (−0.20)	−0.02 (−0.12)	0.17 (0.66)	0.20 (0.84)
0.3 < SPR ≤ 0.4	0.04 (0.22)	0.02 (0.11)	0.05 (0.29)	0.08 (0.51)	−0.22 (−0.94)	−0.22 (−0.94)	−0.13 (−0.35)	−0.04 (−0.12)	0.33 (0.70)	0.18 (0.35)
0.4 < SPR ≤ 0.5	−0.10 (−0.95)	−0.08 (−0.77)	−0.05 (−0.39)	−0.06 (−0.54)	0.08 (0.61)	0.07 (0.53)	−0.14 (−1.14)	−0.16 (−1.47)	0.18 (0.94)	0.14 (0.78)
0.5 < SPR ≤ 0.6	0.02 (0.10)	0.01 (0.02)	0.18 (1.17)	0.16 (0.99)	0.26 (1.10)	0.27 (1.16)	−0.14 (−0.54)	−0.22 (−0.92)	−0.09 (−0.30)	−0.15 (−0.46)
0.6 < SPR ≤ 0.7	0.08 (0.44)	0.06 (0.34)	−0.27 (−1.48)	−0.30 (−1.68)	−0.29 (−1.18)	−0.36 (−1.49)	0.08 (0.39)	−0.17 (−0.86)	0.18 (0.58)	0.13 (0.44)
0.7 < SPR ≤ 0.8	0.18 (0.83)	0.09 (0.42)	−0.25 (−1.32)	−0.20 (−1.06)	0.09 (0.40)	0.09 (0.43)	−0.08 (−0.45)	−0.13 (0.80)	0.27 (1.17)	0.25 (1.25)
0.8 < SPR ≤ 0.9	−0.14 (−0.41)	−0.12 (−0.36)	0.07 (0.25)	−0.01 (−0.05)	−0.91 (−3.34)	−0.91 (−3.40)	0.00 (0.00)	−0.07 (−0.37)	0.19 (0.85)	0.22 (1.06)
0.9 < SPR ≤ 1.0	−0.31 (−1.62)	−0.40 (−2.08)	−0.15 (−0.88)	−0.17 (−0.99)	−0.10 (−0.45)	−0.12 (−0.55)	−0.23 (−1.83)	−0.18 (−1.49)	0.07 (0.36)	0.11 (0.65)
R^2:	0.12	0.17	0.14	0.16	0.12	0.14	0.22	0.34	0.26	0.35
Number of observations:	1708	1708	1660	1660	1077	1077	719	719	594	594

Notes: Table entries are regression coefficients (with t-statistics in parentheses). In Model 1, the log of the term insurance award is regressed on loss of income insured, wealth, indicator variables for self-reported risk, and the following proxies for bequest motives: number of grandchildren, number of children, age of youngest child, average age of children, number of siblings, age of spouse, and an indicator variable for married. Model 2 is the same as Model 1 but with age and indicator variables for female and smoker added as regressors. In HRS, self-perceived risk was reported as an integer between 0 and 100. In AHEAD, self-perceived risk was reported as an integer between 0 and 100. Group A reports self-perceived risk over a range of 11–13 years. For Group B, the range is 14–15 years. The omitted category is reported mortality risk of zero.

Table 12.7   Equilibrium demand and actual risk in HRS (dependent variable: log of term insurance award)

Independent variable	Model 1	Model 2	Model 1	Model 2
Actual risk (upper bound)	1.51	−1.07		
	(0.80)	(−0.54)		
Actual risk (lower bound)			−0.17	−0.89
			(−0.10)	(−0.53)
R^2:	0.05	0.07	0.05	0.07
Number of observations:	3360	3360	3360	3360

Notes: Table entries are regression coefficients (with *t*-statistics in parentheses). In Model 1, log of term insurance award is regressed on loss of income insured, wealth, actual risk, and the following proxies for bequest motives: number of grandchildren, number of children, age of youngest child, average age of children, number of siblings, age of spouse, and an indicator variable for married. Model 2 is the same as Model 1 but with age and indicator variables for female and smoker added as regressors. Actual risk is the likelihood of death, estimated from a logit regression of mortality on demographic characteristics. Attrited sample members are assumed to be dead in the upper bound of mortality and alive in the lower bound.

use the lower bound instead of the upper bound of actual risk. While the beliefs of buyers may not be highly correlated with actual risk, the important question for insurance markets is how well correlated they are with the beliefs of sellers. We suggest a test for relative knowledge: estimate how well self-reported mortality risk explains actual mortality, controlling for the price of the insurance. If the insured are relatively better informed about their mortality, then their beliefs should explain actual mortality risk holding constant the premia the consumer is charged. Table 12.8 reports regressions of actual risk on self-perceived risk, controlling for premia using HRS. The table suggests that consumer beliefs of mortality explain little actual mortality beyond life insurance premia. Premia themselves are not highly correlated with actual one-year mortality risk. Only for roughly a quarter of the risk groups is the correlation statistically significant and positive.

III.   CONCLUSION

Using direct evidence of not only the quantities and prices of insurance, but also of the self-perceived and actual risk of persons demanding life insurance, this paper derived implications of the theory of insurance under asymmetric information and evaluated the empirical support for the theory. It is difficult to interpret the data described in this paper as generated by standard models of

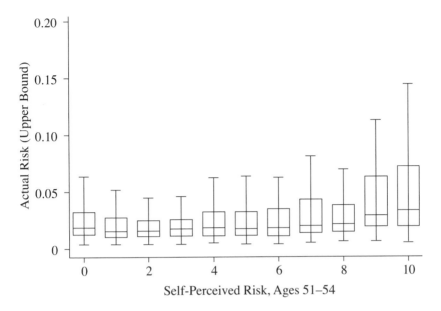

Notes: Each box extends from the 25th to the 75th percentile (the interquartile range), and the line in the middle of each box marks the median. The whiskers emerging from each box extend to the upper and lower adjacent values, defined as three-halves of the interquartile range, rolled back to where there are data.

Figure 12.5 Self-perceived and actual risk in HRS

insurance under asymmetric information. In the largest private insurance market in the world, we found evidence of bulk discounts, multiple contracting, and a negative covariance between risk and quantity. Each of these is the opposite of the predicted pattern.

One potential interpretation of the negative relationship we find between risk and quantity is that insurers can distinguish risks through underwriting and observing systematic patterns in claims over time and then limit coverage to high-risk, instead of low-risk, individuals. We do not claim to have provided direct evidence in support of this hypothesis, but we consider it a potential explanation for our findings. Producers in this market, as in many others, may know their costs of production better than consumers.[33]

More generally, it may be that standard arguments about adverse selection in insurance greatly exaggerate the relative superiority of the information of the demand side. Producers can overcome such problems, and if they do not attempt to, it may be because it is not worthwhile. This may be because of low costs of information production on the supply side. One explanation for why

Table 12.8   Actual and self-reported risk from the HRS data

Self-perceived risk (SPR)	Age 51–54 Females Nonsmokers	Females Smokers	Males Nonsmokers	Males Smokers	Age 55–58 Females Nonsmokers	Females Smokers	Males Nonsmokers	Males Smokers	Age 59–61 Females Nonsmokers	Females Smokers	Males Nonsmokers	Males Smokers
A. Dependent Variable = Actual Risk (Upper Bound):												
0.0 < SPR ≤ 0.1	0.00 (−1.66)	−0.01 (−1.52)	0.00 (−0.82)	0.01 (0.88)	−0.01 (−1.69)	0.00 (−0.15)	0.00 (0.58)	0.00 (−0.01)	−0.01 (−2.06)	0.00 (−0.42)	−0.01 (−2.51)	−0.01 (−1.52)
0.1 < SPR ≤ 0.2	0.00 (−1.98)	0.00 (−0.31)	−0.01 (−2.07)	0.00 (0.03)	−0.01 (−1.93)	0.02 (1.50)	0.00 (0.43)	−0.02 (−1.40)	−0.01 (−3.76)	−0.01 (−2.06)	−0.01 (−2.11)	−0.01 (−1.72)
0.2 < SPR ≤ 0.3	0.00 (−1.07)	0.00 (0.48)	−0.01 (−2.74)	0.00 (−0.68)	−0.01 (−1.40)	0.00 (−0.38)	0.00 (0.06)	0.01 (0.69)	0.00 (−0.28)	0.02 (1.37)	0.01 (0.52)	0.00 (−0.12)
0.3 < SPR ≤ 0.4	0.00 (−0.46)	0.00 (−0.31)	−0.01 (−1.74)	−0.02 (−1.85)	0.00 (−0.64)	−0.01 (−1.09)	0.02 (2.05)	0.00 (−0.46)	0.01 (1.30)	−0.01 (−0.91)	0.01 (0.52)	−0.01 (−1.19)
0.4 < SPR ≤ 0.5	0.01 (1.55)	0.01 (−0.25)	0.00 (0.08)	0.00 (0.54)	0.00 (−0.79)	0.00 (0.41)	0.00 (1.18)	0.02 (0.70)	0.00 (−0.66)	0.00 (0.06)	0.00 (−0.23)	0.00 (−0.34)
0.5 < SPR ≤ 0.6	0.00 (−0.68)	−0.01 (−1.49)	0.00 (−0.44)	0.00 (−0.45)	0.01 (0.81)	0.01 (0.59)	0.00 (−0.38)	−0.02 (−2.42)	−0.01 (−1.42)	−0.02 (−2.63)	0.00 (0.34)	0.10 (14.70)
0.6 < SPR ≤ 0.7	0.01 (1.15)	0.02 (0.98)	−0.01 (−3.66)	−0.01 (−0.75)	−0.01 (−1.29)	0.00 (0.05)	0.03 (2.67)	−0.03 (−4.16)	0.00 (0.38)	−0.01 (−2.12)	0.00 (−0.16)	0.01 (0.74)
0.7 < SPR ≤ 0.8	0.00 (0.05)	0.00 (−0.25)	0.00 (0.37)	0.01 (0.63)	0.02 (1.32)	0.02 (1.49)	0.01 (0.79)	−0.01 (−0.52)	0.00 (−0.07)	−0.01 (−1.28)	0.01 (1.18)	0.02 (1.06)
0.8 < SPR ≤ 0.9	0.04 (2.16)	0.00 (0.31)	0.00 (−0.08)	0.00 (−0.02)	−0.01 (−1.27)	−0.01 (−0.24)	0.02 (1.75)	0.00 (−0.15)	0.00 (−0.21)	−0.02 (−2.81)	0.03 (9.50)	0.08 (1.26)
0.9 < SPR ≤ 1.0	0.01 (1.26)	0.02 (1.78)	0.01 (1.78)	0.01 (1.94)	0.02 (2.12)	0.05 (1.68)	0.03 (1.39)	−0.01 (−1.60)	0.01 (0.69)	0.01 (1.06)	0.01 (1.52)	0.02 (1.06)
Unit price of insurance	0.00 (0.64)	0.00 (4.71)	0.00 (0.42)	0.23 (3.39)	0.02 (2.70)	0.17 (1.53)	0.01 (0.90)	0.00 (−1.10)	0.00 (0.56)	0.00 (0.51)	0.11 (2.23)	0.03 (0.65)
R²:	0.07	0.08	0.04	0.15	0.09	0.16	0.08	0.07	0.06	0.18	0.06	0.19
Number of observations:	480	166	440	216	453	134	410	139	287	84	286	95

262

B. Dependent Variable = Actual Risk (Lower Bound):

	(1)	(2)	(3)	(4)	(5)	(6)	(7)	(8)	(9)	(10)	(11)	(12)
0.0 < SPR ≤ 0.1	0.00 (−0.23)	0.00 (−1.55)	0.00 (−1.10)	0.00 (0.47)	0.00 (−1.59)	0.00 (−0.30)	0.00 (0.47)	0.00 (−0.81)	−0.01 (−1.84)	0.00 (0.49)	0.01 (−1.75)	0.00 (−0.03)
0.1 < SPR ≤ 0.2	0.00 (−0.02)	0.00 (−0.83)	0.00 (−1.68)	0.00 (0.39)	0.00 (−1.17)	0.01 (1.35)	0.00 (0.12)	0.00 (−1.12)	−0.01 (−1.88)	−0.01 (−2.16)	0.00 (−1.49)	0.00 (0.22)
0.2 < SPR ≤ 0.3	0.00 (0.36)	0.00 (−0.23)	0.00 (−1.32)	0.00 (−0.77)	0.00 (−0.96)	0.00 (−0.59)	0.00 (0.40)	0.00 (0.20)	0.01 (0.50)	0.01 (1.03)	0.01 (1.11)	0.01 (0.59)
0.3 < SPR ≤ 0.4	0.00 (−0.14)	0.00 (−0.98)	0.00 (−1.55)	0.00 (−0.76)	0.00 (−0.74)	0.00 (−1.12)	0.02 (1.17)	0.01 (1.64)	0.00 (0.20)	−0.01 (−1.30)	0.00 (0.33)	0.00 (0.39)
0.4 < SPR ≤ 0.5	0.00 (1.49)	0.00 (0.07)	0.00 (0.29)	0.00 (−0.40)	0.00 (−1.00)	0.00 (−0.88)	0.00 (1.46)	0.01 (0.80)	0.00 (−0.28)	0.01 (1.11)	0.01 (1.18)	0.00 (−0.12)
0.5 < SPR ≤ 0.6	0.00 (−1.00)	0.00 (−0.69)	0.00 (−2.73)	0.00 (−0.93)	0.01 (1.00)	0.02 (1.03)	0.00 (−1.00)	0.00 (−1.09)	−0.01 (−1.57)	−0.01 (−2.34)	0.01 (−0.93)	0.05 (12.03)
0.6 < SPR ≤ 0.7	0.01 (2.45)	0.01 (0.76)	0.00 (−1.24)	0.01 (0.85)	0.00 (−2.06)	0.01 (1.06)	0.03 (1.74)	−0.01 (−3.69)	0.00 (−0.06)	−0.01 (−2.73)	0.01 (0.53)	0.03 (1.39)
0.7 < SPR ≤ 0.8	0.00 (−2.08)	0.00 (0.40)	0.01 (1.04)	0.01 (1.33)	0.02 (1.17)	0.02 (1.69)	0.00 (0.34)	0.00 (−0.41)	0.00 (0.27)	−0.01 (−2.30)	0.02 (1.83)	0.01 (1.22)
0.8 < SPR ≤ 0.9	0.03 (1.74)	0.00 (0.57)	0.01 (1.26)	0.01 (5.05)	0.00 (−1.08)	−0.01 (−0.79)	0.01 (1.46)	0.00 (−0.08)	0.00 (0.17)	−0.01 (−2.36)	−0.01 (−4.14)	0.10 (1.30)
0.9 < SPR ≤ 1.0	0.01 (1.71)	0.01 (1.08)	0.00 (1.63)	0.01 (2.17)	0.01 (1.83)	0.05 (1.51)	0.05 (1.15)	0.00 (0.19)	0.00 (−0.09)	0.04 (1.84)	0.02 (1.69)	0.01 (0.52)
Unit price of insurance	0.00 (2.69)	0.00 (−1.65)	0.00 (0.19)	0.06 (1.98)	0.02 (3.77)	0.14 (1.32)	0.01 (0.98)	0.00 (−1.00)	0.00 (−0.44)	0.00 (1.16)	0.04 (0.72)	0.01 (0.62)
R^2:	0.08	0.04	0.04	0.09	0.08	0.18	0.08	0.06	0.03	0.31	0.05	0.22
Number of observations:	480	166	440	216	453	134	410	139	287	84	286	95

Notes: Actual mortality risk was regressed on insurance premia and indicator variables for self-reported risk. Table entries are regression coefficients (with t-statistics in parentheses).

unit prices fall involves fixed costs of production, but these fixed costs may well be the result of supply-side investments in information, such as underwriting.[34] Regardless of their sources, declining prices with coverage are inconsistent with the risk-sorting in the separating equilibrium described by the theory of insurance under asymmetric information.

Production of information prior to contracting also occurs in many other markets in which information has been argued to reduce trade, e.g., inspection markets in housing or credit checks in lending.[35] Generally, it seems that the size of the surplus forgone by walking away from a trade because of asymmetric information should be bounded above by the cost of producing the information through underwriting. Since the costs of real-estate inspections, credit checks, and medical exams are a very small fraction of the surplus generated when buying a home, taking out a mortgage, or having one's life insured for one's children, the patterns we find may generalize to even more markets as the information age further reduces underwriting costs.

NOTES

1. Cawley: Department of Economics, University of Chicago, 1126 East 59th Street, Chicago, IL 60637; Philipson: Irving B. Harris Graduate School of Public Policy Studies, Department of Economics, and the Law School, University of Chicago, 1126 East 59th Street, Chicago, IL 60637 (e-mail: t-philipson@uchicago.edu). Please address all correspondence to Philipson. We thank anonymous referees of the *Review* for comments that improved the chapter. Gary Becker, Michael Boozer, Pierre-Andre Chiappori, Daniel Hamermesh, James Heckman, Joseph Hotz, Magnus Johannesson, Don Kenkel, Brigitte Madrian, Casey Mulligan, Charles Mullin, Derek Neal, John Riley, Sherwin Rosen, and George Zanjani also provided valuable input. Seminar participants at the 1997 AEA Meetings, Brown University, the University of Chicago, DELTA-Paris, the 1996 and 1997 NBER Summer Institutes on Social Insurance and Health Care, Lund University, Stockholm School of Economics, and Rand-UCLA also provided helpful comments. This project was supported by N.I.A. Grant No. T32 AG00243, the George Stigler Center at the University of Chicago, and a Faculty Research Fellowship from the Alfred P. Sloan Foundation. We thank LIMRA, CompuLife, and the Society of Actuaries for discussions and for providing data, although the arguments and analysis here should not be attributed to any of these organizations.
2. See American Council of Life Insurance (1994) and Swiss Reinsurance Company (1997).
3. See e.g., Michael Rothschild and Joseph E. Stiglitz (1976) or David M. Kreps (1990 Ch. 17). For a discussion of the moral hazard effects of life-insurance products, see Philipson and Gary S. Becker (1998).
4. For example, see George A. Akerlof (1970, pp. 12–14) and Stiglitz (1988, pp. 332–33).
5. Although our discussion generalizes, we focus on Rothschild and Stiglitz (1976), the most often discussed model of insurance under asymmetric information.
6. The price differential creates an incentive for smokers to masquerade as nonsmokers in order to pay lower premia. The potential for such adverse selection is eliminated through underwriting on the basis of urine and blood tests, which make nicotine consumption common knowledge. Furthermore, insurance companies reserve the right to limit awards if misreporting of customers becomes evident after the death of the insured.
7. Surprisingly, the magnitude of these discounts is such that, at certain quantities, one can pay less for a higher quantity of insurance. For example, it is cheaper to buy a policy for $250 000 than for $225 000.

8. We describe this figure in more detail in Section II, subsection A.
9. In a separating equilibrium, the low-risk individuals may subsidize the contracts of the high-risk individuals in order to increase the size of the low-risk contract while preserving the separating equilibrium. Such subsidies can reduce the rise in unit price with quantity but cannot eliminate the rise without destroying the separating equilibrium (see Rothschild and Stiglitz, 1976).
10. The incentive-compatibility constraints imposed by screening models are discussed in John G. Riley (1979), Russell Cooper (1984), and George Mailath (1987).
11. For a practitioner's perspective on this type of contracting, see R. Barney (1995).
12. Philipson and George Zanjani (1998) provides a more precise analysis of when underwriting implies bulk discounts and a negative covariance between risk and quantity.
13. Term policies are available for varying term lengths. We analyze only one-year term policies in our CompuLife sample. We do not know the length of the term policies in the HRS and AHEAD surveys.
14. The extent of multiple contracting is consistent across age, gender, and smoking status.
15. Note that positive covariance between quantity and risk alone does not imply a convex total price schedule. With fixed costs of production, unit prices may initially fall but eventually must rise.
16. For a complete description of the survey, see LIMRA International (1994).
17. We find the same pattern when we disaggregate by the income of the insured.
18. Our discussions with actuaries and life-insurance agents confirmed that prices are computed through linear formulas.
19. Produced by the University of Michigan Survey Research Center.
20. In both studies, spouses of age-eligible respondents were interviewed. We drop observations on spouses who were not themselves age-eligible. We also dropped from our sample those who are unsure whether their life insurance is whole life or term; however, we also estimated our models with such people included in our sample, and the results were not significantly different.
21. Both HRS and AHEAD oversampled African-Americans, Hispanics, and residents of Florida, but we use sample weights to produce a nationally representative sample.
22. Measurement error is a concern with any expectations data, although the theory of insurance under asymmetric information implies that consumers should have no difficulty recording their risk beliefs.
23. Hamermesh and Hamermesh (1983), Hamermesh (1985), Hurd and Kathleen McGarry (1995), and Hurd et al. (1996) conclude that subjective survival functions are close to life-table averages and covary with health and socioeconomic variables in the same manner as actual survival curves. In addition, Viscusi (1990, 1992) examines the correlation between smoking activity and perceptions about lung-cancer risk. Although both smokers and nonsmokers are found to greatly overestimate the risk of lung cancer associated with cigarette smoking, those who perceive a greater risk are less likely to smoke.
24. In a previous version of this paper (Cawley and Philipson, 1996), the beliefs about survival over several years were converted into one-year hazard rates. We abandoned this approach because the magnitude (although not the signs) of the coefficient estimates were very sensitive to the parameterization.
25. In AHEAD, respondents were asked about the characteristics of their largest term policy only. In the HRS, respondents were asked to report the total award and premia of all of their term policies.
26. The regressors in the logit regression include age, squared age, height, weight, the first principal component of three measures of cognitive awareness, and indicator variables for female, black, white, married, diabetes, smokes now, ever smoked, drinks alcohol, cancer, lung disease, heart disease, stroke, psychiatric problems, arthritis, asthma, back problems, kidney ailments, ulcers, high cholesterol, broken bones after age 45, high blood pressure, eyeglasses, and a hospital stay in the last year.
27. In AHEAD, total family income represents the couple's combined income, before taxes, for the year 1992 or 1993, depending on the time of the interview. In HRS, total family income equals the total household income for 1991; this is the sum of earnings, unemployment and workers' compensation, pensions, annuities, supplemental security income, welfare, capital

income, disability income, and unspecified 'other' income. In AHEAD, the loss of income from the death of the insured was directly measured and was defined to include the pretax wages of the insured in 1992/1993 plus the net annual loss that death would cause in the top three regular income sources (e.g., pensions, veterans' benefits, and annuities). Net loss can be determined because respondents were asked the current amount of the payments, and how much their spouses would continue to receive from that source if they were to die. In HRS, the loss of income from death of the insured was estimated as the insured's annual income from veterans' benefits, pensions, annuities, supplemental security income, wages and salaries, bonuses, overtime, tips and commissions, professional practice, second jobs, military reserves, unemployment compensation, workers' compensation, and Social Security (including disability, survivors' benefits, and retirement). Unlike AHEAD, HRS does not record how much income a spouse would continue to receive from these sources if the insured dies. The wealth variable constitutes assets minus debts. Assets include retirement accounts, savings accounts, checking accounts, stocks, mutual funds, certificates of deposit, bonds, Treasury bills, money-market funds, annuities, other investments, accounts receivable, real estate, cars, boats, airplanes, businesses, jewelry, and unspecified 'other' assets. Debts include mortgages, credit-card balances, medical debt, loans from relatives, life-insurance policy loans, and unspecified 'other' debt.

28.   For the AHEAD sample we used the following instruments, which we believe are correlated with mortality risk but not with unobserved components of wealth and loss: height, the age of each parent at death, age, and indicator variables that equal 1 if the respondent has living parents. In AHEAD, age is assumed to be uncorrelated with unobservable income because sample members are at least 70 years old and generally on annuitized income. For the HRS sample we used the same instruments with the exception of age; we could not use age as an instrument because the HRS sample is of working age, and age is presumably correlated with unobserved income. Our instruments are weakly correlated with unit price; the R^2 value is roughly 0.1 in both the HRS and AHEAD samples. These instrumented unit price regressions are presented in Cawley and Philipson (1996).

29.   Tables are available from the authors upon request.

30.   These mortality rates were computed from the age conditional survival data reported in US Department of Health, Education, and Welfare (1970, 1975).

31.   See Society of Actuaries (1980) for a description of the 1980 CSO table.

32.   Note that there is no omitted-variable problem here; the respondent's beliefs take into account all of the relevant information that he possesses.

33.   Philipson and Zanjani (1998) discusses a theory with predictions that are consistent with the findings discussed here.

34.   The classic reference on how to use systematic knowledge about customer characteristics to set premia is P. Shepherd and A. Webster (1957). See also K. Clifford and R. Iucolano (1987) for a more recent discussion.

35.   Although life insurance and annuity products both concern mortality risk, they may have different features that seem to make underwriting by insurers more desirable for the former than the latter. Benjamin M. Friedman and Mark J. Warshawsky (1990) estimate the share of annuity prices attributable to adverse selection by comparing the mortality experience of annuity demanders with that of the overall population. However, no existing analysis predicts that markups are related to adverse selection. In addition, applying their methodology to our data suggests that the adverse selection markup in life insurance is negative!

REFERENCES

Akerlof, George A. 'The Market for Lemons: Quality Uncertainty and the Market Mechanism.' *Quarterly Journal of Economics*, August 1970, 84(3), pp. 488–500.

American Council of Life Insurance. *1994 life insurance fact book*. Washington, DC: American Council of Life Insurance, 1994.

Barney, R. 'To Split or Not to Split, That Is the Question.' *Canadian Money Saver*, February 1995, pp. 69–72.

Bond, Eric W. 'A Direct Test of the Lemons Model: The Market for Used Pickup Trucks.' *American Economic Review*, September 1982, 72(4), pp. 836–40.

Cawley, John and Philipson, Tomas. 'An Empirical Examination of Information Barriers to Trade in Insurance.' National Bureau of Economic Research (Cambridge, MA) Working Paper No. 5669, 1996.

Clifford, K. and Iucolano, R. 'AIDS and Insurance: The Rationale for AIDS-Related Testing.' *Harvard Law Review*, May 1987, 100(7), pp. 1806–25.

Cooper, Russell. 'On Allocative Distortions in Problems of Self-Selection.' *Rand Journal of Economics*, Winter 1984, 15(4), pp. 568–77.

Foster, Andrew D. and Rosenzweig, Mark R. 'A Test for Moral Hazard in the Labor Market: Contractual Arrangements, Effort, and Health.' *Review of Economics and Statistics*, May 1994, 76(2), pp. 213–27.

Friedman, Benjamin M. and Warshawsky, Mark J. 'The Cost of Annuities: Implications for Saving Behavior and Bequests.' *Quarterly Journal of Economics*, February 1990, 105(1), pp. 135–54.

Genesove, David. 'Adverse Selection in the Wholesale Used Car Market.' *Journal of Political Economy*, August 1993, 101(4), pp. 644–65.

Hamermesh, Daniel S. 'Expectations, Life Expectancy, and Economic Behavior.' *Quarterly Journal of Economics*, May 1985, 10(2), pp. 389–408.

Hamermesh, Daniel S. and Hamermesh, F. W. 'Does Perception of Life-Expectancy Reflect Health Knowledge?' *American Journal of Public Health*, August 1983, 73(8), pp. 911–14.

Hurd, Michael and McGarry, Kathleen. 'Evaluation of the Subjective Probabilities of Survival in the Health and Retirement Study.' *Journal of Human Resources*, 1995, Supp., 30, pp. S268–92.

Kreps, David M. *A course in microeconomic theory*. Princeton, NJ: Princeton University Press, 1990.

LIMRA International. *The 1994 buyer's study: A market study of new insureds and the ordinary life insurance purchased*. Windsor, CT: LIMRA International, 1994.

Mailath, George. 'Incentive Compatibility in Signaling Games with a Continuum of Types.' *Econometrica*, November 1987, 55(6), pp. 1349–65.

Philipson, Tomas J. and Becker, Gary S. 'Old-Age Longevity and Mortality-Contingent Claims.' *Journal of Political Economy*, June 1998, 106(3), pp. 551–73.

Philipson, Tomas and Zanjani, George. 'A Theory of the Production and Regulation of Insurance.' Working paper, University of Chicago, 1998.

Riley, John G. 'Informational Equilibrium.' *Econometrica*, March 1979, 47(2), pp. 331–59.

Rothschild, Michael and Stiglitz, Joseph E. 'Equilibrium in Competitive Insurance Markets: An Essay on the Economics of Imperfect Information.' *Quarterly Journal of Economics*, November 1976, 90(4), pp. 630–49.

Shepherd, P. and Webster, A. *Selection of risks*. Chicago, IL: Society of Actuaries, 1957.

Society of Actuaries. 'New Mortality Tables for Valuation.' *Transactions of the Society of Actuaries*, 1980, 33, pp. 617–74.

Stiglitz, Joseph E. *Economics of the public sector*. New York: Norton, 1988.

Swiss Reinsurance Corporation. 'World Insurance in 1995: Premium Volume Exceeds USD 2000 Billion for the First Time.' *Sigma Report*, 1997, (4).

Teachers Insurance and Annuity Association (TIAA), Life Insurance Planning Center. *Official life insurance handbook*. New York: TIAA, 1997.

U.S. Department of Health, Education, and Welfare. *Vital statistics of the United States*, Vol. 2, Pt. A. Washington, DC: US Government Printing Office, various years.

Viscusi, W. Kip. 'Do Smokers Underestimate Risks?' *Journal of Political Economy*, December 1990, 98(6), pp. 1253–69.

Viscusi, W. Kip. *Smoking: Making the risky decision*. New York: Oxford University Press, 1992.

13. A direct test of the 'lemons' model: the market for used pickup trucks

Eric W. Bond[1]

This chapter provides an empirical test of one of the implications of models of markets with asymmetric information. In the seminal paper on markets with asymmetric information, George Akerlof (1970) pointed out two possible outcomes that may occur where sellers have better information about the quality of products than do buyers. One possibility is that bad products will drive out good products. If buyers cannot distinguish quality until after the purchase has been made, there will be no incentive for sellers to provide good quality products, and the average quality in the market will decline. In the case of cars, an often-cited example of this phenomenon, owners who discover that they have a 'lemon' will attempt to sell it in the used car market to an unsuspecting buyer. The owner of the 'creampuff' will not sell his car, since it is indistinguishable from a lemon to buyers and must therefore sell for the price of a car of average quality. The effect of quality uncertainty is to reduce the volume of transactions in the used car market below the socially optimal level.

A second possibility suggested by Akerlof is that institutions may develop to counteract the effects of quality uncertainty. Warranties and brand names can be used to give the buyer some assurance of quality. These institutions may prevent good products from being driven from the market, but they will not necessarily eliminate the inefficiency. These institutions may be costly, and sellers may overinvest in signaling the quality of their product to buyers (for example, see Akerlof, 1976).

The purpose of this chapter is to test whether bad products drive out good products in the market for used pickup trucks, a market similar to the used car market. The measure of quality chosen here is the amount of maintenance required on a truck, with a lemon being a truck that requires significantly more maintenance than average. Owners will have an idea of the truck's quality from past maintenance experience, but it may be difficult for a potential buyer to predict future maintenance from inspecting the truck. If this informational asymmetry is significant and counteracting institutions do not develop, the lemons model would predict that owners of high maintenance trucks would sell them in the used market. The used truck market would then become a market for lemons, with the abundance of high maintenance trucks driving out sellers of low maintenance trucks as described above. The empirical implication of this model is that a sample of trucks that has been purchased used should have required more maintenance (since it should contain more lemons) than a sample of trucks with similar characteristics that have not been traded. Section I reports the results of such a test using data form the *1977 Truck Inventory and Use (TIU) Survey.*

The results indicate that if the effects of age and lifetime mileage on maintenance are controlled for, there is no difference in maintenance between trucks acquired new and trucks acquired used. This leads to a rejection of the hypothesis that bad products have driven out good, since there is no evidence of an overabundance of lemons among used trucks. One explanation for this finding is that the counteracting institutions of the type discussed by Akerlof may have developed. The provision of warranties on used trucks and the seller's concern about his reputation may prevent sellers from supplying low quality products. A second possible explanation is that buyers are able to obtain enough information from search to eliminate the asymmetry. While the finding that the average quality of original owner and used trucks is the same is consistent with the operation of an efficient market for used trucks, the market could still be inefficient if the informational asymmetry is eliminated through costly counteracting institutions or costly search by buyers.

I. TESTING THE LEMONS MODEL

As discussed above, the hypothesis that the used truck market contains an overabundance of lemons was tested by comparing the frequency of maintenance between trucks that were acquired used and those that were acquired new in the *TIU Survey*. This section describes the data obtained from the *TIU Survey* and reports the results of the test.

The *TIU Survey* is part of the Census of Transportation. It is based on a stratified probability sample of all trucks registered at motor vehicle departments in the fifty states, and requests information about the characteristics and usage of the trucks. With regard to maintenance, respondents were asked whether their truck had required major maintenance in any of five categories (engine, transmission, brakes, rear axle, and other) in the preceding 12 months.[2] Since the maintenance variable is a dichotomous variable, the frequency of maintenance of a given type in a sample of trucks can be modeled with a binomial distribution if the trucks in the sample are similar. The *TIU Survey* contains information on model year and lifetime mileage, so that it is possible to control for the effects of these observable factors on maintenance.

If these factors are controlled, the sample proportion will be an estimate of the probability of maintenance among trucks of that type.

Pickup trucks were selected for study because pickup trucks have the largest noncommercial demand of any trucks in the survey. In the sample, 59 percent of the pickups are used for personal transportation, 21 percent are in agriculture, and the remainder are in various commercial uses (primarily construction, services, and retail trade). It was felt that the large household demand would increase the likelihood of asymmetric information in second-hand markets, since one would expect that household purchasers have less expertise in evaluating used trucks than commercial purchasers.

In addition, several other bits of evidence suggest similarities with the automobile market. Pickup trucks are produced by the major automobile producers (both foreign and domestic), and are sold by many car dealers. The retail markup over dealer cost on a pickup is comparable to that of a full-size car. Finally, the frequency of trading of pickups is comparable to that of autos. Of the trucks purchased during 1976, 60 percent were purchased used. Although data for the same year are not available for automobiles, the 1972 survey of household durable purchases (Department of Commerce, 1973) indicates that 65 percent of automobiles purchased in that year were used.

One question that had to be addressed was the choice of model years to study. Enough time must be allowed for owners to become aware that their trucks are lemons, but if the model year studied is too old, many of the lemons may already have been scrapped.[3] Since the lemons model gives no guidance on this point, trucks that were from one to five years old in 1977 (model years 1972–76) were studied to give a fairly wide range of time for the lemons effect to occur.

Table 13.1 shows the number of pickups in the survey, the percentage acquired, used, and the proportion of new and used trucks that required major

Table 13.1   Summary statistics of the sample

Year	Number In Sample	Acquired Used	Proportion Requiring Engine Maintenance	
			New	Used
1976	2137	0.11	0.08	0.05
1975	1602	0.27	0.10	0.11
1974	2261	0.37	0.11	0.13
1973	2085	0.48	0.15	0.15
1972	1839	0.53	0.13	0.15

engine maintenance for each model year. The proportion requiring maintenance is slightly higher for used trucks in three of the years. However, this
comparison is biased against used trucks since used trucks had significantly
higher lifetime mileage in each model year.

If the lemons hypothesis is true, the probability of maintenance should be
higher for secondhand trucks than for trucks with similar characteristics that
were acquired new. The effects of observable characteristics were controlled
for by grouping trucks according to model year and lifetime mileage. Let P^n_{ijk}
be the probability of maintenance of type i for trucks of model year j and
mileage group k that were acquired new, and let P^u_{ijk} be the corresponding
proportion for trucks acquired used. The first test of the lemons model was to
test the null hypothesis of no difference in quality between trucks acquired
new and trucks acquired used, $P^n_{ijk} = P^u_{ijk}$. If the number of observations is large
enough, the difference in group means will be normally distributed. Due to the
low frequencies of several types of maintenance and the small number of used
trucks in the 1975 and 1976 model years, larger mileage groupings had to be
chosen to make the assumption of normality for those years.[4]

The advantage of the test for equality of individual group means is that it
allows testing of the hypothesis that only some segments of the market operate inefficiently. For example, suppose that the unreliability of service and
large amount of down time associated with operating a lemon precludes its
being used very intensively. A buyer of a high mileage truck would then be
certain that he was not getting a lemon. If lifetime mileage can be used as a
signal for unobservable quality, some portions of the market might not contain
lemons.

The results of the tests on group means are reported in Table 13.2, with the
number of groups in which the used trucks were judged to be inferior at a 10
percent level of significance shown in column 2. The results indicate almost
no support for the lemons model in any of the model years. In fact, equally
strong support could be found for the hypothesis that trucks in the used market
are superior (shown in column 3). There was no evidence that the cases where

Table 13.2 Tests of differences in proportions requiring maintenance

	Number of Tests	Used Inferior (10 percent level)	Used Superior (10 percent level)
1976	19	1	2
1975	27	0	2
1974	44	2	3
1973	57	3	1
1972	67	2	1

used trucks were inferior were concentrated in any particular segment of the market.

The data indicated that the probability of maintenance generally increased with the lifetime mileage of the truck, as one would expect.[5] Since maintenance is a dichotomous variable, the relationship between maintenance and mileage can be estimated using a logit model:

$$ln\,[P_i/(1-P_i)\,] = \alpha_i + \beta_i\,x + \varepsilon_i \tag{1}$$

where P_i is the probability of maintenance of type i and x is lifetime mileage. A second test of the lemons model was performed by estimating (1) separately for both used and original owner trucks, and then testing whether the slope and constant terms were equal for the two equations. This provides an overall test of whether used trucks and original owner trucks have any difference in quality.

The presence of a market for lemons would be indicated by a constant term in the equation for used trucks that was significantly greater than that for trucks acquired new, or by a combination of differing slope and constant terms that indicate greater maintenance for used trucks over the relevant range. The model was estimated by grouping the data by mileage for both new and used trucks, and then using the group means to estimate (1) with the weighted least squares approximation to the logit discussed by D.R. Cox. Equations were estimated for all five types of maintenance for model years 1973 and 1975. In none of the equations were either the slopes or constant terms significantly different at the 5 percent level between original owner and used trucks. This test provides further support for the hypothesis that there is no dilution of quality in the used market.

II.   CONCLUSION

The main finding of this chapter is that trucks that were purchased used required no more maintenance than trucks of similar age and lifetime mileage that had not been traded. This leads to a rejection of the hypothesis that the used pickup truck market is a market for lemons, which would have required used trucks to show significantly more maintenance. However, it should be noted that the failure to find an overabundance of lemons in the used market is not inconsistent with the commonly expressed notion that cars and trucks are traded when they become 'too costly' to maintain. Suppose that there are two types of buyers in the market: one group with high maintenance costs and a second group of handymen with low maintenance costs. As trucks age and require more maintenance, high maintenance cost owners will prefer to sell to low maintenance cost buyers rather than to continue to operate the truck them-selves.[6] While it might appear to members of the former group that used trucks are too costly to maintain, this results not from the existence of a market for lemons, but from the reallocation of the stock of assets to those individuals who value them most highly.

NOTES

1. Assistant professor of economics, Pennsylvania State University. I thank Roger McCain, Richard Butler, Arnie Raphaelson and an anonymous referee for helpful comments on this chapter. Wayne Morra and John Fund provided computational assistance.
2. It would be preferable to have information on actual maintenance expenditures, since the quality depends not only on the probability of maintenance but also on the costliness of repairs. Unfortunately, expenditure data were not available. However, the costliness of repairs will be partially captured by the fact that the respondents are asked only to indicate major maintenance.
3. The median age of pickup trucks in the TIU Survey was seven years. By the time trucks were five years old, more than 50 percent had been traded at least once.
4. In order for the binomial distribution to be approximately normal, the expected frequency of maintenance should be at least five in each group (see R. Hogg and A. Craig). In order to satisfy this condition, it was necessary to expand the size of the mileage groups for the more recent model years (where relatively few trucks were used) and for transmission and rear axle maintenance (which were more rare events). For the 1972–74 data, the mileage groups were in intervals of 10 000 miles for most maintenance tests. For the 1975–76 data, the groups had to be expanded to 15–20 000 miles intervals for all maintenance tests except the 'other' category.
5. An exception to this was maintenance in the 'other' category, which was negatively related to lifetime mileage.
6. A complete model of used asset markets with complete information and different types of consumers is presented in my working paper, which also presents evidence that buyers who do their own maintenance are more likely to buy used trucks.

REFERENCES

Akerlof, George A., 'The Market for "Lemons": Quality Uncertainty and the Market Mechanism,' *Quarterly Journal of Economics*, August 1970, 84, 488–500.

Akerlof, George A., 'The Economics of Caste and of the Rat Race and Other Woeful Tales,' *Quarterly Journal of Economics*, November 1976, 90, 599–617.

Bond, Eric W., 'A Theory of Trade in Used Equipment,' working paper 1-81-2, Pennsylvania State University, 1981.

Cox, D.R., *Analysis of Binary Data*, London: Methuen, 1970.

Hogg, R. and Craig, A., *Introduction to Mathematical Statistics*, New York: MacMillan, 1978.

US Department of Commerce, Bureau of the Census, *Current Population Reports; Consumer Buying Indicators*, p. 65, No. 45, Washington: USGPO, 1973.

14. Public choice experiments

Elizabeth Hoffman

A number of important issues in public choice have been addressed in experimental research.[1] This chapter summarizes experimental research on the role of allocation mechanisms and agent behavior in the ability of groups of agents to achieve optimal allocations of public goods and externalities when there are gains from cooperation and coordination. This line of research includes studies of the free-rider problem with voluntary contributions; studies of the ability of small and large bargaining groups to achieve Pareto-optimal allocations of externalities or public goods; and studies of the design and behavioral implementation of synthetic allocation mechanisms for the allocation of public goods, externalities, and complex commodities.

1. THE FREE-RIDER PROBLEM WITH VOLUNTARY CONTRIBUTION MECHANISMS

The free-rider problem is a central focus of experimental research in public choice.[2] Economists, psychologists, and sociologists have jointed the debate, answers to which are central to a number of larger issues in public choice. The basic premise of economists is that individuals, acting in their own self-interest, will underprovide public goods and positive externalities and overprovide negative externalities, relative to those quantities that would maximize social welfare. In the limit, with pure public goods and appropriability, no public goods will be provided. Psychologists and sociologists counter both with arguments criticizing the basic assumptions of economic models and with the observation that societies do provide public goods for themselves, sometimes without governmental intervention. Economists, themselves, subscribe to two different 'remedies' to the free-rider problem. One group suggests that the only solution is for government to provide public goods and tax citizens to pay for them. The problem then becomes determining the optimal quantity of public goods and the optimal tax structure. The other group, drawing on the seminal work of Ronald Coase (1960) suggests that individuals will realize the benefits from collective action and form private organizations to provide public goods and collect funds to support them. This section outlines the basic voluntary contribution experiments and reviews some results. These experiments address two important problems with voluntary contribution. First, how serious is the free-rider problem under conditions similar to those prevailing in naturally occurring public goods allocation systems? Second, what policies tend to increase or decrease voluntary contributions to public goods provision? The next section outlines and discusses experiments designed to test the Coasian proposition that groups will privately provide public goods for themselves.

The current literature on voluntary contribution begins with a series of articles by Marwell and Ames (1979, 1980, 1981), two sociologists at the University of Wisconsin. Observing that public goods do seem to get provided, they asked the question whether free-riding was a characteristic more of economists than of society as a whole. They designed their experiment as follows. They recruited high school students by telephone. Each student was given a set of paper tokens that could be redeemed for money. Each student was asked to make one decision, allocating tokens to two accounts. The private account provided a return of one cent per token invested. The group account (the public good) returned to individuals as a function of the total number of tokens invested in the group account by all members of the group. At low investment levels, each individual token contributed to the group account earned less than one cent to the individual contributing, but larger investments by all participants led to higher payoffs for all participants. Subjects were told they were assigned to groups of either four or 80 participants. In reality, all groups had four participants. A companion experiment (Marwell and Ames 1981) substitutes graduate students in economics for high school students. Marwell and Ames found that, in general, subjects in their experiments contributed about half their tokens to the group account. The only exception was the economics graduate students who contributed very little. They concluded that the free-rider problem was not as serious for non-economists as economists were suggesting.

These results prompted economists to initiate experimental research on the free-rider problem. Three papers directly motivated by Marwell and Ames' results (Isaac, Walker, and Thomas 1984; Kim and Walker 1984; Isaac, McCue, and Plott 1985) led to an extensive research agenda on voluntary contributions mechanisms (e.g., Isaac and Walker 1988a, 1988b, 1991; Isaac, Schmidtz, and Walker 1989; Isaac, Walker, and Williams 1994; Laury, Walker, and Williams 1995). Economists had several criticisms of the Marwell and Ames experiments. First, the use of telephone surveys and deception about group size called into question the experimentalists' control of the experimental incentives. Second, the one-shot nature of the experiment did not allow subjects to learn about the possible free-riding behavior of other subjects and adjust their behavior accordingly. This applies both to learning within an experimental session and to learning across different experimental sessions. Third, the subject payoff tables did not generate a single Nash equilibrium strategy. Thus, the results could not provide conclusive evidence about free-riding. In fact, contributing half one's tokens to the group account was a clear focal point in the payoff structure.

Isaac, Walker, and Thomas (1984) defined the experimental design that has become the standard for this research agenda. In their experiment, students at the University of Arizona were recruited to come to a PLATO computer laboratory at a certain time. Each subject sat at a private terminal and read through a set of instructions explaining a task quite similar to that in the Marwell and Ames experiments. Each subject was given a set number of experimental tokens and could invest those tokens in either an individual or group account. The individual account returned one cent for each token invested by the individual. The group account returned less than one cent for each token contributed by the group. These initial incentives were designed so that contributing zero tokens to the group account was a Nash equilibrium, but contributing 100 percent was Pareto optimal. Subjects knew how many other subjects were in the group because they could see them in the room. Consistency was maintained because they all read the same instructions. Each group of subjects participated in ten consecutive decisions; experienced subjects were brought back to participate with other experienced subjects in new sequences of decisions.

Isaac, Walker, and Thomas (1984) considered group sizes of four and ten subjects, individual returns to the group account of 0.3 or 0.75 of a cent, and subject experience. The results do not settle the debate. First, subjects in their experiments continued to contribute well in excess of the Nash equilibrium prediction of zero to the group account. Averaging over replications of the same treatment, contributions ranged from 40 percent to 60 percent of tokens in period 1 to 20 percent to 40 percent of tokens in period 10. Occasionally a group contributed zero tokens in one or more periods, but this was not a predictable or consistent outcome. Certain treatments did encourage or discourage contribution to the group account. Subjects tended to contribute less with repetition or experience, and with a lower individual return from contribution to the group account. Holding individual payoffs constant, group size did not have a significant effect.

These results have led to a significant change in the focus of research on voluntary contribution among economists. The initial thrust was to test the economic model and to show sociologists and psychologists that free-riding really was a serious problem. Now the emphasis is on determining what factors contribute to more or less free-riding. From a policy perspective, this research has led to a renewed emphasis on the possibility of private solutions to the public goods allocation problem.

For example, Isaac and Walker (1988a) study the effect of communication on free riding in an experiment essentially identical to that reported in Isaac, Walker, and Thomas (1984). They consider two experimental treatments. In one subjects begin each of the first ten decisions with a group discussion of how much each subject should contribute. Each decision is made privately. After ten decisions with communication they make ten decisions without communication. In the other the subjects begin with ten decisions with no communication and end with ten communication decisions. They find that communication unequivocally reduces free riding (increases contribution to the group account), even though all decisions are made in private. Groups that begin with communication typically achieve nearly 100 percent contributions to the group account. Contributions diminish once the group ceases communication each period. Groups that begin with no communication take longer to achieve high levels of contribution with communication, but contributions do increase.

Isaac, Schmidtz, and Walker (1989) consider the effect of having a threshold level of the public good, a provision point. Any contributions below the provision point are lost. Contributions equal to or above the provision point go to the group account as in the previously described experiments. The idea is that provision of a public good generally involves raising enough funds to pay for purchase or construction. If insufficient funds are raised the public good is not provided. Isaac, Schmidtz, and Walker (1989) find that higher provision points are associated with greater contributions to the group account, thus suggesting that provision points improve provision. However, they also find that higher provision points also reduce the probability the provision point will be achieved.

Isaac, Walker, and Williams (1994) study the effect of group size with very large groups. Using a clever experiment design, in which they substitute extra credit points for money in large introductory economics classes, they find that very large groups generally achieve higher levels of contributions than groups of size four or ten. Contributions still decline with repetition and with lower private returns to group contributions. Laury, Walker, and Williams (1995) find that subject anonymity, from one another and from the experimenter, do not change average contributions by treatments.

We are now at a crossroads in understanding the role of the free-rider problem in public choice. On the one hand, in the experiments described above, subjects chose the Pareto-optimal allocation of 100 percent of the tokens invested in the group account in few experimental sessions. Generally, subjects contributed 50 percent of their tokens or less. However, it is also true that subjects chose the Nash equilibrium allocation of zero contributions on fewer occasions. Communication prior to each decision round and greater personal benefit from investment in the group account improved provision.

Repetition, without communication, tended to reduce group investment, but the effect was not consistent. Changes in group size were ambiguous. Some groups were more cooperative (invested more in the group account), others were less so.

In summary, we can say that, without frequent reinforcing communication, voluntary contributions to the provision of public goods result in positive, but suboptimal, levels of provision. Fund drives with specific goals raise more funds but still may not raise sufficient funds to provide the public goods. However, all these experiments have the characteristic that subjects cannot enforce any agreements made during communication. In the next section we consider experiments with both communication and enforcement. These deal with the allocation of externalities (not public goods), but the experiments with large bargaining groups have similar free-rider problems.

2. COASIAN BARGAINING EXPERIMENTS

In the previous section we considered private voluntary contributions to the provision of a public good, where the optimal provision was generally not known to the participants. In this section we outline experiments in which subjects can bargain to the Pareto-optimal provision of a negative externality and enforce compliance on all parties. This research began as an experimental test of the Coase theorem in the simplest possible environment: two parties to a bargain, no transactions costs, no wealth effects, clearly defined interior Pareto-optimal allocation, contracts signed and strictly enforced.[3]

These initial experiments proceeded as follows. Two subjects who did not know one another sat in a room across a table; a monitor was present. The subjects were presented with a payoff table that associated a payment to each participant with each of a series of numerical outcomes. One subject would be paid nothing for the lowest numerical outcome and 12 dollars for the highest numerical outcome. The other subject would be paid 12 dollars for the lowest numerical outcome and nothing for the highest numerical outcome. One outcome yielded 14 dollars for the two subjects jointly. All other outcomes yielded 12 dollars or less for the two jointly. By a flip of a coin, one subject was chosen to be the 'controller.' The controller had the right to make the decision of which number to choose without consulting the other person. This right was clearly explained in the instructions. The other subject could persuade the controller, possibly by monetary transfer, to choose some other number. Any bargain involving monetary transfer was to be signed by both parties and enforced by the monitor.

Analyzing this experiment as a game, we can see that the core of the game is for the two subjects to agree to 14 dollars and for the controller to get at least

12 dollars. Considering this as an externality/public goods experiment, the controller becomes the individual with the right to do harm to the other person. The outcome that yields 14 dollars is the predicted outcome, regardless of which subject is selected as controller. That outcome should always be selected and the controller should always earn at least 12 dollars.

In these initial experiments we ran some subjects through a sequence of one-shot decisions with different partners and some through two successive decisions with the same partner. Half the subject pairs had full information about the payoffs of both subjects; the other half knew only his or her own personal payoffs. Almost every subject pair chose the joint-profit maximizing outcome, providing strong support for the Coase theorem and for the ability of pairs of subjects to achieve an optimal allocation of an externality through private bargaining.

We followed this initial experimental study with a thorough examination of bargaining to achieve an optimal allocation of an externality with groups of 3, 4, 10, and 20 subjects (Hoffman and Spitzer, 1985b). Each of these experiments required subjects to agree to the distribution of taxes and benefits as well as the allocation of the externality. For example, the three-person experiments involved either one controller against two other parties or two joint-controllers against one other party. The joint-controllers would have to agree to a distribution of any benefits derived from the other party; the other party would have to agree to divide the payment to the single controller to achieve a Pareto-optimal allocation of the externality. The four-person experiments involved either three subjects against one, or two against two; the ten-person experiments involved either five against five, or nine against one; the 20-person experiments involved 19 against one. The four- and ten-person experiments were conducted with both full and private information. The 20-person experiments were conducted with private information only. The only substantive difference between the experiments reported in Hoffman and Spitzer (1982) and in Hoffman and Spitzer (1985b) is that the right to be the controller or joint-controllers was determined by winning a game of nim, not by the flip of a coin. We effected that change because we discovered that controllers were more likely to demand their individual maximum if the right to be controller was won in a game of skill and then reinforced by the experimenter (see Hoffman and Spitzer, 1985a).

The results of these experiments with large bargaining groups reinforce the two-person bargaining results. Almost all the bargaining groups selected the joint-profit maximum. Moreover, even with large numbers of joint-controllers or with groups having to agree to transfer earnings to controllers, subjects succeeded in agreeing to distributions of taxes or benefits. Thus, with communication and enforceable contracts, subjects solved the free-rider problem through negotiation.

In a recent extension, Blake, Guyton, and Leventhal (1992) study Coasian bargaining in a different environment. In their experiments groups of three subjects are presented with a bargaining problem involving selecting from among several specific alternative allocations of subject profits. All sets of allocations contain one selection that is Pareto optimal, but only half the subjects bargain over sets of allocations including a core allocation. In addition, half the subject groups bargain face-to-face and half bargain only through computerized messages. They find that subjects bargaining over sets of allocations containing a core are generally able to reach the Pareto-optimal/core allocation as well as subjects in the Hoffman and Spitzer experiments were. However, subjects bargaining over sets of allocations in which there is no core are significantly less likely to agree on a Pareto-optimal allocation. These results are not significantly affected by the technology of bargaining. Thus, these results suggest caution in extending Hoffman and Spitzers results to more general bargaining environments.

3. THE DEVELOPMENT OF NEW MECHANISMS FOR ALLOCATING PUBLIC GOODS AND EXTERNALITIES

William Vickrey (1961) outlined a new auction mechanism, the second-price auction, and showed that participants in such an auction would have a dominant strategy incentive to bid their true values. The reasoning is simple. In a second-price auction the highest bidder wins the auction but only pays the second-highest bid price. Since the winner does not have to pay his or her bid price, the best strategy is to truthfully reveal his or her true value.

Vickrey's result was virtually ignored in the economics literature until it was rediscovered independently by Clarke (1971) and Groves (1976), who were exploring the possibility of designing synthetic mechanisms for achieving Pareto-optimal allocations of public goods and externalities. Clarke and Groves suggested that Vickrey's insight could be applied to the allocation of public goods and externalities by creating a mechanism in which each participant reveals his or her marginal benefit from the public good and is then assessed a personalized tax as a function of the values revealed by the other participants.

To apply the Clarke tax the government asks each consumer for a schedule of his or her marginal willingness to pay for different quantities of the public good. Using those revealed schedules, the government determines the optimal quantity of the pubic good to provide. Each consumer is then assessed a tax equal to the total cost of providing the public good, minus the sum of the marginal values revealed by the other participants. If consumers have utility functions with no wealth effects on the public good, it can be shown that each consumer has an individual incentive to reveal his or her true marginal willingness to pay schedule.[4]

The only problem with the Clarke tax is that the government runs a deficit. The taxes collected do not cover the cost of providing the public good. The Groves mechanism solves that problem by developing a separate lump-sum tax for each participant that is also calculated independent of the participant's responses.

The work of Clarke and Groves initiated a line of research, which continues today, on the design and implementation of synthetic mechanisms for the optimal allocation of public goods and externalities. At first, the emphasis was on designing mechanisms with the strict incentive properties of the Clarke and Groves mechanisms. For example, the Groves–Ledyard (1977) mechanism requires subjects to submit messages to a dispatch center, indicating a marginal quantity of the public good they wish to contribute and their marginal willingness to pay. The center then adds the marginal proposed quantities to form a total quantity and taxes each participant as a function of the cost of providing that quantity and the responses of the other participants. However, Vernon Smith discovered early, through laboratory experimental research on implementation, that the behavioral properties of synthetic mechanisms do not always correspond to their theoretical incentive properties (Smith 1979).

Smith (1979) compares the performance of the Groves–Ledyard mechanism with the performance of a new mechanism, the Smith auction mechanism, which formalizes the voluntary contribution mechanism discussed above. In the Smith auction mechanism each subject submits a message to a dispatch center, indicating how many units of the public good the subject wants the group to provide and how much he or she is willing to contribute to that provision. The dispatch center then calculates the average quantity proposed by the members of the group, the sum of the individual contributions, and whether or not the contributions cover the cost of provision. The center reports back to each participant that average quantity and a proposed cost share calculated as the total cost of that provision minus a prorated sum of the other participants' contributions. A subject can either ratify that proposal by sending that message back to dispatch or change his or her proposal. Several different stopping rules have been proposed, including unanimity voting on the final allocation and repetition of the last proposal by all participants.

While this mechanism does not have the strong incentive properties of a Groves mechanism or a Groves–Ledyard mechanism, Smith finds that subjects participating in such a mechanism generally select the Pareto-optimal allocation of a public good and volunteer to contribute a sufficient amount to provide it. Moreover, he finds that the Groves–Ledyard mechanism is difficult to implement, despite its stronger incentive properties. In particular, subjects find it difficult to operationalize the requirement that they submit messages indicating the marginal quantities of the public good they wish to provide and their marginal willingness to pay.

Binger, Hoffman, and Williams (1987) study another allocation mechanism with incentive properties similar to the Smith auction mechanism. Their mechanism operationalizes a Lindahl tâtonnement mechanism, without the obvious incentive to underrepresent characteristic of a Lindahl mechanism. In the Binger, Hoffman, and Williams mechanism the dispatch center presents each participant with a proposed personalized lump sum and per-unit tax as a contribution toward provision of the public good. Each participant then sends a message to the center indicating how many units of the public good he or she wants the group to provide, given the proposed taxes. If all participants suggest the same quantity, the center reports back that quantity and the proposed taxes as an allocation, and the participants vote whether to accept that allocation. If the vote is unanimous, the allocation is implemented; if it is not unanimous, the process continues. If all participants do not propose the same quantity, the center adjusts the personalized taxes using an indirect tâtonnement process and then reports back the set of proposed quantities and the new proposed personalized taxes. The process continues until all the participants agree on a quantity and a set of personalized taxes. Binger, Hoffman, and Williams test the behavioral properties of this mechanism in laboratory experiments using a wide variety of preference profiles and degrees of subject experience. They find the mechanism generally leads subject to select a quantity of the pubic good close to the Pareto-optimal quantity, leading to average efficiencies greater than 90 percent.

Recently, research on synthetic mechanisms has focused on designing computer-assisted 'smart' markets for the allocation of externalities and complex, networked commodities, requiring coordination similar to that required for the optimal allocation of public goods. These new markets draw upon the insights gained from research on the design and implementation of mechanisms for allocating public goods. For example, the allocation of electric power to end users involves a complex network of generators serving large numbers of customers and interconnected distribution lines. Because of the complexity of the distribution problem, the large capacity of generators required for efficient operation, and the public goods nature of the coordination problem, electric power used to be referred to as a natural monopoly requiring either government provision or, at least, direct government regulation. Similar goods include natural-gas pipeline distribution; airline takeoff, docking, and landing slots at interconnected airports; and the distribution of water through canals in arid lands.

In the mid-1980s, Vernon Smith and his colleagues at the University of

Arizona Economic Science Laboratory became interested in the possibility of designing a computer-assisted market to allocate such goods.[5] The idea can be illustrated with reference to electric power distribution on the western United States grid. Electricity is produced in large coal and hydroelectric generating plants, generally located far from major population centers, and then distributed to communities that purchase power for their consumers over high-voltage transmission lines. Once power is sent to the transmission line it is a public good. Any community with access to the line can withdraw power. Moreover, power is lost in transmission as a function of resistance and distance traveled.

Smith and his colleagues suggested that one could design a networked market mechanism with the following characteristics. First, communities that wished to purchase power could submit schedules of bids to buy quantities of power at specified prices. Second, producers of power could submit schedules of offers to sell quantities of power at specified prices. Third, owners of transmission lines could submit offers to transmit power over specified distances. Fourth, a computer model would incorporate all the engineering information regarding transmission losses, distance, and the need for a system wide power reserve to determine prices at each node and prices for transmission that maximized the gains from exchange in the system. Finally, buyers and sellers that could trade profitably at the prices dispatched from the center would do so.

They proposed using a two-sided extension of the Vickrey auction as their market mechanism: a uniform price, double auction market. In this market, buyers submit limit orders to buy specified quantities of the good at specified prices. Sellers submit limit orders to sell specified quantities at specified prices. The computer algorithm combines the buyer and seller bids and offers with transmission offers and engineering information on transmission losses to suggest prices at each node that maximize the revealed gains from exchange. Buyers and sellers can revise their limit prices for a prescribed length of time until the market closes. Dispatch continuously updates proposed market-clearing prices on the basis of new information. When the market closes all buyers who bid greater than or equal to the market price (including transmission costs) purchase units and all sellers who offer to sell at prices less than or equal to the market price sell units. Excess demand or supply at the market price can be rationed in a variety of ways, including random selection and first into the market.

Smith and his colleagues have designed a market model for an electric grid, a gas pipeline network, an airport-slot allocation problem, and a work-assignment problem. They have also studied the behavioral properties of the uniform price double auction market in a simple induced demand and supply environment and are discussing designing a market for water allocation in arid lands. They find that buyers and sellers generally underreveal the value of inframarginal units in such markets. That is to say, buyers generally bid less than the true value of inframarginal units and sellers generally offer prices greater than their true cost. However, the market mechanism tends to force buyers and sellers of marginal units to truthfully reveal the value of those units or be forced out of the market. In general, these markets converge to prices and quantities that maximize the true gains from exchange within a few trading periods.

This success in designing and testing laboratory prototypes of smart markets has led to considerable interest in implementing such markets for the sale of real commodities. For example, the Arizona Stock Exchange, established in 1992, is the first fully computerized stock exchange to use a uniform price, double auction market to trade stocks daily after the close of the New York Stock Exchange. Large investors, such as TIAA/CREF, use the market heavily because they can trade for less than one-eighth the commission charged by New York Stock Exchange traders. The owners of the Arizona Stock Exchange maintain a working relationship with the University of Arizona Economic Science Laboratory to test any proposed trading mechanisms.

There is also considerable interest in the electric power and gas pipeline markets by governments interested in privatization of public utilities. Vernon Smith has traveled to Eastern Europe, Australia, New Zealand, and China to demonstrate the power and efficiency of these proposed market mechanisms. The state of California is privatizing both electric power and water, and is interested in exploring alternative market mechanisms.

4. CONCLUSION

Experimental research in public choice has generated important results on the behavioral implications of mechanisms for allocating public goods and externalities. Voluntary contribution mechanisms, which theoretically result in zero contributions, generally result in positive, although suboptimal contributions. If participants can communicate face-to-face prior to making private contributions, however, contributions rise to near optimal levels. On the other hand, the Groves–Ledyard mechanism, which should lead to optimal contributions, is not reliable behaviorally. In addition, Coasian bargaining yields optimal allocations when a core exists, despite the potential for a public goods problem in coordinating large numbers of bargainers.

Experimental research in public choice is also valuable in the design and testing of new allocation mechanisms that might be implemented for public goods, externalities, or complex commodities. Using experimental techniques, a scholar can design a new mechanism, determine its theoretical incentive properties, and then study its behavioral properties in a controlled laboratory environment. Participants in existing allocation mechanisms for electricity, natural gas, or water are not likely to change to smart markets without large-scale testing of these market mechanisms. The experimental laboratory provides the first test site.

NOTES

1. Interested readers should also consult Davis and Holt (1993), Hoffman and Plott (1994), and Ledyard (1995).
2. Ostrom and Walker (1997) also address voluntary contribution mechanisms.
3. Hoffman and Spitzer (1982).
4. General conditions under which such mechanisms create dominant strategy incentives to reveal truthfully one's marginal willingness to pay are summarized in Hurwicz (1979), and Green and Laffont (1980).
5. See McCabe, Rassenti, and Smith (1991) for a survey of the literature on smart markets up to 1991.

REFERENCES

Binger, B.R., Elizabeth Hoffman and A.W. Williams. 1987. *Implementing a Lindahl Mechanism with a Modified Tatonnement Procedure.* Economic Science Association.

Blake, E.L., J.L. Guyton and S. Leventhal. 1992. 'Limits of Coasean Bargaining in the Face of Empty Cores.' *Public Choice*/ESA Meetings.

Clarke, Edward H. 1971. 'Multipart Pricing of Public Goods.' *Public Choice* 11: 17–33.

Coase, Ronald H. 1960. 'The Problem of Social Cost.' *Journal of Law and Economics* 3: 1–44.

Davis, Douglas D. and Charles A. Holt. 1993. *Experimental Economics.* Princeton: Princeton University Press.

Groves, Theodore. 1976. 'Information, Incentives, and the Internalization of Production Externalities.' In S.A.Y. Lin, ed., *Theory and Measurement of Economic Externalities.* New York: Academic Press, 65–86.

Groves, Theodore and John O. Ledyard. 1977. 'Optimal Allocation of Public Goods: A Solution to the "Free Rider" Problem.' *Econometrica* 45: 783–809.

Hoffman, Elizabeth and Charles R. Plott. 1994. *Bibliography of Research in Experimental Economics.* Manuscript.

Hoffman, Elizabeth and M.L. Spitzer. 1982. 'The Coase Theorem: Some Experimental Tests.' *Journal of Law and Economics* 25: 73–98.

Hoffman, Elizabeth and M.L. Spitzer. 1985a. 'Entitlements, Rights, and Fairness: An Experimental Examination of Subjects' Concepts of Distributive Justice.' *Journal of Legal Studies* 14: 259–97.

Hoffman, Elizabeth and M.L. Spitzer, 1985b. 'Experimental Tests of the Coase Theorem with Large Bargaining Groups.' *Journal of Legal Studies* 15: 149–71.

Isaac, R. Mark, Kenneth McCue and Charles R. Plott. 1985. 'Public Goods Provision in an Experimental Environment.' *Journal of Public Economics* 26: 51–74.

Isaac, R. Mark, David Schmidtz and James M. Walker. 1989. 'The Assurance Problem in a Laboratory Market.' *Public Choice* 62: 217–36.

Isaac, R. Mark and James M. Walker. 1988a. 'Communication and Free-Riding Behavior: The Voluntary Contribution Mechanism.' *Economic Inquiry* 26: 585–608.

Isaac, R. Mark and James M. Walker. 1988b. 'Group Size Effects in Public Goods Provision: The Voluntary Contributions Mechanism.' *Quarterly Journal of Economics* 103: 179–99.

Isaac, R. Mark and James M. Walker. 1991. 'Costly Communication: An Experiment in a Nested Public Goods Problem.' In Thomas R. Palfrey, ed., *Laboratory Research in Political Economy*. Ann Arbor: University of Michigan Press, 269–86.

Isaac, R. Mark, James M. Walker and Susan Thomas. 1984. 'Divergent Evidence on Free Riding: An Experimental Examination of Some Possible Explanations.' *Public Choice* 43: 113–49.

Isaac, R. Mark, James M. Walker, and Arlington W. Williams. 1994. 'Group Size and the Voluntary Provision of Public Goods: Experimental Evidence Utilizing Large Groups.' *Journal of Public Economics* 54: 1–36.

Kim, Oliver and Mark Walker. 1984. 'The Free Rider Problem: Experimental Evidence.' *Public Choice* 43: 3–24.

Laury, Susan K., James M. Walker and Arlington W. Williams. 1995. 'Anonymity and the Voluntary Provision of Public Goods.' *Journal of Economic Behavior and Organization* 27: 365–80.

Ledyard, John O. 1995. 'Public Goods: A Survey of Experimental Research.' In A.L. Roth and J. Kagel, eds, *The Handbook of Experimental Economics*. Princeton: Princeton University Press.

Marwell, Gerald, and Ruth E. Ames. 1979. 'Experiments on the Provision of Public Goods I: Resources, Interest, Group Size, and the Free Rider Problem.' *American Journal of Sociology* 84: 335–60.

Marwell, Gerald and Ruth E. Ames. 1980. 'Experiments on the Provision of Public Goods II: Provision Points, Stakes, Experience and the Free Rider Problem.' *American Journal of Sociology* 85: 926–37.

Marwell, Gerald and Ruth E. Ames. 1981. 'Economists Free Ride: Does Anyone Else?' *Journal of Public Economics* 15: 295–310.

McCabe, K.A., S.J. Rassenti, and V.L. Smith. 1991. 'Smart Computer-Assisted Markets.' *Science* 254: 534–8.

Ostrom, Elinor and James Walker. 1997. 'Neither Markets nor States: Linking Transformation Processes in Collective Action Arenas' in Dennis C. Mueller, ed., *Perspectives on Public Choice: A Handbook*. Cambridge: Cambridge University Press, 35–72.

Smith, Vernon L. 1979. 'Incentive Compatible Experimental Processes for the Provision of Public Goods.' *Research in Experimental Economics* 1: 59.

Vickrey, William. 1961. 'Counterspeculation, Auctions, and Competitive Sealed Tenders.' *Journal of Finance* 16: 8–37.

15. Non-prisoner's dilemma

Gordon Tullock[1]

1. INTRODUCTION

The prisoner's dilemma, since it was introduced more than 50 years ago,[2] has led to a very large amount of both theoretical and experimental work.[3] Its general importance for many purposes is real, but most of our transactions in the real world do not involve prisoners. I can choose the store that I buy from, and, in theory if they wanted to they could refuse to sell things to me. In dealing with other people in general, I am not prevented from communicating with them and I am not forbidden from choosing my partners. I am also not prevented from changing partners at will. In all of these ways real life in most cases differs substantially from the case of the prisoners.

Most experiments have followed the prisoner's model in producing the dilemma. The people playing are selected by the experimenter, are not permitted to communicate, and cannot 'fire' their partner. It is not true that all of the existing experiments follow this pattern, but most of them do and most of them are designed to determine something other than the effect of these particular restrictions.

2. MATRIX INSTRUCTIONS

Some time ago I wrote a paper in which I argued that a very large part of real world interactions do not occur in prisoner's dilemma situations.[4] I argued that most commercial and social dealings do not meet these strict conditions for the prisoner's dilemma, and different results should be expected. There are not infrequent cases which fit the prisoner's dilemma problem and the public good variant of the prisoner's dilemma is the basic justification for the existence of government. Nevertheless, most of our normal dealings do not meet the rather stringent conditions of the prisoner's dilemma.

Theoretically, as I mentioned in the article referred to in note 4, this should lead to different results. I took advantage of a visit to Washington to run my own experiment in which people were permitted to choose their partners, communicate freely, and change partners if they wished. When I had to be absent from

Table 15.1   Prisoner's dilemma experiment Tullock conducted 10 August 1998 and on 10 November 1998[a]

	Column	Row
Team 1	20	20
Team 2	20	20
Team 3	19	19
Team 4	20	20
Team 5	18	15
Team 6	19	19
Team 7	20	20
Team A1	20	20
Team A2	20	20
Team A3	20	20

Note: [a]Full details are available from the author.

Arizona a few weeks later, I had two students repeat my experiment with an even smaller set of players. Not to my surprise we got heavily cooperative play.

The instruction sheet and matrix is attached as an appendix of this chapter. At the beginning of the experiment the 14 players in Arlington selected their partners and were given $10, as were the four spares sitting in the rear of the room. They then played the game with my student assistants after each round either collecting some money or handing it out in accord with the selected strategy. The same method was used in Tucson. The total payoff for each player is show in Table 15.1. The first seven pairs were in Arlington and the remaining three marked A in Tucson.

If the two team members cooperated from the beginning as was the case with teams 1, 2, 4, 7, A1, A2, and A3 they each got $20. Teams 3 and 6 tried non-cooperative plays at first but quickly settled down to cooperative play for the last eight rounds. They each received only $19.

The one team, 5, which did badly, I believe, was the result of a genuine lack of understanding by the row player. I think this man actually did not understand how you calculated the pay off from the two strategies. I base this judgement from watching the play, I did not cross-examine anyone. Column then tried to deal with his erratic play. He eventually learned and the last three rounds were cooperative.

The main significance of this experiment is to point out that people in most natural environments, can (and will) engage in cooperation. There are certain cases where we cannot choose our partners. France and Germany for example, cannot decide that they do not want to be neighbors.

Further, a more significant reason for limited communication is the desire to keep certain things secret from the person that you are bargaining with. When I bought my house I did not reveal my reservation price to the seller, and the course of the negotiations indicated pretty clearly that he did not reveal his reservation price to me. As a result of this there was a good deal of wasted effort during the negotiations.

If each of us revealed honestly our reservation price, and then split the difference there would have been a large saving. The problem would be that itwould not have been rational to honestly reveal the reservation price. Genuine prisoner's dilemma cases of this sort are not uncommon, for example, settlement for lawsuits. Still, most inter-human dealings follow the conditions of my experiment, not the traditional pattern.

The point of this brief article is simply that a very large part of human interactions lead to cooperation. Even in the last play of each series, my subjects were genuinely cooperative, and in fact, there was even more cooperation in the last plays than in the earlier ones.

The experimental subjects in Arlington were students in an undergraduate course in constitutional law who had never heard of the prisoner's dilemma. In Tucson they were undergraduates in my Law and Economics course. I did not explain the last play problem to them and it would appear that either they did not figure it out for themselves, or perhaps, they thought the profit from cheating on the last play was not great enough to compensate for dealing with irritated other participants in class for another month. Thus it would not really be the last play. In real life the prospect of further interaction continues till death in most situations, so this is realistic.

I would like to say that this is a highly important experiment, but actually I do not think that it is. I do think it is different from the other experiments and that the difference is significant.

APPENDIX

The purpose of this game is to test experimentally certain economic theories. These theories are not secret, but it would take too much time to explain them now. After the experiment is over, we will suggest some reading for the curious.

Twelve of the 15 subjects now in the room should choose to pair up according to your preferences. This will leave three unpaired participants. Each pair consists of a row player and a column player. The pairs should decide which one is to be row and which column. This is an unimportant decision but necessary for the rest of the experiment. Flip a coin if you have difficulty.

Each participant will be given ten $1 bills; this is their capital. At the end of experiment most of you will have more than $10 to take home, but possibly some will have less.

The 12 paired participants will play ten rounds. Any one of them may, however, decide to change partners, selecting one of the people who were not paired at the beginning at any time during play.

Play is simple. If you are a row player check which row you want. If you are a column check the column you prefer. The intersection of the chosen row and column selects a square. The row player will receive the amount in the lower left of the selected square if it is positive and pay if it is negative. The column player will receive or pay the amount in the upper right. An assistant will collect the slips and pay or collect the amount from each player after each round. Once this is completed there will be another round. To repeat, any player may decide to change partners at any time.

Any questions? There will be two practice rounds before you risk your money.

	1	2
1	1 / −1	
2	−1 / 2	0 / 0

NOTES

1. I took a ten-week course in Economics in the Law School, University of Chicago, in 1939. After military service, and finishing my law degree, I joined the foreign service, and became a China expert. I switched to academic economics in about 1960, and am currently a distinguished fellow of the American Economic Association.
2. Although they did not invent it, R. Duncan Luce and Howard Raiffa introduced most students to it. Luce and Raiffa, 1957, *Games and Decisions*.
3. It is now in elementary texts. See Browning and Zupan, 1999, *Microeconomic Theory and Applications*.
4. Tullock, 1985. Adam Smith and the prisoner's dilemma.

REFERENCES

Browning, E.K., Zupan, M.A., 1999. *Microeconomic Theory and Applications*, Addison-Wesley, New York, pp. 363–369.

Luce, R.D., Raiffa, H., 1957. *Games and Decisions*, John Wiley, London, pp. 94–97.

Tullock, G., 1985. 'Adam Smith and the prisoner's dilemma'. *Quarterly Journal of Economics*, 402, pp. 1073–1081. Reprinted in: Klein, D. (ed.), *Reputation: Studies in the Voluntary Elicitation of Good Conduct, Economics, Cognition and Society Series*, University of Michigan Press, Ann Arbor, MI, 1997.

16. Group size and the voluntary provision of public goods: experimental evidence utilizing large groups

R. Mark Isaac, James M. Walker and Arlington W. Williams[1]

1. INTRODUCTION

Over the past decade, the use of computer-based laboratory experiments to study resource allocation mechanisms for both private and public goods has proliferated. The vast majority of this research has employed the same basic procedural framework for executing experiments: a relatively small (e.g. ten-person) group of subjects arrive at the lab at the same time, participate in the experiment, are paid a performance-based cash reward at the experiment's conclusion, and leave. This standard framework presents two distinct problems when one wishes to focus on 'large' (e.g. 100-person) decision-making groups: physical constraints rooted in the size of the lab and number of computer workstations available, and financial constraints rooted in the magnitude of the subject payments necessary to motivate a large group of participants. It is thus quite understandable that small-group experiments predominate and, in the absence of evidence to the contrary, are implicitly assumed to characterize behavior in similar, large-group decision-making environments. The validity of this assumption is critical if 'parallelism' between the laboratory and a naturally occurring environment (with many decision-making agents) is essential to the relevance of the research. This is presumably the case in experimental research focusing on public policy issues.

The research reported here has two primary objectives. The first objective is to explore the extent to which results from previous small-group experiments on the voluntary provision of a pure public good survive in a large-group setting. The second objective is methodological – to document and discuss the general procedural framework used to overcome the problems associated with conducting large-group experiments mentioned above. We compare the use of cash versus extra-credit point incentive structures, and experiments lasting about an hour versus experiments lasting several weeks.

Our interest in the first objective is motivated in part by the common premise in economics and other social sciences that the suboptimality of the provision of a public good will increase with increases in group size. The logic and empirical evidence which might support this premise is not always clearly specified. Evidence from field studies is flawed by a lack of control over critical environmental parameters and the inability to observe preferences and hence to measure the degree of suboptimality. Evidence from laboratory studies is based primarily on data from literally thousands of two-person games and a smaller set of *N*-person games with group sizes that have rarely exceeded ten. These are very small decision-making groups in comparison with the group sizes one might expect to find in many field environments. Thus, the common premise that free riding becomes more severe as group size increases, *ceteris paribus*, does not appear to be based on an extensive empirical foundation.

Building on research presented by Isaac and Walker (1988), this chapter presents new evidence regarding the existence of a pure group size effect in the provision of a pure public good. Our experiments utilize group sizes ranging from 4 to 100 and provide replicable results that contradict the widely held view that a group's ability to provide the optimal level of a pure public good is necessarily inversely related to group size. The next section summarizes the components of the voluntary contribution mechanism and briefly reviews the experimental literature on public goods provision utilizing this institution. Section 3 describes the experimental environment and procedural framework developed for our new experiments. Section 4 reports our initial experimental results. Section 5 presents possible explanations for the inconsistency between these results and the predictions of the standard complete information Nash equilibrium model. Section 6 reports the results from additional experiments designed to provide further insight into the observed discrepancies between the standard Nash model and our results. Finally, section 7 summarizes our experimental results.

2. THE VOLUNTARY CONTRIBUTION MECHANISM

The essence of the Voluntary Contribution Mechanism (VCM) is that each individual in a group must decide how to allocate an endowment of a productive factor between a private good (where consumption benefits accrue only to the individual) and a group good (where consumption benefits accrue to all group members).

2.1 Experimental Implementation

The laboratory version of VCM utilized in the experiments presented here was implemented in a sequence of ten decision-making rounds. At the start of each round, individual i was endowed with Z_i tokens which had to be divided between a 'private account' and a 'group account.' Tokens could not be carried across rounds. Each token placed in the private account earned p_i cents with certainty.[2] For a given round, let m_i represent individual i's allocation of tokens to the group account and Σm_j represent the sum of tokens placed in the group account by all other individuals ($j \neq i$). Each individual earned $[G(m_i + \Sigma m_j)]/N$ cents from the group account. Because each individual received a $1/N$ share of the total earnings from the group account, the group account was a pure public good. This specification of the group account payoff function is one of many that could be utilized to create a laboratory public good. Thus, a representative individual's utility function in any one period can be written as $U_i[p_i(Z_i-m_i) + (G(m_i+\Sigma m_j)/N)]$. The marginal per-capita return from the group account ($MPCR$) is defined as the ratio of benefits to costs for moving a single token from the individual to the group account, or $[G'(\bullet)/N]/p_i$. In the experiments reported here, p_i and the function $G(\bullet)$ were chosen so that the Pareto Optimum (defined simply as the outcome that maximizes group earnings) was for each individual to place all tokens in the group account (i.e. to set $m_i = Z_i$). The single-period dominant strategy for each individual i, however, was for each subject to place zero tokens in the group account because p_i and $G(\bullet)$ were chosen so that the $MPCR < 1$. Given the finite number of decision rounds, the outcome $m_i = 0 \; \forall \; i$ is also the unique, backward unravelling, complete information, multi-period Nash equilibrium. This will be referred to as a complete free-riding outcome.

Each individual's information set included: the number of rounds, Z_i (i's own token endowment for each round), ΣZ_i (the groups' aggregate token endowment for each round), p_i (earnings per token from i's private account), N (group size), and $G(\bullet)/N$ (per-capita earnings function for the group account presented in tabular form).[3] It was explained that the decisions for each round were binding and that end-of-experiment rewards would be based on the sum of earnings from all rounds. Prior to the start of each round, participants were shown information on their own earnings for the previous round as well as the total number of tokens placed by the entire group in the group account. During each round, subjects could view their personal token allocations, earnings, and total tokens placed in the group account for all previous rounds.

2.2 Previous Experimental Results

A large body of experimental research addresses the empirical validity of the free-rider hypothesis utilizing various implementations of the voluntary contributions mechanism. See, for example, Marwell and Ames (1979, 1980, 1981); Kim and Walker (1984); Isaac, Walker and Thomas (1984); Isaac, McCue and Plott (1985); Isaac and Walker (1988); Andreoni (1989); Brookshire, Coursey, and Redington (1989); and Dorsey (1992). This work demonstrates two points: (1) the early findings of Marwell and Ames', who report substantial levels of contributions to the public good, are replicable under certain experimental conditions, and (2) very different (replicable) results showing far more free-riding can be found under alternative parametric and institutional conditions.

The results presented by Isaac and Walker (1988), hereafter IW, are of particular relevance to the research presented here. IW investigate different concepts of group size in the context of the standard conjecture that larger groups have a more difficult task in providing public goods. A natural question is: why should free riding increase in severity as the group size is increased? A logical response is that as the size of the group increases, the marginal return from the group good declines (due to crowding). Alternatively, public goods provided in large group settings may be characterized naturally by 'small' marginal returns. These are both explanations which depend on a smaller marginal benefit from the public good with increases in group size. Is there, however, a 'pure numbers' effect which influences the efficiency of public goods provision? In a framework where $G(\bullet)$ increases linearly (as in IW and here), a pure numbers effect can be examined by varying $G'(\bullet)$ so that the *MPCR* remains constant as N increases. Alternatively, group size effects based on crowding or an inherently small *MPCR* can be examined by allowing the *MPCR* to vary with group size.

IW examined the separate and combined influences of a pure numbers effect and variations in the *MPCR* in groups of size 4 and 10. Their primary conclusion was that a higher *MPCR* leads to less free-riding and thus greater efficiency in the provision of the public good. IW found no statistical support for a pure numbers effect. In fact, to the extent that there was any qualitative difference in the data, it was in the direction of the groups of size 10 providing larger levels of the public good than the groups of size 4. IW did find support for a crowding effect; larger groups exhibited more free riding if increases in group size generated a smaller *MPCR*.

One critique of IW's results is that a ten-person group is not large enough to be behaviorally distinct from a four-person group. According to this very informal argument, a much larger group, of say 100, would be required to capture any behavioral properties inherent in very large groups. Unfortunately, the effective size of laboratory experiments has been limited by both the expense of subject payments and by the capacity constraints of existing laboratories. The initial phase of the research reported here focused on the development of experimental procedures designed to facilitate large group experiments. These procedures are implemented utilizing new software on the NovaNET computer system. This chapter reports results from groups of size 4, 10, 40, and 100. We believe that the 100 person groups are the largest salient reward, public goods experiments conducted to date.

3.   EXPERIMENTAL PROCEDURES AND PARAMETERS

Most of the experiments presented here employ two important procedural modifications relative to the earlier IW research: (1) decision-making rounds last several days rather than a few minutes, and (2) rewards are based on extra-credit points rather than cash. We refer to experiments composed of rounds lasting several days as 'multiple session' (MS) experiments. This contrasts with the 'single session' (SS) experiments of IW, typical of laboratory experiments in economics where all decision rounds occur in sequence over a relatively brief time span, usually an hour or two.

3.1   Framework for Computerized Multiple-Session Experiments

Figure 16.1 shows a flow chart of the steps which comprise our multiple-session VCM experiments using a salient reward structure based on extra-credit points (VCM-MS-XC).[4] Subjects participating in VCM-MS-XC experiments were volunteers from undergraduate microeconomic theory classes at Indiana University and the University of Arizona. All students attending these classes received a handout explaining the rules for participation [Ed.'s note: the handout can be found in Appendix A of the original version of this paper]. In summary, the handout informed students: (1) of the basic nature of the group decision-making exercise, (2) that participation is voluntary and will result in their earning extra-credit points rather than cash, (3) of the specific formula used to convert the cash earnings reported to them by the computer into extra-credit points, (4) of the days associated with each of the ten decision rounds, and (5) of the specific procedures for accessing the experiment on NovaNET. The following specific points describe the multiple-session procedure.

(1) The NovaNET VCM software handles many decision-making groups running simultaneously. Before beginning the experiment, the experimenter initializes a set of parameters for each decision-making group (called a design cell). For example, a class of size 350 might have one group of 100, three groups of 40, and several groups of 10 and 4 running simultaneously.

(2) Upon logging onto the computer for the first time, subjects are assigned to a design cell via a quasi-random rotation procedure unknown to the subjects. This reduces the probability that several acquaintances who access

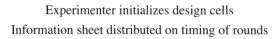

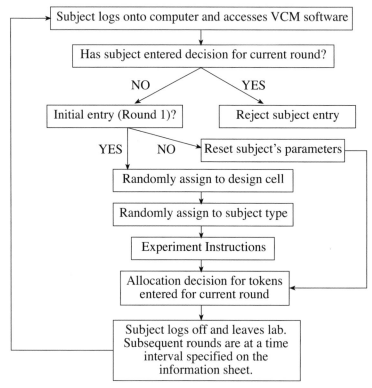

Figure 16.1   Flow of multiple-session experiments

Round 1 at the same time will be assigned to the same group. As part of the initialization process, the experimenter designates each design cell as either 'primary' or 'secondary.' All primary design cells are filled before remaining subjects are assigned to secondary cells. Inevitably, some students fail to meet the deadline for entering their Round 1 decision and are thus excluded from further participation.

(3) After logging in for the first time, subjects work through a set of instructions at their own pace and then enter their allocation decision for Round 1 of the experiment.[5] After entering their decision subjects log off the computer and leave the lab.

(4) Subjects are allowed to proceed to the next round only after the experimenter advances the 'current round' parameter to allow for the continuation

of the experiment. Upon logging on for subsequent rounds, subjects are shown the results of the previous round and then routed directly to the decision entry display for the current round. At this point, subjects have the option to review the instructions and to view the results from all prior rounds. It is important to note that subjects are *not* shown preliminary information on the aggregate tokens allocated to the group account for the current round. Information on aggregate token allocations is disseminated only for completed rounds.

(5) We cannot guarantee that *all* subjects will make an allocation decision in each round (a similar problem exists in many field experiments). For this reason, the software allows the experimenter to specify a default allocation decision for each subject. This procedure for handling defaults is explicitly explained to subjects in the instructions. An obvious setting for the default decision is to place zero tokens in the group account since lack of participation can be interpreted as a decision to free ride. There are certainly other reasonable default specifications – the method for handling default decisions is an interesting research question which can potentially influence aggregate outcomes in multiple-session experiments. For all VCM-MS-XC experiments reported here, *the default decision for each subject was for all tokens to be invested in the individual account* (private good). Thus, this specific VCM-MS-XC implementation contains an additional element which lowers the cost of free riding behavior.

The experimental procedures outlined above represent a logical link between standard single-session laboratory experiments and actual field experiments. Certainly some experimental control is lost relative to a strictly controlled laboratory setting; however, the gain in feasible group sizes, the real time between allocation decisions, and the more 'natural' communication opportunities available in this environment add an element of parallelism with non-experimental settings that could have important methodological and behavioral ramifications.

3.2 Extra-credit Performance Index

As explained in the class handout, subject i's experimental dollar earnings were converted into the following 'performance index' prior to being converted into extra-credit points:

$$\frac{i\text{'s actual earnings} - i\text{'s minimum possible earnings}}{i\text{'s maximum possible earnings} - i\text{'s minimum possible earnings}}$$

which can range from 0 to 1 for each individual. At the end of the final round, this fraction was computed for each individual (based on earnings in all rounds), multiplied by 3, and added to the subject's final grade average. Thus, the range of possible extra-credit points was [0, 3]. The performance index was used so that the maximum and minimum possible extra-credit earnings did not depend upon the design cell assignment. All classes from which subjects were drawn utilized a 100-point scale and, with minor modifications, used a standard mapping of point totals into letter grades (A = 90's, B = 80's, etc.). Furthermore, Indiana University (where 64 of 74 of the extra-credit experiments were conducted) allows + and – letter grades, so a unique letter grade typically comprised a three to four point interval.

We have spent a great deal of time considering questions of practicability and fairness in the use of extra-credit points as a motivator. It is important to realize that our extra-credit experiments always have a clear pedagogical objective and become an integral part of our in-class discussions of private vs. external benefits, public goods provision, and free-riding. Our research procedures were thoroughly reviewed and approved by the Indiana University Committee for the Protection of Human Subjects. On the issue of fairness, we can report that, of the thousand of students who have participated in VCM-MS-XC experiments, there have been no grade appeals in which these extra-credit points were an issue. In fact, feedback from students (and from other faculty who have adopted similar experiments for purely pedagogical purposes) has been quite positive.[6]

3.3 Experimental Parameters

The data reported here are based on 87 new experiments involving 1908 subjects.[7] Of these experiments, 77 were multiple-session, extra-credit reward experiments (VCM-MS-XC) and 10 were single-session, cash reward experiments (VCM-SS-$). Table 16.1 categorizes the new experiments according to twelve unique initializations utilized in this research. The first three columns in Table 16.1 correspond to specific components of an initialization: the sequencing-reward procedure (MS-XC or SS-$), group size ($N$), and marginal per-capita return (*MPCR*) from a token allocated to the group account. The fourth column lists the total number of experiments conducted under each initialization. In addition, two initialization parameters were held constant across all experiments and are thus not listed in Table 16.1; p_i (*i*'s return per token from the private account) is \$0.01 and Z_i (*i*'s token endowment in each round) is 50.

4. INITIAL EXPERIMENTAL RESULTS

The presentation of the results from our initial experiments will be organized around three subsections: subsection 4.1, a baseline comparison of VCM-MS-XC

Table 16.1   Listing of experiments by initializations

Procedure Used for Sequencing – Motivation	Group Size	MPCR	Number of Experiments
MS-XC	4	0.75	10
MS-XC	4	0.30	17
MS-XC	10	0.75	10
MS-XC	10	0.30	16
MS-XC	40	0.75	6
MS-XC	40	0.30	6
MS-XC	40	0.03	6
MS-XC	100	0.75	3
MS-XC	100	0.30	3
SS-$	40	0.30	3
SS-$	40	0.03	1
SS-$	10	0.30	6

small group ($N = 4$, $N = 10$) experiments with the VCM-SS-$ experiments reported by IW; subsection 4.2, a presentation of large group ($N = 40$, $N = 100$) experiments using both extra-credit and cash incentives; and subsection 4.3, an overview of variations in individual behavior.

The baseline experiments reported in subsection 4.1 were critical for establishing that the basic IW small-group results were replicable in the VCM-MS-XC experimental environment. Having confirmed that small-group behavior in VCM-MS-XC is qualitatively similar to the behavior reported by IW, subsection 4.2 examines large-group behavior. These results are particularly interesting in that: (1) they suggest that large groups may be more efficient at providing public goods than small groups (holding *MPCR* constant), and (2) the positive correlation between *MPCR* and efficiency observed in small groups appears to vanish in large groups (for the [0.30, 0.75] *MPCR* domain previously studied). This correlation is shown, however, to reappear in groups of size 40 with an *MPCR* of 0.03. Subsection 4.3 documents the tremendous diversity in individual subject behavior, giving the reader a more thorough perspective on the aggregate results presented in previous subsections.

4.1   Small-Group Baseline Comparison

The results presented in this subsection are from 53 VCM-MS-XC experiments conducted with small groups ($N \in [4,10]$). Figures 16.2 and 16.3 present a time-series comparison of the IW and the VCM-MS-XC aggregate data. The

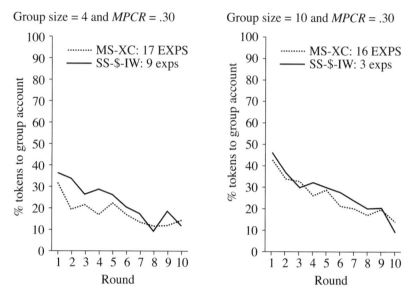

*Figure 16.2   Comparison of new (MS-XC) data with Isaac–Walker (SS-$)
data:* MPCR = 0.30

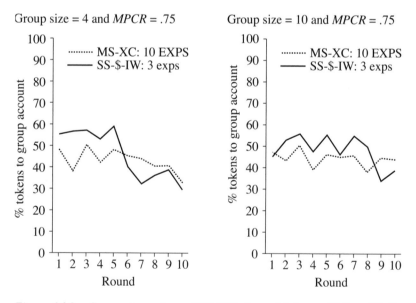

*Figure 16.3   Comparison of new (MS-XC) data with Isaac–Walker (SS-$)
data:* MPCR = 0.75

extent to which the VCM-MS-XC experiments reproduce the results of IW is striking.

> *Observation 1.* For a specific group size and *MPCR*, the aggregate pattern of token allocations in the VCM-MS-XC environment and the VCM-SS-$ environment studied by IW are very similar.

This observation is supported by two sample *t*-tests on data for each decision round. Of the 40 *t*-values (4 design cells x 10 rounds), a significant difference in the percentage of tokens allocated to the group account is observed in only one round. Analysis of the VCM-MS-XC data using both OLS and Tobit estimation techniques lend additional support to Observation 1 by reconfirming the positive correlation between *MPCR* levels and efficiency reported by IW.

The results of this baseline comparison are important for two reasons. First, they demonstrate that the IW results are robust to changes in experimental procedures and the reward medium. Second, the VCM-MS-XC environment does not exhibit any obvious behavioral anomalies which would preclude its use as a procedure for exploring the large-group properties of VCM.

4.2 Large-Group Experiments

This subsection begins by focusing on the large-group experiments using extra-credit incentives. The time series data for groups of size 40 and 100 are shown in Figures 16.4 and 16.5. These figures present 90 percent confidence bands for the mean allocation to the group account for the experiments within each of the four group size and *MPCR* combinations. The data summarized in these figures support the following observation.

> *Observation 2.* For groups of size 40 and 100, with *MPCR* = 0.30 or 0.75, a positive correlation between the percentage of tokens allocated to the group account and *MPCR* does not exist.

OLS and Tobit regressions of *MPCR* dummy variables on the percentage of tokens allocated to the group account support this observation. This is in stark contrast to groups of size 4 and 10, where a positive *MPCR* effect is consistently present over the range 0.30 to 0.75. The next subsection focuses in more depth on why the *MPCR* effect appears to vanish in large groups for the [0.30, 0.75] *MPCR* domain.

Figure 16.6 presents the sequence of mean percentage of tokens allocated to the group account for each of the VCM-MS-XC initializations using a 0.30 or 0.75 *MPCR*. The data summarized in this figure lead us to the following two observations.

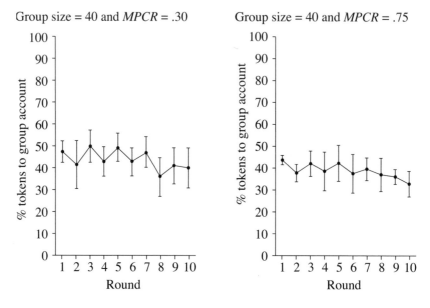

Figure 16.4   90% confidence bands: group size = 40

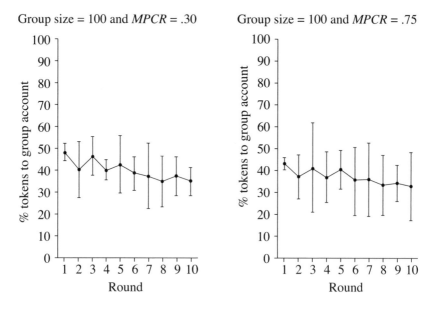

Figure 16.5   90% confidence bands: group size = 100

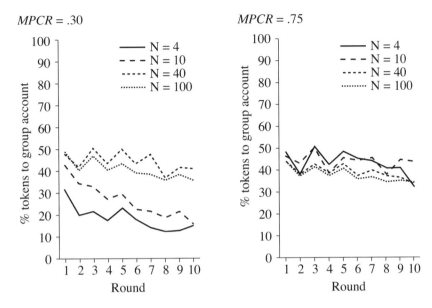

Figure 16.6   *Group size comparison for low (0.30) and high (0.75)* MPCR *cells*

Observation 3. For the case of *MPCR* = 0.30, groups of size 40 and 100 allocate more tokens to the group account on average than do groups of size 4 and 10.

Observation 4. For the case of *MPCR* = 0.75, there is no discernable difference in allocations to the group account on average across group sizes.

These results (supported by OLS and Tobit regressions) are particularly striking, since they do not support the existence of the traditionally assumed pure group size effect. In fact, the *MPCR* = 0.30 data supporting Observation 3 exhibit an *increase in efficiency when moving from smaller groups to larger groups*.

The possibility that large-group behavior is an artifact of the VCM-MS-XC procedures seems unlikely given the data from the smaller groups, but nonetheless required some empirical confirmation. Reported next are the results of three 40-person VCM-SS-$ (single-session, cash reward) experiments using *MPCR* = 0.30. As discussed previously, in single-session experiments the ten decision-making rounds occur during a single experimental session lasting one to two hours. Given the limited seating capacity of our laboratories, these 40-person experiments had to be conducted 'multi-site'

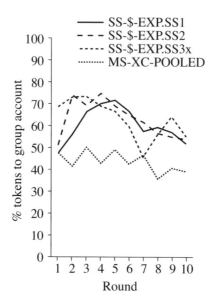

Figure 16.7 Cash (SS-$) versus extra-credit (MS-XC) rewards: group size
= 40, MPCR = 0.30

with subjects participating simultaneously at Indiana University and the
University of Arizona through NovaNET. These cash payment experiments
were quite expensive. In spite of the fact that we utilized an 'experiment
dollar' to US dollar exchange rate of $\frac{1}{2}$, each experiment cost over $900.[8]

Figure 16.7 compares allocations to the group account for these three N =
40, *MPCR* = 0.30, VCM-SS-$ experiments (SS1, SS2, SS3x) with the means
of the six corresponding VCM-MS-XC experiments. SS1 and SS2 used
subjects who had not previously participated in a VCM experiment, while
SS3x used experienced subjects randomly drawn from SS1 and SS2. The high
percentage of tokens allocated to the group account clearly is not an artifact of
the VCM-MS-XC procedures. In fact, for these few exceptions using cash
rewards, the percentage of tokens allocated to the group account is higher than
in the experiments using extra-credit rewards.

4.3   Diversity in Individual Behavior

Figures 16.8 and 16.9 document several features of individual subject behavior typical to many of our VCM experiments. Figure 16.8 reports the time-
series behavior for each subject in two 4-person VCM-MS-XC experiments.
These data are typical of small-group VCM behavior in that: (1) they show a
pattern of token allocations which is *not* bimodal between the two extremes of

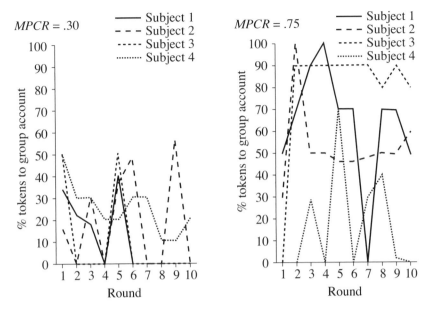

Figure 16.8   Examples of individual subject decisions: group size = 4

0 percent and 100 percent of tokens placed in the group account; and (2) there is a shift in allocations associated with the *MPCR* conditions. With larger groups, presenting individual time-series behavior for each subject is unmanageable. Figure 16.9 presents frequency polygons illustrating the empirical distribution of token allocations for all subjects within two groups of size 100 during Rounds 1 and 10. The behavior again is clearly not bimodal in Round 1. By period 10, many subjects (35–40 percent) have moved to a complete free-riding allocation of zero tokens to the group account; however, a secondary peak (15–20 percent) in frequency appears at the 100% allocation level. Finally, it is common in all treatment conditions to observe individuals whose allocations to the group account may vary substantially from round to round. Such 'pulsing' behavior could be interpreted as attempts to influence others' allocations through signalling.

Recall that one of the parameters specified for each subject type in multi-session experiments is the 'default decision' which is entered automatically for any subject who fails to enter a decision for any round. In the experiments reported here, the default decision is a zero allocation of tokens to the group account (complete free riding). Figure 16.10 displays the time-series of the mean percentage of defaults for group size 4 and 100 under each *MPCR* condition. Several (tentative) conclusions can be drawn from the default data we have studied to date. With group size equal to 100, the percentage of defaults

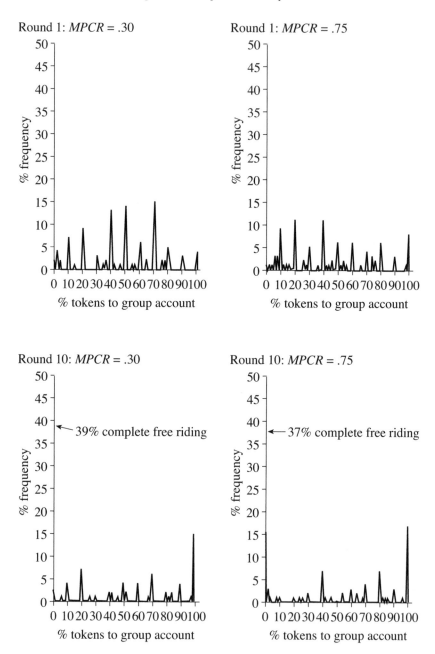

Figure 16.9   Frequency polygons of tokens allocated to group account:
          group size = 100

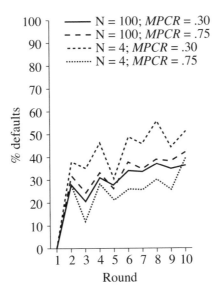

*Figure 16.10   Mean percentage of default decisions: group size = 4 and
100*

is relatively low, nearly identical for both *MPCR* treatments, and quite stable over Rounds 6 through 10 (35–45 percent). In conjunction with this default rate, recall that allocations to the group account were in the 30–40 percent range for these groups. In contrast, with groups of size 4 there are distinctly higher defaults in the low-*MPCR* treatment relative to the high-*MPCR* treatment. In low-*MPCR* groups, the default rate averages as high as 60 percent in the later rounds, whereas high-*MPCR* groups reach a maximum default rate of approximately 40 percent in Round 10. These default rates are consistent with the result that lower *MPCR* tends to correspond to lower token allocations to the group account for 'small' groups. Finally, note that we do observe subjects actually entering (non-default) decisions of zero tokens allocated to the group account.

5.   FACTORS THAT SHAPE BEHAVIOR: IF NOT NASH, THEN WHAT?

The results presented above are generally inconsistent with the complete information Nash equilibrium (NE) prediction. In the final decision round, it is a dominant strategy for an individual to allocate all tokens to the private account. In prior periods, the unique complete information multi-period NE is also complete free-riding. Over the range of parameter variations investigated here, neither changes in group size nor changes in *MPCR* alter these predictions. The NE model correctly predicts the observed failure of our groups to achieve the Pareto Optimum. Furthermore, in some treatments, decisions show a marked tendency to decay toward the NE prediction. Even in the final rounds, however, there is a notable allocation of tokens to the group account in most experiments. Given the inconsistency between observed behavior and the complete information NE prediction, it is natural to examine what assumptions of the natural standard model may not be met in the experiments or whether alternative modelling approaches might help explain the observed behavior. Subsection 5.1 focuses on several standard assumptions which may break down in the VCM experimental environment. In subsection 5.2, several nonstandard modelling approaches are discussed.

5.1   Potential Breakdown of Standard Nash Assumptions

5.1.1   Incomplete information

The NE model assumes complete information, but in fact two pieces of information were not provided to participants in our experiments: others' token endowments and others' per-token return from the private account. Because the return from the private account is necessary to compute the opportunity cost of token allocations to the group account, one might conjecture that an incomplete information process along the lines of that described by Kreps, et al. [1982] (for the finitely repeated Prisoner's Dilemma) is responsible for the pattern of the data. There are, however, some problems in ascribing these results entirely to the domain of incomplete information. The structure of our experiments, although similar to a two-person Prisoner's Dilemma, is not identical. In addition, Isaac and Walker (1989), using a four-person, *MPCR* = 0.3 design identical to that of VCM-SS-$ reported here, found no difference in results when it was publicly announced that token endowments and returns from the private account were identical across all individuals. However, it may be that the incomplete information occurs at a deeper level than simply the structure of the payoffs. For example, there may be uncertainty as to the rationality of other players.

5.1.2   Learning

Using a standard model as the basis for evaluating our data leaves open the question of how quickly individuals are expected to behave in accordance with the NE model. One interpretation of the typical decay process observed in VCM is that of a 'learning' phenomena (see, for example, Andreoni [1988]). Even in dominant strategy decision environments, evidence exists that some individuals must learn the strategic nature of the optimization problem.[9] Furthermore, in nondominant strategy settings, individuals may have to learn to make decisions that are consistent in the sense of a Nash Equilibrium. Recently, there has been a growing literature on formal models of how individuals 'learn' to play Nash equilibria (see Fudenberg and Kreps [1988], Moreno and Walker [1993], and Milgrom and Roberts [1991]). Whether these models can be adapted to have implications for the VCM environment is an open question for further research.[10]

5.1.3 Failure of backward induction

The essence of the standard NE model is that individuals choose their actions noncooperatively. In certain classes of infinitely repeated games, however, seemingly cooperative outcomes can be supported by noncooperative strategies which specifically incorporate the multi-period nature of the game. Such outcomes are theoretically ruled out here by backward induction from the known end-point. Failure of some individuals to behave in a manner consistent with the logic of backward induction is one possible explanation for deviations from complete free riding.

5.1.4 Incorrectly represented preferences

In our experiments, the theoretical prediction of complete free riding is based on the assumption that each individual is maximizing a utility function which is monotonically increasing in experiment earnings. The standard model further assumes that one's own earnings are the sole determinant of utility. This may not be a correct representation of actual preferences in the stage game. This observation is not new to this paper. For example, Palfrey and Rosenthal (1988) model 'uncontrolled preferences' which derive from 'acts of social cooperation or contribution, the utility of altruism, or social duty.' Likewise, Andreoni [1989] develops the notion of a 'warm glow' from contributions to collective goods. In addition to warm glow effects, 'fairness' considerations (Kahneman, Knetsch, and Thaler [1986a, 1986b]) may play a role in the formation of individual decisions.

The 'incomplete information' and 'learning' explanations for the inconsistency between our results and the complete information NE prediction can be further addressed with additional experiments. Section 6 reports the results of several new cash payment experiments utilizing a large number of decision rounds and enhanced strategic information. The 'failure of backward induction' and 'incorrectly represented preferences' explanations require a fundamental change in the approach to modelling behavior in the VCM environment.

5.2 Alternative Modelling Approaches

The inconsistency between observed behavior in the VCM environment and the complete information NE prediction has led to the development of several alternatives to the standard Nash model. This subsection briefly summarizes two approaches by Ledyard (1990) and Miller and Andreoni (1991). This is followed by the development of a simple binary choice modelling approach designed to highlight the potential gains from cooperation, and a more complex nonbinary approach based on forward-looking behavior.

Ledyard (1990) has proposed an equilibrium model in which individuals 'get some satisfaction (a warm glow) from participating in a group that implicitly and successfully cooperates.' (In modelling a 'warm glow,' Ledyard's assumption is related to the work of Andreoni [1989]). Individuals are distinguished by types, based upon the strength of their 'warm glow' preferences. Under certain assumptions on the population distribution of preferences, Ledyard finds that (1) there can be deviations from complete free riding even in a single-shot game, and (2) individuals will be more likely to deviate from complete free riding in large groups.

Miller and Andreoni (1991) present an interesting nonstandard model based on the adaptive behavior of replicator dynamics. Their approach is consistent with our finding that the percentage of tokens allocated to the group account appears to be directly related to both group size and *MPCR*. The replicator dynamic approach also predicts continuous decay toward complete free riding and, ceteris paribus, identical time paths for designs in which $(N \cdot MPCR)$ is constant (eg. $N = 4$, $MPCR = 0.75$ and $N = 10$, $MPCR = 0.30$). While the Miller–Andreoni model does capture some of the characteristics of our aggregate VCM data, neither of the two predictions mentioned above is entirely consistent with our data.

Below, two alternative nonstandard VCM modelling approaches are presented: a simple all-or-nothing (binary) symmetric choice approach, and a more complex (nonbinary) asymmetric choice approach. The intent of the first approach is simply to focus on how changes in group size and *MPCR* change the magnitude of the groups' gains from deviating from complete free-riding. The intent of the second approach is to outline a more detailed decision-theoretic explanation of the VCM data.

5.2.1 A symmetric binary choice approach

This subsection focuses on the determinants of the gains from cooperation in a given period under the simplifying assumption that individuals choose to allocate either zero tokens (play Nash) or all tokens (fully cooperate) to the group account. Recall, the strategy space in our experiments allows for greater variation than 'all tokens' or 'zero tokens' and all or nothing allocations are not generally consistent with the data. This assumption, however, provides useful insight into how the group size and *MPCR* treatment variables affect the gains from cooperation, defined as the difference in experimental dollar earnings between the Pareto Optimal and the NE outcomes.[11]

Simplifying the notation developed in section 2.1, let $Z_i = Z$ (the individual token endowment), $p_i = 1$ (the 1 cent per token return from the private account), and recall that N is the group size, $G' > 1$ is the return to the group from a token placed in the group account, and $G'/N < 1$ is the *MPCR*. Note that: (1) individual earnings at the Pareto Optimum (E^{PO}) are $G'Z$, and (2) individual earnings at the Nash Equilibrium (E^{NE}) are Z. Thus, if a group moves from the Nash Equilibrium to the Pareto Optimum the gains to one individual from full cooperation can be expressed as:

$$E^{PO} - E^{NE} = G'Z - Z = Z(G'-1) = Z[(MPCR \cdot N) - 1]$$

which varies directly with both group size (holding *MPCR* constant) and *MPCR* (holding group size constant).[12] Further, the gains from cooperation are invariant to changes in *MPCR* and N when the product term ($N \cdot MPCR$) is constant.

Table 16.2 displays the numerical value of $E^{PO} - E^{NE}$ for $N = 4, 10, 40, 100$ and *MPCR* = 0.75, 0.30. The most striking calculation is that $E^{PO} - E^{NE}$ increases dramatically as group size increases from 4 to 100 for both *MPCR* conditions. To the extent that participants are aware of the general nature of these relationships and tend to increase token allocations to the group account as the gains to group cooperation increase, then we expect to see allocations to the group account increase with increases in $E^{PO} - E^{NE}$. Our Observation 3 is consistent with this approach. Furthermore, at the extremes, this approach correctly predicts that allocations to the group account will be greater with $N = 100$, *MPCR* = 0.75 than with $N = 4$, *MPCR* = 0.3. On the other hand, our results are not consistent with this approach as reported in Observation 2 and Observation 4 in section 4. That is, for groups of size 40 and 100, with *MPCR* = 0.30 or 0.75, a positive correlation between the percentage of tokens allocated to the group account and *MPCR* does not exist, and for the case of *MPCR* = 0.75, there is no discernable difference in allocations to the group account on average across group sizes.

Table 16.2   Gains from cooperation

	MPCR = 0.75	*MPCR* = 0.30
N	$E^{PO} - E^{NE}$	$E^{PO} - E^{NE}$
4	1.00	0.10
10	3.25	1.00
40	14.50	5.50
100	37.00	14.50

This simple binary choice approach is useful as a starting point for characterizing the joint importance of group size and *MPCR* as factors that shape behavior in our VCM environment. In the next subsection, we begin the task of generalizing this simple approach into a more formal model of individual behavior which allows for nonbinary asymmetric decisions.

5.2.2 An asymmetric, forward-looking, non-binary approach

Given that a *unilateral* increase in tokens to the group account by an individual will *always decrease* that individual's earnings in the current round, what plausible rationale exists for an individual to deviate from full free-riding? We propose a rationale based on the individual's perception of the expected intertemporal gains from placing tokens in the group account. Gains are 'expected' due to uncertainty regarding the actions of others. The standard modelling approach based on backwards induction rules out equilibria containing intertemporal signalling. The modelling approach suggested here deviates from the logic of backwards induction, assuming instead that individuals view themselves as involved in a *forward-looking intertemporal decision problem*.

This approach is composed of three principle components: (1) the assumption that individual i believes his decisions have signalling content to others; (2) a benchmark earnings level for measuring the success of signalling; and (3) the formulation of a subjective probability function for evaluating the likelihood of success.

For purposes of exposition, suppose that individual i believes his allocation decisions have signalling content and considers the implications of his actions only one period into the future, with no discounting. Individual i is contemplating the possibility of allocating m_i tokens to the group account in both the current and the next period, and he considers this effort a 'success' if his earnings in the next period are greater than his earnings at the complete free-riding equilibrium (Z). This definition of success is clearly *ad hoc* and one of numerous possible benchmarks.

Let $M_j^*(m_i)$ be the aggregate allocation of tokens to the group account by the $N-1$ other individuals such that individual i's earnings equal Z when he invests m_i. Note that the formulation of M_j^* does not require symmetric allocations to the group account. Solve for $M_j^*(m_i)$ as follows:

$$(Z-m_i) + MPCR(m_i+M_j^*) = Z,$$

$$M_j^* = m_i[(1-MPCR)/MPCR].$$

Notice that M_j^* varies inversely with *MPCR*. Furthermore, the average number of tokens per person required to generate M_j^*, $M_j^*/(N-1)$, varies inversely with group size.

Table 16.3   Values of M*$_j$/(N–1) when m$_i$ = 1

N	$M^*_j/(N-1)$	
	MPCR = 0.75	MPCR = 0.30
4	0.112	0.778
10	0.037	0.259
40	0.009	0.060
100	0.003	0.023

Let $\alpha^t_i(m_i, \Omega^t)$ be individual i's conditional subjective probability at period t that a positive allocation of m_i tokens will succeed. Ω^t is a vector of characteristics of the institution and environment at time t which could include the history of other individual's behavior and an individual's 'homegrown' expectations about the effects of signalling. The approach developed here assumes that Ω^t includes $M^*_j/(N-1)$, and that $\alpha^t_i(m_i, \Omega^t)$ and $M^*_j/(N-1)$ are negatively related. Our principal conjectures are that: (1) an individual will be more likely to signal in those experimental conditions in which $\alpha^t_i(m_i, \Omega^t)$ is greater, and (2) the observed m_is will be negatively related to $M^*_j/(N-1)$.

Table 16.3 shows numerically how $M^*_j/(N-1)$ varies with the parameters used in our experiments for $m_i = 1$. Notice that the absolute difference between the two *MPCR* columns is greatest at $N = 4$ and diminishes as N increases. Consider the case of $N = 10$ and *MPCR* = 0.30 where $M^*_j/(N-1) = 0.259$. Assume that individual i allocates $m_i > 0$ tokens to the group account in rounds t and $t+1$. The average allocation to the group account of the nine other individuals must exceed $0.259m_i$ tokens in round $t+1$ for i's non-zero round t allocation to be viewed as a successful signal (that is, individual i earns greater than Z in round $t+1$).

This model of asymmetric behavior is consistent with several (but not all) aspects of our data. First, it is common in all treatment conditions to observe individuals whose allocations to the group account vary substantially from round to round. Such 'pulsing' behavior could be interpreted as attempts to influence others' allocations through signalling. Second, as reported in Observation 3 for the case of *MPCR* = 0.30, groups of size 40 and 100 allocate more tokens to the group account on average than do groups of size 4 and 10. Third, moving from the design condition of ($N = 10$, *MPCR* = 0.30) to ($N = 4$, *MPCR* = 0.75), the value of (*MPCR·N*) is constant but $M^*_j/(N-1)$ decreases. As predicted by this approach, average group allocations for the $N = 4$, *MPCR* = 0.75 experiments consistently exceed those observed under the condition of $N = 10$, *MPCR* = 0.30. The Miller–Andreoni replicator dynamic approach and the simple binary choice approach predict no difference in behavior across designs where ($N \cdot MPCR$) is held constant. Finally, both OLS and Tobit regressions demonstrate the importance of $M_j^*/(N - 1)$ as an explanatory variable for aggregate allocations to the group account. Pooling the data across all group sizes and $MPCR$ conditions, $M_j^*/(N - 1)$ is negatively and significantly correlated with allocations to the group account. Thus, $M_j^*/(N - 1)$ appears in a statistical sense to incorporate the combined impact of N and $MPCR$. No significant difference in allocations to the group account is observed: (1) for groups of size 40 and 100 with $MPCR = 0.30$ or $MPCR = 0.75$ (Observation 2), and (2) across all group sizes for the case of $MPCR = 0.75$ (Observation 4). These results are inconsistent with the predictions of the asymmetric non-binary approach, the symmetric binary approach, and the Miller-Andreoni replicator approach. In addition, there is no discernable difference in aggregate allocations for the cases of ($N = 40$, $MPCR = 0.75$) and ($N = 100$, $MPCR = 0.30$) even though $M_j^*/(N - 1)$ changes. Since ($MPCR \cdot N$) is constant for these parameters, the Miller-Andreoni and binary choice approaches correctly predict no difference in aggregate allocations.

In summary, for $MPCR$ values in the domain of $[0.30, 0.75]$, significant differences in aggregate allocations are observed when: (1) group size is small (4, 10) and $MPCR$ changes, and (2) $MPCR = 0.30$ and group size changes from the small-group (4, 10) to the large-group (40, 100) domain. It is in these conditions that the largest absolute changes in $M_j^*/(N - 1)$ occur. Given the potential for large variations in α_i across individuals and over time, statistically significant differences in Σm_i between N and $MPCR$ treatment groups are unlikely to be observed in small samples unless there are large differences in $M_j^*/(N - 1)$ across the treatment groups. This suggests a direction for new experimentation – large groups with considerably larger differences in $M_j^*/(N - 1)$ across treatment conditions. Such experiments are presented in section 6 below.

Up to this point, individual i has been assumed to contemplate the signal value of $m_i > 0$ for only one period in advance. This need not be the case in an expanded version of the non-binary asymmetric choice approach. If multiple-stage signalling is allowed, then the following conjecture seems reasonable: as the final round approaches, the expected gains from signalling diminish. Thus, in contrast with a purely adaptive or learning model where the number of rounds completed is central to behavioral dynamics, this expanded forward-looking approach suggests that the *number of rounds remaining* is an important determinant of behavior in the current round. Varying the number of rounds across experiments allows one to address this issue. If the number of rounds remaining is positively correlated with subjects' expectations that signalling will be successful, then the aggregate allocation to the group account in round t should be larger, *ceteris paribus*, in experiments with a longer time horizon. Section 6 below presents several VCM experiments with a much longer time horizon than any previously reported.

The forward-looking logic embodied in this approach suggests that, as the final round of the experiment approaches, the expected gains from cooperation diminish since fewer rounds remain. In the final round, the signal content of m_i is irrelevant and all individuals have a dominant strategy of $m_i = 0$. The data, however, show many deviations from this strategy. Thus, any forward-looking model based on signalling must be complemented with an explanation for positive allocations to the group account in the final round. The literature suggests two likely candidates: fairness considerations and warm-glow effects.

Clearly, this more complex forward-looking approach to modelling VCM behavior has limitations as currently developed. The benchmark for success is arbitrary, and the approach does not differentiate between 'barely' succeeding and 'substantially' succeeding. Furthermore, no consistency requirements have been imposed on the α_j's. The articulation of a formal, fully developed, forward-looking model is left as a challenge for future research.

6. ADDITIONAL EXPERIMENTAL RESULTS

This section presents two additional series of experiments. The first set examines behavior in groups of size 40 with an $MPCR = 0.03$ and is motivated by the disappearance of the $MPCR$ effect in large groups. The second set examines behavior when subjects are provided with additional payoff information and participate in a large number of decision rounds. These experiments are motivated, in part, by the 'incomplete information' and 'learning' explanations for the failure to observe complete free riding. In addition, they allow for further testing of the forward-looking approach presented above.

6.1 Large-Group Experiments with a Low *MPCR*

Recall that in groups of size 100 and 40 there was no significant separation in Σm_i for $MPCR = 0.30$ versus $MPCR = 0.75$. In groups of size 40 and 100, however, $MPCR$s of 0.30 and 0.75 yield values of $M_j^*/(N-1)$ which are quite close in an absolute sense. In a large-group experiment with a *very* low $MPCR$, one can recapture the feature of the small-group $MPCR = 0.30$ experiments of a relatively large value of $M_j^*/(N-1)$. Specifically, in a 40-person group with $MPCR = 0.03$, $M_j^*/(N-1) = 0.83m_i$. This implies that the average allocation of tokens to the group account by the $(N-1)$ other individuals must be greater than $0.83m_i$ for individual i's earnings to be greater than E^{NE}. Thus, such experiments should exhibit lower Σm_i than those with $MPCR = 0.30$ or $MPCR = 0.75$.

The results of seven 40-person $MPCR = 0.03$ experiments are reported in this subsection; six using the VCM-MS-XC procedures and one using the

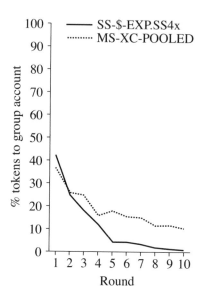

*Figure 16.11   Experiments using group size 40 and a very low (0.03)
              MPCR*

VCM-SS-$ procedure. The subjects in the later experiment (SS4x) were randomly drawn from the group of 80 subjects who participated in experiments SS1 and SS2 reported above.[13] Figure 16.11 displays the mean results of the VCM-MS-XC experiments and the data from the single VCM-SS-$ experiment. As predicted, these 40-person groups exhibit a substantial decay in allocations to the group account. Thus, the *MPCR* effect does appear to exist in 40-person experiments for *MPCR* values much smaller than those used by IW.

6.2   Experiments with Additional Payoff Information and a Larger Number of Decision Rounds

The single-session experiments reported in this section all employ cash rewards, $N = 10$, and $MPCR = 0.30$. There are two design changes relative to the previously reported experiments. First, subjects were provided with a handout explicitly stating the conditions in which: (1) an individual receives the maximum possible earnings, (2) an individual receives the minimum possible earnings, (3) the group as a whole receives the maximum possible earnings, and (4) the group as a whole receives the minimum possible earnings. Second, the number of decision rounds varied from 10 in three experiments to 40 in two experiments to 60 in one experiment. The subjects in the

40-round experiments were drawn from a pool of subjects with experience in ten-round VCM experiments. The subjects in the 60-round experiment were drawn from the two 40-round experiments.[14]

Figure 16.12 summarizes the results from these additional experiments. The top panel displays the sequence of mean allocations to the group account from two series focusing solely on the effect of additional payoff information. The first series, SS-$-IW, were previously reported in section 4. The second series, SS-$-INFO, are the new ten-round experiments in which subjects received the additional payoff information. Examining each decision round separately, *t*-tests indicate that the differences in means are insignificant.

The bottom left panel reports the results of two experiments with 40 decision rounds and the additional payoff information. These experiments exhibit a pattern of allocations to the group account in which group allocations begin at a mean of 57.5 percent and decay slowly (but not monotonically) to a mean of 6.8 percent by round 40. The bottom right panel reports the results of one experiment with 60 decision rounds and the additional information. In this experiment, group allocations begin at 51 percent of total endowment and decay slowly (but not monotonically) to 19.2 percent by round 60.

These experiments supplement our VCM database in several interesting ways. Even with a richer information environment, highly experienced subject groups continue to follow a pattern of behavior inconsistent with the predictions of the complete information Nash model. Thus, the results reported in section 4 are not an artifact of limiting decisions to ten rounds. Furthermore, the rate of decay of allocations to the group account is inversely related to the number of decision rounds. For example, compare rounds 8–10 in the ten-round experiments to rounds 8–10 in the 40- and 60-round experiments. Or, compare rounds 35–40 in the 40-round experiments to rounds 35–40 in the 60-round experiment. Clearly, the rate of decay is faster the shorter the time horizon of the experiment. This result is inconsistent with backward induction models, and purely adaptive or learning models based on the number of rounds completed. This aspect of the VCM data is consistent with a forward-looking modelling approach based on the potential gains from cooperation.

The diversity in individual behavior is illustrated in Figure 16.13 which displays the group allocation decisions for three subjects from the 60-round experiment. These three subjects typify three types of behavior we regularly observe. Subject 1 characterizes 'slow decay with pulsing' and follows a pattern generally consistent with the aggregate data observed in many experiments. Subject 2 characterizes 'weak free-rider with pulsing.' Finally, subject 10 characterizes 'strong pulsing.' It is worth emphasizing that the subjects in this 60-round experiment were 'super experienced,' having participated in an

10 decision rounds

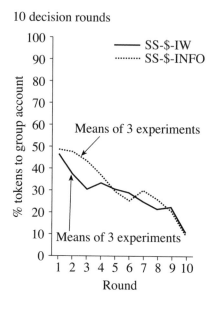

40 decision rounds

60 decision rounds

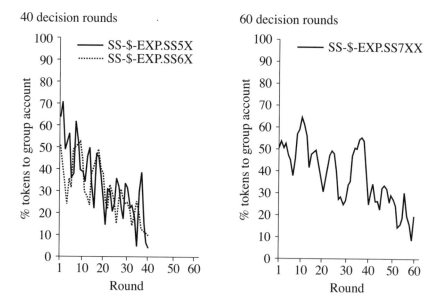

*Figure 16.12   Experiments with additional payoff information and a larger
number of decision rounds*

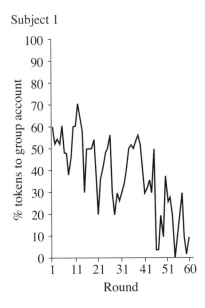

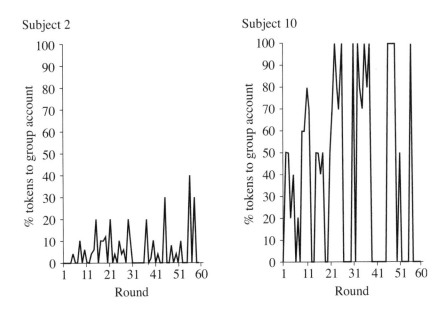

Figure 16.13   Illustrative individual subject data

initial ten-round trainer experiment without the additional payoff information (not reported here), one of the ten-round experiments with additional payoff information, and one of the 40-round experiments with additional payoff information. Clearly, no simple symmetric choice model can capture the individual behavior observed in the VCM environment.

7. SUMMARY OF RESULTS

This chapter presents new evidence on the existence of group size effects in the provision of a pure public good via voluntary contributions. In order to overcome the methodological difficulties associated with large-group experiments, 'multiple-session' experimental procedures and the use of extra-credit rewards are explored. Decision-making groups of size 4, 10, 40, and 100 provide replicable results contradicting the widely held premise that a group's ability to provide the optimal level of a pure public good is inversely related to group size.

The results of a series of (extra-credit, multiple-session) baseline experiments with groups of size four and ten are consistent with the (cash, single-session) experimental results reported by Isaac and Walker (1988) that a higher marginal benefit from the public good leads to less free riding and thus greater efficiency. This is in spite of the fact that, in this experimental setting, the single-period dominant strategy is a zero allocation of resources to the public good.

Our experiments with groups of size 40 and 100 yield several surprising results (see Table 16.3). First, the impact from variations in the magnitude of the marginal per-capita return from the public good (*MPCR*) appears to vanish over the range [0.30, 0.75]. Second, with an *MPCR* of 0.30, groups of size 40 and 100 provide the public good at higher levels of efficiency than groups of size 4 and 10. Third, with an *MPCR* of 0.75, there is no significant difference in efficiency due to group size.

Several additional experiments utilizing cash rewards and standard single-session procedures suggest that the unexpectedly high efficiency levels generated by large groups are not simply an artifact of extra-credit rewards or multiple-session procedures. 40-person experiments with a very low *MPCR* of 0.03 yield the low efficiency levels previously observed with small groups and an *MPCR* of 0.30. The existence of an '*MPCR* effect' is thus reconfirmed for large groups. Our research reveals, however, that behavior is influenced by a subtle interaction between group size and *MPCR* rather than simply the sheer magnitude of either. Experiments using both additional payoff information and as many as 60 decision rounds provided further evidence of the failure of the standard backward induction model.

NOTES

1. Research support from the National Science Foundation under grants #SES-8820897 and SES-8821067 is gratefully acknowledged as is the research assistance provided by Susan Laury (Indiana University), Bradley Cloud, and Curtis Libor (University of Arizona). The authors thank John Ledyard and Mark Walker for their extensive comments and the numerous colleagues and students who have provided constructive criticisms of this research. The experimental data are permanently archived on the NovaNET computer system. Contact the authors for information on accessing the data archive via microcomputer dial-up.

2. In the experiments reported here $p_i = \$.01$ for all i. This need not be the case. Fisher, Isaac, Schatzberg, and Walker (1988) report experiments in which the p_i's vary from person to person.

3. Note that we do not explicitly announce other subjects' p_i values nor the distribution of tokens. Isaac and Walker (1989) report no obvious difference in behavior in similar experiments where this information was common knowledge.

4. An alternative multiple-session procedure was used in the public goods experiments of Kim and Walker (1984). Other examples of multiple-session procedures exist in the social science literature. Such experiments are rare, however, relative to single-session experiments.

5. Instructions are available upon request from the authors.

6. In terms of formal, anonymous feedback, students in Williams' Fall 1989 introductory and Intermediate Microeconomic Theory classes were given an end-of-semester course evaluation that included an item stating that the experiment 'was an interesting and constructive supplement to this course.' The average responses were 2.89 and 2.87; where 'Strongly agree' = 4, 'Agree' = 3, 'Neither agree nor disagree' = 2, 'Disagree' = 1, and 'Strongly Disagree' = 0. In addition, there were no written comments complaining that the method of awarding extra-credit points was in any way unfair.

7. Subjects were enrolled in introductory and intermediate microeconomic theory classes ranging in size from about 40 to over 350. On average, 87 per cent of the students enrolled chose to participate in the VCM extra-credit exercise. The subjects' major area of study varied widely – the majority were *not* economics majors. Indiana subjects accessed the experiment through a public microcomputer facility while Arizona subjects accessed the experiment through the Economic Science Laboratory computer room.

8. Subjects earned, on average, about $20 in the experiment plus $3 for keeping their appointment to participate.

9. For example, there is an abundance of evidence that many subjects do not immediately follow the dominant strategy of bidding full value in a second-price sealed-bid auction. See, for example, Cox, Smith and Walker (1985) or Kagel and Levin (1993).

10. Most of this literature, in contrast to the designs reported here, focuses on nondominant strategy NE in the stage games.

11. In the IW and VCM-SS-$ experiments reported here, explicit cooperation in the form of group discussions was strictly prohibited. In the VCM-MS-XC experiments, explicit cooperation is not prohibited since communication among subjects is uncontrolled; however, identifying the other individuals in a specific group would be very difficult.

12. Gains from cooperation also exist for movements from the Nash equilibrium to partial cooperation ($\Sigma m_i < NZ$). Symmetric allocations to the group account by all participants ($m_i = m < Z \,\forall\, i$) leads to gains over E^{NE} of $m(G'-1)$. Asymmetric allocations do not necessarily lead to gains over E^{NE} for all participants.

13. Subjects in SS4x were paid $2 cash for each 'experiment dollar' earned due to the very low *MPCR*. Cash earnings in SS4x were approximately one-half the earnings in the other three single-session experiments.

14. Subjects in the 40- and 60-round experiments were paid in cash $0.50 for each 'experiment dollar' earned due to the large number of decision rounds.

REFERENCES

Andreoni, J. 1988. 'Why Free Ride? Strategies and Learning in Public Goods Experiments.' *Journal of Public Economics* 37, 291–304.

Andreoni, J. 1989. 'Giving With Impure Altruism: Applications to Charity and Ricardian Equivalence.' *Journal of Political Economy* 97, 1447–58.

Brookshire, D., D. Coursey and D. Redington, 1989. 'Special Interests and the Voluntary Provision of Public Goods.' Unpublished Manuscript.

Cox, J., V. Smith and J. Walker. 1985. 'Expected Revenue in Discriminative and Uniform Price Sealed-Bid Auctions.' In *Research in Experimental Economics*, V. Smith, ed. (JAI Press, Greenwich) 183–232.

Dorsey, R. 1992. 'The Voluntary Contributions Mechanism With Real Time Revisions.' *Public Choice* 73, 261–82.

Fisher, J., R.M. Isaac, J. Schatzberg and J. Walker. 1988. 'Heterogenous Demand For Public Goods: Effects On The Voluntary Contributions Mechanism.' Unpublished Manuscript.

Fudenberg, D. and D. Kreps. 1988. 'A Theory of Learning, Experimentation, and Equilibrium in Games.' Unpublished Manuscript.

Isaac, R.M., K. McCue and C. Plott. 1985. 'Public Goods Provision in an Experimental Environment.' *Journal of Public Economics* 26, 51–74.

Isaac, R.M. and J. Walker. 1988. 'Group Size Effects in Public Goods Provision: The Voluntary Contribution Mechanism.' *Quarterly Journal of Economics* 103, 179–200.

Isaac, R.M. and J. Walker. 1989. 'Complete Information and the Provision of Public Goods.' Unpublished Manuscript.

Isaac, R.M., J. Walker and S. Thomas. 1984. 'Divergent Evidence on Free Riding: An Experimental Examination of Some Possible Explanations.' *Public Choice* 43, 179–49.

Kagel, J., and D. Levin. 1993. 'Independent Private Value Auctions: Bidder Behavior in First, Second, and Third Price Auctions with Varying Numbers of Bidders.' *Economic Journal*.

Kahneman, D., J. Knetch and R. Thaler. 1986. 'Fairness and the Assumptions of Economics.' *Journal of Business* 59, S285–S300.

Kahneman, D., J. Knetch and R. Thaler. 1986. 'Fairness as a Constraint on Profit Seeking: Entitlements in the Market.' *American Economic Review* 76, 728–41.

Kim, O. and M. Walker. 1984. 'The Free Rider Problem: Experimental Evidence.' *Public Choice* 43, 3–24.

Kreps, D., P. Milgrom, J. Roberts and R. Wilson. 1982. 'Rational Cooperation in the Finitely Repeated Prisoners Dilemma.' *Journal of Economic Theory* 27, 245–52.

Ledyard, J. 1993. 'Is There a Problem with Public Goods Provision?' *The Handbook of Experimental Economics*. John Kagel and Avin Roth, eds, Princeton University Press.

Marwell, G. and R. Ames. 1979. 'Experiments on the Provision of Public Goods I: Resources, Interest, Group Size, and the Free Rider Problem.' *American Journal of Sociology* 84, 1335–60.

Marwell, G. and R. Ames. 1980. 'Experiments on the Provision of Public Goods II: Provision Points, Stakes, Experience and the Free Rider Problem.' *American Journal of Sociology* 85, 926–37.

Marwell, G. and R. Ames. 1981. 'Economists Free Ride: Does Anyone Else?' *Journal of Public Economics* 15, 295–310.

Milgrom, P. and J. Roberts. 1991. 'Adaptive and Sophisticated Learning in Normal Form Games.' *Games and Economic Behavior* 3, 82–100.

Miller, J. and J. Andreoni. 1991. 'A Coevolutionary Model of Free Riding Behavior: Replicator Dynamics as an Explanation of the Experimental Results.' *Economics Letters* 36, 9–15.

Moreno, D. and M. Walker. 1994. 'Two Problems in Applying Ljung's Projection Algorithm to the Analysis of Decentralized Learning.' *Journal of Economic Theory* 62(2): 420–27.

Palfrey, T. and H. Rosenthal. 1988. 'Private Incentives in Social Dilemmas.' *Journal of Public Economics* 35, 309–32.

17. Cooperation in public-goods experiments: kindness or confusion?

James Andreoni[1]

Theories of free-riding predict that privately provided public goods should have very few contributors, and contributions should be very small. Nonetheless, millions of people give to public goods like the Red Cross and Public Broadcasting, and they generally contribute sizable sums.[2] This observation has caused researchers to re-examine models of giving, and it has become important to understand the role of social and cultural factors like altruism and 'warm-glow.' These issues extend beyond charitable giving, into public goods within the family and intergenerational altruism (see e.g., B. Douglas Bernheim et al., 1985; Bernheim, 1986; Andreoni, 1989; Joseph Altonji et al., 1992).

As with real-world giving to public goods, experiments on free-riding find that subjects are generally more cooperative than predicted, and often much more cooperative. This suggests that the same social and cultural influences thought to affect real-world giving could be at work in experiments. However, the goal of laboratory experiments is to control the incentives of subjects and to remove the social and cultural influences to the greatest extent possible. If the theory being tested is correct, then the cooperation observed should be due to subjects who misunderstand the instructions or the incentives in the experiment. Hence, the cooperation should be caused only by errors and confusion, and not altruism, warm-glow, or other forms of kindness. If confusion is the principal explanation for cooperation, then this justifies the emphasis on 'learning' in the experimental literature.

Unfortunately, it is impossible to tell from existing experiments whether observed cooperation is due to kindness or confusion. For laboratory experiments to be informative on individual motives for giving, it is essential to determine whether there is a significant fraction of giving that is due to kindness. This paper presents an economic laboratory experiment designed to separate kindness and confusion. The experiment strengthens the controls that subtract out the incentives for kindness, leaving confusion as the only explanation for cooperative moves. Comparing subjects in this condition to others who can cooperate either out of kindness or confusion, one can determine what fraction of cooperation can be attributed to each motive.

The results of the experiment are, first, that subtracting the incentives for kindness makes subjects far more likely to choose the dominant strategy of free-riding. Overall, contributions to the public good are about one-third the level observed in the usual public-goods experiment. This means that cooperation cannot be attributed to embarrassing amounts of experimenter or subject error. Second, and more importantly, the experiment shows that on average about half of all cooperative moves can be classified as kindness. This implies that social and cultural propensities for kindness and generosity must clearly be very strong, and that such motives cannot easily be removed from experiments simply by providing neutral environments and pledges of anonymity. Third, the results suggest that the decline in cooperation often observed in the multiple trials of public-goods experiments may not be due to learning, but instead may be due to frustrated attempts at kindness. The weight of the evidence now appears to indicate that experiments should focus on detailed studies of charitable behavior. Experiments can have a positive role in developing and testing alternative theories of giving.

I. BACKGROUND

Many experiments have been conducted to test the free-rider hypothesis (see Douglas D. Davis and Charles A. Holt [1993] and John O. Ledyard [1995] for reviews). The most common design requires groups of four to ten subjects. Each subject is given an endowment which can be 'invested' in a public good. Each subject then receives a constant marginal return from each cent invested in the public good, regardless of which subjects invest. The marginal return from the public good is chosen so that each subject has a dominant strategy to invest zero in the public good, that is, to free ride, while the symmetric Pareto-efficient outcome is for all subjects to invest their entire endowment in the public good.

These experiments typically find that subjects are sensitive to free-riding incentives and are generally closer to the free-riding outcome than the Pareto-efficient outcome. Nonetheless, cooperation is still above that which would validate the theory. In a ten-period iterated game, subjects generally begin by contributing about half of their endowments to the public good. As the game is iterated, the contributions 'decay' toward the dominant strategy level and stand at about 15–25 percent of the endowment by the tenth iteration (R. Mark Isaac and James M. Walker, 1988). Similar patterns of cooperation are observed in experiments where subjects play in repeated single-shot games created by randomising the members of groups, rather than in finitely repeated games (Andreoni, 1988b). This suggests that cooperation in these games is not attributable to reputation-building. Prior experience in public-goods experiments does not appear to eliminate cooperation either. Subjects participating in a second public-goods experiment showed significant cooperation as well, regardless of whether the other subjects in their group were the same or different (Isaac and Walker, 1988; Andreoni, 1988b). Subjects are also sensitive to the experimental parameters, even though these do not affect the equilibrium prediction. In particular, people cooperate more the larger the marginal return from the public good (Isaac and Walker, 1988), and counter to the intuition on free-riding, subjects also cooperate more the larger their group (Isaac et al. 1994). They also appear to be more cooperative when the decision is framed as a public good rather than a public bad (Andreoni, 1995). This persistent and sometimes counterintuitive nature of cooperation has created an important puzzle.

II.   KINDNESS OR CONFUSION?

There are two main hypotheses that could explain the lack of free-riding as a dominant strategy in the laboratory. First, one could conjecture that the free-riding hypothesis, in its pure form, is incomplete. Subjects could have tastes for cooperation that they bring from outside of the experiment and which influence their behavior in the experiment.[3] There are many specific alternatives which could be proposed to capture this. Since these would likely appeal to some notions of benevolence or social custom, this paper will refer to these collectively as *kindness*.

A second hypothesis is that the experimenters have somehow failed to convey adequately the incentives to the subjects, perhaps through poorly prepared instructions or inadequate monetary rewards, or simply that many subjects are incapable of deducing the dominant strategy during the course of the experiment. Since this alternative suggests that subjects have somehow not grasped the true incentives, this alternative will be called *confusion*.

Several experiments have examined the kindness hypothesis. These have generally added manipulations that try to influence cooperation in predictable ways. For example, Palfrey and Howard Rosenthal (1991) have added nonbinding 'cheap talk,' Andreoni (1993) added a 'tax' that would be incompletely crowded out in the presence of kindness, and Robyn M. Dawes et al. (1987) added effects for group identification. All of these experiments produced results consistent with various notions of kindness. By contrast, experiments have not attempted to capture the degree of confusion. It is possible, for instance, that the manipulations just mentioned could be influencing confusion in addition to, or perhaps instead of, kindness and real cooperation.

The confusion hypothesis is potentially very important to the experimental literature. Notice that with an equilibrium prediction of zero contribution to the public good there is only one way a confused subject can err, and that is to contribute too much to the public good. Hence, contributions that are really due to confusion may be mistakenly called cooperation.[4] If instead the prediction were some interior choice, so that an error could also lead one to contribute too little, then errors may be more likely to be averaged out of the aggregate data. Indeed, public-goods experiments are strikingly different from other experiments with externalities, such as oligopoly experiments and common-pool resource experiments. These experiments have interior Nash equilibria and get results much closer to the predictions of the theory than do public-goods experiments.[5] It is distinctly possible, therefore, that the dominant-strategy design of the standard public-goods games is biasing experiments toward rejecting the theory.

This paper will directly examine both hypotheses of confusion and kindness. Instead of adding conditions to encourage kindness, the experiments will subtract off the social, cultural, and strategic incentives for subjects to cooperate, leaving confusion as the most reasonable explanation for cooperation. With this methodology I will be able to estimate what fraction of cooperative moves is due to kindness and what fraction is due to confusion.

III. EXPERIMENTAL DESIGN

The experiment has three conditions. The first, called the *Regular* condition, is the standard public-goods experiment. In a second condition subjects also play a standard public-goods game; however, their monetary payments are not the same as their experimental earnings. Rather, these subjects get paid based on how their experimental earnings rank in comparison to the other subjects in their group. The subject with the highest experimental earnings gets the highest monetary payments, with payments decreasing with rank so that the subject with the lowest experimental earnings gets the lowest monetary payment.[6] If there are ties, those who tie will split the payoffs, keeping the average earnings for each round constant. Note that this payment scheme makes a zero-sum game out of the standard positive-sum public-goods game. This condition will be called the *Rank* condition.

The important feature of the Rank condition is that it preserves the dominant strategy equilibrium of the Regular condition; the way to get the highest rank in the group is to be the biggest free rider, that is, to contribute zero. The Rank condition, however, offers no incentives for cooperation. If three subjects cooperate they can all raise their own experimental earnings, but these three subjects will raise the experimental earnings of the other subjects by even more. Hence, mutual cooperation only assures the cooperators of the lowest possible payoff. Not only are there no monetary gains from cooperation, the potential for kindness or altruism would also appear to be largely eliminated. The incentives for any reciprocal altruism have surely been removed. The zero-sum nature of the Rank payoffs also makes it much less likely that any one subject would consciously wish to make the least amount of money possible: someone has to get the highest Rank payoff – why not me? However, if such selflessness exists it will lead experimenters to overstate confusion. Another possibility is that an interest in equality could lead all subjects to wish to choose identical contributions, so that all subjects get identical earnings. But the focal choice for such an ethic would seem to be zero contributions, since it reaches the goals of equality and is cheat-proof. Hence, this would be unlikely to generate significant amounts of cooperation. Finally, since paying subjects by rank introduces another layer of complexity for subjects it may actually increase the level of confusion. To the extent that this exists, it will increase the estimates of confusion, and as will be seen, it reduces the calculation of kindness.

A potential problem with comparing the Rank condition and the Regular condition is that there are really two differences between them. First, the Rank subjects have information about their rank, while the Regular subjects do not. Second, Rank subjects are paid according to rank, while the Regular subjects get paid their experimental earnings. It is possible that the information on rank, apart from the payment by rank, could alter behavior. Giving information about rank, for instance, could sharpen the subjects' focus on the incentives and could help clear up their confusion. Also, the information on rank could distract attention away from natural tendencies for helping one another and direct the attention toward finishing first. Hence, the information alone may squelch some kindness.[7]

For this reason one needs a third condition, called *RegRank*. In this condition subjects get all the same information on their rank (and whether there are ties) that the Rank subjects get, but they get paid according to their experimental earnings, just like the Regular subjects do. Hence, the only difference between Regular and RegRank is the information on rank. This will make it possible to measure the difference on cooperation due only to information on rank. The RegRank and Rank conditions have all of the same information, but differ on the method of payment. Comparing these two conditions will allow me to focus on the effect of paying by rank alone. As a result, the differences in cooperation between RegRank and Rank will provide a measure of the minimum amount of cooperation that would be attributable to kindness. The cooperation seen in the Rank condition will provide a measure of the minimum amount of cooperation that is attributable to confusion. This leaves the change in cooperation due simply to information on rank (i.e., the difference between Regular and RegRank) which could be attributable to either kindness or confusion.

IV. RESULTS

The public-goods paradigm used here is similar to that used in Andreoni (1988b). Subjects play in groups of five. They are given budgets of 60 tokens in each iteration. A token invested in the private good yields the subject one cent of experimental earnings. A token invested in the public good earns every subject in the group one-half cent of experimental earnings. Hence, investing nothing in the public good is the dominant strategy, while investing everything in the public good is Pareto efficient. The experiments reported below are conducted as follows. On a given day, 40 subjects are recruited from intermediate-level economics classes. The subjects are divided randomly into two rooms of 20 each. In each room a different condition of the experiment is conducted. This is done to maintain the greatest control over random assignments to conditions. In a particular room, the subjects again are assigned randomly to numbered desks. They are given instructions and a packet of ten 'investment decision forms,' which subjects use to record their decision. One computer and printer is in the back of each room. In each iteration of the game, the experimenter collects the decision forms from each subject and enters the decisions into the computer. The computer is programmed to assign subjects randomly to groups of five and calculate payoffs. It then prints an 'earnings report' for each subject. These reports are returned to each subject. The earnings report tells subjects their investment decision, the group's investment in the public good, their experimental earnings, and their monetary earnings. In the RegRank and Rank conditions the earnings report also lists their rank, for example, 'Rank 3 tied with 2 others.' All of the parameters of the experiment are known to all subjects, but the information on individual payoffs is all private. The subjects are assigned randomly to new groups each iteration. This is important in order to avoid the possibility of reputation-building. Each experiment lasts about 50 minutes, with average earnings of $8.68 per subject. A copy of the subjects' instructions is included in the Appendix of this paper.

Subjects in the Rank condition were given the schedule for payments shown in Figure 17.1. They were told that if they tried, they would receive the average of the rank payoffs. For instance, if three tied for first rank, they would each get paid $(0.95 + 0.87 + 0.80)/3 = \$0.873$. The median rank payoff of $0.80 was determined on the basis of a pilot study and was set to be equal to the average earnings per round in a pilot run of the RegRank condition. This was done to minimize differences due to income effects. The actual earnings per round for the RegRank condition reported here were $0.8007. As can be seen, the range of the rank payoffs is 30 cents. This amount was chosen because this is the maximum difference in earnings in any one round between the highest and lowest earnings from the public good in the Regular and RegRank conditions. This means that the difference in earnings for a subject who goes from

Your Cash Earnings Based on Your Rank				
Highest				*Lowest*
Your Rank	1	2	3	4	5
Your cash earnings	.95	.87	.80	.73	.65

Figure 17.1   Monetary earnings for subjects in the rank condition

contributing all of his endowment to contributing none of his endowment is identical regardless of whether subjects are in the Rank, Regular, or RegRank condition.[8] This basic procedure was conducted three times, using 40 subjects for each condition; hence, a total of 120 subjects were used in this experiment.

With this design, subjects in the Regular condition are expected to be the most cooperative, and subjects in the Rank condition are expected to be the least cooperative. Table 17.1 lists the average percentage of the endowment contributed to the public good in each round. The first thing to note is that the Regular condition conforms to the pattern of earlier experiments, with cooperation in round 1 of 56 percent, decaying to 26 percent by round 10. This compares to nearly identical experiments reported in Andreoni (1988b) in which cooperation went from 51 percent to 24 percent. Next note that, as predicted, Regular subjects are more cooperative than RegRank subjects, and RegRank subjects are more cooperative than Rank subjects. The significance of these differences can be tested with a Mann-Whitney rank-sum U test, which has a normal distribution. This test organizes the data by subjects.[9] It shows that the differences in mean contributions across all three conditions are significant: comparing Regular and RegRank, $z = 3.772$; and comparing RegRank and Rank, $z = 3.580$.

Similar results hold when looking at the number of subjects choosing zero contributions to the public good. The percentage of free riders in any one round is given in the top panel of Table 17.2. As predicted, Rank subjects free ride the most, and Regular subjects the least. Differences between these conditions are also statistically significant, with U tests of $z = 2.281$ for Regular versus RegRank, and $z = 4.200$ for RegRank versus Rank.

The outcome for the Rank condition is strikingly different from that for the Regular condition. By round 4 the subjects in the Rank condition are contributing less than 10 percent of their endowment to the public good, and by round 10 they are contributing only 5.4 percent, while the Regular subjects never contribute less than 25 percent in any single round. Likewise, by round 2 over 50 percent of Rank subjects free ride, which is a higher rate than the Regular subjects reach in any one round. By the end of the experiment, all but three of 40 Rank subjects (7.5 percent) are free-riding, but 22 of 40 Regular subjects (55 percent) contribute something to the public good. Although there

Table 17.1   Percentages of endowment contributed to the public good per round

Condition	Round										All
	1	2	3	4	5	6	7	8	9	10	
Regular	56.0	59.8	55.2	49.6	48.1	41.0	36.0	35.1	33.4	26.5	44.07
RegRank	45.8	45.4	32.6	25.0	23.1	17.8	11.3	9.5	8.3	9.0	22.79
Rank	32.7	20.3	17.7	9.9	9.2	6.9	8.1	8.3	7.1	5.4	12.55
RegRank – Rank	13.2	25.1	15.0	15.1	13.9	11.0	3.2	1.3	1.2	3.6	10.24
As percentage of Regular	23.5	42.0	27.1	30.4	28.9	26.7	8.9	3.6	3.6	13.5	20.82

Table 17.2 Percentage of subjects contributing zero to the public good per round

Condition	Round										All
	1	2	3	4	5	6	7	8	9	10	
Regular	20	12.5	17.5	25	25	30	30	37.5	35	45	27.75
RegRank	10	22.5	27.5	40	35	45	50	67.5	70	65	43.25
Rank	35	52.5	65	72.5	80	85	85	85	92.5	92.5	74.50
Kindness:											
Rank – RegRank	25	30	37.5	32.5	45	40	35	17.5	22.5	27.5	31.25
As percentage of 100 – Regular	31.3	34.3	45.5	43.3	60.0	57.1	50.0	28.0	34.6	50.0	43.41
Confusion:											
100 – Rank	65	47.5	35	27.5	20	15	15	15	7.5	7.5	25.50
As percentage of 100 – Regular	81.3	54.3	42.4	36.7	26.7	21.4	21.4	24.0	11.5	13.6	33.33
Either:											
RegRank – Regular	–10	10	10	15	10	15	20	30	35	20	15.5
As percentage of 100 – Regular	–13.0	11.4	12.1	20.0	13.3	21.4	28.6	48.0	53.8	36.4	23.26

is not complete free-riding among the Rank subjects, the data are much closer to the predicted values than in any other conditions. Using the evidence in these two tables one could reasonably conclude that the behavior of the subjects in the Rank condition, unlike the Regular condition, is broadly consistent with the predicted behavior, especially after round 4 of the experiment.

The data in Table 17.2 permit a closer look at the motivations of the subjects. Recall that the Rank and RegRank conditions are identical except for the method of payment; hence their difference provides an estimate of the number of subjects who understand the incentives but cooperate out of kindness. Likewise, the amount of cooperation in the Rank condition provides a measure of subjects who are confused. The decline in cooperation from Regular to RegRank could be classified as either kindness or confusion, since it is solely due to RegRank subjects receiving information about the rank. The bottom of Table 17.2 separates cooperation into each of the other three motives for every round. Confusion is by far the dominant motive in round 1 of the experiment, accounting for 81 percent of all cooperation. However, confusion falls rapidly over rounds 1–5 to only 26.7 percent, and then continues in a more slow decline to a mere 13.6 percent in round 10. Kindness, on the other hand, doubles from its round-1 level to its peak in rounds 5 and 6 of around 60 percent. After round 6, however, kindness sputters to its low of 28 percent in round 8 before returning to 50 percent of all cooperation in round 10.

The measures of kindness and confusion in Table 17.2 suggest an interesting pattern. Over rounds 1–6 the total amount of cooperation is rather stable. However, over the same period the amount of confusion is declining rapidly, and the amount of kindness is increasing. After round 6, confusion is rather stable, but kindness falls. This points to a possible explanation for the 'decay' phenomenon often observed in public-goods experiments. When individuals who start off confused finally learn the dominant strategy, it appears that they may first try to cooperate but then eventually turn to free-riding.[10] This could suggest that, for some subjects, kindness may depend on reciprocity.

Note that Table 17.2 also reveals that a number of subjects could not be classified as either cooperating from kindness or confusion. This number is relatively stable at about 10–15 percent, until round 7 when it roughly doubles. Surely some of these subjects belong in the kindness category and some in confusion. A conservative approach would be to classify all of these subjects as confused. This means that the kindness measured in Table 17.2 is a lower-bound estimate of the amount of kindness present. Hence, combining the confusion and the 'either' categories, one could say that, on average, cooperation is about 43 percent kindness and 57 percent confusion. Alternatively, one could get an upper-bound estimate of kindness by combining the 'either' category with the kindness category. Doing this, we find that cooperation is no more than 67 percent kindness on average, with 33 percent confusion. A rough characterization of these findings is that cooperation is about half kindness and half confusion.

To obtain a different measure of confusion, all subjects were also given a postexperiment questionnaire which was designed to determine whether subjects understood the incentives. Subjects were presented with two hypothetical situations similar to those that they could encounter in the experiment and were asked what choice would yield the highest experimental earnings. They were also asked for verbal descriptions of their strategies. In each condition, exactly two subjects failed to answer these questions correctly. Hence, there were no systematic differences across conditions in the ability to discern incentives by round 10. All of the errant subjects in the Regular and RegRank conditions were also cooperators in round 10. Of the two Rank subjects who erred on the questionnaire, one was a cooperator in round 10, and one was not. Two other Rank subjects who did cooperate in round 10 were able to answer the questionnaire correctly. For one of these subjects the questionnaire itself may have cleared up some confusion. In the other's verbal explanation of his strategy, however, the subject indicated that he chose the dominant strategy for the first half of the experiment, but then switched to giving all his endowment to the public good in order to 'give others a chance.' For this subject, a clear motive of kindness is classified as confusion in Table 17.2. On balance, however, the amount of confusion shown in the table for round 10 generally corresponds to the results of the direct questionnaire.

There is a final surprising contrast that can be found between Tables 17.1 and 17.2 concerning the RegRank condition. As seen in Table 17.1, over rounds 7–10 the fraction of the endowment contributed to the public good by RegRank subjects is very close to that contributed by the Rank subjects, 9.5 percent versus 7.3 percent, while it is far from the fraction contributed by Regular subjects, who contribute 30.2 percent. In Table 17.2, by contrast, the fraction of subjects who contribute *something* to the public good over rounds 7–10 is 36.9 percent in the RegRank group, which is almost exactly halfway between the 63.1 percent in the Regular group and the 11.3 percent in the Rank group. Hence, conditional on giving at all, the average contribution of the RegRank contributors is actually lower than that of the Rank contributors. This means that information about rank decreases the amount given much more than it decreases the number of givers. It is unclear what this implies about the way information affects kindness and confusion, but it remains a striking puzzle that future work may address.

V. DISCUSSION

The significant presence of both kindness and confusion in public-goods experiments suggests that both merit greater consideration. Kindness in experiments corresponds to a large body of evidence from privately provided public goods, like charitable giving, which indicates that people contribute more than the theory predicts. Several alternative models have been suggested to explain this, and these models could be adapted to experimental environments to help inform the theory. For instance, one hypothesis is that subjects may be purely altruistic, that is, they care directly about the payoffs of the other subjects. A more general hypothesis is that subjects also care about the act of being nice to each other, that is, they are 'warm-glow' givers (Andreoni, 1989, 1990). Other alternative models are based on moral arguments, such as reciprocity (Robert Sugden,1984), group ethics (Howard Margolis, 1982), and fairness (Matthew Rabin, 1993). These models could be examined experimentally.

The significant presence of confusion presents a much different challenge to experimenters. Confusion is especially apparent in this experiment because errors can only be in one direction and, hence, will not be averaged out of the aggregate data. This suggests that experiments with interior equilibria could potentially overstate the extent to which subjects understand incentives. Since games with interior equilibria generally do not have dominant strategies, it is much more difficult to classify exactly when a subject is making an error. An assumption of no error may mistakenly lead experimenters to be overly confident of their theories.

One example of this is illustrated in a recent public-goods experiment published in the *American Economic Review* (Andreoni, 1993).[11] This experiment offered subjects a payoff matrix for a public good for which there was an interior Nash equilibrium. One matrix, however, reflected 'taxation,' and the tax revenue was added to the public good. If subjects either have altruism toward other subjects or get warm-glows from giving, then theory suggests that the subjects with the tax should provide more public goods than the subjects without the tax. The alternative of no altruism or no warm-glow predicts the same equilibrium contribution in both conditions. The experiment revealed that there was indeed a significant difference between these conditions, indicating a presence of altruism or warm-glow. However, neither condition by itself was significantly different from the no-warm-glow equilibrium prediction, even though the two conditions were significantly different from each other. Hence, if either condition were conducted in isolation, the experimenter might mistakenly conclude that altruism or warm-glow is not present.

This fact may also reconcile the standard public-goods experiments with the broader literature on externalities mentioned in Section II. Experiments on externalities, which have interior equilibria, generally cannot reject the theory. The results of the current paper raise the possibility that the confusion in these experiments may create enough variance in the data to mask any influence of kindness. If controls are added in an effort to manipulate or measure kindness, then perhaps it will be identified.

Finally, the presence of kindness in public-goods experiments is consistent with evidence for fairness found in bargaining experiments. In particular, Forsythe et al. (1994) compare ultimatum and dictator games and find a significant tendency for people in dictator games to give away money, even when there is not the threat of retribution found in ultimatum games. Since the dictator game is not very confusing, this generosity is thought to be due to kindness. In a related study, Bolton (1991) followed up on a study by Ochs and Roth (1989) in which bargainers often made counteroffers that were worse for themselves than offers they had already rejected. Bolton found that a rank-order treatment substantially reduced these 'disadvantageous counterproposals,' again indicating that fairness, as well as some confusion, may be at play in bargaining experiments.

VI. CONCLUSION

The persistent and sometimes counterintuitive nature of cooperation in public-goods experiments has presented an important puzzle for economists. In general, laboratory experiments are designed to control the incentives of subjects and to restrict social and cultural influences. Hence, many experimenters have focused on learning hypotheses as potential explanations for cooperation. In contrast, studies of giving and cooperation that are based on real-world data have increasingly focused on social influences, such as fairness and warm-glow, to understand giving behavior. In order to use experiments to learn about giving in real situations it is important to understand whether the experiments are indeed identifying only confusion by subjects, or whether kindness is also fundamental to the strategies.

The experiment presented in this paper is the first systematic attempt to separate the hypotheses of kindness and confusion. It reveals that on average about 75 percent of the subjects are cooperative, and about half of these are confused about incentives, while about half understand free-riding but choose to cooperate out of some form of kindness. This demonstrates that kindness and confusion are equally important in generating cooperative moves in public-goods experiments and suggests that the focus on 'learning' in experimental research should shift to include studies of preferences for cooperation.

It is important to note that laboratory experiments are designed to be neutral and to minimize social effects like kindness. Hence, regular public-goods experiments may already be eliminating a large amount of subjects' natural tendency to be cooperative. In the real world a much larger fraction of people may naturally be cooperative than this experiment indicates. Admittedly, the stakes for kindness are often higher in the real world, so comparisons cannot be direct. Nonetheless, the striking importance of these effects in the laboratory and the parallel of these findings with real-world evidence on giving point to a promising area of research. Is it possible to test alternative models of kindness in the laboratory as well as with real world data?

One should also note the importance of confusion. Most of the learning in this experiment was accomplished in the first five rounds. However, this reduction in confusion was replaced by a growth in kindness, leaving total cooperation fairly stable. The movement toward the equilibrium in the last half of the experiment appeared to be due to frustrated attempts at kindness, rather than learning the free-riding incentives. This, rather than learning *per se*, could explain the decay of cooperation often observed in public-goods experiments.

In summary, this paper goes beyond showing that subjects tend to cooperate too much in free-finding experiments; it identifies the part of this cooperation that needs explanation with behavioral models, and the part that may be due to methodological issues in experiments. The findings of this experiment indicate that future research, both theoretical and experimental, should focus on developing reliable predictive models of charitable and altruistic behavior.

APPENDIX: SUBJECTS' INSTRUCTIONS [EXACT TRANSCRIPT]

Welcome

This experiment is a study of group and individual investment behavior. The instructions are simple. If you follow them carefully and make good investment decisions you may earn a considerable amount of money.

The money you earn will be paid to you, in cash, at the end of the experiment. A research foundation has provided the funds for this study.

The Investment Opportunities

You have been assigned to a group of five people. Each of you will be given an investment account with a specific number of tokens in it. These are then invested to turn them into cash. *All tokens must be invested to earn cash from them.*

You will be choosing how to divide your tokens between two investment opportunities:

1. THE INDIVIDUAL EXCHANGE

Every token you invest in the Individual Exchange will earn you a return of one cent.

Example. Suppose you invested 55 tokens in the Individual Exchange. Then you would earn $0.55 from this exchange.

Example. Suppose you invested 148 tokens in the Individual Exchange. Then you would earn $1.48 from this exchange.

Example. Suppose you invested 0 tokens in the Individual Exchange. Then you would earn nothing from this exchange.

2. THE GROUP EXCHANGE

The return you earn from the Group Exchange is a little more difficult to determine.

What you earn from the Group Exchange will depend on the total number of tokens that you and the other four members of your group invest in the Group Exchange. The more the group invests in the Group Exchange, the more each member of the group earns. The process is best explained by a number of examples:

Example. Suppose that you decided to invest no tokens in the Group Exchange, but that the four other members invested a total of 100 tokens. Then your earnings from the Group Exchange would be $0.50. Everyone else in your group would also earn $0.50.

Example. Suppose that you invested 40 tokens in the Group Exchange and that the other four members of your group invested a total of 80 tokens. This makes a total of 120 tokens. Your return from the Group Exchange would be $0.60. The other four members of the group would also get a return of $0.60.

Example. Suppose that you invested 60 tokens in the Group Exchange, but that the other four members of the group invest nothing. Then you, and everyone else in the group, would get a return from the Group Exchange of $0.30.

As you can see, every token invested in the Group Exchange will earn one half of a cent for every member of the group, not just the person who invested it. It does not matter who invests tokens in the Group Exchange. Everyone will get a return from every token invested—whether they invest in the Group Exchange or not.

Table A1   Returns from the group exchange

Total investment by your group	Return to each member of your group
0	0
10	5
20	10
30	15
40	20
50	25
60	30
80	40
100	50
120	60
140	70
160	80
180	90
200	100
220	110
250	120
280	140
310	155

Table A1 can be used to help you calculate your earnings from the Group Exchange.

The Investment Decision

Your task is to decide how many of your tokens to invest in the Individual Exchange and how many to invest in the Group Exchange. You are free to put some tokens into the Individual Exchange and some into the Group Exchange. Alternatively, you can put all of them into the Group Exchange or all of them into the Individual Exchange.

Stages of Investment

There will be 10 decision rounds in which you will be asked to make investment decisions. At the end of each round your payoff will be recorded by the experimenter. After the last round you will be paid the total of your payoffs from all 10 rounds.

At the beginning of each round you will be given a fresh investment account. You will also be given an INVESTMENT DECISION FORM. You are to record your decision using this form. Be sure that your investment in the Individual Exchange plus your investment in the Group Exchange equals the number of token in your account. You must make your investment decisions *without* knowing what the others in your group are deciding.

Do not discuss your decision with any other participant!

The experimenter will collect the form when you have filled it out. The experimenter will then calculate your earnings from the Individual and Group Exchanges, and calculate your total payoff. This information will be conveyed to you on an EARNINGS REPORT.

IMPORTANT NOTICE: The Earnings Report tells you the total investment in the Group Exchange and your personal earnings. It will also tell you where your investment earnings ranked in comparison to the other 4 members of your group. 1 is the highest rank, and 5 is the lowest rank. In case of ties for rank, the highest number will be reported. Your earnings report does not tell you the investment decisions or earnings of the other members of your group. YOUR INVESTMENT DECISIONS AND EARNINGS ARE CONFIDENTIAL.

Your Investment Account

The number of tokens in your Investment Account is indicated on your Investment Decision Form. You and every other member of your group will have 60 tokens in your investment account each decision round. The total number of tokens in each group in every decision round is 300.

Your Group

The composition of your group will be changing *every* decision round. After each decision round you will be **reassigned** to a **new group** of 5 participants. The 5 group members will never have been members of the same group in the past. The chance that any other participant will ever be in a group with you more than one time is very small.

At no point in the experiment will the identities of the other members of the group be made known to you, nor will your identity be made known to them.

Your Payoff

Your monetary payoff from your investment *will not* be the same as your investment earnings. Instead, your payoff from each investment decision will depend on how your investment earnings compare to the investment earnings of the other subjects in your group. If your investment earnings are the highest among the 5 subjects in your group, then your payoff will be $0.95. If your earnings are second highest, your payoff will be $0.87. If your earnings are third highest, your payoff will be $0.80. If your earnings are fourth highest, your payoff will be $0.73. If your earnings are fifth highest, your payoff will be $0.65. For example, suppose five subjects in your group had investment earnings of 100, 80, 60, 40, and 20. Then they would receive payoffs of $0.95, $0.87, $0.80, $0.73, and $0.65, respectively. If two people have the same investment earnings – so they have the same rank – then they will earn the average payoff from the tie. For example, suppose the second and third highest investors both earned 70 from their investments. Then each of them would receive a payoff of (0.87 + 0.80)/2 = $0.835. Suppose instead that the first, second and third highest investment earnings were all equal to 75. Then all three players would receive a payoff of (0.95 + 0.87 + 0.80)/3 = 2.62/3 = $0.873.

The following table can help you determine your payoff:

Your Cash Earnings Based on Your Rank				
Highest				*Lowest*
Your Rank 1	2	3	4	5
Your cash earnings .95	.87	.80	.73	.65

GOOD LUCK!
You may begin completing the first Investment Decision Form.

NOTES

1. Department of Economics, University of Wisconsin, Madison, WI 53706. I am grateful to the National Science Foundation and the Alfred P. Sloan Foundation for financial support. I am also grateful to Paul Brown and to two anonymous referees for many helpful comments.
2. See Andreoni (1988a) on how the public-goods model fails to explain privately provided public goods observed in the real world.
3. See Colin Camerer and Keith Weigelt (1988), Richard D. McKelvey and Thomas R. Palfrey (1992), John Neral and Jack Ochs (1992), and Andreoni and John H. Miller (1993) for related discussions regarding finitely repeated games. For a related discussion of the presence of fairness in sequential games see Ochs and Alvin E. Roth (1989), Vesna Prasnikar and Roth (1992), Ernst Fehr et al. (1993), and Robert Forsythe et al. (1994).
4. This has also been recognized recently by Isaac and Walker (1992), and Palfrey and Jeffrey E. Prisbrey (1992).
5. Oligopoly experiments find that only four or five subjects are required to generate prices at competitive levels (see Jon Ketcham et al. [1984], Dan Alger [1987], and the summary by Davis and Holt [1993 Ch. 4]). Common-pool resource experiments also find rapid dissipation of the resource, again with relatively small groups (see Walker et al. [1990], Walker and Roy Gardner [1992], and a related study by Charles R. Plott [1983]). I have examined this difference directly (Andreoni, 1995) and found that framing decisions as negative rather than positive externalities greatly reduces cooperation.

6. Paying subjects by their rank was also done by Gary E. Bolton (1991).
7. It is important to note that the directions were deliberately written to avoid any suggestion of tournament-style behavior. See the Appendix for a copy of the instructions.
8. To the extent that there may be ties, the marginal difference between contributing all or nothing to the public good may be smaller in the Rank than in the Regular or RegRank conditions. To the extent that this fails to encourage maximizing behavior it will bias downward the estimate of kindness.
9. The test is conducted by first calculating the mean contribution for each subject and ranking these means for the joint sample. Under a null hypothesis of no difference between conditions, the sum of the ranks should be equal across conditions (see John E. Freund, 1971 pp. 357–49).
10. A stricter view of confusion would assume that a person is confused if that person cooperates at any time in the future, even if he or she does not cooperate in the current period. An earlier version of this paper (available from the author upon request) also considers this definition, and the results are very similar to those reported here.
11. See Kenneth Chan et al. (1993) for a replication of this result.

REFERENCES

Alger, Dan. 'Laboratory Tests on Equilibrium Predictions with Disequilibrium Data.' *Review of Economic Studies*, January 1987, 54(1), pp. 105–45.

Altonji, Joseph, Hayashi, Fumio, and Kotlikoff, Laurence. 'Is the Extended Family Altruistically Linked?' *American Economic Review*, December 1992, 82(5), pp. 1177–98.

Andreoni, James. 'Privately Provided Public Goods in a Large Economy: The Limits of Altruism.' *Journal of Public Economics*, February 1988a, 35(1), pp. 57–73.

Andreoni, James. 'Why Free Ride? Strategies and Learning in Public Goods Experiments.' *Journal of Public Economics*, December 1988b, 37(3), pp. 291–304.

Andreoni, James. 'Giving with Impure Altruism: Applications to Charity and Ricardian Equivalence.' *Journal of Political Economy*, December 1989, 97(6), pp. 1447–58.

Andreoni, James. 'Impure Altruism and Donations to Public Goods: A Theory of Warm-Glow Giving?' *Economic Journal*, June 1990, 100(401), pp. 464–77.

Andreoni, James. 'An Experimental Test of the Public Goods Crowding-Out Hypothesis.' *American Economic Review*, December 1993, 83(5), pp. 1317–27.

Andreoni, James. 'Warm Glow vs. Cold Prickle: The Effect of Positive and Negative Framing on Cooperation in Experiments.' *Quarterly Journal of Economics*, February 1995, 110(1), pp. 1–21.

Andreoni, James and Miller, John H. 'Rational Cooperation in the Finitely Repeated Prisoner's Dilemma: Experimental Evidence.' *Economic Journal*, May 1993, 103, pp. 570–85.

Bernheim, B. Douglas. 'On the Voluntary and Involuntary Provision of Public Goods.' *American Economic Review*, September 1986, 76(4), pp. 789–93.

Bernheim, B. Douglas, Shleifer, Andrei, and Summers, Lawrence. 'The Strategic Bequest Motive.' *Journal of Political Economy*, December 1985, 93(6), pp. 1045–76.

Bolton, Gary E. 'A Comparative Model of Bargaining.' *American Economic Review*, December 1991, 81(5), pp. 1096–136.

Camerer, Colin, and Weigelt, Keith. 'An Experimental Test of the Sequential Equilibrium Reputation Model.' *Econometrica*, January 1988, 56(1), pp. 1–36.

Chan, Kenneth, Godby, Rob, Mestelman, Stuart, and Muller, Andrew. 'Boundary Effects and Voluntary Contributions to Public Goods.' Working paper, McMaster University, 1993.

Davis, Douglas D., and Holt, Charles A. *Experimental Economics*. Princeton, NJ: Princeton University Press, 1993.

Dawes, Robyn M., van de Kragt, Alphons, and Orbell, John M. 'Not Me or Thee but We: The Importance of Group Identity in Eliciting Cooperation in Dilemma Situations.' Mimeo, Carnegie Mellon University, 1987.

Fehr, Ernst, Kirchsteiger, Georg, and Riedl, Arno. 'Does Fairness Prevent Market Clearing? An Experimental Investigation.' *Quarterly Journal of Economics*, May 1993, 108(2), pp. 437–60.

Forsythe, Robert, Horowitz, Joel L., Savin, N.E., and Sefton, Martin. 'Fairness in Simple Bargaining Experiments.' *Games and Economic Behavior*, May 1994, 6(3), pp. 347–69.

Freund, John E. *Mathematical Statistics*, 2nd Ed. Englewood Cliffs, NJ: Prentice Hall, 1971.

Isaac, R. Mark, and Walker, James J. 'Group Size Effects in Public Goods Provision: The Voluntary Contributions Mechanism.' *Quarterly Journal of Economics*, February 1988, 103(1), pp. 179–200.

Isaac, R. Mark, and Walker, James J. 'Nash as an Organizing Principle in the Voluntary Provision of Public Goods: Experimental Evidence.' Mimeo, University of Arizona, 1992.

Isaac, R. Mark, Walker, James M., and Williams, Arlington W. 'Group Size and the Voluntary Provision of Public Goods: Experimental Evidence Utilizing Large Groups.' *Journal of Public Economics*, May 1994, 54(1), pp. 1–36.

Ketcham, Jon, Smith, Vernon J. and Williams, Arlington W. 'A Comparison of Posted-Offer and Double-Auction Pricing Institutions.' *Review of Economic Studies*, October 1984, 51(4), pp. 595–614.

Ledyard, John O. 'Public Goods: A Survey of Experimental Research,' in J. Kagel and A.E. Roth, eds., *The Handbook of Experimental Economics*. Princeton, NJ: Princeton University Press, 1995.

Margolis, Howard. *Selfishness, Altruism, and Rationality*. Cambridge: Cambridge University Press, 1982.

McKelvey, Richard D. and Palfrey, Thomas, R. 'An Experimental Study of the Centipede Game.' *Econometrica*, July 1992, 60(4), pp. 803–36.

Neral, John, and Ochs, Jack. 'The Sequential Equilibrium Theory of Reputation Building: A Further Test.' *Econometrica*, September 1992, 60(5), pp. 1151–70.

Ochs, Jack, and Roth, Alvin E. 'An Experimental Study of Sequential Bargaining.' *American Economic Review*, June 1989, 79(3), pp. 335–84.

Palfrey, Thomas R., and Prisbrey, Jeffrey E. 'Anomalous Behavior in Linear Public Goods Experiments: How Much and Why?' Working paper, California Institute of Technology, 1992.

Palfrey, Thomas R. and Rosenthal, Howard. 'Testing for Effects of Cheap Talk in a Public Goods Game with Private Information.' *Games and Economic Behavior*, May 1991, 3(2), pp.183–220.

Plott, Charles R. 'Externalities and Corrective Policies in Experimental Markets.' *Economic Journal*, March 1983, 93(369).

Prasnikar, Vesna and Roth, Alvin E. 'Considerations of Fairness and Strategy: Experimental Data from Sequential Games.' *Quarterly Journal of Economics*, August 1992, 107(3), pp. 865–88.

Rabin, Matthew. 'Incorporating Fairness into Game Theory and Econometrics.' *American Economic Review*, December 1993, 83(5), pp. 1281–303.

Sugden, Robert. 'Reciprocity: The Supply of Public Goods Through Voluntary Contributions.' *Economic Journal*, December 1984, 94(376), pp. 772–87.

Walker, James M. and Gardner, Roy. 'Probabilistic Destruction of Common-Pool Resources: Experimental Evidence.' *Economic Journal*, September 1992, 102(414), pp. 1149–61.

Walker, James M., Gardner, Roy, and Ostrom, Elinor. 'Rent Dissipation in a Limited-Access Common-Pool Resource: Experimental Evidence.' *Journal of Environmental Economics and Management*, November 1990, 19(3), pp. 203–11.

Index